English Reformation Literature

ENGLISH REFORMATION LITERATURE

The Tudor Origins of the

Protestant Tradition

JOHN N. KING

Princeton University Press

To My Mother and Father

Contents

Contents

List of Figures
(following page 142)

[ix]

LIST OF FIGURES

Acknowledgments

This study argues that a distinctively Protestant literary tradition appeared in England during the radical phase of the Tudor Reformation and then influenced the writings of such authors as Spenser, Donne, Herbert, and Milton. The inquiry began in bewilderment when I encountered Robert Crowley's 1550 text of *Piers Plowman* (3rd edition), with its mystifying preface and marginalia. Literary tradition, it seemed, could not explain the significance of Crowley's apparatus. Rather it appeared that the answer must lie in the little-known territory of English Reformation polemical practices and biblical commentary—somewhere, perhaps, in the vast domain of early Protestant social complaint, political theory, and millennial prophecy. I became convinced, however, that Crowley's mid-Tudor edition was an immediate ancestor of Book One of Spenser's *Faerie Queene.* Eventually I wrote the present book about a lost or forgotten period of Renaissance English literature.

It was Richard C. Wood, now of Southwestern at Memphis University, who first aroused my interest in Tudor poetry and also in the entire range of English literature. I could not have completed this book without the guidance of William A. Ringler, Jr., Senior Research Associate at the Huntington Library, to whom I owe my greatest debt. David Bevington and the late Arthur Heiserman of the University of Chicago influenced the early development of this project. The manuscript received careful criticism at various stages from J. Scott Colley of Vanderbilt University, Elizabeth Hageman of the University of New Hampshire,

Acknowledgments

Arthur F. Kinney of the University of Massachusetts at Amherst, D.G.E. Norbrook of Magdalen College, Oxford, Dale B.J. Randall of Duke University, John T. Shawcross of the University of Kentucky, and John N. Wall, Jr., of the University of North Carolina at Raleigh. In addition to reading sections of the manuscript, George Walton Williams of Duke University brought into focus my work on woodcuts and bibliographical problems. Jennifer Loach of Somerville College, Oxford, brought to the text the much-needed perspective of a Tudor historian.

At appropriate points in the text, I acknowledge special contributions made by others. I should like to include here the names of Katharine F. Pantzer of the Houghton Library of Harvard University and Paul Morgan, Assistant Librarian at the Bodleian Library, for offering generous assistance and access to the typescript and page proofs of the *STC* revision. David Paisey, Assistant Keeper of Printed Books at the British Library, and Giles Dawson, Curator Emeritus of the Folger Shakespeare Library, aided substantially. Michael Curley of the University of Puget Sound assisted with Latin. Rosemary Weinstein of the Tudor and Stuart Department at the London Museum answered questions about the London book trade. David Watters of the University of New Hampshire commented on the development of Puritanism. A. C. Hamilton of Queen's University (Ontario), James K. McConica of All Souls' College, Oxford, Barbara K. Lewalski of Brown University, and the late Richard Sylvester of Yale University offered generous counsel and encouragement.

For assistance in research I am indebted to the staffs of the Bodleian Library, British Library, Cambridge University Library, English Faculty Library at Oxford University, Guildhall Library (London), Records Office of the Corporation of London, Folger Shakespeare Library, Huntington Library, Newberry Library, Beinecke Library of Yale University, and Houghton and Widener Libraries of Harvard University. Librarians at the following institutions were very helpful: All Souls' College, Corpus Christi College, Exeter College, and Merton College of Oxford University; Emmanuel College and St. John's College of Cambridge University; and Manchester College (Oxford), the British and Foreign Bible Society, Society of Antiquaries, Lincoln Cathedral, University of Chicago, Duke University, University of North Carolina at Chapel Hill, and Bates College. Kathleen Cann, Archivist at the British and Foreign Bible Society, Barbara Smith, Assistant Librarian at Manchester College, and Jane Fowler, Thomas Hayward, and LaVerne Winn of the Ladd Library at Bates College were of particular assistance.

For permission to reproduce the illustrations, I acknowledge the following: Bodleian Library (Figures 4-8, 11, 13, 15, 17-19); British Library (Figures 1-3, 14, 16); British and Foreign Bible Society (Figures 9-10); and National Portrait Gallery (Figure 12). Chapter 7 incorporates the text of two of my articles in a form that is substantially revised and expanded: "Robert Crowley's Editions of *Piers Plowman*: A Tudor Apocalypse," *Modern Philology*, 73 (1976), 342-52, reprinted by permission of the University of Chicago Press; "Robert Crowley: A Tudor Gospelling Poet," reprinted from the *Yearbook of English Studies*, 8 (1978), 220-37, by permission of the Modern Humanities Research Association and the editors of the *Yearbook of English Studies*. Papers based on parts of the manuscript were given at the Southeastern Institute of Medieval and Renaissance Studies (1976), the Folger Renaissance and Eighteenth-Century Studies Colloquium at the Folger Shakespeare Library (1980), and meetings of the Modern Language Association (1979 and 1980). At the invitation of Tibor Klaniczay and Robert Dan, I delivered a lecture drawn from this text at the Renaissance

Seminar of the Hungarian Academy of Sciences in Budapest (1981). A grant from the Southeastern Institute as well as a sabbatical leave from Bates College contributed to the completion of the manuscript.

James Hepburn of Bates College has always supported my work with consistent encouragement and wise counsel; I am grateful. Special thanks are not sufficient to repay my debt to Sophie and Robert Gore, Lucy and Mark Le Fanu, and John and Elizabeth Cowen, one-time residents of 35 Argyll Road, for unfailing friendship, hospitality, and encouragement during repeated visits to London. Lady Verney of 38 Argyll Road extended her hospitality as well. Robert and Catherine Brawer have always offered generous assistance and a cordial welcome. Martine W. Brownley of Emory University helped out in the bitter winter of 1979 during my sabbatical leave at Oxford University. Ann B. Scott of Bates College and David W. Luter assisted in the final preparation of the manuscript. Julie Bourisk and Amy Greene typed it with patience and diligence. Marjorie Sherwood of Princeton University Press has guided this book during its journey into print. Judith May provided meticulous editorial direction at the Press. My father, Luther Waddington King, greatly improved the manuscript with his editorial skills. Toward the end my mother, Alba Iregui King, and my aunt, Esther V. King, assisted with proofreading. Of course I am solely responsible for all remaining errors and faults.

Unless otherwise noted translations are my own and reference is made to the earliest printed edition, manuscript, or entry in contemporary records concerning the texts under study. Contractions are expanded. The modern use of i/j and u/v has been followed.

Oxford
14 May 1982

[xiv]

Abbreviations

Unless otherwise specified, London is the place of publication, and reference is to the first edition. The abbreviation sig. is omitted from signature references. Journal abbreviations follow *NCBEL*, I and the *PMLA* annual bibliography.

A & M (1563)	John Foxe, *Actes and Monuments of these Latter and Perillous Dayes* (1563).
A & M (1570)	———, 2nd ed., rev. and enlarged, 2 vols. (1570).
A & M	———, *Acts and Monuments*, edited by S. R. Cattley, 4th ed., rev. and corrected by J. Pratt, 8 vols. (1877).
Annales	John Stow, *Annales, or a Generall Chronicle of England* (1631). Continued by Edmund Howes.
BCP	*The First and Second Prayer Books of Edward VI*, introduction by Douglas Harrison (1968).
B.L.	British Library, Reference Division, Departments of Manuscripts and Printed Books.
Bodl.	Bodleian Library, Oxford University.
Catalogus, I	John Bale, *Scriptorum Illustrium maioris Brytanniae . . . Catalogus* (Basel, 1557).
Catalogus, II	———, *Scriptorum Illustrium maioris Brytanniae posterior pars* (Basel, 1559).
C.U.L.	University Library, Cambridge University.
DNB	*Dictionary of National Biography*, edited by Leslie Stephen and Sidney Lee (1885-1900).
EETS	Early English Text Society.

Index	John Bale, *Index Britanniae Scriptorum*, edited by Reginald Poole and Mary Bateson (Oxford, 1902).
NCBEL, I	*The New Cambridge Bibliography of English Literature*, edited by George Watson, Vol. 1 (Cambridge, 1974).
OED	*A New English Dictionary on Historical Principles*, edited by J.A.H. Murray et al. (Oxford, 1884-1933).
STC	*A Short-Title Catalogue of Books Printed in England, Scotland, & Ireland, and of English Books Printed Abroad, 1475-1640*, compiled by A. W. Pollard and G. R. Redgrave (1926).
STC	————, 2nd ed., rev. and enlarged by W. A. Jackson and F. S. Ferguson, completed by Katharine F. Pantzer, Vol. 2 (1976). Vols. 1 and 3 are forthcoming. This edition assimilates entries from the original, with corrections. Decimalized listings refer to revisions or additions. Besides the texts themselves, Vol. 2 and the typescript and page proofs of Vol. 1 of the revised *STC* are the basic bibliographical sources concerning the early printed works studied in this book.
Summarium	John Bale, *Illustrium maioris Britanniae scriptorum summarium* (Wesel, Cleves, 1548).

English Reformation Literature

PROLOGUE

> . . . it shalbe but a little more lost time to inquire why England
> (the Mother of excellent mindes) should bee growne so hard a step-
> mother to Poets, who certainly in wit ought to passe all other. . . .
>
> Sidney, *An Apology for Poetry* (c. 1583)

The English Protestant literary tradition emerged and
flourished during the radical Reformation in the middle of
the sixteenth century. The core of this inquiry provides the
first substantial review of the literary climate and produc-
tivity during the reign of Edward VI (1547-53). The argument is twofold: that there was significant literary activity growing out of a medieval heritage later denied in part
by the humanists and the Italianate Renaissance culture under Elizabeth I; and that this literature introduced Protestant themes and a plain style that would continue to influence English literature throughout most of the seventeenth
century. Little work has been done on the early literature
of the English Reformation; this investigation therefore
aims to encourage interest in this badly neglected period
of the English literary Renaissance. It surveys mid-Tudor
Protestant literature, by genre and theme, and traces the
development of conventions, techniques, and styles. Analysis of the writings of Edwardian authors is grounded in
a more general consideration of Protestant literature and
thought from Tyndale's time until the Elizabethan Compromise (c. 1525-75). Forgotten texts from the reign of
Queen Mary (1553-58) receive closer scrutiny than later

writings. The study places literary work squarely in the context of religious, social, and political history. It isolates the most imaginative literature of the period—by Luke Shepherd, Nicholas Grimald, John Harington, Robert Crowley, John Bale, William Baldwin, and many other little-known contemporaries—and provides readings of individual texts. Commentary on the art of the printed book, woodcuts, and book design suggests ancillary methods of literary criticism.

The reign of Edward VI is a major watershed in the development of Renaissance literature. Edwardian authors drew their inspiration from a body of interrelated themes, conventions, and techniques that emerged out of pietistic and devotional literature at the close of the Middle Ages. Late medieval modes underwent a sea change when the Protestant school applied them to a set of radically different historical, political, and religious circumstances. The origins of Reformation literature may be traced back to the writings of John Wyclif and his fourteenth-century Lollard followers. Their most important texts were the Wyclifite Bible and *Piers Plowman*, an orthodox prophecy tinged with Lollardry. Because of their alleged heterodoxy, these fourteenth-century writings were prohibited by the heresy and treason statutes of Henry VIII. Perhaps because they were preoccupied with the inhospitable policies of an absolute monarch, Henrician Protestants produced scarcely any imaginative literature. It was as both biblical translator and author of tracts and polemics that William Tyndale dominated the first generation of English Protestant intellectuals (c. 1525-36). Disciples such as Simon Fish, John Frith, and Robert Barnes followed their master in turning out sub-literary rhetorical forms, including appeals to the monarch, complaints against religious and social abuses, and barely fictionalized dialogues.

[4]

John Bale, a recently converted Carmelite friar, is the notable exception. Before embarking on a long series of polemical tracts and editions, Bale composed a large corpus of anti-Catholic plays under the patronage of Thomas Cromwell, who served Henry VIII during the 1530s as vicegerent (deputy) in religious affairs. Bale's extant plays synthesize the biblical form of the medieval mystery cycles with the allegorical conventions and psychomachia plot of the Tudor moralities and interludes. The fall of his patron drove Bale into exile; radical authors such as Thomas Becon, William Turner, John Hooper, and Miles Coverdale joined him on the Continent or went into hiding in England.

When Edward VI succeeded to the throne as a minor, the king's uncle Edward Seymour led a faction of Protestant courtiers and aristocrats in seizing power. Their relaxation of crown censorship triggered an explosion of radical Protestant publication. Even before Bale's return from exile (c. 31 July 1548), his overseas printer issued three of his plays in print for the first time (c. 1547-48). Imported copies influenced the composition and production of a large body of Protestant interludes, most of which remained in manuscript until Elizabeth's reign. A great variety of reformist poetry, dialogues, and satires, including what may be the first true novel written in English, circulated in both manuscript and print. This emphasis on works of fiction and imaginative literature represents a sharp break with the practice of Henrician Protestant authors. The Protestant lords lifted the ban on publication of both Lollard works and the social and religious complaints of the radical reformers. Private citizens wrote pamphlets and treatises calling for the thorough reform of church doctrine and ritual along the lines of Lutheran, Calvinist, and Zwinglian ideas. Translations of the Continental reformers appeared openly for the first time. Aristocratic and royal patronage encouraged the dissemination of revolutionary works and ideas. The only parallel to Edward's reign, as a time of intellectual ferment, is the early period of the Puritan Commonwealth, prior to the reimposition of censorship restrictions. In alliance with Thomas Cranmer, Archbishop of Canterbury, Seymour attempted to channel public discussion by sanctioning vernacular translations of the Bible and mandating public conformity to the *Book of Homilies* and *Book of Common Prayer*.

Mid-Tudor Reformation literature is significant not only for its intrinsic merit but even more because of its vast influence on later authors. It provides the foundation for very nearly all English Protestant literature through the Restoration. The reformers forged a broad consensus concerning doctrine and devotional life, based upon the central tenets of justification by faith alone and the absolute primacy of the scriptures. This consensus underlies the central tradition of Protestant literature and art. Later disagreements among Anglicans, Puritans, and sectarians largely derive from nondoctrinal questions concerning ecclesiastical polity, ritual, discipline, and piety. Although some Edwardian radicals later joined the fledgling Puritan movement during the first decade of Elizabeth's reign, all Protestant groups united in support of reforms implemented in the name of Edward VI. Regardless of factional disagreements, no Protestant questioned the authority of the boy king and his prelates to impose an essentially Protestant settlement in religion. Throughout the reign of Queen Elizabeth, Protestant authors such as John Foxe, Sir Philip Sidney, and Edmund Spenser preserved the Edwardian synthesis of royalist politics and reformist art. The Protestant poetics that emerged during the reign of Edward VI generated a common literary tradition capable of accommodating minor differences between the literary modes of later Anglicans and Puritans. Virtually all Protestant authors absorbed the cadences of both the Tudor Bible translations and Cranmer's prayer book and homilies. The legacy of the biblical and visionary poetics of the earliest Protestant authors may be traced through the writings of John Donne and George Herbert, Henry Vaughan and Thomas Traherne, John Milton and John Bunyan, and even Isaac Watts and William Blake.

Within the broad spectrum of Protestant literary tradition, the passage of time brought shifts in style, fashion, and taste. In her ground-breaking study of English Protestant poetics, Barbara K. Lewalski investigates the flowering of the devotional lyric in response to the general acceptance of the Bible as a literary and artistic model.[1] Her conclusions, however, refer to religious poetry written by seventeenth-century Anglicans and Puritans; the present study deals with the origins and early development of the tradition analyzed in her book. Although Tudor Protestant authors address religious questions, they tend to avoid the mode of lyric devotion. The general impulse of the sixteenth century was toward public reformation of church and state rather than private sanctification. This emphasis helps to account for the paucity of Tudor Protestant lyrics and the fashion for the public forms of satirical, visionary, and heroic verse.

The Puritan literature of England and New England inherits the reformist tradition established by the early Protestants. Faced with the ritualistic, Anglo-Catholic practices of Charles I and Archbishop Laud, English Pu-

---

[1] *Protestant Poetics and the Seventeenth-Century Religious Lyric* (Princeton, 1979). See the related argument of Andrew D. Weiner, *Sir Philip Sidney and the Poetics of Protestantism: A Study of Contexts* (Minneapolis, 1978).

ritans evolved increasingly into a party opposed to royalty and prelacy. In opposing both bishop and king, however, such nonconformists as John Lilburne, John Goodwin, Henry Parker, and William Walwyn argued for a return to the consensus supported by king, bishop, and radical reformer during the reign of Edward VI. The intellectual shift during the intervening century is as much political as theological. The separatist tendencies of New England, coupled with intolerance toward Presbyterians, Anglicans, Quakers, and others, do, however, reflect theological as well as political differences with English Puritanism. Despite the passage of time, the biblical poetry of such New England Puritans as Anne Bradstreet and Edward Taylor is thoroughly rooted in Reformation theology. Although the preface to "The Bay Psalm Book" acknowledges the sacrifice of the nature of the Hebrew poetry to the English ballad tradition, the American translators nevertheless follow the Reformation practice of paraphrasing the Psalms in common measure. Even in its metrics, Michael Wigglesworth's *The Day of Doom* differs in no material respect from Robert Crowley's biblical prophetic poetry. After the close of the Puritan epoch, the apocalypticism of Jonathan Edwards continued to echo the concerns of the Edwardian reformers.[2]

[2] Few critical studies of English and American Puritanism probe the area of pre-1590 English Protestant literature or theology. On the immense later influence of Foxe's *Actes and Monuments*, see William Haller, *Foxe's Book of Martyrs and the Elect Nation* (1963). Also see the essays by various hands in Sacvan Bercovitch, ed., *The American Puritan Imagination: Essays in Revaluation* (Cambridge, 1974), esp. "The Literary Consequences of Puritanism" by Larzer Ziff. Nancy Beaty's *The Craft of Dying: A Study in the Literary Tradition of the "Ars Moriendi" in England* (New Haven, 1970) traces a seventeenth-century Puritan genre back to sixteenth-century Reformation sources. Her argument concerning seventeenth-century England can be applied to America. Sacvan Bercovitch goes back to

This book is a survey of the emergence and early development of an enduring tradition of English and American literature. The outline of the history of ideas in the first part details the historical, political, and religious background, an understanding of which is necessary to comprehend the discussion of the Protestant literature and literary ethic formulated during the English Reformation. The second part then examines the varying genres of the literature and traces the development of themes, conventions, techniques, and styles. The entire study is based upon primary material not readily available, both manuscript evidence and early printed books that exist in only one or few known copies. A major purpose of the whole investigation is to isolate problems and questions concerning future literary development. Detailed analysis of pioneering authors and works should lead toward a better understanding of the Protestant literary tradition throughout the sixteenth and seventeenth centuries. The very existence of this school of English Reformation authors, however, with its large body of literary texts, raises a critical problem of major importance. How could so many authors and works, of such significance and influence, remain unknown to most Renaissance literary scholars?

THE CRITICAL PROBLEM

Traditional scholarship pays scant attention to English literature of the mid-sixteenth century.[3] We are told that the

---

Bale and Foxe in *The Puritan Origins of the American Self* (New Haven, 1975).

[3] Most standard bibliographies and critical studies ignore the period or exclude it from their chronological limits. William A. Ringler's bibliography of Tudor poetry (*NCBEL*, I, cols. 1079-1162) and the revised *STC* recover many forgotten works. The only critical studies to approach mid-

English Renaissance effectively begins with the "new poetry" of Spenser and Sidney. Various explanations have been offered for the apparent dearth of early Tudor literature. R. W. Chambers restates the traditional view that Henry VIII stopped the poets' music and that all learning ceased at the death of Thomas More.[4] On the basis of stylistic criteria, C. S. Lewis declares that the "Drab Age" began with the late Henrician poetry of Wyatt and Surrey and continued until the " 'Golden' Age" initiated by Spenser and Sidney. For Lewis mid-Tudor verse was marred by metrical regularity, plain diction, short lines, and simple "clumsiness." He is particularly hostile to poulter's measure and fourteener couplets. Yet he provides few objective grounds for his assertion that most writing before Sidney's time is "bad." Despite Lewis's disclaimer that his terminology is neither "dyslogistic" nor "eulogistic," he echoes the common enthusiasm for the last two decades of Elizabeth's reign as that time when English literature escaped from decadent conventionality into a flowering of "ingenuous" art that is "naturally delightful."[5] Others find that the English Reformation was inimical to fiction and art. L. B. Campbell, for example, delivers the commonplace opinion that the Protestant reformers supplanted courtly love poetry with prosaic metrical Psalms.[6] Thus the mid-sixteenth century is seen as an age of artless controversy

---

Tudor literature in any detail are L. B. Campbell's *Divine Poetry and Drama in Sixteenth-Century England* (Berkeley, 1959); David Bevington's *From "Mankind" to Marlowe: Growth and Structure in the Popular Drama of Tudor England* (Cambridge, Mass., 1962) and *Tudor Drama and Politics: A Critical Approach to Topical Meaning* (Cambridge, Mass., 1968); and C. S. Lewis's *English Literature in the Sixteenth Century Excluding Drama* (Oxford, 1954).

[4] *Thomas More* (1935), p. 379.

[5] *Sixteenth Century*, pp. 64-65, and passim.

[6] *Divine Poetry and Drama*, pp. 41-45.

during which the Reformation snuffed out the Renaissance. Such critics contend that after the destruction of traditional art forms by English reformers, further development in poetry and fiction proved impossible until Sidney formulated a new aesthetics suitable to the changed circumstances of his time.

The received opinion that the period before the 1579 publication of *The Shepheardes Calender* constitutes a "dark age" of Tudor literature has gone unchallenged by almost all literary scholars.[7] Yet reassessment of the statements of Sir Philip Sidney, George Puttenham, and their Elizabethan contemporaries, who decry the decadence of their English predecessors, reveals that these critics are united by a new disdain for medieval literature and native vernacular tradition. Their scorn derives from the imported standards of Continental literature which, by the 1580s, had supplanted the native English tradition as the basis of Elizabethan poetics. Sidney's *Apology for Poetry*, making few exceptions, rejects early Tudor literature because of its lack of metrical sophistication and failure to conform to neoclassical canons. He censures even Spenser for his imitation of "an old rustick language" in *The Shepheardes Calender*; Sackville and Norton err because they violate the unities in *Gorboduc*. According to Puttenham, the chief distinction of the "new company of courtly makers" led by Wyatt and Surrey was the reformation of the "rude & homely maner of vulgar [vernacular] Poesie" by means of the introduction of the "sweete and stately measures and stile of the Italian Poesie." Puttenham's misunderstanding of the writings of two earlier authors, William Langland and John Skelton, epitomizes the late Elizabethan shift in literary taste. By lumping these poets together Puttenham

---

[7] For a strenuous dissent see John T. Shawcross, "The Bridge between the Towers: Tudor Poetry, 1557-1579," forthcoming.

shows that he cannot differentiate between their highly varied techniques of language, metrics, and style.[8] He can neither comprehend nor appreciate alliterative conventions and the fourteenth-century dialect employed by Langland. We must test traditional shibboleths and discover the principles of Tudor literature by an inductive examination of the works themselves. One cannot deny that late sixteenth-century authors believed that they were participating in the rebirth of English literature. Late Elizabethan disdain for earlier Tudor literature, like the modern lack of sympathy, springs from a retrospective application of imported standards of Italianate criticism to older native traditions. In fact, it is from Sidney, Puttenham, and their contemporaries that C. S. Lewis and other modern critics inherit the stylistic criteria that they continue to apply to the earlier literature. In challenging these Italianate concepts, A. C. Hamilton rightly calls for a reassessment of the literary Renaissance in England in terms of the assumptions of contemporary English readers.[9]

Mid-Tudor taste contradicts Puttenham's judgment of the earlier literature. The interest of Englishmen of the mid-century was sufficient to justify four editions of *Piers Plowman*; Robert Crowley published three editions in 1550, and Owen Rogers reprinted the text in 1561. After that date, *Piers Plowman* remained out of print until the nineteenth century. Similarly, although in 1557 John Bale could praise Skelton as "a second Lucian or Democritus" because of his "worthiness and eloquence both in prose and verse"

---

[8] G. G. Smith, ed., *Elizabethan Critical Essays* (Oxford, 1904; 2 vols.), II, 62-63, 64-65.

[9] "On the Concept of the English Literary Renaissance," in *Medieval and Renaissance Studies: Proceedings of the Southeastern Institute of Medieval and Renaissance Studies*, Summer 1976, vol. 8, ed. Dale B.J. Randall (Durham, N.C., 1979), pp. 119-40.

and because of the pleasant "mordancy" of his satires,[10] Puttenham thirty years later denied him any "great worthines."[11] Bale and his audience evidently appreciated older standards of complaint and satire that clashed with the Italianate canons of the 1580s. Skelton's art depends upon the deliberate mixture of older conventions and techniques of satire that would appear primitive and barbaric to any neoclassical critic.[12] His poems were reprinted frequently until the appearance in 1568 of John Stow's edition of the collected works, the last complete Skelton edition to appear for 168 years.

The present investigation challenges the accepted history of sixteenth-century English literature and the traditional canon of Tudor literary texts; it relates Protestant authors and their works to each other and demonstrates that they fit together into a coherent configuration. Detailed examination of Edwardian literature disproves the notion that this time is part of an awkward limbo between the Middle Ages and the Renaissance. Radical reformers participated in a "Renaissance" by returning to original sources in order to revive them through application to immediate contemporary conditions.[13] By scrutinizing radical Reformation literature within its broad mid-Tudor context, this argument provides a bridge between our understanding of the rise of humanism under the early Tudor kings (Henry VII and Henry VIII) and the renaissance of poetry and

---

[10] *Catalogus*, I, 651.

[11] *Essays*, ed. Smith, II, 62.

[12] Arthur Heiserman, *Skelton and Satire* (Chicago, 1961).

[13] In recent years Tudor historians have supported this viewpoint from the perspective of intellectual history. See James K. McConica, *English Humanists and Reformation Politics under Henry VIII and Edward VI* (Oxford, 1965), hereafter cited as McConica; and A. B. Ferguson, *The Articulate Citizen and the English Renaissance* (Durham, N.C., 1965).

drama under Queen Elizabeth. The exceptional force of religious and social reform under Edward VI, coupled with the intense reaction against that reform under Mary and the reinstatement of reform efforts early in Elizabeth's reign, gives the writing of this period properties that differentiate it from the literature of the reign of Henry VIII and the later years of Elizabeth I. A major purpose of this study is to establish the integrity of mid-Tudor literature as a distinct segment of Tudor literary history, with its own particular significance for the study of the English literary Renaissance.

Edwardian literature contradicts the stereotype that Protestant radicals were intrinsically hostile to images and art. During Edward VI's reign, relaxation of restraints on the English Bible permitted the proliferation of varied secular and religious works. The Bible offered the Protestant author a literary model that he could imitate on the assumption that it resolved the potential conflict between truth and art. The reformers believed that the Bible was a storehouse of precedents concerning diction, genres, and figurative language. Protestant ideals did lead to widespread iconoclasm at this time. Instead of snuffing out all art, however, the Protestant prohibition of Roman Catholic iconography and ritual encouraged sanctioned forms of literature. Thus at the same time that the reformers destroyed some literary modes on grounds of religious error, they adapted old genres and conventions and formulated new ones. Early Tudor themes and conventions undergo a sea change during the reign of Edward VI. In fact, the principles of English Reformation literature result from a fusion of unbroken and continuous native traditions with new Protestant ideas. One may extrapolate the principles of Protestant aesthetics from examination of such extra-literary materials as sermons, letters, biblical commentaries, and political pamphlets. Early Protestants approved of the arts so long as they conformed to their ideals of religious truth. In the manner of Spenser and Milton, they rejected any substitution of artifice for truth.

The radical reformers, whose works are analyzed in this study, became known as "gospellers" because of the extreme scripturalism of their style and thought. (Critics would not apply the term "Puritan" to such radicals until the 1560s, after their return from the Marian exile.) Their detractors applied the term "gospeller" as a pejorative epithet for the extremist members of the Protestant faction that controlled England under Edward VI. In R. Wever's interlude *Lusty Juventus* (c. 1550), for example, the Catholic Vice Hypocrisy mocks the Protestant hero ironically as "a great gospeller in the mouth" for listening to sermons and carrying a New Testament in his pocket. Government support for the gospellers encouraged the Edwardian vogue for scriptural literature. An Elizabethan account states that the

> . . . worde [Bible] at that time had the pryce & bare the bell awaie througheoute the whole lande. With that were all pulpettes filled, Churches garnished, printers shoppes furnyshed, and every mans house decked. With gods word was every mans mouth occupied, of that wer al songes, enterludes, and plaies made.[14]

Gospelling literature integrates profuse biblical quotation, allusion, paraphrase, and marginal commentary with native literary forms, techniques, and conventions. Particular works may consist of moralistic plots studded with scriptural tags and examples, gospel stories, or metrical

---

[14] Introduction by E. P., translator of Cranmer's *Confutation of Unwritten Verities* (1558), A4ʳ.

paraphrases of the Bible. Protestant interludes, the dialogues of William Turner, sermons by Hugh Latimer and John Hooper, and poems by Robert Crowley and others are often little more than patchworks of Bible verses.

Devotion to the scriptures led the Protestants to forbid apocryphal forms of literature and art; thus they mandated a cultural revolution. Protestant emphasis on the printed text as the embodiment of divine truth contradicted the rich variety of medieval adaptations of the Bible to contemporary life. Widespread illiteracy and the sacerdotal assumptions of the late medieval church had commonly led to the substitution of sacred legends for Bible reading. Until Edward's reign, the Vulgate Bible remained the property of clerics and Latin-educated laymen. In place of the vernacular Bible, lay devotion had centered upon saints' lives and images, shrines, the folk art of the mysteries and carols, illuminated books of hours, crucifixes and rosaries, images of Christ and the Virgin, and elaborate allegorical visions. The popularity of Caxton's translation of *The Golden Legend* (1483) is an indication of late medieval piety. In the eyes of the Protestant reformers, medieval tradition subordinated the text of the Bible to a variety of sensational and pictorial objects of art. For example, the actors who played Mak, Gib, and Gill in the *Secunda Pastorum* in the Towneley cycle would have portrayed themselves, and the audience would have recognized them as fellow countrymen. They reenacted the nativity in a medieval English setting that had lost touch with its biblical prototype. The reformers felt that such adaptations shifted emphasis away from the Bible itself.

Reformation literature presupposes a major shift in mimetic theory. In opposition to the artistic externalization of religious feelings, Protestant subjectivity demands inner faith predicated upon spiritual understanding. The un-

[16]

varying principle of Edwardian literature is the primacy of the Bible; thus the reformers deny that artificial figures contain the spiritual truth that they imitate. Insisting that truth inheres in the literal text, the Protestants used the Bible as the touchstone for their experience in the world. Neither secular nor religious forms subordinate biblical texts to images or other pictorial forms. Unlike medieval adaptations of the Bible to contemporary circumstances, Protestant art uses the scriptures as a paradigm for present life. Providential patterning guides the dramatization of individual experience by reference to universal biblical models such as the ever-popular topics of conversion, exile, and martyrdom. Insisting on a radical distinction between biblical history and contemporary life, Edwardian Protestants find in biblical events archetypal patterns for current action. They preserve the Pauline distinction between the planes of nature and grace. In the fallen world, human action and art should be dark reflections of primordial truth.

The literary achievement of the mid-Tudor reformers manifests itself through a great variety of genres, including both the courtly and popular interlude, allegory and satire, and millennial prophecy and biblical paraphrase. The major authors were Robert Crowley, William Baldwin, John Bale, Luke Shepherd, and Thomas Cranmer. They were joined by a host of minor poets as well as by the anonymous authors of dialogues and interludes. Such writers as Crowley and Baldwin, Nicholas Udall and R. Wever created complex and allusive works like *Philargyrie of Greate Britayne*, *Beware the Cat*, *Ralph Roister Doister*, and *Lusty Juventus*. Cranmer's great liturgical texts (the prayer book and *Book of Homilies*) employ an eloquent, colloquial style suited to the capacities of both high- and low-born members of the congregation. These Reformation authors strenuously affirmed the validity of fiction and a variety of literary forms. Like their Protestant successor, Sir Philip Sidney, they acknowledged the capacity of literature for correct use or abuse. Playwrights explored the comedic possibilities of eschatological drama. Satire, in particular, captured the imagination by bringing to life the bitter controversies of the time by means of equally violent paradoxes and verbal abuse. Prophecies, parables, and Psalms were at this time the dominant genres of biblical literature. Musical scores were printed with metrical paraphrases of the scriptures so that they might be recited as lyrical song. In imitation of the English Bible and Cranmer's books, Protestant writers fashioned a plain style that furnished the basis for the prose manner of seventeenth-century Puritanism.

The Reformation is a complicated time of literary transition, birth, and growth. We have tended to look with wonder at *The Shepheardes Calender*, seeing it as an example of a "new poetry" that appeared full-grown out of a dormant epoch. Spenser's pastoral eclogues, however, and the succeeding poetry and drama of the great Elizabethan flowering, are built upon the advances of the preceding generation of English Protestant authors. Native conventions and techniques continued to appear in the works of various non-Italianate authors of the 1590s. Marston, for example, retains the snarling diction and invective manner of John Bale and his contemporary reformers, although stylistic harshness has lost its cutting polemical edge. With their abstract ethical sentiments and lack of figurative complexity, Sir Walter Raleigh's lyrics perpetuate the stylistic flatness of mid-Tudor verse. The achievement of the seventeenth-century devotional lyric and Milton's biblical epics grows out of a richly complex, living reformist tradition. The mid-Tudor Protestants looked not to the sword but to the book as the source of freedom and justice—and it is through the books of the entire English Protestant literary tradition that we may discover the power, and the beauty, of unadorned truth.

A HISTORICAL OVERVIEW

A unique set of historical circumstances offered occasion for the sudden growth of Protestant publication and the emergence of the Reformation literary tradition. A standard view of history might attribute the more tolerant climate of the mid-century to the monarch who set the general tenor for his reign. Such reasoning would lead to emphasis on entertainment and intellectual life at the royal court rather than to study of aristocratic patronage, radical Protestant publication, or the new Protestant liturgy. The conditions of Edward's reign were, however, without parallel during the whole of the English Renaissance. Edward, as a minor ruler, was never more than a figurehead. Examination of his manuscript letters, notebooks, and journal reveals no evidence of original thought or influence on the culture and politics of his time. The royal government was controlled first by the king's uncle Edward Seymour, Duke of Somerset and Protector of the Realm, and second by John Dudley, Duke of Northumberland and President of the Privy Council. Both regents ruled through the king in succession, Seymour by means of personal government that circumvented the council and Dudley through skillful manipulation and control of the king and loyal councilors. The course of Edward's reign, then, was determined by both the victory of the Protestant lords, who seized control when Henry VIII died, and the internal power struggle between partisans of the two dukes.

Because an accurate understanding of the turbulent history of the reigns of Edward VI and Mary Tudor has resisted even the efforts of specialists in the field, it is necessary to outline the sequence of events in ecclesiastical and political history in order to clarify related developments in literature.[15] The literary critic and intellectual historian need to understand how Edward Seymour, with the support of Archbishop Cranmer, became the dynamic political force behind the Protestant ascendancy at court, the aristocratic patronage of Protestant literature, and the explosion of radical reformist publication during Edward's reign. This survey will provide a broad perspective for detailed analyses of the following: the early Tudor origins of the Reformation literary tradition (Chapter 1); the literary and cultural consequences of Seymour's coup d'état, especially his encouragement of propaganda favoring his controversial policies (Chapter 2); the generation and literary impact of the fundamental texts of the Reformation church settlement: the English Bible, *Book of Homilies*, and *Book of Common Prayer* (Chapter 3); and the iconographic image of the godly prince, which was perpetuated by panegyrics, emblematic woodcuts, civic pageantry, and courtly drama and spectacle (Chapter 4). The ordering of chapters in Part I reflects the causal movement from the rise to power of a tightly knit faction of Protestant lords and prelates to their exploitation of book publication, the liturgy, and the carefully controlled idealization of a boy monarch as different vehicles for implementing a religious and cultural revolution.

Edwardian authors built upon groundwork that had been laid by writers, preachers, and politicians ever since the appearance of the Tyndale New Testament (1525). Until

[15] For further detail see both G. R. Elton, *Reform and Reformation England, 1509-1558* (1977), hereafter cited as Elton, and A. G. Dickens, *The English Reformation* (1967; 2nd ed., rev.).

Tyndale's time, Lollard dissent had been driven underground, although bitter anticlericalism made London and the southeastern counties fertile areas for the spread of new Lutheran ideas. Discussion of religious reform underwent a slow gestation in the secure atmosphere of Oxford and Cambridge, notably the latter, where at the White Horse tavern a group of scholars sympathetic to reform, which included Tyndale, Thomas Cranmer, Hugh Latimer, John Frith, Robert Barnes, and Miles Coverdale, met for regular discussion. Lord Chancellor Thomas Wolsey, Archbishop of York, attempted to halt the spread of Lollard heresy and the smuggling of Lutheran texts by means of executions and book burnings. Henry VIII himself issued his *Assertio septem sacramentorum* (1521), a confutation of Luther that may reflect the thinking of Thomas More. When Wolsey's career foundered on his failure to secure a divorce or annulment for his master, More was the obvious successor as Lord Chancellor.

Thomas More zealously continued Wolsey's defense of the church, by persecuting heretics and burning Lutherans, until his opposition to the king's divorce led him to resign his office. For almost one decade, William Tyndale was More's chief antagonist in religious matters. His radical Erasmianism and translation of the New Testament into English brought this Lutheran convert to exile himself in Antwerp and other European locations. From his Continental base he began to issue polemical works in English, many of which bore the false imprint "Marlborowe in the lande of Hesse" (i.e., Marburg). Two 1528 "Marburg" tracts, the *Parable of the Wicked Mammon* and *Obedience of a Christen Man*, respectively argue Tyndale's case for the Lutheran doctrine of justification by faith alone and for the obligation of Christian rulers to obey divine will. In a series of massive replies and counterarguments,

More attempted to rebut the Protestant attack mounted by Tyndale and his disciples, William Roy, Robert Barnes, John Frith, and George Joye. Of particular interest is Simon Fish's attack on the clergy, *A Supplicacyon for the Beggars* (c. 1529). Fish saw ecclesiastical corruption as a social rather than a theological problem; his call for the confiscation of church property and its redistribution to the poor prepared the way for the outburst of Edwardian complaints by Robert Crowley, Thomas Becon, Thomas Lever, and others. Tyndale was eventually tracked down and executed by Imperial authorities for treason and heresy, but not before More's own refusal to accept royal supremacy in religious affairs led him to the scaffold.[16]

As Henry VIII's chief minister, Thomas Cromwell constructed the Acts of Succession and Royal Supremacy (1534) in opposition to which More went to his death. Cromwell collaborated with Cranmer, the recently named primate of the Church of England, in effecting the royal divorce and ensuring the succession of a legitimate heir. Although Cromwell and Cranmer leaned toward Protestantism, their administrative reforms left unchanged all matters of doctrine and ritual. Henry became an English pope, whose supremacy over the church ensured that its hierarchy would serve the crown and its ministers. Cromwell ruthlessly dissolved the monasteries and redistributed their wealth not to the poor commons but to the crown and royal favorites. During a brief interval during the late 1530s, when Cromwell gathered around him a circle of young Protestant publicists including John Bale, some moderate Protestant advances were achieved through both the sanctioning of the English Bible and the campaign against pilgrimages and religious images. The king and his ministers ap-

[16] See J. A. Guy, *The Public Career of Sir Thomas More* (New Haven, 1980), chap. 8.

pointed Protestant bishops such as Latimer, Barlow, and Robert Holgate. Cromwell's fall into disfavor and eventual execution, however, brought with it the defeat of the Protestant faction. Thomas Howard, third Duke of Norfolk, and Stephen Gardiner, Bishop of Winchester, became the king's chief advisers following Cromwell's fall. Although both men supported the Henrician Reformation—Gardiner's *De vera obedientia* (1535) articulated a strong defense of the royal supremacy—they fervently opposed Protestantism and guided the king into a policy of religious reaction. Aided by the Lord Chancellor Thomas Wriothesley and by Edmund Bonner, Bishop of London, Howard and Gardiner led in the passage of the Act of Six Articles (1539), which even before Cromwell's fall reimposed rigid Catholic orthodoxy and assigned the harshest penalties for heresy. Latimer and other Protestant bishops resigned their sees in response, while Coverdale, Bale, Turner, Hooper, and other reformers left England for Antwerp, Strasbourg, and Zurich.

Despite the administrative victory of the reactionaries, two related Protestant groups came to dominate the court during Henry VIII's last years (c. 1540-47). Both owed their position to marriage alliances with the king and the birth in 1537 of Prince Edward. By 1546 the rising reformist faction surrounding Edward Seymour, Earl of Hertford, had defeated the Catholic courtiers led by Gardiner and Howard. Seymour's position was due solely to kinship with his sister Jane, the late queen, and his nephew Edward, the heir apparent. The circle surrounding Catherine Parr, Henry's last queen, was well known for its moderate Protestantism and Erasmian pietism. Perhaps at the recommendation of Cranmer, the queen brought to court as tutors to Prince Edward a group of distinguished Protestant scholars from St. John's College of Cambridge University: Sir John Cheke, Roger Ascham, and William

Grindal. With the assistance of other Erasmians, these tutors created a humanist academy for Edward and his sister Princess Elizabeth, which was modeled on Erasmus's *Institutio Principis Christiani* and the educational ideas of Juan Luis Vives. Sir Thomas Smith, the first Regius Professor of Civil Law at Cambridge, and William Cecil, another graduate of St. John's, may have arrived at court via the Parr connection; Cecil had been Cheke's student.[17] The outstanding members of this second generation of Protestant intellectuals had already tangled with Gardiner. Smith and Cheke, England's foremost Greek scholars, had been muzzled by the bishop, who was Cromwell's successor as Chancellor of Cambridge University, when they attempted to introduce a more "modern" and correct Erasmian standard for Greek pronunciation. This conflict between "new" and "old" learning followed the lines of developing religious controversies.

In Henry VIII's last year, when it became obvious that the king's death was imminent, a struggle arose for succession between the Howard-Gardiner group and the Seymour-Parr faction. The division between them brought the backers of reaction and reform into direct conflict. The reformers gained the upper hand, partly through their links to Prince Edward and partly through Thomas Howard's fall from favor because of the disgrace of his niece, Catherine Howard. William Paget, who dominated the administration as the king's principal secretary, took sides with Seymour. The conservatives made the first move when they attempted to implicate Catherine Parr, the Duchess of Suffolk (Catherine Brandon), and Seymour's wife Anne Stanhope in heresy accusations made against Anne Askew, a Lincolnshire gentlewoman. Prominent reformers such as

---

[17] See McConica, chap. 7.

Hugh Latimer came under suspicion. Gardiner presided at the Privy Council's two formal examinations of Anne Askew, which became a reformist *cause célèbre* because of the use of the full rigor of torture, an unheard-of practice in Tudor England. Gardiner and Wriothesley operated the rack. Although Askew was burned at Smithfield on 16 July 1546, the conservative attempt to bring down the Protestant faction ultimately backfired. Gardiner's fall from favor led to his exclusion, along with that of Bonner, from the council of regency set up by Henry VIII's will in order to govern England during Edward's minority. The Duke of Norfolk and his eldest son Henry Howard, the Earl of Surrey, were arrested by the end of the year when the turbulent Surrey was charged, on the basis of dubious evidence, with contesting the prince's claim to the throne. For at least a decade, Surrey and Seymour had been rivals at court. The younger Howard died at the block, and his father would have followed had Henry VIII not died on 28 January 1547 before the sentence could be carried out. The elder Howard spent Edward's reign in the Tower of London, where Gardiner eventually joined him.

Henry's death left the Protestant lords poised to seize power. Edward VI was insulated from the outer world by a court filled with reformist tutors and aristocrats. On 31 January 1547 the council of regency elected Seymour Lord Protector, the traditional assignment of the king's eldest uncle during a minority. Seymour was created Duke of Somerset on 16 February at the same time that John Dudley became Earl of Warwick. Seymour's coup d'état allowed him to rule effectively as king, and, in violation of the royal will, to replace the legitimate council of regency with a Privy Council that he selected personally. Contrary to the traditional interpretation, this council did not unite in support of Seymour's religious reforms. The protector

acted without consulting other councilors, sometimes fal-
sifying council records to suit his political purposes. The
ultimate failure of his government resulted from fundamental administrative error and his overbearing circum-
vention of the Privy Council, which gradually alienated
almost all his original supporters.[18] The disastrous campaign to conquer Scotland weakened Seymour, and the
Thomas Seymour affair paved the way for his own downfall. The younger Seymour challenged control at court by
first marrying Catherine Parr and then, when the dowager
queen had died in childbirth, courting Princess Elizabeth,
a strong claimant to the throne. By permitting John Dudley and his fellow councilors to move against his ambitious
brother through attainder rather than trial, Seymour undermined his own authority. His failure to save his brother
from execution left Seymour in a precariously isolated position when the councilors turned against him during the
1549 rebellions.

As protector, Seymour permitted an unprecedented degree of religious toleration and freedom of speech, reading, and publication. The protectorate was the only time
during the Tudor age when no one was executed on grounds
of heresy. Printers turned out a huge volume of Protestant
pamphlet literature, which had been forbidden so long as
Henry VIII had lived. Seymour's *de facto* relaxation of
censorship brought him into direct confrontation with Gardiner, whose Winchester diocese was disturbed by outbursts of iconoclasm. Lutheran writings and inflammatory
Protestant tracts went openly on sale in the Winchester
market, including Bale's account of the persecution of Anne
Askew which singled out the bishop as the *bête noire* of
English reformers. In an extraordinary series of letters,

[18] D. E. Hoak, *The King's Council in the Reign of Edward VI* (Cambridge, 1976), pp. 167, 177-79, 189-90, and passim.

Seymour defended scriptural authority and individual freedom of conscience as the sole arbiters in matters of faith. Gardiner reaffirmed Thomas More's defense of the external authority of the church as an infallible guide to scriptural interpretation and salvation. Inheriting Cromwell's bent for patronage and propaganda, Seymour included the radical poets William Gray and William Samuel among his retainers. He gave positions in his own household to the returned exiles Thomas Becon and John Hooper, who served as chaplains; William Turner became the protector's personal physician. Miles Coverdale found a place at court as a royal chaplain. The four bookmen edited reformist texts and wrote sermons, plays, dialogues, and tracts defending Seymour and his policies. The prominent printers Richard Grafton and Edward Whitchurch issued Protestant propaganda on behalf of the crown. Grafton as King's Printer seems to have underwritten the activities of Robert Crowley, the most active Edwardian publicist. Crowley's editions of writings attributed to Wyclif and Tyndale complemented his landmark edition of the underground classic *Piers Plowman*. His apocalyptic prophecies and millennial tracts epitomized the expectant mood of the reformers. Crowley's own compositions, in verse and prose, continued the tradition of commonwealth complaint established by Simon Fish's *Supplicacyon for the Beggars* and Henry Brinkelow's *Complaynt of Roderyck Mors* (Strasbourg?, c. 1542). Seymour's pulpit spokesman Hugh Latimer and Thomas Lever similarly preached the old-fashioned attack on avarice.

In collaboration with Archbishop Cranmer, Seymour embarked on a sweeping program of Protestant reform in church doctrine and ritual. Exiled preachers returned home as England gained a reputation as a refuge for fugitive foreign reformers. The Protestant aristocracy extended patronage and protection as the influx swelled. Hugh Latimer began to preach as a crown spokesman at both St. Paul's Cathedral and the royal court. John Hooper swayed London congregations; Thomas Becon and Thomas Lever preached before the king at Westminster. Widespread iconoclasm erupted in London and other towns. In addition to sanctioning unrestricted public access to the vernacular Bible, the Royal Injunctions ordered all clergy to use the English translation of Erasmus's *Paraphrases* and to read from the *Book of Homilies*. The same orders revived the Cromwellian attack against relics, pilgrimages, and traditional religious images. Gardiner's isolated opposition incurred arrest and imprisonment in the Tower, from which he issued repeated protests against the introduction of changes in religion during a royal minority. By the end of the first year of the new regime, Parliament had abolished the chantries, swept away the Act of Six Articles and previous heresy statutes, and approved a program of radical reform that dismantled the Anglo-Catholicism of Henry VIII. The doctrines of purgatory and clerical celibacy went out of use. During 1548 the Privy Council abolished many religious ceremonies (including the use of holy candles, ashes, and palms) and encouraged the iconoclastic attack on religious images. Cranmer permitted the gradual introduction of an English church service. Parliament authorized the prayer book, which came into use throughout England on 9 June 1549 (Whitsunday). The new rite abolished the Latin service and broke down the traditional division between clergy and laity. Although it rejected transubstantiation, the compromise document retained an English mass, clerical vestments, and other elements of the traditional ritual. Introduction of this new service led to rebellion in Cornwall as well as lesser risings in Yorkshire and Oxfordshire. The insurrection in East Anglia, on the other hand, resulted from lower-class demands for agrarian reform that were tinged with traditional anticlericalism.

This turbulence gave John Dudley his occasion to over-throw Seymour. His coup d'état (10 October 1549) re-established government by council. Contrary to the pre-vailing view that the Edwardian council abandoned the governmental reforms of the 1530s, Dudley was the ad-ministrative heir of Thomas Cromwell. After his coup, Dudley, who became Duke of Northumberland on 11 Oc-tober 1551, perceived a threat from the conservatives; they had regained their position at the royal court and in coun-cil, and Dudley feared a plot to install Princess Mary as regent. Dudley's uneasiness explains his puzzling decision to join the radical reformers after he had deposed Sey-mour; it also accounts for his even more surprising deci-sion to release his rival from prison. The motives of Dud-ley, who appears to have been a conservative in religion, were entirely political. After consolidating his position, Dudley again arrested Seymour, who, acquitted of treason, was executed for felony on 22 January 1552. Seymour died a popular hero whose reputation was to develop into the legend of the "good duke." Dudley, as the head of the Privy Council, manipulated Edward VI and created the fiction that the king was able to engage in personal rule. After a brief period out of favor, William Cecil returned to a central role in Edwardian government. In moving from Seymour's household into the inner circle of Dudley's council, Cecil first displayed his flair for political sur-vival.[19]

Dudley cast in his lot with the Protestant extremists. John Hooper used his enhanced prominence at court to advance Zwinglian ideas. Conservative prelates, including Bonner and Gardiner, were deprived of their sees and dis-placed by radical bishops: Hooper, Coverdale, Nicholas Ridley, John Ponet, and John Scory. The see of Ossory in

[19] Ibid., pp. 241-58.

Ireland went to John Bale. Unlike their Anglican successors, these evangelical bishops returned to the apostolic ideal of the bishop as pastor and chief minister. Ridley and Hooper led the way in ordering the removal of rood screens and replacing altars with communion tables placed in the chancel. Cranmer organized the attack on sectarians that resulted in the burnings of Joan Bocher (Joan of Kent) and other Anabaptists. At his combined see of Gloucester and Worcester, Hooper attacked the Anabaptists and, in a prelude to the Puritan agitation of the 1560s, protested the use of clerical vestments. Parliament ordered the extirpation of all Catholic service books and religious images, including roods. Cranmer revised the prayer book under pressure from English radicals (notably Hooper) and Continental divines at Oxford and Cambridge (chiefly Martin Bucer). The second prayer (after 27 October 1552) did away with the mass, the host, altars, and chasubles. The canon of the mass was so altered to make it clear that no veneration of the sacrament was involved. The Privy Council overruled Cranmer when it inserted the "Black Rubric," which denied that kneeling at communion implied adoration, transubstantiation, or the Real Presence of Christ. Shortly before the king's death, the government issued the Forty-two Articles, which established an essentially Protestant settlement in religion. On 6 July 1553, after a lingering illness, Edward VI finally died at Greenwich.

There was never any real doubt concerning Mary's accession—despite her Catholicism, Protestant gentry and aristocrats acclaimed her as the Tudor heir. Dudley failed in his attempt to place his daughter-in-law Lady Jane Grey on the throne; had he succeeded, he would have retained control of the government and ensured a Protestant succession. The foreign reformers fled, and English radicals such as Bale, Crowley, Ponet, and Foxe left England for the Continent. Mary reinstalled the Catholic bishops, making

Stephen Gardiner her Lord Chancellor. Cardinal Pole returned from Rome as primate of the Church of England. The two Marian Acts of Repeal undid first the Edwardian and then the Henrician Reformation. The heresy laws were first used in February 1555 to condemn a Protestant, John Rogers, to the stake. Many other convictions followed, including those of Cranmer, Latimer, Ridley, and Hooper. By the time Mary died on 17 November 1558, more than three hundred Protestants had died for their faith.

The reformers hailed the restoration of Protestantism at Elizabeth's succession to the throne.[20] Surviving exiles such as Crowley and Bale returned to England. Although the Seymours never regained their lofty preeminence, the Protestant line of John Dudley's younger son Robert, Earl of Leicester, thrived through the influence and favor of the queen. Mary had reigned too briefly to destroy the new faith, and John Foxe shaped his account of her persecutions into an extraordinarily potent attack on the papacy and English Catholicism. Elizabeth inherited the outlines of her religious settlement from Henry VIII and Edward VI. She revived the royal supremacy, even though she controlled the church as "supreme governor" rather than "supreme head." The chantries had already disappeared, and Elizabeth easily reversed Mary's restoration of monasticism. Edward's reign contributed the fundamental body of reformed doctrine and ritual. The *Book of Homilies* was reimposed and expanded through addition of a second volume. The Elizabethan prayer book assimilated the 1552 revisions. The Thirty-nine Articles revised and reissued the Edwardian doctrinal articles without any significant modifications. The Elizabethan settlement was most conservative in the area of ornaments and vestments—the or-

---

[20] On the Elizabethan reestablishment of Protestantism, see Penry Williams, *The Tudor Regime* (Oxford, 1979), chap. 8.

naments of the church and clergy were to be those in use "in the second year of the reign of King Edward VI."

Although Queen Elizabeth skillfully ensured that England would remain a Protestant nation, she could not impose uniform acceptance of her Anglican compromise. The 1560s brought attempts by Puritans, who inherited the ideas of Latimer and Hooper, to abolish what they perceived to be Roman Catholic survivals, including kneeling at holy communion, the use of organ music in services, and especially the wearing of vestments. For their refusal to wear the prescribed vestments, Robert Crowley and many other Puritan clergy were suspended from office. By the 1580s the government began to harry the Jesuit missionaries and recusants; at the same time it attempted to silence the Protestant radicals. Late in the reign, Archbishop Whitgift fiercely persecuted both the Puritans, led by Thomas Cartwright, and the restless Catholics. The seeds of Elizabethan disunity and of the violent controversies of the seventeenth century lay in the factional disputes of the English Reformation of the mid-sixteenth century. Lines of conflict had been drawn that were to develop into the Puritan Revolution.

PART I

THE REFORMATION
BACKGROUND

CHAPTER I

The Emergence of Protestant Literary Tradition

For lyke as golde passeth in valewe alle other metalles, so thys legende excedeth alle other bookes.

Caxton, Epilogue to *The Golden Legend*

LATE MEDIEVAL LITERATURE AND PIETY

By the eve of the English Reformation, a controversy had erupted over the relative merits of native literary tradition and the neoclassical modes of European humanism. That literary taste had undergone little change from the time of Chaucer to the beginning of the Tudor age is evident from the fact that William Caxton catered to an elite clientele with a fondness for the courtly tradition of medieval English literature. During the next generation, humanists such as Thomas More turned toward classical and Continental models. In asserting the validity of native vernacular tradition, early Protestants resisted this shift; they chose, in part, to popularize the elite tradition of Caxton's time. Thomas Cromwell, for example, patronized the publication of the English Bible and literary works that appealed to a broad popular audience. He did so in defense of the Henrician Reformation of the 1530s, which concentrated on questions of ecclesiastical polity rather than theological doctrine. Henry VIII presided over a political revolution that substituted his authority for that of the pope. Examination of the development of native vernacular tradition through Henry's reign will permit assessment of the distinctively Protestant literature that would follow.

Caxton's publications mirror aristocratic taste at the end of the fifteenth century. After opening his shop late in 1476, he remained in business as England's first printer and publisher under four kings: Edward IV, Edward V, Richard III, and the first Tudor monarch, Henry VII. The location of his shop within the precincts of Westminster Abbey documents his dependence on aristocratic and crown patronage, for he chose a site where courtiers and members of Parliament would pass his door. That he entered his new trade under Yorkist patronage is suggested, if not proved, by the Huntington Library copy of his translation of Raoul Le Fevre's *The Recuyell of the Historyes of Troy* (Bruges, c. 1475), which contains a unique engraved frontispiece showing a kneeling author presenting his book to Margaret of York, Duchess of Burgundy and sister of Edward IV.[1] This copy belonged to the king's wife, Elizabeth Woodville. Caxton dedicated Jacobus de Cessolis's *The Game and Play of Chess* (Bruges, 1475) to the king's brother, George, Duke of Clarence. Later dedications to Lady Margaret Beaufort, mother of Henry VII, and to Prince Arthur show that Caxton survived the fall of the dynastic houses of York and Lancaster by acquiring new patrons at the court of Henry VII.

As a scholar-publisher, Caxton published most of the major works of Middle English verse. Issuing many other medieval works in translations that he made or commissioned, he supplied prologues and epilogues that comment

[1] Margaret Kekewich, "Edward IV, William Caxton, and Literary Patronage in Yorkist England," *MLR*, 66 (1971), 481-87.

on the significance of each text as literature. Like any modern critical editor, he showed shrewd judgment in choosing manuscripts and prepared good copy for the press. He tailored his publications to a select audience of aristocratic laymen, thus satisfying demand rather than shaping his readers' tastes. Publication of works by Chaucer, Gower, and Lydgate shows that courtly taste had changed little during the previous century. These authors had written under auspices similar to the patronage that Caxton himself later enjoyed. Chaucer wrote his poems during the period when he received appointments from Edward III and then Richard II. Gower composed the first version of *Confessio Amantis* at the command of Richard II. Lydgate received commissions from a variety of courtly figures including Henry V and his brother, the great fifteenth-century patron Humphrey, Duke of Gloucester.

Piers Plowman and the Wyclif Bible are the most striking omissions in Caxton's series. Langland's absence may be attributed in part to Caxton's general avoidance of works that held little appeal for his patrons. The popular conventions of unrhymed alliterative meter violated the courtly style of Chaucer, Gower, and Lydgate. Because of its association with fifteenth-century Lollard traditions, however, *Piers Plowman* also fell under the prohibition on Wyclifite texts imposed by the 1408 Oxford Synod. Nevertheless, the survival of a rich manuscript tradition shows that readers continued to value the allegory until Robert Crowley published the poem in 1550. Although the 1408 sanctions prevented publication of the Wyclif Bible, an elite audience, including royalty and clergy, read the unauthorized translation. Scribes copied the text frequently throughout the fifteenth century. At least two copies were once held in the royal library. Henry VI donated a fine folio manuscript to the Carthusian monastery north of London (Bodl. MS Bodley 277, fol. 375^r).

Except for a brief interval under Henry VIII, the only vernacular form in which English laymen could approach the Bible prior to Edward VI's reign was Caxton's translation of Jacobus de Voragine's *The Golden Legend*. This collection of saints' lives occupied a place in late medieval lay devotion similar to that which the Bible had held in the early Christian period. Caxton evaded the prohibition against an English Bible by printing a series of stories condensed from the life of Christ in a separate introductory section and by supplementing his received Latin text with a similar series of Old Testament lives. But his intermingling of biblical narrative with medieval commentary makes even indirect interpretation of the Bible difficult. Caxton's tale of Adam, for example, assimilates prophecies of Noah's Flood and the union of Christ with the church into the account of Adam's lust "as Methodius saith" (e6^r). The Bible stories disappear into the vast collection of saints' lives. The pervasive sacerdotalism of the text dictates the subordination of biblical stories to the ecclesiastical calendar. The feasts of Corpus Christi and Dedication of the Church, for example, receive emphasis equal to that placed on events in the life of Christ. The many stories about Mary reflect late medieval devotion to the Blessed Virgin, and the various lives of the saints emphasize their intercessory role between God and man through repeated accounts of miracles, visions, and relics. The work even includes the classicized myth of the Seven Sleepers. Caxton's version concludes with a didactic account of transubstantiation and the mass beginning with the incipit: "Here begynneth the noble historye of thexposicion of the masse."

Publication of *The Golden Legend* exemplifies Caxton's accommodation of medieval classics to aristocratic taste. After completing the translation under the patronage of William, Earl of Arundel, Caxton illustrated the text in a manner that reflected his concern with aristocratic patronage. He modeled this and other books on the fourteenth-century Burgundian fashion for large illuminated manuscripts of vernacular works. Nobles who had commissioned these manuscripts chose to hear readings from vernacular literature, just as their English counterparts heard Chaucer read his poems at court. The illuminated Flemish manuscripts were designed to be read by a reader standing at a lectern at the same time as a noble patron looked at the miniatures. In a similar fashion, Caxton illustrated the folio text of *The Golden Legend* with eighteen large woodcuts for important scenes from the Bible and other stories. In contrast to his small stereotyped images of saints with their emblems, which he used throughout the book, Caxton designed the large illustrations to fit specific sections of text.[2]

In all probability, Caxton included woodcuts as objects of devotion rather than as purely ornamental embellishments. His prologue identifies the collection as a whole with the doctrine of justification by good works, for he derives its authority from the recommendation of St. Jerome that one "do alweye somme good werke to thende that the devyl fynde the not ydle. . . ." ([–5ʳ]). Reading or hearing such a text was considered a pietistic deed. Caxton's Dutch contemporary Gheraert Leeu explains that he prints related illustrations in his treatise on the seven sorrows of the Virgin Mary "in order to evoke stronger and greater devotion in people . . . with the aim that laymen who cannot read will, when beholding the images, experience devout feelings. For images are the laymen's books."[3]

---

[2] Edward Hodnett, *English Woodcuts: 1480-1535* (1935), nos. 237-308 and figs. 5, 6, 11. Hereafter cited as Hodnett.

[3] *Ghedenchenisse van den VII Weeden oft droefheyden onser liever Vrouwen* (Antwerp, 1492), as quoted in Bibliothèque Royale Albert Iᵉʳ, *Le cinquième centenaire de l'imprimerie dans les anciens Pays-Bas* (Brussels, 1973), no. 130. Dr. Lotte Helinga of the British Library kindly translated the passage from the Dutch.

In his edition of *Rosarium Mariae* (Gouda, c. 1484), Leeu states that he includes woodcuts because laymen can read along with the text through the pictures.

Although Caxton designed *The Golden Legend* for aristocratic readers, it appealed to a much wider audience. In 1848 the Bodleian Library acquired a damaged copy of the first edition that had been sold from the parish library of Denchworth, Berkshire.[4] During the fifteenth and early sixteenth centuries, the copy was chained for public reading in the parish church. The absence of three complete signatures at the beginning and one complete signature at the end of the heavily worn Denchworth copy is consistent with its having been in continual use by parishioners. As their aristocratic predecessors had heard poems read at court, illiterate laymen looked over the shoulders of their companions who could read aloud from the book. The woodcut images of the saints, the crucifixion, and the Corpus Christi procession served as objects of lay devotion; thus they were analogous to items that were displayed in medieval churches and shrines, such as sculptures of saints, crucifixes, and decorated monstrances (see Figure 1).

The use of images by illiterate Englishmen conformed to the sixth-century directive of Gregory the Great:

> . . . in the same thing [i.e., picture] they read [the truth] who do not understand letters. Whence and especially to the [common] people the picture is in place of reading.[5]

Although Gregory had sanctioned the use of artistic images in lay religious instruction, he did not intend that they

---

[4] Bodl. Arch. G. b. 2. See William D. Macray, *Annals of the Bodleian Library Oxford* (Oxford, 1890; 2nd ed., rev.), p. 494.

[5] ". . . in ipsa legunt qui litteras nesciunt. Unde et praecipue gentibus pro lectione pictura est," Epistola 13: "Ad Serenum Massiliensem Epis-

should supplant the Bible. He recognized the danger of confusing the visual image with its scriptural prototype. Gregory acted in response to linguistic change that had already transformed Latin into a hieratic language known only to monks and scholars. By the end of the sixth century, Latin had all but disappeared as a popular language. The *Historia Francorum* (c. 590) shows that even such a scholar as Gregory of Tours had lost touch with classical Latin. Lay speakers of the new vernacular languages were almost universally illiterate and could not understand oral readings from the fourth-century Vulgate Bible. St. Jerome had originally translated the scriptures into Latin because it was still a living vernacular tongue. During the Middle Ages, however, the Vulgate evolved into a text sacred in itself that the people could understand only indirectly through clerical interpretation; collections of saints' lives and a variety of nonscriptural images came to fill the place that the Bible had originally occupied in lay devotion.

illiterate laypersons

Caxton and his contemporaries subordinated or replaced Bible texts with woodcut images as sensational, visual objects of lay devotion. For example, the *Biblia pauperum* (Netherlands, c. 1465) condenses Bible stories into a series of woodcut illustrations that accompany an allegorical commentary cut into the same block. The text emphasizes the suffering of Christ and the Virgin Mary. One hand-colored copy stresses Christ's agony through the vivid red of his wounds (Bodl. Auct. M. III. 13). Many illustrated indulgences bear similar coloration. One image of the crucified Christ surrounded by such instruments of the passion as the crown of thorns, scourges, dice, and nails promises pardon "to þem þat before þis ymage off pyte. Devoutly

picture Bible books

copum," in *Patrologiae cursus completus. Series latina*, ed. J. P. Migne (Paris, 1844-64; 221 vols.), LXXVII, col. 1128.

.v. tymes say. pater noster & ave. Pit[eous]ly beholding
þies ar[mes of Chris]tes passion. Ar [granted . . .] ii. M.
vii. C [. . . years] off pardon."[6] Emotional response to
such pictures through passionate formulaic prayer supplanted the scriptural reading recommended by the church
Fathers. A rare example of an intact text survives in one
image of pity: "To them that before this ymage of pyte
devoutly say fyve Pater noster fyve Aveys & a Credo py-
tously beholdyng these armes of Christ's passyon ar graunted
xxxii M. vii. C. & lv. yeres of pardon."[7] Such indulgences assured penitent devotees of absolution.

THE HUMANISTIC ATTACK ON NATIVE
ENGLISH LITERATURE

By the early sixteenth century, a new school of English
humanists began to attack the native literary traditions of
Caxton and early Tudor authors like Stephen Hawes and
John Skelton. The humanists seized in particular on what
they regarded as the stylistic failures of their predecessors.
Under the influence of Lorenzo Valla and his followers,
such scholars as John Colet and Thomas More advocated
the reading of classical Greek and Latin texts as the core
of the curriculum and as models of literary imitation. Although the Middle Ages had inherited some works of classical literature, not until Valla's time had they been treated
as models of stylistic purity. The humanists condemned
medieval literature in both Latin and the vernacular because of their strong distaste for what they perceived as
barbaric and "gothic" language and style. Although as a
youth Thomas More had written a handful of vernacular
poems including *A Mery Gest* (c. 1503), in maturity he

---

[6] England, c. 1490 (Bodl. Arch. G. e. 35; *STC* 14077c.7).

[7] England, c. 1500 (*STC* 14077c.13), pasted into Bodl. MS Rawlinson
D. 403, fol. 2ᵛ.

reserved English for the invective of his attacks on Luther and Tyndale. When he wrote the serious fiction of *Utopia* (1516), he addressed his international audience in an elegant Latin style.

Utopia lodges an oblique attack on all native tradition, in England and on the Continent. Under the guise of the advent of printing in Utopia, More describes the rebirth of classical learning in Western Europe. Despite the mockery in his portrait of Raphael Hythlodaeus, the chest of books that the philosopher-voyager carries with him to Utopia supplies an index of humanistic taste. The omissions are significant. Hythlodaeus easily ignores every book printed by Caxton. One book alone, a grammar of Constantine Lascaris (d. 1501), is by a medieval or modern author; all of the others are by classical Greek authors, whose works constitute the essential sources of humanistic scholarship. Lucian, Aristophanes, Homer, Euripides, and Sophocles are the only poets. As a Greek purist, Hythlodaeus denies the utility of all Latin literature except some writings by Cicero and Seneca. His companion Tricius Apinatus carries medical treatises by Galen and Hippocrates. Easily learning both Greek and the art of printing from their European callers, the Utopians soon publish thousands of copies of these texts. Although they possess no other books, in the eyes of the humanists the Utopians need no other works of secular learning.[8]

The strictures of the humanists were not, however, accepted without argument. John Skelton, for example, defended the native tradition of English language and literature, as well as medieval literature in general, against the new classical standards of the humanists. He lists thirty-six poets in his roster of great writers in *A Garlande of*

[8] *Utopia*, ed. E. Surtz and J. H. Hexter, vol. 4 of *The Complete Works* (New Haven, 1963- ; 14 vols.), ed. R. S. Sylvester et al., pp. 180-85.

Laurell (1523). By poetry Skelton means anything written or created, rather than only works of fiction. His list includes works in classical and vernacular languages written by ancient, medieval, and modern authors. He treats many of the Greek authors cited in *Utopia* as part of an unbroken literary tradition. Medieval authors of romances and theological commentaries jostle Boccaccio and Petrarch. Gower, Chaucer, and Lydgate welcome Skelton into their company in the same manner that Homer, Virgil, Ovid, Horace, and Lucan greet Dante in the *Inferno* (IV. 82-90). In defending his right to a place of honor among English poets and in praising his predecessors for enriching the vernacular, Skelton thus attacks the imported criteria of Continental humanism.

THE PROTESTANT DEFENSE OF ENGLISH LITERARY TRADITION

The influence of Erasmus on the native literary tradition, in contrast to that of Thomas More, was positive rather than negative. Erasmian writings had immense impact on English authors and readers, an effect that was deeply penetrating and long lasting. Erasmus issued the first critical edition of the Greek New Testament (1516), with a translation into modern Latin, during the same year that *Utopia* appeared. *Paraclesis* ("Exhortation"), the introduction to this New Testament, advocates Bible translation and the writing of popular scriptural literature. Because of the enthusiastic response of Tyndale and his followers, Erasmus, an orthodox Catholic, could appeal to both Protestant radicals and conservative Catholics. Erasmus's defense of vernacular language and literature is unusual for a humanist scholar; his call for religious reform through recovery of the scriptures by means of translation from the original tongues is intrinsically a defense of vernacular tradition, both ancient and modern. Protestants in particular responded by producing a great variety of literary forms in the language of the people, ranging from scriptural translation to biblical ballads and devotional songs. This return *ad fontes* denies the validity of such objects of formalistic lay devotion as pilgrimages, relics, and saints' images.

On the model of St. Jerome, Erasmus advocated translation of the Bible into the vernacular so that "even the lowliest women" could study the scriptures for themselves. Shifting emphasis from scholastic logic to gospel ethics, *Paraclesis* argues that only the "philosophia Christi" can undo the Fall and restore "human nature originally well formed." If people were illiterate, oral reading of the Bible and recitation of biblical stories should encourage universal lay understanding of the scriptures. Erasmus advocates the setting of biblical texts to popular tunes:

> Would that, as a result, the farmer sing some portion of them at the plow, the weaver hum some parts of them to the movement of his shuttle, the traveller lighten the weariness of the journey with stories of this kind!

Such songs would accommodate the Bible to lay illiteracy in very much the manner in which Gregory had approved of images as "laymen's books." Recited in the proper manner, the Bible could provide an anthology of popular literature. Vernacular Bible reading would undermine the validity of visual modes of devotion:

> But why do we not venerate instead the living and breathing likeness of Him in these books? . . . any paltry image . . . represents only the form of the body . . . but these writings bring you the living image of His holy mind and the speaking, healing, dying, rising Christ

himself, and thus they render Him so fully present that you would see less if you gazed upon Him with your very eyes.[9]

Paraclesis inspired William Tyndale to translate the New Testament that he produced at Cologne and Worms (c. 1525). In *The Obedience of a Christian Man*, he defended his choice of popular style and idiom:

> The sermons which thou readist in the Actes of the apostles & all that the apostles preached were no doute preached in the mother tonge. Why then mighte they not be written in the mother tonge? . . . Saynt hierom also translated the bible into his mother tonge. Why maye not we also? (B7ʳ⁻ᵛ)

Despite its Erasmian foundation, Tyndale's edition presupposes distinctively Protestant tenets. The prologue to Romans, for example, articulates the Lutheran doctrine of justification by faith alone. Henry VIII attempted to suppress the translation because it lacked royal authority and carried Tyndale's inflammatory notes. The illustrations for the edition also part from Erasmian practice, deriving rather from the woodcut series, attributed to Lucas Cranach, for Luther's translation of the New Testament (Wittenberg, 1522). Such illustrations in the Lutheran tradition serve as a companion to the text rather than as autonomous devotional images. The initial capitals depict the evangelists and apostles with their medieval emblems of quill and book. In imitation of classical images of poets and philosophers, the iconography of the author and his book had emerged by early Christian times in portraits of canonical authori-

---

[9] Desiderius Erasmus, *Christian Humanism and the Reformation: Selected Writings*, ed. John C. Olin (New York, 1965), pp. 97, 100, 105-106.

ties.[10] Cranach modeled his series of twenty woodcuts for Revelation on Dürer's magnificent engravings (Nuremberg, c. 1498). Cranach's incorporation of papal tiaras into his illustrations of the dragon, seven-headed beast, and Whore of Babylon assimilates Lutheran propaganda. In illustrating the measurement of the temple in chapter eleven, for example, he contrasts a dragon crowned with the papal tiara and an altar bearing a single candle in an otherwise bare church (compare Figure 10).

Restoration of the Bible as the sole spiritual authority was a limited solution to reforming nonscriptural abuses. This shift away from the nonscriptural traditions of the Middle Ages raises the implicit problem of how laymen are to interpret the scriptures. As Gabriel Josipovici states, "no text, whether it is the Book of God or the portrait of Pantagruel's ancestor, is self-explicating. If it means something then that meaning was put into it by someone, but by itself it is dumb to tell what the meaning is."[11] Erasmus and Tyndale meant different things by defining the Bible as a layman's book. Although he advocated individual reading and interpretation, Tyndale still channeled his readers' interpretation through his textual apparatus. Erasmus's annotations to his Greek New Testament were more or less factual, but he preferred noncontroversial paraphrase as a superior form of commentary that adheres closely to the literal sense of the text. Erasmus identifies under-

[10] Kurt Weitzmann, *Late Antique and Early Christian Book Illumination* (1977), plates 33, 35, 37, and 42. Pictures of the evangelists and apostles are not in themselves distinctive of Protestant tradition. Because these individuals are associated with the writing and transmission of scriptural texts, their portraits survived the Reformation attack on the medieval array of sensational images of Christ crucified, the Virgin Mary, saints, and martyrs. The surviving images often symbolize the Protestant concern for scripturalism, textual fidelity, and the return *ad fontes*.

[11] *The World and the Book: A Study of Modern Fiction* (1971), p. 48.

standing with the experience of individual reading or hearing, whereas Tyndale, in an apparent paradox, directs his readers toward an established interpretation.

Publication of an authorized version of the English Bible required the support of a new kind of patron: Thomas Cromwell. He had won Henry VIII's favor because of his success in imposing the royal supremacy on the Church of England. During the 1530s he dissolved the monasteries and reorganized crown administration. As political rather than doctrinal changes, Henrician church reforms substituted the king for the pope as head of the church. Like Thomas Cranmer, Archbishop of Canterbury, Cromwell supported reform along moderate Protestant lines. As the king's deputy in religious affairs, Cromwell skillfully manipulated a broad, popular audience as a vehicle of government policy.[12] By commissioning a series of works intended for the reading public rather than a coterie audience, Cromwell turned away from established patronage practices. Until his time, authors and printers had cultivated the approval of wealthy aristocrats. Cromwell reversed this relationship by taking Protestant authors into his service and commissioning propaganda that attacked conservative opposition to religious change. Authors continued to depend on grants of money and appointments to offices in order to earn a living, because they received few, if any, proceeds from the sale of books.

Cromwell's circle consisted for the most part of impoverished humanist scholars. John Foxe later described the group:

> . . . [Cromwell] always retained unto him and had about him such as could be found helpers and furtherers of

[12] McConica, chap. 6; also see W. Gordon Zeeveld, *Foundations of Tudor Policy* (Cambridge, Mass., 1948), pp. 111-12, and Dickens, *English Reformation*, pp. 187-91, 236-38.

the same; in the number of whom were sundry and divers fresh and quick wits, pertaining to his family; by whose industry and ingenious labours divers excellent both ballads and books were contrived and set abroad, concerning the suppression of the pope and all popish idolatry. (*A & M*, V, 403)

William Gray of Reading composed antipapal ballads for his patron. Thomas Starkey and Richard Morison wrote pamphlets in defense of the royal supremacy. Richard Taverner's translations converted Erasmus into an advocate of Protestant moderation.[13] John Bale went into Cromwell's service soon after converting to Protestantism. When Archbishop Lee of York indicted the former Carmelite friar for heresy, Cromwell freed him because of the comedies that he had written.[14] For performance at Cranmer's house during Christmas 1539, Bale wrote both a set of Protestant mystery plays and *King Johan*, a history play that represents the medieval king as a reforming prototype of Henry VIII. He also translated Thomas Kirchmeyer's *Pammachius* (Wittenberg, 1538), with a dedication to Cranmer. The latter seems to have inspired Bale's activities, whereas Cromwell provided the group of players who performed the plays.[15]

Cromwell's apologists were related to a tradition of social complaint that came out of the radicalized Protestant tradition of Erasmian humanism. Styling themselves as the voice of the people, the radical social reformers applied the precepts of such figures as Sir Thomas Elyot and, indeed, Thomas More to appeals to Parliament and the king's council

---

[13] John K. Yost, "Taverner's Use of Erasmus and the Protestantization of English Humanism," *RQ*, 23 (1970), 268-69. See Yost, "Protestant Reformers and the Humanist *Via Media* in the Early English Reformation," *JMRS*, 5 (1975), 187-202.

[14] ". . . ob editas comoedias me semper liberavit" (*Catalogus*, I, 702).

[15] Bevington, *Drama and Politics*, pp. 97-98.

for the redress of grievances. Like their Lollard forebears they saw church wealth as the root cause of its spiritual failure—their anticlerical outbursts recognized no distinction between religious abuses and economic, social, and political problems. Thus Simon Fish presented *A Supplicacyon for the Beggars* as a fictionalized plea by the poor against members of the mendicant orders who competed with them for alms. He went out of his way to attack purgatory and the proliferation of chantries founded to perpetuate prayer for the dead. Disillusionment followed upon the dissolution of the monasteries when the reformers discovered that a new Protestant elite had simply supplanted the friars and monks in exploiting the commonwealth. They argued that by distributing church property to the aristocracy rather than the poor, Henry VIII preserved or worsened such age-old forms of oppression as rack-renting and price increases. Although Cromwell's fall silenced many reformers, the furious outbursts of Simon Fish and Jerome Barlow would be heard again in Henry Brinkelow's *Complaynt of Roderyck Mors*. The satirical colophon of Brinkelow's *Lamentacion of a Christian against the Citie of London* (1542), a second complaint by "Roderyck Mors," censured the government for dissipating the potential for reform brought by the dissolutions: "printed at Jericho in the land of Promes by Thome Trauth [i.e., Truth]." These arguments were to be heard once more during the reign of Edward VI when such preachers as Hugh Latimer and Thomas Becon attacked "possessioners" as "greedy cormorants" and "caterpillars of the commonweal." Robert Crowley would issue his dire prophecies and denunciations as the direct heir of Simon Fish.

Genuine and supposititious works ascribed to Chaucer and other medieval writers appear to have been published in support of Cromwell's dissolution of the monasteries. Thus at the same time that native literature fell into disrepute with the humanists, many earlier writers began to acquire reputations as crypto-Protestants. Under the Cromwell administration, reformers first eluded censorship by disguising the virulently anticlerical *Plowman's Tale* (c. 1535) as a gathering out of a legitimate Chaucer edition. Sixteenth-century reformers adapted the fifteenth-century Lollard poem through the addition of a crude Chaucerian prologue. Ecclesiastical opposition had prevented William Thynne, a favorite retainer of Henry VIII, from including the forgery in the first printed edition of Chaucer's works "with dyvers workes never in print before" (1532); the work did appear as a separate imprint during the middle 1530s.[16] Publication of the piece in the 1542 Thynne edition took place only by means of royal protection and an act of Parliament declaring that Chaucer's "woorkes had byn counted but fables."[17]

The reformers fully identified *Piers Plowman* and its tradition of medieval complaint with the cause of religious and social change. John Leland confused *The Plowman's Tale* with *Piers Plowman* when he included "*Petri Aratoris fabula*" in the *Canterbury Tales*. Describing Chaucer as a reformist theologian and disciple of Wyclif, Leland explains the earlier suppression of the tale because "it vigorously inveighed against the bad morals of the priests."[18] Although it voiced an orthodox call for religious reform,

[16] Andrew Wawn, "The Genesis of *The Plowman's Tale*," *YES*, 2 (1972), 36, 40, and "Chaucer, *The Plowman's Tale* and Reformation Propaganda: The Testimonies of Thomas Godfray and *I Playne Piers*," *Bulletin of the John Rylands Library*, 56 (1973), 174-84. In *The Renaissance Chaucer* (New Haven, 1975), Alice Miskimin minimizes the gradual assimilation of apocryphal works into the Chaucer canon.

[17] Francis Thynne, *Animadversions uppon the Annotaciouns and Corrections of Some Imperfections of Impressiones of Chaucers Workes*, ed. G. H. Kingsley (1875), p. 7.

[18] *Commentarii de Scriptoribus Britannicis*, ed. Anthony Hall (Oxford, 1709), p. 423.

Piers Plowman remained under the old ban against Wyclifite texts. Piers himself disappeared in *Jack Upland*, but the persona of the simple and devout countryman remained. This Lollard attack on the friars received treatment similar to that of *The Plowman's Tale* when it appeared disguised as a gathering "compyled by the famous Geoffrey Chaucer" (c. 1536). It too lent support to the Cromwellian attack on the religious houses. *The Pilgrim's Tale*, yet another crude Chaucerian imitation, appeared under Cromwell in *The Court of Venus* (c. 1536). The ideas of Simon Fish would reappear in *Pyers Plowmans Exhortation, unto the lordes, knightes and burgoysses of the Parlyamenthouse* (c. 1550).

Miles Coverdale's translation of the first complete printed Bible in English (Cologne?, 1535) was a landmark in the development of early Protestant literary tradition. Its title-page border implies that the volume appeared with authorization from the crown (Figure 2). In actual fact the edition was unsanctioned. Engraved under Cromwell's patronage, Holbein's woodcut recognizes that the translation can circulate only by tacit permission of the crown. Bishops and lords kneel before a figure of the king enthroned above the royal arms. This illustration reverses the traditional iconography of such dedication portraits as the Huntington frontispiece for Caxton's *Receuil*. Instead of receiving the book from its translator, the king confers the text on the kneeling prelates. The royal portrait assimilates the stereotyped pose of the evangelists and apostles found in Protestant New Testaments. Occupying an intermediary position between God and man, the king supplants the pope as apostolic successor to Christ. The proliferation of keys in the inset portrait of Christ and the apostles undercuts the papal claim to primacy as the inheritor of the keys of St. Peter.

Cromwell felt the need to produce a Bible translation that could appear unambiguously under crown auspices. It is an irony of history that this "new," authorized version conflated the suspect work of both Tyndale and Coverdale. Only the associations of the earlier translations with religious and political dissent, in particular Tyndale's polemical annotations, made their work unacceptable to Henry VIII. Cromwell's second set of Royal Injunctions (1538) ordered the purchase of "one book of the whole Bible of the largest volume, in English" (hence the epithet "great"). The people were permitted free access for the "reading or hearing" of chained copies of this text. The injunctions juxtaposed approval of the English Bible as a "layman's book" with a prohibition on "idolatry" or the abuse of images. Images were permitted so long as they were used in the strict manner recommended by Gregory the Great: ". . . images serve for none other purpose but as to be books of unlearned men that cannot know letters, whereby they might be otherwise admonished of the lives and conversation of them that the said images do represent."[19]

Under Cromwell's patronage, Richard Grafton and Edward Whitchurch printed the Great Bible (1539) stipulated by Henry VIII's injunctions to transmit the scripture to English laymen. Its Holbein title page, which derives from his 1535 woodcut, symbolizes the royal supremacy and the conservatism of crown policy (Figure 3). The five levels of the woodcut preserve a graded hierarchy in which Henry replaces the pope as the temporal intermediary between God and man. Kneeling in the upper right-hand corner, the king as a latter-day Moses receives the law directly from God in the form of divine revelation. On

---

[19] *The Reformation in England to the Accession of Elizabeth I: Documents of Modern History*, ed. A. G. Dickens and Dorothy Carr (1967), pp. 82-83.

Spiritual Hierarchy
King/Bishops
Nobles/Clergy
Public

the second level, Cranmer and Cromwell accompanied by bishops and nobles receive "Verbum Dei" from the king. The lower levels portray the transmission of the text to clergy and laity. Aristocrats are distinguished by their ability to call out "Vivat Rex," while the tiny, almost childlike figures of commoners shout "God Save the King."

As epitomes of the Henrician Reformation, the Holbein title pages make it clear that the vertical process of reform is a royal prerogative. A reduced array of ideal types replaces the complex ecclesiastical and social hierarchy featured in such medieval works as *The Canterbury Tales* and *Piers Plowman*: the king, the bishop, the magistrate, the preacher, and the true subject. Comparison with the frontispiece of Caxton's *The Golden Legend* (Figure 1) clarifies this radical simplification of the traditional spiritual hierarchy. Caxton's illustration portrays the Trinity by means of human figures. Down below, a crowded throng of canonized bishops, popes, kings, friars, and queens stands ready to intercede for mankind. Unlike the woodcuts in Protestant Bibles, which contain emblematic images for the Bible or visual representations of specific texts, Caxton's woodcut includes such conventional symbols as axes, castles, crosses, and wheels. Few woodcuts in Caxton's edition contain biblical emblems.

By supplying a prologue for the second edition of the Great Bible—this volume and its successors are also known as "Cranmer's Bible"—Archbishop Cranmer fully integrated Erasmian ideals with the cause of moderate reform under the crown. In this reworking of *Paraclesis*, he yokes popularization of the scriptures with caution against the diversity of opinion that so troubled Henry VIII. His main purpose is to cite precedents for translation of the Bible into the vernacular:

> . . . it is not muche above one hundreth yeare ago, sence scripture hath not been accustomed to be read in the vulgare tonge within this realme, and many hundred yeares before that, it was translated and read in the Saxones tonge, which at the time was our mother tonge: wherof there remaine yet dyverse copyes founde lately in olde abbeys, of suche antique maners of wrytyng and speakyng, that fewe men nowe been able to reade and understand them. (1549 edition; **ᴿ)

A related goal is identification of the reader as an elect Christian. In acknowledgment of the conservative fear that the laity may misunderstand the "depe & profounde mysteries of scriptures," Cranmer echoes Erasmus's insistence that the Word be spoken in the language of the people in such a way as to level class distinctions. Free of the neoclassical hierarchy of styles, God addresses high and low together in the popular idiom. Because there can be no semantic distinction between the most simple and sublime passages, Cranmer identifies the biblical *sermo humilis* with the plain style of native English literature. Dependent on no authority external to itself, the Bible should be a self-explicating text that admits no ambiguity when it is read in good faith. As a dynamic process, Bible reading demands response from the reader: movement toward right action. The text in effect creates its own audience of readers who adopt its ideal pattern of Christian life. In understanding the Bible, the Christian should explicate himself.

The Cromwellian liberty ended quickly. The Act of Six Articles (1539) ensured the conservative nature of the Henrician settlement in religion by making it a heretical offense carrying the penalty of death to deny transubstantiation, clerical celibacy, or other traditional doctrines. The conservative leaders Thomas Howard, Duke of Norfolk, and Stephen Gardiner, Bishop of Winchester, appeared to win their final victory during the following year, when Cromwell lost favor and went to the block. The Protestant faction at court seemed to be on the verge of extinction. Protestant bishops like Nicholas Shaxton and Hugh Latimer resigned their sees and gave up preaching in the face of this defeat. The Protestant publicist Thomas Becon withdrew to the north of England, where he wrote tracts under the pseudonym Theodore Basille. Cromwell's protégés Miles Coverdale, John Rogers, and John Bale fled into exile on the Continent. The 1543 Act for the Advancement of True Religion finally withdrew permission for most commoners to read the Bible. The act restricted access to the Great Bible to an elite audience made up of the nobility, clergy, gentry, and merchants. Despite this retrenchment, with its harsh penal measures, Henry VIII extended protection to the Protestant courtiers closest to the throne: Catherine Parr, Edward Seymour, and Thomas Cranmer. Evidence to be brought forward at the interrogation of Anne Askew would even suggest that these privileged reformers underwrote the activities of such exiles as John Bale.

JOHN BALE: THE PROTESTANT EXILE

John Bale was the most active English Protestant author to survive Cromwell's fall. His prolific career as a public author effectively began with his flight from England; his earlier polemical plays were either lost or remained in manuscript. Through an extraordinary series of works, he became the most influential English Protestant author of his time. The writings that he produced during two exiles and three periods of royal favor enable one to chart the evolution of English Protestant thought throughout the mid-century (c. 1536-63). Because the works that he wrote during his Henrician exile constitute a paradigm for all his writings during the rest of his career, he may be approached most effectively as a precursor of the Reformation flowering. After his return to England under Edward VI, his writings offer variations in a pattern of apocalyptic conflict that he had worked out during exile.

Despite his contemporary esteem, Bale has suffered more than most mid-Tudor authors from the 1580s reaction against the native literary tradition. He has attracted relatively little critical attention, and what little there is has been directed to biographical, historical, or bibliographical questions. Later critics treat him as little more than an exaggerated prototype for such stage Puritans as Tribulation Wholesome and Zeal-of-the-Land Busy. Critical judgment rarely tests the assertion that Bale was a radical Protestant with a violent temper who had a flair for vilification and scurrilous attack upon his enemies. As a Carmelite friar he is said to have been sheltered from the intellectual nourishment of new humanistic learning, but as an apostate Protestant he could not shake himself loose from the impure style and diction of the "medieval" past. Later studies assert that immoderation and bad taste led him to make salacious imputations of sexual misconduct and perversion against the Roman clergy. Even students sympathetic to Bale approach their subject apologetically and argue his case on grounds of historical importance rather than literary merit. Few studies make any claim for him as a serious artist, and no study provides a thorough analysis of Bale's art or recognition of the literary techniques and forms through which he achieved his polemical effects. [20]

[20] W. T. Davies renewed Bale scholarship in "A Bibliography of John Bale," *Oxford Bibliographical Society, Proceedings and Papers*, 5 (1936),

Bale's later reputation had become established by the early seventeenth century. In a catalogue silently modeled on Bale's bibliographies, John Pits accused Bale of plagiarism, libeling the Roman clergy, and employing a barba-

201-80. In addition to a well-documented biography, he lists all works that Bale claims to have written, Bale's extant works in manuscript and print, and Bale's works in conjectural chronological order. Despite the thoroughness of his study, Davies voices the traditional lack of sympathy with his subject: "It must be confessed that he is more important than readable. At times Bale seems to be not so much writing as barking in print, and frequently the most charitable thing we can find to say . . . is that his bark is worse than his bite" (203). In covering the same ground as Davies, J. W. Harris's judgments are typical: "Of his numerous productions, these are the least reprehensible . . ."; ". . . for even Bale has a redeeming point in his literary character"; ". . . [in a] life otherwise filled with bitterness and disillusionment" (*John Bale: A Study in the Minor Literature of the Reformation* [Urbana, Ill., 1940], pp. 110-11). Honor McCusker supports the Davies-Harris interpretation in *John Bale: Dramatist and Antiquary* (Bryn Mawr, Pa., 1942). F. J. Levy and May McKisack approach Bale fruitfully as a pioneering historian who greatly influenced the historiography of the Tudors and German reformers (*Tudor Historical Thought* [San Marino, Calif., 1967], pp. 89, 94-99, and *Medieval History in the Tudor Age* [Oxford, 1971], pp. 1-25). Rainer Pineas approaches Bale as an important literary figure in his own right; however, his studies stress historical and theological subject matter at the expense of analysis of literary form, convention, and technique: "John Bale's Nondramatic Works of Religious Controversy," *Studies in the Renaissance*, 9 (1962), 218-33; "Some Polemical Techniques in the Nondramatic Works of John Bale," *Bibliothèque d'Humanisme et Renaissance*, 24 (1962), 583-88; and "William Tyndale's Influence on John Bale's Polemical Use of History," *Archiv für Reformationsgeschichte*, 53 (1962), 79-96. In "*The vocacyon* [*sic*] *of Johan Bale* and Early English Autobiography," *RQ*, 24 (1971), 327-40, Leslie Fairfield demonstrates the utility of Protestant themes and conventions in the literary analysis of Bale's works. He mars his succeeding study, *John Bale: Myth-maker for the English Reformation* (W. Lafayette, Ind., 1976), with repetitious and uncritical argument for the presence in Bale's works of "mythic" and "epic" patterns. These patterns may be approached more plausibly as commonplace biblical paradigms.

rous Latin prose style.[21] In attacking him as a violent fanatic who was "unable to command his own passion," Thomas Fuller attached an unforgettable epithet to Bale: "*Biliosus Balaeus* passeth for his true Character."[22] The Restoration antiquary Anthony à Wood ranked antipapal animus as a lesser sin than Bale's corruption of John Leland's elegant Ciceronian style with a barbaric Latin "full of scurrilities" and "full of ill language." According to Wood, the "old and rude English" of Bale's vernacular style marked no improvement over his Latin.[23] The handing down of these colorful accusations characterized eighteenth- and nineteenth-century scholarship. The *DNB*, for instance, did little more than repeat Fuller's charge: "He was known as 'Bilious Bale.' " Similarly, the account of "foul-mouthed Bale" by C. H. and T. Cooper echoed Wood's charges.[24]

Yet during his own lifetime, Bale received wide acclaim as an author and found many patrons. Laurence Humphrey, the celebrated Elizabethan Latinist, eulogized Bale over and above Continental reformers:

> Plurima Lutherus patefecit, Platina multa,
> Quaedam Vergerius, cuncta Baleus habet.[25]

Richard Hakluyt cited him as one of his few useful native sources. Moreover, Bale's Latin works won him a greater international reputation than was enjoyed by any of his

---

[21] *Relationum Historicarum de Rebus Anglicis* (Paris, 1619), a5ʳ, G3ʳ.

[22] *The History of the Worthies of England* (1662; 4 pts.), iii, 61.

[23] *Athenae Oxonienses* (1691-92; 2 vols.), I, cols. 70, 174; II, col. 135.

[24] *Athenae Cantabrigienses* (Cambridge, 1858-1913; 3 vols.), I, 226.

[25] As quoted from *Vaticinium de Roma* (n.p., n.d.) in Andrew Kippis, *Biographia Britannica* (1747-66; 6 vols.), I, 429, with the following translation: "Luther and Platina discovered many things, and Vergerius some; but Bale detected them all; *viz.* the errors and frauds of the Papists."

English contemporaries. The Swiss reformer Conrad Gesner called him a writer of greatest diligence ("vir diligentissimus") and modeled later editions of his universal bibliography on Bale's catalogues.[26] Matthias Flacius may have modeled his *Magdeburg Centuries* on the same works. Despite Bale's poor reputation during later centuries, a few scholars attempted to correct the prevailing view. Notable among them is the eighteenth-century antiquary Thomas Hearne, who defended Bale against Wood's accusations. According to Hearne, Bale's bibliographies constitute an original composition that is "a most valuable and judicious performance, and far preferable to the less perfect one that was left by Leland."[27] In *Reliques of Ancient English Poetry* (1765; 3 vols.), Bishop Thomas Percy relies on Bale as an essential authority and demonstrates thorough knowledge of his works.

The radical shift in opinion concerning Bale argues that later hostility results, at least in part, from anachronistic application of the literary canons of succeeding generations. The endemic complaints about Bale's barbaric style are of the same order as Jeremy Collier's attacks on Wycherley and Dryden, Dryden's comment about Chaucer's faulty metrics, and Johnson's censure of Shakespeare's vulgar diction. By the Restoration, linguistic change and neoclassical decorum had rendered obsolete the vigorous colloquial diction of Bale, Tyndale, Latimer, and their Tudor contemporaries. Similar strictures had been voiced as early as Sidney's qualification concerning Spenser's "old rustick language." Sixteenth-century Ciceronianism made Bale's Latin prose style, which descended from the learned tradition of medieval universities and monasteries, seem old-

---

[26] *Bibliotheca Instituta et Collecta* (Zurich, 1574), F2ᵛ.

[27] As quoted in *Athen. Oxon.*, 3rd ed., rev. and enlarged by Phillip Bliss (1813-20; 4 vols.), I, 202.

fashioned; the extravagances of humanistic Latin similarly killed Latin as a living language. Although Bale found in the mid-Tudor reading public an audience eager for his works, at the end of the sixteenth century his writings tended to go unread. His literary career had been obscured by a legend about Bale the man, and his works were not to be reprinted until the antiquarian revival of the eighteenth century.

Bale's most influential publication is *The Image of Both Churches*, which contains the first full-length Protestant commentary on Revelation. Written during the course of his first exile (c. 1541-47), the text is an excellent example of the divisive interpretation so feared by Henry VIII. In domesticating Continental traditions of apocalyptic thought, the *Image* exerted a profound influence on John Foxe and later English writers by applying to English history the twelfth-century identification of Antichrist with the papacy made by Joachim de Fiore. Bale also received the Joachimist interpretation indirectly through Martin Luther's reading of Revelation as a prophecy of the Reformation.[28] Bale's commentary states the key doctrine that informs all of his writings as well as those of many contemporaries. According to the *Image*, mankind is divided into the two "churches" of the Christian elect and the reprobate followers of Antichrist (see Figure 4). Christian history traces the dualistic conflict between the faithful descendents of the primitive, apostolic church and the Roman church whose apostasy dates back to the time of Boniface III and Emperor Phocas. Bale's millennial ideas gained wide circulation prior to their condensation in Edwardian Bible editions printed by John Day. His historical vision became ingrained in the Renaissance consciousness through assim-

[28] Katharine Firth, *The Apocalyptic Tradition in Reformation Britain: 1530-1645* (Oxford, 1979), pp. 32-41, 61, 67-68.

ilation into such major texts as the Geneva Bible, Foxe's *Actes and Monuments*, and Book One of Spenser's *Faerie Queene*.

As a Protestant exile, Bale dramatizes his spiritual distress as a latter-day St. John. His epigraphs (Genesis 19:14, Revelation 18:4, and Jeremiah 50:8) claim for him status as an apostolic witness who has fled from the land of iniquity. Comparison between himself and John, who went into exile on the island of Patmos, functions as a recognizable hallmark in other works from Bale's two exiles. Here as elsewhere his urgent concerns are to console the English Protestants during their current time of suffering, which constitutes a state of spiritual exile, and to convey a vivid sense of Reformation warfare that surrounds the besieged faithful with enemies. Despite his incessant return to contemporary persecution, he never attacks Henry VIII directly. Even from exile, he still looks to the king as the sole source of reform: "In no wise rebel I here against any princely power, or authority given of God, but against antichrist's filthy titles."[29] Instead he attributes responsibility for the Henrician retrenchment to the conservative prelates Stephen Gardiner and Edmund Bonner, Bishop of London. Unlike his seventeenth-century Puritan successors, he can be at the same time loyal to the monarch and hostile to the sitting bishops as the agents of Antichrist.

The key term in the title for *The Image of Both Churches* stresses the figurative nature of the Apocalypse. Deriving from the Latin *imago* ("imitation, copy, likeness"), the word implicitly raises the problem of interpretation. Although the richly poetic imagery of Revelation functions to conceal the truth from the reprobate, it makes a powerful appeal

[29] *Select Works*, ed. Henry Christmas (Cambridge, 1849), p. 263. Hereafter cited as *Image*.

to the reader's imagination. According to Bale's interpretation, Apocalypse should be read as a visionary picture book full of "pleasant figures and elegant tropes" (p. 252). The title implies that the problem of discrimination between images of truth and falsehood is central to the Reformation. Spenser makes the same point when Archimago, a figure for Antichrist as the source of false images, confounds the Red Cross Knight. In his inability to discriminate between Una and Duessa, the knight embodies the sixteenth-century dilemma. Guided by faith, the elect Christian reader should see in Revelation his own individual history and the history of mankind. The scriptures offer an image of the divine, an image of past human history, and an image of one's own personal condition. Throughout his commentary on Revelation, Bale insists that literal interpretation of the biblical text must underlie all historical application. Revelation may unlock human history, but history does not clarify the scriptures: "Yet is the text a light to the chronicles, and not the chronicles to the text" (p. 253). Medieval devotional objects substituted image for archetype, but Bale's Pauline doctrine insists on the radical distinction between historical events and the archetypal truth that they reflect imperfectly.

Bale constructs a Protestant theory of history by means of his Joachimist argument that the seven ages outlined by the opening of the seven seals and the blowing of the seven trumpets contain the cyclic pattern of history. The preaching of the gospel by Christ's apostles characterized the first age of the primitive church. The persecutions of Diocletian marked the second age, which was followed by the third age of martyrdom and heresy. The fourth and fifth ages saw the synchronous conflict between the followers of Antichrist and the faithful members of the true church. The triumph of such nonscriptural traditions as clerical celibacy, devotion to images, and the use of candles, ashes, and palms characterized the temporary victory of Antichrist during the sixth age. This epoch has lasted until the present moment. During this Age of Locusts, Wyclif and Hus fought for a return to apostolic traditions of gospel purity, but the triumph of the papacy, monasticism, and scholastic philosophy overcame them. Bale modifies Luther's reading when he associates the locusts with the papacy. For Luther, the third woe (Revelation 11:14) represents the "princely papacy," whereas the locusts represent Arius and his followers (or the medieval scholastics who introduced "heresy" in the church). Evidently Bale conflates Wyclif's scholastic antagonists with the triumphant papacy in general. The age of scholasticism continued until the advent of reform during Bale's own lifetime. The Reformation conflict may be read "as in a glass . . . under this sixth seal opening" (p. 340; see Revelation 6:12-17). The imminent opening of the seventh seal should lead to the fall of Babylon (papal Rome) and the restoration of the true, pure faith of the apostolic church (see Firth, pp. 42-43).

Bale attributes a reflexive quality to Revelation imagery, for the sealed book is the Bible, of which Revelation is the summary (p. 252). He finds in the opening of the seven seals both a visual image for biblical exegesis as a whole and the concrete unraveling of the conflict between the apostolic church and the papacy. As an analogue to the truth read in the unsealed book, the image of the temple symbolizes the true Christian church of the militant reformer (chapters 11, 14-16). Measurement of the temple (chapter 11) symbolizes the Reformation effort to reconstruct the church. It contains "the ark of God's holy testimony," that is, the book figured forth in chapters 5-8. The temple represents the physical church or, during time of retrenchment, the heart of the individual Christian (p. 403).

Bale's role as biblical commentator foreshadows the manner in which he dramatizes his own consciousness in other works. Because all true books are refractions of the Book, his authorial stance of the fighting preacher comprehends his other literary roles of dramatist, pamphleteer, editor, and translator. Bale's writings conceal a consistent literary strategy and rhetorical art that were later forgotten. His polemical art makes up in sheer force and power for what it lacks in humanistic polish and finesse. Bale generally evades the need to align his position with that of attacking opponents in the traditional point-for-point confutation of scholastic disputation. He does so by creating carefully designed, typical *personae* for himself or for the reformers whose works he edits. The verbal violence of Bale's polemics should come as no surprise to anyone familiar with the charges and countercharges hurled by Luther, Tyndale, and More. In fact he never sinks to the level of invective and scatological innuendo indulged in by those predecessors. His *Expostulation* (c. 1552) is typical of his autobiographical writings in styling Bale as a fighting evangelist. His unnamed antagonist, the "franticke papyst of Hamshyre," remains a generalized, dramatized figure whom Bale may have abstracted out of many particular experiences. Their antagonism recreates the apocalyptic conflict of Revelation.

Bale's tendency to dramatize and fictionalize his own experience is the definitive feature of his polemical art. His earliest printed works appeared under such pseudonyms as James Harrison and Henry Stalbridge. He exploits the practical necessity of concealing himself from crown authority by adopting the role of a bluff, plain-speaking Englishman. The device confers a dramatic quality on his ideas that would have eluded him had he written *in propria persona*. Bale defines pseudonyms as a witty means of fictionalizing polemics when he states that Walter Map "played with made-up names, such as Bishop Golias, or John the Abbot, or John of Corbirius, or Walter of Ireland, and similar ones."[30] His ability as a playwright won him Cromwell's patronage. In addition to his clearly defined role as author, Bale styles himself as one of the participants ("interlocutores") within his dramatic trilogy. In each play, an actor representing "Baleus Prolocutor" steps forward to deliver a prologue directly to his "most Christen audience." Such titles as *An Expostulation agaynste a Franticke Papiste of Hamshyre* or *The Apology agaynste a Ranke Papyst* (c. 1552) make it clear that dialogue, either explicit or implied, is Bale's characteristic mode. He generally assumes the role of an underdog advocate who defends the true church from unjust attack. Because his name appears in the imprint of *The Vocacyon of Johan Bale* (Wesel?, 1553), he could not possibly have designed the false colophon "Rome, before the castell of S. Angell" as a device for preserving anonymity. The spurious colophon reduces the Reformation controversy to a simple dramatic confrontation between the truth-telling Englishman and Roman heresy.

Bale's activities as England's first significant literary historian brought together concerns that he had addressed piecemeal in earlier works. Although his first bibliography, *Illustrium maioris Britanniae scriptorum summarium* (Wesel, 1548), appeared during Edward VI's reign, Bale compiled the work in exile on the basis of research completed before he fled to the Continent. The full title boldly declares his intention of chronicling the native literary tradition from its origins to the present day. By arranging authors in chronological order into five *"centuriae"* or

---

[30] "Sed fictis nominibus lusit, ut Goliae pontificis, vel Ioannis de Abbatia, vel Ioannis de Corborio, vel Gualteri de Hybernia, ac similibus" (*Catalogus*, I, 253).

groupings of one hundred, Bale imposes on the text a correspondence between the development of English literature and the pattern of the seven historical ages expounded in *Image*, a work that he wrote as he completed *Summarium* (3Q1^r-2^v). Despite its obvious Protestant bias and inclusion of mythical figures (his list includes Brutus Albion, Dares Phrygius, and Merlin), this catalogue and Bale's later revisions are indispensable sources for the study of early English literature. In assuming the validity of Geoffrey of Monmouth, Bale shares with such later contemporaries as Spenser and Shakespeare a belief in the legendary history of Britain.

Bale tried to catalogue and preserve manuscripts that were endangered by the destruction of ancient monastic libraries after the dissolution of the abbeys. Despite the longstanding tradition that Bale plagiarized from Leland's manuscripts,[31] he clearly distinguishes his own additions from the Leland manuscript that he edited for publication.[32] The Renaissance lacked a modern sense of literary ownership and, by the almost nonexistent standards of his time, it is difficult to accuse Bale of piracy. Despite inevitable errors, his Latin translations of titles and incipits are usually correct. Andrew Maunsell's catalogue (1595), the only comparable contemporary source for Tudor bibliography, lacks the scope of Bale's work. Very often *Summarium* is the sole external source concerning Tudor authors and texts, as well as the single record of lost manuscripts and printed books.

Bale had no native models for his project because of England's failure to catalogue its authors. Conrad Gesner's

---

[31] F. J. Levy's charge in *Tudor Historical Thought* that Bale "ransacked the manuscripts of Leland and John Boston of Bury" is typical (p. 95).

[32] *The Laboryouse Journey & Serche for Englandes Antiquitees* (1549); see McKisack, *Medieval History*, p. 15.

Bibliotheca (Zurich, 1545) supplied a foreign model. In rejecting the humanistic condemnation of medieval literature, Bale goes so far as to deny the validity of classical philosophy and literature (*Image*, p. 515). Discussion of Caedmon and the Anglo-Saxon makers, as well as praise for the satires of Nigel Wireker and Walter Map, shows catholicity unusual for his time. He praises Caxton for printing texts by Bede, Geoffrey of Monmouth, and other "good authors" including Chaucer, Gower, and Lydgate (3F4ᵛ). With the exception of R. W. Chambers,[33] few modern scholars assert the existence of an unbroken literary tradition from Old English to modern times. *Summarium* vividly embodies that continuity.

Bale's rhetorical theory of composition emphasizes authorship and the relationship between author and reader. It leads him to treat authors as exemplary types within an apocalyptic matrix. Because one cannot separate the life of particular authors from their works, each entry consists of three elements: biography and character (praise or blame); bibliography; and historical context with the "correct computation of the years through all ages from Japhet the most virtuous son of Noah to A.D. 1548" (A1ʳ). Correct attribution, biography, and chronology enable Bale to assign writers to a specific place in the conflict between the two churches. Although Bale approves of the satirical use of pseudonyms, genuinely anonymous works posed a real problem. Such had been the case when he discovered the Latin manuscript of *Apocalypsis Goliae*, "written by a certain Englishman," which he published as *Rhithmi vetustissimi de corrupto ecclesiae statu* (Antwerp, 1546). The preface to that work recounts Bale's strenuous efforts to recover the author's name. Of two possibilities, John of Salisbury

---

[33] "The Continuity of English Prose from Alfred to More and His School," in Nicholas Harpsfield, *The Life of More*, ed. E. V. Hitchcock (1932; EETS, o.s. 186), pp. xlv-clxxiv.

and Robert Grosseteste, he concludes that the latter attribution is more probable. Despite the doubtful ascription, the manuscript's contents show that the Medieval Latin author is "yet another faithful man in an age of darkness." In the spirit of Elias, the poet attacks the Roman church by means of apocalyptic prophecy and vision (*Rhithmi*, A2ʳ-3ᵛ). By 1548 Bale had decided that John of Salisbury had written the goliardic satire (*Summarium*, Z4ʳ), and it was not until 1557 that he finally concluded that Walter Map had written the poem (*Catalogus*, I, 253). Matthias Flacius Illyricus (Mattias Vlachich) accepted Bale's attribution when he included an edition of the poem in *Varia doctorum Piorumque Virorum, De Corrupto Ecclesiae Statu, Poemata* (Basel, 1557; i3ʳ-k3ʳ).

The authorial role that Bale assigns to himself most often is that of "compiler" or "collector," terms that denote derivation from a variety of sources. "Compiler" designates a more active and creative role, as in the ascription for the plays in his trilogy: "Compiled by Johan Bale. Anno M.D. XXXVIII." He even "compiled" his autobiographical narratives out of his own experience. Derived from the Latin verb *compilere* ("to collect, put together"), the epithet *compilator* was originally used to denigrate Virgil's imitation of Homer. By the time of Isidore of Seville, the word had acquired its medieval sense of one who constructs a work that is legitimate in its own right (*Etymologiarum*, 10. 44). In assuming the latter definition, Bale associates himself with medieval commentary traditions that presuppose incremental accumulation and assimilation of the work of predecessors. In an age that defined rhetorical invention as the mastery of traditional commonplaces, "compilation" was a respectable literary activity. The word encompasses a conception of "authorship" derived from its Latin root *augere* ("to increase, augment").

Bale defines apostleship as the highest category of authorship. According to *Summarium*, the most important British authors are the spiritual apostles, whose true Christian authority contradicts papal claims to primacy. The authority of Protestant apostles derives from their role as transmitters of the Bible text. According to Bale's legendary materials, Christianity was transmitted to Britain from the original gospel source by Joseph of Arimathea, a secret disciple of Christ. His arrival during the first age predated St. Augustine's mission from Rome. On the basis of Joseph's apocryphal letters to the British church ("Ad ecclesias Britannorum, Epi. Plu."), Bale accords him apostolic authority similar to that of St. Paul and St. John the Evangelist (D1^v-2^v). In converting the Saxon invaders, on the other hand, Augustine's mission supplanted the native British church. Apostolic authority survived in a few men of faith such as Bede and Alcuin. As the spiritual successor to Joseph, Bede has quasi-patristic authority equivalent to that of Augustine of Hippo, Jerome, and Chrysostom (N2^r-4^r; see *Catalogus*, I, 94).

In Bale's history, John Wyclif emerges as the central English author. Aside from the dedicatory portraits of Bale himself, the woodcut of Wyclif is the only image of a British author in *Summarium* (Figures 5-7). Both Wyclif and Bale are seen in the evangelical pose with book in hand. Wyclif's Bible translation accomplished the apostolic transmission of the Bible; Bale styles himself as Wyclif's direct successor in pursuing his evangelical mission to the English people. Bale praises Wyclif because "in the middle of impious locusts of darkness he stood for his [Christ's] truth" (2Q2^v). Just as the posthumous burning of Wyclif's manuscripts and bones conferred symbolic martyrdom upon him, as witnesses to faith his books survive as the Protestant equivalent of relics. It is as the author of fiction that Bale's Wyclif differs most from Joseph and Bede. Bale ascribes to Wyclif *Piers Plowman* (*"Petrus Agricola"*) and the recently published "Jack Uplande, *seu Ioannem a rure*" (R1ʳ; see *Index*, p. 274). His later correction of these attributions in *Catalogus* makes it improbable that he intended deliberate deception. Bale accepts Chaucer's reputation as a Lollard disciple of Wyclif. Implicit in Bale's effort to reconstruct a circle of Wyclifite poets is a desire to exploit the polemical possibilities of fiction. During his own age, Bale sees Tyndale as the direct successor to Wyclif: "in learning, faith, and clear innocence of life, he is the first that has been in this region after John Wyclif" (314ᵛ).

Bale fits two other authors into the apostolic mold of *Summarium*: Sir John Oldcastle and Anne Askew. His editions of their martyrologies attribute to them the status of Protestant saints. Oldcastle's reputation lacks basis in historical fact. Bale can, however, document Askew's career as a contemporary reformer who denied transubstantiation and the mass. Her prosecution under the Act of Six Articles was unprecedented in its application of the full rigor of torture and the rack. Stephen Gardiner and Thomas Howard had attempted to use the notorious Askew controversy as the vehicle for demolishing the Protestant courtiers who were poised to assume power at Henry VIII's long-awaited death. Such conservatives as Thomas Wriothesley and Edmund Bonner supported their intrigue to use Askew's testimony as evidence for the presence of heresy in Henry VIII's inner circle. They tried to trace support for the Lincolnshire martyr to Catherine Parr and aristocratic ladies surrounding her (such as Anne Stanhope, the Duchess of Suffolk, and Lady Denny). By attempting to undermine the protected circle surrounding the king, however, Gardiner and Howard overreached themselves. Their failure left the conservatives stripped of all power and authority as Henry VIII entered the final stages of his last illness (see McConica, pp. 222-27).

The first part of Askew's *Examinations* was printed in Wesel in November 1546, soon after she died at the stake on 16 July 1546. Bale designed the text as virulent anti-government propaganda. By absolving Henry VIII of responsibility for her death, he treats Askew's antagonists, the Lord Chancellor Wriothesley, Richard Rich, Thomas Howard, and the "syttynge Byshoppes" Gardiner and Bonner, as monstrous villains. Her account charges that Gardiner and Rich "toke peynes to racke me [with] their owne handes, tyll I was nygh dead" (II, F5^r). In addition to concealing his location in the Duchy of Cleves, Bale's spurious colophon ("Imprented at Marburg in the lande of Hessen") designates himself as the apostolic successor to William Tyndale, who had issued a series of Antwerp imprints under "Marburg" colophons.

Bale clearly distinguishes between his commentary and Askew's first-person narrative. As he states in *Summarium*: "She wrote this in her own hand and I illustrated it with prefaces and notes."[34] We have no reason to doubt Bale's account of the smuggling of the manuscript out of England: ". . . lyke as I receyved it in coppye, by serten duche merchauntes commynge from thens, whych had bene at their burnynge. . . . First out of the preson she wrote unto a secrete frynde of hers, after thys maner folowynge" (II, B3^r). As a Protestant saint, she left no relics for the witnesses of her execution except "a bundell of the sacred scriptures enclosed in ther hartes . . ." (II, A5^v). Bale's rapid acquisition of the manuscript suggests that it was sent directly to him and that he was in close contact with English reformist circles. If the patronage that he would later

---

[34] "Scripsit haec propria manu, quos & ego praefationibus ac scholiis illustravi" (3M1^r).

receive from the Duchess of Richmond predated Edward VI's reign, she or other Protestant women close to Catherine Parr may indeed have encouraged Bale's activities during his exile.

Bale's commentary places Askew in the universal context of sacred history. The title-page woodcut presents the affair as another skirmish in the apocalyptic conflict by portraying Askew in the evangelical pose with "Biblia" in her right hand and a quill pen in her left. She comes under attack from a dragon wearing a papal tiara. As a contemporary refraction of the Woman Clothed with the Sun (Revelation 12:1; see Figure 4), she represents the beleaguered church in general as well as each individual Christian. Bale's two epigraphs interpret the portrait. Psalm 117:2 refers to archetypal truth that transcends time and space: "The veryte of the lorde endureth forever." The second legend applies that text by treating the particular historical incident as a worldly manifestation of divine truth: "Anne Askewe stode fast by thys veryte of God to the ende." The biblical paraphrase in the epilogue dramatizes her spiritual condition as a recapitulation of the faithful soul in battle with the enemies of the Lord: "The voyce of Anne Askewe out of the 54. Psalme of David, called Deus in nomine tuo" (I, F7^r).

Bale's commentary dramatizes the circumstances of the text. His hyperbole contrasts with such examples of Askew's understated colloquial diction as the following:

> Then on the sondaye I was sore sycke, thynkynge no lesse than to dye. Therfore I desyred to speake with Latymer it wolde no be. Then was I sent to Newgate in the extremyte of syckenesse. For in all my lyfe afore, was I never in soch payne. (II, C7^v)

Bale shapes the narrative by comparing it to Eusebius's account of Blandina, who suffered under Emperor Antoninus Verus (I, ✤7ʳ⁻ᵛ). In assuming the role of a Reformation Eusebius, Bale defines the office of the martyrologist as a significant form of authorship: "No lesse necessarye is that offyce now, though fewe men attempt it, nor no lesse profytable to the christen commonwealth than it was in those terryble dayes" (II, A2ᵛ). According to Eusebius, examinations and answers were the worst forms of imperial persecution. Conventional elements in Bale's account include the testimonial of faith under duress (Eusebius notes Blandina's distress at being unable to confess her faith in a sufficiently loud voice because torture has exhausted her) and the pattern of the martyr as a fighting Christian (*Ecclesiastica historia*, 5. 1. 17-19, 37-42).

The encounter between accuser and accused is implicitly dramatic in its use of dialogue. The term "martyr" referred to early Christians who had been "faithful unto death" (Revelation 2:10). Such witnesses must speak from firsthand experience; juxtaposition of Askew's narrative with Bale's commentary suggests rhetorical dialogue. He implicitly assumes a role as an interlocutor in the text. Directing his outbursts against Gardiner and Bonner, Bale casts the bishops as satanic villains in the drama. Askew's temptation and racking by "the great Cayphas of Wynchestre" stress the Christlike nature of her suffering and of martyrdom in general. Although the advantage may seem to lie with the attacker, Bale converts the martyr's suffering posture into one of attack against unjust accusers. The providential signs cited in Bale's conclusion develop the crucifixion parallel:

> Credyblye am I infourmed by dyverse duche merchauntes whych were there present, that in the tyme of their sufferynges, the skye abhorrynge so wycked an acte, sodenlye altered coloure, and the cloudes from above gave a thonder clappe, not all unlyke to that is written,

Psal. 76. . . . . And lyke as the Centuryon with those that were with hym, for the tokens shewed at Christes deathe, confessed hym to be the sonne of God, Math. 27. So ded a great nombre at the burnynge of these martyrs, upon the syght of thys open experyment, afferme them to be hys faythfull members. . . . Neyther were the vii. thonderynges whych gave their voyces, Apoc. 10. anye other than mysteryes at their tymes to be opened. . . . (II, I3^{r-v}, I5^r)

Because they were printed in Wesel on 16 January 1547, copies of the second part of Anne Askew's *Examinations* could not possibly have been smuggled into England prior to the death of Henry VIII on 28 January. The Howards had fallen during the previous month. Having written his final poems in the Tower of London, the Earl of Surrey died by the axe on 19 January. Surrey's father, the third Duke of Norfolk of the Howard house, would have followed on the 28th had Henry not died early that morning. By excluding Gardiner and Bonner from Edward VI's council of regency, the late king's will ensured a Protestant succession. The conservative courtiers were powerless observers at the spectacle of the Protestant lords, who held power collectively, electing Edward Seymour Lord Protector. The boy king had been educated by reformist tutors in the pietistic academy organized by Catherine Parr. By historical accident, the printed homage ("God save the king") concluding the second part of *Examinations* could apply in all sincerity to King Edward. His father's death might seem to have rendered the text obsolete, yet it played an important role during the new reign. But the story of this sequel properly belongs to the next phase of our study, which concerns the literary context of the truly doctrinal Protestant Reformation effected under Edward VI.

CHAPTER 2

Print, Patronage, and Propaganda

Therewith she spewd out of her filthy maw
A floud of poyson horrible and blacke,
Full of great lumpes of flesh and gobbets raw,
Which stunck so vildly, that it forst him slacke
His grasping hold, and from her turne him backe:
Her vomit full of bookes and papers was,
With loathly frogs and toades, which eyes did lacke,
And creeping sought way in the weedy gras:
Her filthy parbreake all the place defiled has.

Spenser, *The Faerie Queene* (1590)

FREEDOM OF THE PRESS AND RELIGIOUS TOLERATION

The Edwardian abolition of the heresy legislation permitted previously unheard-of freedom of speech and publication as well as a flood of Protestant controversial literature. It was Edward Seymour's seizure of power that permitted a Protestant revolution to radiate outward from the inner circles of the royal court. As the only time during the Tudor age when no one was condemned for heresy, the Seymour protectorate marked a period of unprecedented toleration. Although Edward VI played no role in the setting of policy, the young king's uncompromising zealotry doubtless encouraged the overall progress of religious reform. Seymour, as the eldest uncle of the king, was the

[76]

natural choice of the council of regency to serve as Protector of the Realm and Governor of the King's Person during the royal minority. Under his leadership the Protestant lords and prelates had emerged victorious from the factional intrigues that followed Cromwell's beheading. Seymour epitomizes the Edwardian liberty as the man in power when censorship restrictions were lifted. As an intellectual and man of letters, he was the greatest patron of letters during an age dominated by mighty Protestant patrons. He collaborated with Cranmer in the introduction of genuinely Protestant doctrine and ritual. They abolished the chantries and promulgated the vernacular liturgy in the *Book of Common Prayer*. A Protestant communion service replaced the Medieval Latin mass. At their invitation, Martin Bucer and a host of Protestant theologians immigrated from the Continent. Seymour's lenience toward dissent contributed to the 1549 rebellions, which led to the coup d'état organized by John Dudley. Yet more radical Reformation followed Seymour's fall. Dudley's attempt to perpetuate a Protestant regime was to fail when Mary succeeded to the throne at Edward's death. Her effort at counterreformation would in turn be reversed by the Elizabethan settlement in religion. This compromise attempted to arbitrate between the Protestant doctrine of Edward's reign and conservative ritual and church polity.[1]

Seymour's overthrow of Henrician policy forced Stephen Gardiner to bring their decade-long rivalry into the open. Their underlying political conflict came to the surface in a controversy over whether to reimpose traditional restrictions on reading, speech, and publication. Their debate crystallized the shift in government policy toward the

[1] See prologue for an overview of Reformation history. Division of thinkers into radical, moderate, and conservative groupings follows the terminology in Elton, p. 137, n. 15, and pp. 158-60, 301, 317-20.

press. In theory they disagreed over the definition of authority, both spiritual and temporal. In opposition to Seymour's Protestant assumption that the individual conscience should arbitrate spiritual problems on the basis of scriptural authority, Gardiner reaffirmed the external authority of the church to determine matters of faith. These had been the positions taken, respectively, by William Tyndale and Thomas More in their earlier arguments. In a letter dated 21 May 1547, Gardiner demanded suppression of "two books set forth in English by Bale": his edition of Anne Askew's *Examinations* and his translation of a German account of Luther's death. Gardiner's ostensible motive is opposition to dissent and to open circulation of books "without authority":

> Certain printers, players, and preachers, make a wonderment, as though we knew not yet how to be justified, nor what sacraments we should have. And if the agreement in religion made in the time of our late sovereign lord be of no force in their judgment, what establishment could any new agreement have? . . . where every man will be master, there must needs be uncertainty. (*A & M*, VI, 30-31)

Seymour rejected Gardiner's arguments. His tolerant attitude toward the press is unique for a ruler of Renaissance England:

> The world never was so quiet or so united, but that privily or openly those three which you write of, printers, players, and preachers, would set forth somewhat of their own heads, which the magistrates were unawares of. And they which already be banished . . . dare use their extreme license or liberty of speaking. . . . There have foolish and naughty rhymes and books been made and set forth . . . but yet, after our mind, it is too sore

and too cruelly done, to lay all those to our charge, and
to ask as it were account of us of them all. . . . In the
late king's days of famous memory . . . there were that
wrote such lewd rhymes and plays as you speak of . . .
who were yet unpunished, because they were unknown
or ungotten. (*A & M*, VI, 34-35)

Gardiner had a less disinterested motive for continued
protest regarding copies of *Examinations* that had been seen
in circulation in Winchester: "some with leaves unglued,
where Master Paget was spoken of; and some with leaves
glued." John Bale had designed this edition as a bitter *ad
hominem* attack on Gardiner and the conservative councilors who led the heresy investigation. Bale's commentary
praises Anne Stanhope, Seymour's wife, for assisting Anne
Askew. This reputed link between Askew and the Seymour
circle brings us to the heart of the affair. Gardiner and
conservative councilors had tried to implicate Anne Stanhope and three other Protestant ladies in the heresy charges.
Having lost out in this factional struggle, Gardiner was
excluded by Henry's will from any political role during
his son's minority. Despite Bale's effort to link him to the
conservative faction, however, Sir William Paget, who assisted in the Protestant takeover, retained Seymour's confidence as Secretary of State.

Although book distributors left intact Bale's vilification
of Gardiner, someone converted the text into progovern-
ment propaganda by skillfully altering *Examinations* in order to exonerate Paget. The pasting together of two leaves
in the second part conceals Bale's attack on Paget for urging Anne Askew to recant.[2] The open sale of this inflam-

---

[2] C7ʳ. In B.L. G 11657 and C.21.a.4, as well as a copy at Manchester
College, Oxford, four lines at the top of folio C7 have been cut out so that
C6ᵛ and C7ʳ could be glued together without any apparent break in the
text. The leaves have been separated in the B.L. copies. Other copies were
never altered.

matory text in Winchester market shows that distributors deliberately shipped copies into Gardiner's own diocese in order to attack the bishop. The account of Luther's death, on the other hand, had been brought to Winchester "by an honest gentleman, to whom it was . . . given at London for news" (*A & M*, VI, 39).

Edwardian publishers helped to turn the Askew affair into a *cause célèbre* that Gardiner could not live down. Their reprints of *Examinations* cultivated the new government by omitting Bale's commentary, with its attack on Paget. In *Confutation of Nicolas Shaxton* (1548), Robert Crowley attacked Shaxton for preaching the recantation sermon at the burning of Anne Askew. But his exoneration of Latimer's one-time colleague for preaching under duress turned the text into an attack against Gardiner. Crowley's publisher John Day enlivened his point-by-point refutation by inserting a separately printed fold-out illustration of the execution. The title prominently alludes to "the burning of mestres Anne Askue, which is lively set forth in the figure folowynge" (Figure 8). The printer went to great expense to embellish the inexpensive octavo text. In a rare example of a tailor-made woodcut, the engraver follows Bale's account of the execution. As Shaxton preaches from a portable pulpit, the councilors who participated in the interrogation sit on a dais in front of the church of St. Bartholomew the Great. The bolt of lightning alludes visually to Bale's commentary.

Some Tudor historians have objected recently that the tolerance implicit in Seymour's reply to Gardiner is disingenuous. M. L. Bush makes such a claim in his revision of the traditional interpretation of Seymour as a forward-looking idealist who anticipated modern notions of religious toleration and social justice.[3] Although Bush substan-

---

[3] *The Government Policy of Protector Somerset* (1975), pp. 58-63. Bush

tiates many of his arguments, he neglects the Gardiner-Seymour correspondence in concluding that Seymour subordinated government policy to an uncompromising commitment to Scottish conquest. His economic analysis does prove that Seymour offered little more than traditional shibboleths against the enclosure movement to which he and other landlords were a party. The *DNB* and earlier sources document his assertion that Seymour was a proud man guilty of acquisitiveness and maladministration.

Bush fails to offer any evidence in support of his refutation of the argument that Seymour extended relative freedom of speech, publication, and reading. No necessary dichotomy exists between Seymour's personal pride and property ownership, on the one hand, and a tolerationist policy on the other. During the same age as Thomas Wolsey, Thomas More, and Stephen Gardiner, Seymour's mixture of idealism with practicality is not unique. Bush does not explain why Seymour pursued liberty of the press and public discussion to the extent that he alienated former supporters including Paget and Cranmer. "Persecution" inaccurately defines Seymour's handling of Gardiner, Bonner, and Princess Mary (p. 3). After Seymour tolerated an unprecedented degree of opposition, Dudley imposed harsh penalties on the three.

Bush attacks Seymour's pursuit of a "virtuous reputation" (p. 57). The present study argues instead that Seymour's cultivation of the image of a good man was itself a

---

attacks the interpretation of Seymour as a social reformer advanced by A. F. Pollard and W. K. Jordan in *England Under Protector Somerset: An Essay* (1900) and *Edward VI* (Cambridge, Mass., 1968-70; 2 vols.). Jordan's view in particular is revised in Elton; Hoak, *King's Council*; and B. L. Beer, *Northumberland: The Political Career of John Dudley, Earl of Warwick and Duke of Northumberland* (Kent, Ohio, 1973). The best study of Mary's reign is D. M. Loades's *The Reign of Mary Tudor* (1979).

major element of policy. Reliance on modern secondary sources leads Bush to conclude that the repeal act constituted an inevitable reaction against the harshness of the old regime caused by Seymour's "desire to appear virtuous and to be held in esteem" (pp. 5, 55, 57, 67, 88). Yet if one examines manuscript and early printed sources for evidence concerning patronage, book commissions, and press controls, one discovers a concerted effort to issue propaganda in defense of religious reform during the royal minority. Patronage for this propaganda and many of the works themselves may be traced to Seymour and prominent Protestant lords. Seymour excelled every other Tudor governor in exploiting the potential power of the press. If one returns to the original documents, one discovers that the Pollard-Jordan interpretation relies uncritically on a tradition of praise going back to Seymour supporters, notably Becon, Crowley, and Foxe. Protestant partisans united in praise of Seymour as the ruler who relaxed the Henrician terror and permitted them freely to exercise their own beliefs. Any attempt to demolish the "good Duke" must lay its charges against works of mid-Tudor literature and propaganda.

In pursuing his revisionist thesis, Bush disregards yet another important letter that William Paget wrote to Seymour at Christmas 1548. Paget echoes Gardiner's call for conformity in criticizing Seymour for encouraging extremism through excessive tolerance:

> Extremities be never good, and for my part I have always hated them. . . . in our old majesty's time . . . all things were too straight and now they are too loose; then was it dangerous to do or speak though the meaning were not evil; and now every man hath liberty to do and speak at liberty without danger.

What are and were the causes? Marry, then the prince thought not convenient for the subject to judge or to dispute or talk of the sovereign his matters. . . . the people (which be most inconstant, uncertain, and flexible) vary their sayings and show themselves to like or mislike; so do the ministers change their determinations, contrary to all the rules of policies. The governor is not feared; the noblemen contempted; the gentlemen despised.[4]

For Paget, Seymour's inversion of the traditional relationship between readers and authority poses the threat to hierarchy that Donne saw as a symptom of the modern age in *An Anatomy of the World* (1611). Dryden would voice a similar attack on extremism when he mocked the changeability of the Puritan mob in 1681:

The *Jews*, a Headstrong, Moody, Murmuring race,
As ever try'd th'extent and stretch of grace.
(Absalom and Achitophel, ll. 45-46)

Eighteenth-century orthodoxy attacked the "enthusiastick" sects with Paget's traditional antidemocratic argument.

"Liberty" is the key term in all of the letters by Seymour, Paget, and Gardiner. Sixteenth-century usage retains the Latin sense of *libertas* as freedom from slavery or arbitrary and excessive control: liberty consists of privileges granted to individual citizens by the state. Bale and Crowley praise the restoration of such liberty under Edward VI.[5] Gardiner, Seymour, and Paget agree that authors and speakers transgress limits established by higher

---

[4] B. L. Beer, ed., "A Critique of the Protectorate: An Unpublished Letter of Sir William Paget to the Duke of Somerset," *HLQ*, 34 (1971), 280.

[5] *Summarium*, 3P4^v; *The Way to Wealth* (1550), A7^r.

authority. Seymour implies that discussion had transgressed permissible limits, but that he is unable or unwilling to control public discourse. His denial of tacit consent implies agreement with the general principle of free discussion as well as an unwillingness to seek out illicit forms of discussion. Acceptance of dissent should not imply approval of its content. Seymour clearly tolerates the expression of opinions that he does not himself hold. Opposition to licensing does not, however, condone licentiousness. His letter to Gardiner discriminates between verbal statement and real action in the world:

> Writers write their fantasy [imagined idea], my lord, and preachers preach what either liketh them, or what God putteth in their heads. It is not by and by done, that is spoken. The people buy those foolish ballads of Jack-a-Lent. So bought they in times past pardons, and carols, and Robin Hood's tales. (A & M, VI, 35)

Seymour's paradoxical argument leans toward encouragement rather than control of discussion. The fundamental debate is over the relative merits of internal and external authority. Seymour assumes that truth should be determined by the individual conscience on the basis of scriptural authority. His concept of the permissible derives from a semantic shift rooted in Protestant theology. Seymour accepts Melanchthon's adiaphoristic principle, which distinguishes between divine truth essential to salvation and indifferent human customs.[6] For conservative thinkers like Gardiner, however, individual conscience is prone to error and pluralism of belief. He preserves More's position that the external authority of the church is a necessary guide to scriptural interpretation. As a defender of traditional Cath-

---

[6] John Phillips, *The Reformation of Images: Destruction of Art in England, 1535-1660* (Berkeley and Los Angeles, 1973), pp. 48-49 et seq.

olic practices, Gardiner holds that words and images are objects that embody truth that is effective in justifying the individual for salvation.[7]

Despite Gardiner's opposition, Edward's government renounced all forms of prior censorship. The Royal Injunctions of 31 July 1547 led the way when they "auctorised and licensed" all men to read and interpret the Bible and related writings (b1ʳ). Parliament then repealed all treason and heresy statutes promulgated since the reign of Edward I, including Henry VIII's Act of Six Articles with its prohibition on expression of religious opinion without prior crown approval. Although Parliament demanded more radically libertarian modifications in the legislation (Bush, pp. 145-46), it amended an act proposed by the administration. Seymour did not originate all features of the repeal act, but he did execute the intentions of the radical Protestant faction that controlled both the upper and lower house. His government represented the wishes of reformers who found themselves free of autocratic royal control for the first time. The "legend of the 'good duke'" began not at Seymour's execution but at least as early as the repeal legislation (but see Elton, p. 363). As Foxe states,

Through the endeavour and industry of this man, first that monstrous hydra with six heads (the Six Articles, I mean), which devoured up so many men before, was abolished and taken away: by reason whereof the counsels and proceedings of Winchester [Stephen Gardiner] began to decay. . . . (A & M, V, 703)

The repeal act freed the press of prior censorship. The sole proviso reserved the power to impose posterior censorship under the royal supremacy. Seymour permitted

[7] See Josipovici, *World and the Book*, pp. 47-49.

greater freedom of speech and publication than at any point prior to the period between the opening of the Long Parliament in November 1640 and its issuance of the licensing order of 14 June 1643. Not until the lapse of the Licensing Act in 1695 did general prior censorship cease in England.[8] The restoration of controls by the Privy Council during the 1549 risings signaled the failure of Seymour's program.[9] Immediately after taking power, Dudley reimposed prior censorship and abrogated Seymour's "libertarian" policy.

The royal supremacy forbade public defense of Catholic doctrine and ritual as well as a range of sectarian opinion attributed to the Anabaptists. Judged by present standards, such control appears intolerant and contradictory to Seymour's opposition to licensing. Yet this restraint was imposed after rather than before the fact. If one defines liberty as a natural right to state and practice different forms of political and religious belief, no one in authority during the Renaissance favored complete liberty of speech and press. Liberty in the modern sense may not have existed under Edward VI, but by the standards of his own day Seymour believed in toleration.[10] It is true that in promulgating the 1549 *Book of Common Prayer*, the first Edwardian Act of Uniformity forbade public dissent. Yet within the limits that it prescribes, the prayer book itself defines faith as an inward matter that cannot be dictated by the state.

Randall Hurlestone draws Seymour's antithesis between

[8] Philip Gaskell, *A New Introduction to Bibliography* (Oxford, 1972), p. 185.

[9] J. R. Dasent et al., eds., *Acts of the Privy Council of England*, New Series (London, 1890-1964; 46 vols.), II, 311-12.

[10] Herbert Butterfield, "Toleration in Early Modern Times," *JHI*, 38 (1977), 573-84; see V. Norskov Olsen, *John Foxe and the Elizabethan Church* (Berkeley and Los Angeles, 1973), chap. 6.

Catholic error and toleration of individual belief in dedicating his translation of *Newes from Rome* (c. 1550) to Lord Thomas Howard, the orphan grandson and heir to the attaindered third Duke of Norfolk. He juxtaposes his call for liberty of discussion with an attack on the "blasphemous sacrifice of the papisticall Masse." The Royal Injunctions represent for Hurlestone the reversal of Catholic persecution of the Lollards. Although "fyer, sworde, and roope" could not defeat them spiritually, censorship stripped these "unlerned professours of the gospell" of their only defense against scholastic theologians: "after that men were shutte up from theyr bookes which were published for the edifieng of other, they shuld become as it were unarmed, and naked in everie side . . ." (A2ᵛ-3ʳ).

Despite their requirement of freedom of conscience and religious liberty for themselves, early Protestants refused to grant the same right to others. Seymour's policy articulated the Lutheran notion of liberty of conscience as the freedom to pursue individual salvation rather than the right to accept erroneous beliefs or practice civil liberty.[11] Tyndale assimilated Luther's theory in *Obedience of a Christian Man* (C6ᵛ). In appealing for unlicensed printing, Milton's *Areopagitica* (1644) stops at the exact point where Seymour imposed his limit. Neither Seymour, Hurlestone, nor Milton carried toleration to the extreme of Roger Williams who, in *The Bloudy Tenent, of Persecution, for Cause of Conscience Discussed* (1644), abandoned adiaphorism and demanded complete freedom of religion that would encompass "Paganish, Jewish, Turkish or Antichristian consciences and worships." Williams did follow the Tudor reformers by arguing that such false beliefs only "bee *fought* against with . . . the *Sword* of *Gods Spirit*, the *Word of God*" (a2ᵛ).

---

[11] *Commentary on St. Paul's Epistle to the Galatians*, trans. E. Middleton, ed. J. P. Fallowes (1940), pp. 298-300.

He alone, however, identifies liberty with the content of speech rather than simply the process of discussion. The alternative to the individual search for truth is stasis: Milton's "muddy pool of conformity and tradition." In a letter to Seymour, Gardiner contends that such liberty would remain philosophically alien to his traditional association of word and object:

> But, as one asked, when he saw an old philosopher dispute with another, what they talked on; and it was answered how the old man was discussing what was virtue; it was replied, "If the old man yet dispute of virtue, when will he use it?" so it may be said in our religion, "If we be yet searching for it, when shall we begin to put it in execution?" (*A & M*, VI, 34)

Seymour's libertarian policy led him to permit the massive volume of publication that appeared during the protectorate. Protestant propaganda comprised the bulk of this flood. One cannot attribute the vast array of reformist writings to his direct sponsorship, for the Edwardian publicists built upon an intellectual foundation laid by the previous generation of reformers. Yet Protestant authors acknowledged as their spiritual leader the man who replaced persecution with liberty. Theirs was a symbiotic relationship. English printers produced books at the highest rate ever known prior to the Elizabethan age. Almost as many editions were published between 1548 and 1550 as during the average mid-Tudor decade. More than two hundred editions were published in 1548, representing the crest of this wave. The sharp drop in the number of titles during Dudley's last three years in power, after Seymour's final imprisonment, is consistent with Dudley's reimposition of controls. Although the average annual volume of the Elizabethan press exceeded that under Seymour, it was not until after 1570 that it passed the peak rates of 1548 and 1550.

Most Edwardian publications argued for Protestant reforms. Three out of four books printed under Seymour dealt with religion. Only during the Puritan Revolution did the proportion of religious publications exceed that of the Reformation press. Protestant authors who had been driven into exile by Henrician proclamations returned under Edward. Previously banned works by the following reformers appeared openly: Bale, Barnes, Becon, Bullinger, Frith, Hooper, Luther, Tyndale, Turner, and Wyclif. One out of every ten editions attacked the mass and called for a Protestant communion service in the vernacular. The thirty-one mass tracts published in 1548 supported Cranmer's piecemeal introduction of liturgical reforms. After the Act of Uniformity closed off public discussion in 1549, intramural debate continued between the English and foreign theologians favored by the government.

Protestant tracts inundated the Catholic opposition, which is represented by only four extant pamphlets printed in England. The government silenced Richard Smith and Miles Hogarde for writing these works. Administrative records, Protestant attacks, and increasingly frequent outbursts of violence show that the scarcity of recusant publication is an inaccurate gauge of public resistance to the Reformation. One Hogarde tract survives only because Robert Crowley quoted it in its entirety in *The Confutation of the Mishapen Aunswer to the Ballad Called the Abuse of the Blessed Sacrament* (1548). On 15 May 1547 Seymour forced Smith to recant at Paul's Cross for his defense of traditional doctrine in *A Brief Treatyse Settynge forth Divers Truthes* (1547). This recantation and Smith's public declaration at Oxford University, where he held a Regius

Professorship of Divinity, were printed in the same year in order to reach a wider audience. Smith's anonymous tract *Of Unwryten Verytes* (1548) is the only surreptitious Catholic publication extant from the reign. Hiding, flight, and publication in France were the recourse of those who would not remain silent; Smith's flight to Louvain typified the beginning of the recusant movement. In addition to two pieces that Gardiner smuggled out of the Tower of London, a Smith tract printed in Paris attacked Cranmer's liturgical reforms.[12]

Seymour's success at encouraging Protestant debate resulted in an unexpected outburst of radical dissent. In *The Fal of the Late Arrian* (1549), John Proctor aims to refute "Anabaptistes, Libertines, Marcyonistes . . . Ebbionitts, Arrians, Selentians, Saduces, and Pellagians (A6ᵛ, B5ʳ). Proctor may also have designed his tract as a cryptic attack on Seymour and the Protestant faction for encouraging sectarianism. Bearing a dedication to Princess Mary, this conservative pamphlet is the only Edwardian publication to include a traditional woodcut of the Blessed Virgin. William Turner widens the attack to include the following schismatics in *A Preservative agaynst the Poyson of Pelagius, lately renued by the Annabaptistes* (1551): "Anabaptistes, Adamites, Loykenistes, Libertines, Swengfeldianes, Davidianes, and the spoylers" (A3ᵛ). Christopher Hill has shown that such groupings form part of a continuous underground heretical tradition that links fourteenth-century Lollardry to the proliferation of radical ideas at the time of the English Civil War.[13] As a radical advocate of free

[12] See my article, "Freedom of the Press, Protestant Propaganda, and Protector Somerset," *HLQ*, 40 (1976), 1-9.

[13] *The World Turned Upside Down: Radical Ideas during the English Revolution* (1972), and the unpublished essay "From Lollards to Levellers." See Dickens, *English Reformation*, pp. 40-62, passim.

will against the predestinarian theology of the Edwardian reformers, Henry Hart published tracts advocating separatism and congregationalism.[14]

Traditional anticlericalism surfaced in sectarian dissent. In contrast to the learned Catholic opposition, John Champneys describes himself as "an unlearned laye mane" from Bristol in *The Harvest is at Hand, Wherein the Tares shall be Bound, and cast into the fyre and brent* (1548). This millenarian appeal for the absolute primacy of the Bible is strikingly similar to seventeenth-century Puritan pamphlets. So extreme is Champneys's attack against the licensed Protestant preachers as "marked mounsters of Antichrist" that it is easy to misread it as a tract concerning the allegedly corrupt Roman clergy. He appeals to the king, protector, and council to grant the same "libertie" to men of "smal reputacion & learnyng" as that allowed to the small body of educated, magisterial reformers. The retention of clerical vestments (the "disquysed monstrous garmentes" of Antichrist) signals the failure to purge all vestiges of Roman influence. It is a fundamental paradox of English Protestant tradition that the call for church reform on the model of primitive Christianity invariably produced dissenters who attacked the ensuing reform as a violation of gospel truth. In confirmation of Henry VIII's fears, relaxation of restraint could lead to a rejection of all limits imposed from above. Champneys thus distinguishes between "true catholyke" faith and the Edwardian reforms. Unlike the Puritan revolutionaries, however, he identifies true religion with the king and council "which unfainedly loveth the gospel . . ." ([ᵣA2ʳ]-A4ʳ, B2ʳ, D7ᵛ, E8ʳ, G4ʳ).

Despite the prevalence of dissent, Seymour was the only

[14] Joseph W. Martin, "English Protestant Separatism at its Beginnings: Henry Hart and the Free-Will Men," *Sixteenth Century Journal*, 7, ii (1976), 55-74.

English ruler until his time to eschew capital punishment as a penalty for heresy (*A & M*, V, 704). For example, a Cornish priest was executed on 7 July 1548, but hanging, drawing, and quartering punished him for the treasonous act of murdering a royal commissioner rather than for religious dissent. At his attainder trial, Seymour was charged with encouraging rebellion through excessive lenience; indeed, after the 1549 risings, the Privy Council reimposed traditional penalties. Blaming the 1549 rebellions on the Anabaptists, the nobles imposed the summary justice of martial law. Increasingly frequent executions marked the Dudley regency. Cranmer's 1549 commission against the Anabaptists examined Champneys, Joan of Kent, and a Colchester tanner named Putto. Because they recanted, Champneys and Putto suffered the symbolic penalty of bearing fagots at Paul's Cross. The 2 May 1550 burning of Joan of Kent was the first heresy execution since that of Anne Askew. The Dutch Arian George van Paris was burned on 24 April 1551.[15]

Seymour surrounded himself with reformers who favored toleration and clemency. After his fall from power, they opposed Dudley's punitive policy. The duke's physician William Turner identifies the "material fyre, and faggot" of Smithfield with the arms that "the papists used agaynst us." The only suitable weapon for religious warfare is the "spirituall sworde, the worde of God" (*Preservative*, A3ᵛ-4ʳ). Turner's dedication to Hugh Latimer links his tract to Seymour's pulpit spokesman. Thomas Becon and Thomas Norton, who respectively served as Seymour's chaplain and amanuensis, wrote poems for the text. Randall Hurlestone, who also contributed a poem, also opposes execution in *Newes from Rome*. His dedication of this writ-

[15] *Annales*, 3D3ᵛ, 3D6ʳ⁻ᵛ, 3E1ʳ-2ʳ et seq. See Michael Watts, *The Dissenters* (Oxford, 1978), pp. 9-11.

ing to Thomas Howard the younger suggests the influence of John Foxe, tutor to the Howard heir. Despite his animosity toward the Catholics, Foxe was a lifelong opponent of execution on religious grounds.

The opposition of these reformers to capital punishment and their apparently paradoxical habit of hurling verbal abuse against their enemies clarify the way in which Protestants thought differently from Catholics. Both practices stem from the Reformation belief in reason and individual conscience. Turner and Hurlestone both distinguish between the violent language appropriate to spiritual warfare and their renunciation of execution. The reformers were fond of *sarcasmos* and *illusio*, recognized rhetorical devices for heaping bitter taunts upon an opponent. Finding no inconsistency between a ranting style and a horror of execution, these Protestants resemble the Utopians who brainwashed dissenters rather than killing them. John Bale has earned the epithet "Bilious Bale" for the scabrous charges that he lodged against the Roman clergy. The following passage is typical:

> All wayes of the juste
> The lorde hath discuste
> The prestes dwell in ther dreames
> De reliquerent fontem aque vive, & foderunt   Hie. 2
> In ther donge they lye
> Lyke boores in a stye
> For mudde they leave the streames.
>
> (*Answer*, A8ᵛ-B1ʳ)

Yet there is no evidence that he was anything but a mild man in personal life. English and Continental reformers praised him both for his ideas and his pleasing Latin style.

Reformation mingling of sacred and profane diction contradicts later notions of piety and decorum. Bale himself divorces blasphemy from the obscene in *A Christen Exhortacion unto Customable Swearers* (c. 1543), a text that contrasts impiety with the proper "maner of sayinge grace." Foxe's papers contain a copy of a "Foul mouthed letter" upbraiding Edmund Bonner for cruelty to Protestant prisoners during Mary's reign. It rants, "Oh you bloudy Boner, and idolatrouse Bishop of London, oh thou most cruell Tyrant of Sodoma, and proude painted prelate of Gomorra. . . ." Despite his scurrility, the anonymous writer concludes with "Amen," using the biblical word expressing assent to both curses and prayers (B.L. MS Harley 416, fol. 76). The reformers lived in an age that could still intermingle piety with earthiness, sharing Luther's fondness of invective, jokes, puns, and proverbs. Mid-Tudor Protestant style has more in common with Rabelais's seriocomic mixture of raillery and truth than with the genteel standards of decorum and propriety introduced in the period between Sidney's *Apology* and the *Spectator* essays of Addison and Steele.

THE REFORMATION BOOK TRADE

As a corollary to the relaxation of restraints on publication, Seymour and the Privy Council encouraged Protestant master printers and publishers. A strongly reformist book trade thrived throughout Edward VI's reign. Under their patents royal, Richard Grafton as King's Printer and Edward Whitchurch operated what were virtually government presses. A monopoly protected the editions of the *Book of Homilies* and the prayer book that they published during Edward's reign. In addition to the Great Bible, these printers issued Erasmus's *Paraphrases* under government orders that permitted them to commandeer the workmen and equipment of other printers.[16] As Printer to the Archbishop of Canterbury, Walter Lynne issued his Protestant translations under government protection.[17] Protestant aristocrats supported a great variety of lesser printers and stationers including John Day and his partner William Seres, Anthony Scoloker, Robert Crowley, John Oswen, and John Bale.[18]

Although he was new to the book trade, John Day received marks of high favor. When the Lord Mayor of London, Sir John Gresham, and conservative aldermen harassed Day for printing Luke Shepherd's *John Bon and Mast Person* (1547), the courtier Edward Underhill intervened on his behalf. No records survive of appearances before the Lord Mayor or the Mayor's Court from this period, but a surviving memorandum of a recognizance for Day to appear before the Lord Mayor was taken at the court held on 10 January 1548.[19] Intervention by William Cecil seems to have won Day the very valuable monopoly on printing *A. B. C.*s that he retained for the rest of his

[16] E. J. Devereux, "The Publication of the English *Paraphrases* of Erasmus," *Bulletin of the John Rylands Library*, 51 (1969), 348-67.

[17] King, "Freedom of the Press," pp. 7-8.

[18] Despite his title, Lynne printed none of the books that he published. There is no evidence that Bale ever sold the books bearing his imprint. The word "printer" was used loosely during this period to describe anyone undertaking to have books printed, and colophons often credited stationers with "printing" books that they merely published. Booksellers were at this time gaining ascendancy over printers. Complicated printing and publication arrangements frequently lay behind books with deceptively simple imprints. See W. W. Greg, *Some Aspects and Problems of London Publishing between 1550 and 1650* (Oxford, 1956), p. 83; Edward Arber, ed., *A Transcript of the Registers of the Company of Stationers of London; 1554-1640 A. D.* (1875-94; 5 vols.), I, 114. Imprints and colophons are my basic sources concerning printing and publication.

[19] Corporation of London, Records Office, MS Repertory of the Court of Aldermen, vol. 11, fol. 378.

career.[20] As Lord Burghley, Cecil tended to remain loyal
to his supporters. As late as 13 December 1572, Matthew
Parker, Archbishop of Canterbury, recommended that Cecil intercede on Day's behalf concerning a printing privi-
lege (B.L. MS Lansdowne 15, fol. 99ʳ). Day's printing of
Becon's tracts and the sermons of Latimer and Lever signals the beginning of his lifelong association with Protestant authors.

These master printers collaborated with the Protestant
scholar-publishers Robert Crowley, John Bale, and William Baldwin. Baldwin worked as a corrector for Whitchurch, a job given to educated men who were not printers
by training.[21] Baldwin published *A Treatise of Morall Phylosophie* (1547) and *Canticles or Balades of Salomon* (1549)
as "servaunt with Edwarde Whitchurche." Day printed
several books for Bale, notably the very popular *Image of
Both Churches*. Bale relied on such booksellers as Richard
Foster to sell his publications.

Robert Crowley's career in publication was remarkably
varied. Prior to the 1549 opening of Crowley's bookshop
at Ely Rents in Holborn, Day printed at least five of
Crowley's tracts. Crowley possibly read proof at Day's
shop.[22] After setting himself up as a bookseller, Crowley
published nineteen Protestant texts under his own imprint
between 1549 and 1551, including ten of his own works
and editions. He specialized in the sale of octavo chapbooks. What is surprising is that with the exception of the
single quire of Crowley's *Psalter* that Stephen Mierdman
printed, Richard Grafton printed all of these texts. Crow-

[20] H. S. Bennett, *English Books & Readers, 1475 to 1557* (Cambridge,
1952), p. 39.

[21] Gaskell, *New Introduction*, p. 172.

[22] A. B. Emden, *A Biographical Register of the University of Oxford A. D.
1501 to 1540* (Oxford, 1974), p. 153.

ley made prominent use of his colophons to advertise his role as "printer" and the location of his shop in Ely Rents, but he never acknowledged Grafton's role. Crowley's offerings included biblical poems by William Samuel (a protégé of Anne Stanhope) and Crowley's patroness, Lady Elizabeth Fane. The wife of Sir Ralph Fane, a loyalist who was executed with Seymour in 1552, Lady Fane was later described by Foxe as "a special nurse, and a great supporter . . . of the godly saints, which were imprisoned in queen Mary's time" (*A & M*, VII, 234). These links to Grafton and to Seymour's inner circle suggest that Crowley's shop served as a conduit for controversial works favoring the new regime. An effort to shape public opinion in secret would account for Crowley's silence about Grafton.

Crowley and Bale collaborated as publishers. Bale's *Summarium* provides Crowley's ascription to Wyclif of the prologue to the Wyclifite Bible: "as maye justly be gatherid bi that, that John Bale hath written of him in his boke entitild the Summarie of famouse writers of the Ile of greate Britan."[23] Crowley follows Bale's *Image* in associating the Age of Locusts with the Roman hierarchy of Wyclif's time (A1ᵛ). Crowley used a wood block from *Summarium* for his frontispiece. The lower left corner of the Wesel cut has an incipient break that has widened in the London impression (Figure 7). He even translated the woodcut's legend ("The figure of John Wycklife") from Bale's bibliography. As publisher of *Summarium*, Bale evidently commissioned and retained ownership of his Continental wood blocks. As valuable items of printing equipment, Bale brought at least two Wesel blocks with him when he returned to England. In the 1551 edition of the second part of *Actes of Englysh*

[23] *The True Copye of a Prolog Wrytten about Two C. Yeres Paste by John Wycklife* (1550), attributed to John Purvey.

[97]

Votaryes, he reused the small woodcut showing himself presenting *Summarium* to Edward VI (Figure 6). These highly personalized cuts appear nowhere else. In all probability, Crowley received the Wyclif block directly from Bale.

Crowley published the Bible prologue and other Wyclifite texts as part of Bale's effort to preserve and print medieval British manuscripts. Bale advanced this project in *Summarium* by attempting to enumerate all extant works, in manuscript and print, by British authors. He wished to prevent the destruction of learning due to the breakup of monastic libraries. In *Rhithmi vetustissimi* Bale mentions that it was only by chance that he rescued the manuscript of that text from destruction by an Antwerp bookbinder (A2^r), and in his edition of Leland's *Journey* Bale makes particular mention of the cutting up of manuscripts for use in bookbinding and as wrapping paper (B1^{r-v}). His preface calls for a project to publish manuscripts of Old and Middle English texts as well as translations from medieval Latin writings. Such publication would provide reliable native authorities in place of Catholic sources. As the Henrician Chaucer editions had shown, medieval British texts carried special authority in the rapidly expanding arsenal of Protestant propaganda. A project such as Bale's would necessitate the kind of study that Leland had undertaken of "Bryttyshe, Saxonyshe & Walshe tonges" (B4^v). Crowley published most of the early editions of texts in Welsh.

Someone at court collaborated in the publication of the Wyclifite prologue, for Crowley reports on his title page: "the Originall whereof is founde written in an olde English Bible bitwixt the olde Testament and the Newe. Whych Bible remayneth now in the kyng hys majesties Chamber." George I donated this early fifteenth-century manuscript to Cambridge University in 1715 (C.U.L. MS Mm. 2. 15.).

Crowley's title correctly identifies the location of the prologue (fols. 275-90). He did not use the Cambridge manuscript as his copy text, for it bears neither casting off
marks nor printer's ink. Because it is unlikely that the
manuscript left the royal collection, in all probability
Crowley was admitted to the palace to make his accurate
transcript.[24]

Great significance was attached to the royalist prove-
nance of the Wyclifite prologue. By means of allusions to
Crowley publications, two elegantly illuminated vellum inserts celebrate the discovery of the Wyclif manuscript in
the king's library. With Tudor roses at the corners, the
recto side of the first leaf states the Reformation *topos* of
the Bible as the spiritual sword which Turner also uses in
Preservative: "The holy Bible, the lyvely Worde of the
lyveynge god, the Swerde of the spirite, and lantarne of
lyght to oure foote steppis a treasure more preciouse then
golde and preciouse stonis." Except for the first stanza, the
ballad version of Psalm 82 on the verso side comes from
Crowley's 1549 *Psalter*. As a title for the Wyclifite prologue, the second vellum insert commemorates Crowley's
publication of the printed text. "EDOVERDUS SEX-
TUS" appears in large gold capitals within a blue tablet
on the recto side. The inscription on the verso side refers
to the edition of *The True Copye of a Prolog* that Crowley
dated 28 May 1550:

The true copie of a Prologe whiche John Wicklife wrote
to this Bible which he translatid into Englishe about two
hundred yers past, that was in the tyme of kynge Edwarde the thryd, as may justly be getherid of the men-

---

[24] Crowley entered a marginal gloss on fol. 275ᵛ. The same mid-Tudor
hand entered a 1582 note bearing Crowley's autograph signature in B.L.
MS Add. 38170, fol. 16ʳ.

tion that is had of him in divers ancient Cronicles.—
Anno domini. 1550 (fol. 274^v).

The rhyme royal verses that Crowley placed beneath the
woodcut connect Wyclif to the reign of Edward III as a
halcyon time of faith prior to the Age of Locusts.

In contrast to Caxton's aristocratic folios, Crowley and
Bale produced a popular library of English classics. Most
of their publications appeared in inexpensive octavo format. *True Copye* exemplifies Bale's publication project.
Crowley's preface explains the purpose of popularizing
medieval texts:

> . . . but thou hast it now offered unto the for little coste,
> in a time when true religion biginnith to floryshe. It was
> at the fyrste made common to fewe men that wolde and
> were able to optayne it. But nowe it is made commen to
> all menne, that be desyrouse of it. (A2^v)

Crowley accommodates the Middle English work to contemporary readers through such glosses as "Bygh, is a Collar or gorget" (D5^r). *Piers Plowman* was the most important medieval text that Crowley edited. Although Bale
initially attributed *Petrus Agricola* to Wyclif (*Summarium*,
2R1^r), Crowley states in his preface that he ascribed the
work to Langland after consulting several learned antiquaries. Bale must have been among the scholars Crowley
consulted, because he ultimately agreed with Crowley concerning the problem of authorship (*Index*, pp. 509-10).
Crowley also published a translation of Peter Pateshull's
Vita fratrum mendicantium. Pateshull was an Augustinian
friar who came under Wyclif's influence and preached
against his order (*Index*, pp. 322, 353).

In addition to the London book trade, a large number

of provincial presses operated under Edward VI. Books were printed at Ipswich, Canterbury, Worcester, and Dublin. These operations were an anomaly for the Renaissance and characterize the relatively uncontrolled press of the protectorate as well as government encouragement of Protestant publication. A small number of early presses had operated outside of London at such centers of the medieval manuscript trade as Oxford and York;[25] thus John Mychell printed at Canterbury where he had access to the monastic library.[26] Henry VIII banned provincial printing in 1539 in order to bring the book trade under control.[27] When Mychell went back into operation in Canterbury under Edward VI, he printed predestinarian tracts, Hurlestone's *Newes from Rome*, translations of two Erasmian colloquies by Edmund Becke, and other reformist texts under the patronage of Archbishop Cranmer. After the chartering of the Stationers' Company in 1557, however, printing was centralized in London.

Proximity to monastic libraries does not account for printing at Ipswich, Worcester, and Dublin. The importance of Ipswich as a center of the book trade may be explained by the presence of a large population of literate Protestants[28] and the closeness of the port to the Continent. After London itself, Ipswich was the most convenient en-

---

[25] Paul Morgan, *English Provincial Printing* (Birmingham, 1958), pp. 4-5. See E. Gordon Duff, *English Provincial Printers, Stationers and Bookbinders to 1557* (Cambridge, 1912) for printers' lists.

[26] Mychell could not have printed *A Comparyson bytwene .IIII. Byrdes, the Larke, the Nyghtyngale, the Thrusshe & the Cucko* (c. 1538) by Robert Saltwood, monk of Christ Church, Canterbury, after the dissolution of the monastery (compare *STC* 15192.5).

[27] A. W. Pollard, *Fine Books* (1912), pp. 224, 226.

[28] Dickens, *English Reformation*, pp. 307-308.

trepôt for books shipped from Antwerp, Wesel, and other Protestant printing centers. The colophon of Bale's *Summarium* attributes publication to John Overton, an Ipswich bookseller ("Gippeswici per Ioannem Overton"). This false attribution enabled Bale to circumvent restrictions on the importation of books printed abroad. Bale had close connections to Ipswich. Coming from Dunwich, a Suffolk village twenty-five miles from Ipswich, he headed the Carmelite house in Ipswich during the 1530s. The ascription "Autore Ioanne Balaeo Sudovolca" on the title page of *Summarium* prominently announces his Suffolk origins (see Figure 5). The contact that Bale maintained with Ipswich during exile suggests that his Henrician publications may have been smuggled through that port.

Immediately after the relaxation of censorship, Anthony Scoloker and John Oswen printed a startlingly large number of Protestant books at Ipswich during the single year of 1548. Scoloker printed works of Continental reformers in translations made by himself and Richard Argentine, a physician and Master of the Ipswich grammar school. Chapbooks like John Ramsey's *A Plaister for a Galled Horse* and popular verse by the Protestant artisan-poet Peter Moone show that Scoloker and Oswen catered to a popular audience of literate laymen. After a burst of intense activity, Scoloker and Oswen relocated their presses in 1548. Oswen set up shop in Worcester as King's Printer for Wales. Scoloker went into partnership with William Seres, who also published as partner to John Day. Like Bale, Day had close links to Dunwich and Seres was a Suffolk man. At about this time the Privy Council commissioned Humphrey Powell to move to Dublin as King's Printer for Ireland. Evidently the government wished to sponsor the publication of Protestant propaganda near the marches of Wales and Ireland, each of which had hostile Catholic populations.

PROTESTANT PATRONS AND PATRONAGE

Influential Protestant lords shielded these reformist printers and publishers and offered them patronage. The former worked in the Cromwellian tradition of encouraging inexpensive popular editions rather than expensive folios geared to aristocratic readers. Courtly and native literary traditions still coexisted in elite circles, but only those works that appealed to popular taste tended to go into print. Patrons rarely made outright money payments to their favorites. Their support usually came in the form of protection, preferment to church benefices, and appointments to court offices. Because Tudor dedications represent only requests for support, one cannot assume on the basis of an isolated dedication that a particular author received any form of reward. Although their payments were meager at best, printers sometimes functioned as patrons by offering employment or hospitality to writers. Hospitality that John Day extended to Gabriel Streamer, a fictitious author, is, for example, an important element in William Baldwin's learned satire and publishing hoax, *Beware the Cat*.

Protestant publishers and their aristocratic patrons assumed the existence of a large reading public. They disagreed with Gardiner, who argued for traditional images on the ground that not one layman in one hundred could read.[29] Gardiner's stance represented another survival of earlier medieval attitudes, when only scribes and scholars could read. The Protestant position more closely resembles that of Thomas More, who estimated that more than forty percent of Englishmen could read.[30] Clerical opposition to the vernacular Bible presupposed widespread literacy. The

---

[29] Bennett, *Books and Readers*, p. 28.

[30] J. W. Adamson, "The Extent of Literacy in England in the Fifteenth and Sixteenth Centuries: Notes and Conjectures," *Library*, 4th ser., 10 (1930), 171.

rapid growth of literacy in Reformation Germany followed upon the exhortations that accompanied the German New Testament and Lutheran tracts. The reception of the Wyclif and Tyndale translations of the Bible probably had a similar effect. Advocacy of lay reading may account for the overwhelming sympathy of printers for the Reformation in Germany and England.[31] An explosion of popular culture accompanied the Reformation. Octavo editions of theological tracts, political pamphlets, and verse chapbooks crowded bookstalls. The extreme rarity of so many Edwardian tracts and fugitive pieces is itself a proof of popularity. English readers wore out their pamphlets, proclamations, ballads, broadsides, and other ephemera.

Anthony Scoloker and Richard Argentine operated in Ipswich under the protection of Thomas, first Baron Wentworth, and Edward Grimston, the future Comptroller of Calais. Argentine dedicated his translation of Zwingli's *Certeyne Preceptes* to Grimston, who lived north of Ipswich in Kenton. He dedicated his translation of Luther's sermon on John 20 to Wentworth, who owned a manor northwest of Ipswich at Nettlestead. For many years an ardent reformer, it was Wentworth who had converted John Bale and served as patron to both Bale and Thomas Becon.[32] He was the preeminent peer in East Anglia. Protestant writers looked to him for support. According to Richard Sherry's dedication of his translations of Joannes Brentius's *Exposicion upon the Syxte Chapter of Saynte John* (9 April 1550), he placed himself under Wentworth's protection because of "a general fame . . . that you favoure all good letters, and chiefelye the holie scripture . . ." (A2r-v).

The Edwardian activities of the Duchesses of Somerset,

[31] H. G. Haile, "Luther and Literacy," *PMLA*, 91 (1976), 817.
[32] *Catalogus*, I, 702; McConica, p. 219.

Suffolk, and Richmond confirmed Gardiner's suspicions that they belonged to a circle of Protestant ladies in sympathy with the radicals. They sponsored publishers and writers including Day, Seres, Bale, and Crowley. Although this group of aristocratic women first gathered around Catherine Parr toward the end of Henry VIII's reign, she had relatively little direct impact during her stepson's reign. Young Princess Elizabeth began to attract attention as a Protestant sympathizer after her father's death and during her period of residence at Chelsea House as Catherine Parr's charge. Before he returned to England, Bale edited her translation of Margaret of Navarre's *Godly Medytacyon of the Christen Sowle* (Wesel, 1548). Someone close to the princess probably sent Bale his copy text. Walter Lynne dedicated his translation of Luther's *Frutefull Exposition* (1548) to the princess.

Catherine Brandon, Dowager Duchess of Suffolk, was the great Protestant patroness. The zealous reformer Thomas Wilson worked on *The Rule of Reason* (1551) and *The Art of Rhetorique* (1553) during his period of service as tutor to her sons. John Harington the elder and Thomas Some, the editor of Latimer's sermons, dedicated works to her. After Seymour's fall, Latimer retired to her Lincolnshire estate at Grimsthorpe as household chaplain. The prominent use of her coat of arms in the publications of Day and Seres suggests that she underwrote their activities. Without a significant source of capital, it is unlikely that they could have taken such a large share of the Reformation book trade so soon after starting operation. They printed the Suffolk arms in five editions that appeared in quick succession in 1548 and 1549: the Apocrypha and New Testament, Latimer's *Sermon on the Plowers*, Tyndale's *Exposicion uppon Matthew*, and a translation of Viret's *Exposition of the Apostles creed.* Day dedicated Joannes Epinus's *Exposition upon the XV. Psalme* (c. 1550) to the duchess.

The patronage of Mary Fitzroy, Duchess of Richmond, paralleled that of Catherine Brandon. On Bale's return to England, she lodged him along with John Foxe at her London residence, Mountjoy House. As the surviving child of the imprisoned Duke of Norfolk, the duchess succeeded Wentworth as guardian of Surrey's children. She engaged Foxe to serve as their tutor. It was at Mountjoy House and Reigate Castle that Foxe wrote his earliest published works, Latin treatises in favor of tolerance and against the death penalty: *De non plectendis morte adulteris consultatio* (1548) and *De censura sive excommunicatione ecclesiastica* (1551).

Edward Seymour was the preeminent Reformation patron. A 1547 letter from Roger Ascham addresses him as "literarum patronus maximus" ("the supreme patron of letters"). In addition to sponsoring some writers, he gained a reputation for protecting radical authors in general. Thomas Churchyard acknowledged Seymour's assistance "when I was troubled before the Lords of Counsell, for writing some of my first verses." Although he was the direct successor to Thomas Cromwell in sponsoring Grafton and Whitchurch, Coverdale, William Gray of Reading, and other Protestant writers, Seymour extended patronage on a far more sweeping scale. Unlike other Protestant lords, he controlled crown patronage. He surpassed his predecessors in manipulating the press. It was in service to Seymour that William Cecil gained his first experience as a patron, which he later applied on behalf of Elizabeth as the queen's chief minister. The queen's confidant Robert Dudley, Earl of Leicester, was the other great patron at the end of the century.[33]

[33] The best studies of Tudor patronage are in McConica and in Eleanor Rosenberg, *Leicester, Patron of Letters* (New York, 1955).

The very large number of book dedications that Seymour received attests to his standing as a patron of arts and letters as well as a sponsor of government propaganda. His manuscript dedications portray him as a discerning man of learning. Although no writings were dedicated to him under Henry VIII, Seymour received twenty-five dedications under Edward VI. Members of his immediate family, notably Anne Stanhope, received twelve dedications. Seventeen of these dedications came in publications by Grafton, Whitchurch, Lynne, Day and Seres, and Scoloker. William Baldwin dedicated his *Treatise of Morall Phylosophie* to Seymour's son Edward as a text suitable for the education of youth. Such immigrant theologians as Martin Bucer, Peter Martyr Vermigli, and Bernardino Ochino dedicated works to the protector and king.

Although not all of these authors received support, their dedications acknowledge Seymour's central position as a Protestant patron. Out of 123 dedications that went to Edwardian royalty, courtiers, and peers, Seymour, along with his immediate family, and Edward VI received 88 acknowledgments. Some authors praised Seymour in simple gratitude for his policy of liberalization. During the protectorate, Edward VI received fifteen book dedications, ten of which were in pamphlets authorized by Seymour and published by Grafton, Lynne, and Whitchurch. During the Dudley regency, the king received seventeen more printed dedications. Fifteen manuscripts were dedicated or addressed to him as king. As Prince of Wales, Edward had received dedications in only one manuscript and one printed book. All but one of Dudley's seven dedications were in works of noncontroversial scholarship; he received no manuscript dedications. When one considers that Seymour was the real power behind the throne during the protectorate, his true stature as a patron is apparent. He continued to receive dedications and requests for patronage after he fell from power.[34]

Seymour's eclecticism exemplifies the fluidity of courtly and popular auspices during the Reformation. By the 1580s, critics like Sidney and Puttenham would attempt to seal off aristocratic literature from "rustick" native influences. Seymour's protégés included radical, moderate, and conservative writers. Such gospellers as Thomas Becon and John Hooper lived in Seymour's household as chaplains at the same time that William Turner served as his personal physician. Hugh Latimer gained great notoriety by preaching at Paul's Cross as well as the royal court. Although they were overshadowed in the public sphere by the gospellers, moderate humanists like Cheke, Smith, and Cecil occupied positions of authority at court, in the church, and at the universities. No radicals occupied policy-making positions. Such conservative Erastians as Nicholas Udall retained Seymour's confidence. In his own household, Seymour shared the concern of Catherine Parr and Princess Elizabeth for the study of languages and the humanistic piety of Margaret of Navarre. Latin verses on Margaret's death by the three eldest Seymour daughters were printed in

---

[34] For general documentation, see my article "Protector Somerset, Patron of the English Renaissance," *PBSA*, 70 (1976), 307-31, with its index of Reformation book dedications. Additional book dedications are cited above, pp. 90, 104-106, and below, pp. 216, 239, and 466. Franklin B. Williams, Jr., *Index of Dedications and Commendatory Verses in English Books Before 1641* (1962) is the standard source concerning printed dedications. Appendix I, below, lists manuscript dedications. The remainder of the present discussion goes beyond the *PBSA* essay. M. L. Bush offers no proof for his conjecture that the "key to his [Seymour's] beliefs in the period of the protectorate lies in his protégés and associates rather than his words and reputation" (*Government Policy*, p. 104; also see pp. 66, 68-70, 104-12). The present chapter assembles evidence concerning Seymour's thought.

Paris.[35] Seymour owned a fine illuminated manuscript copy of a French translation of Boccaccio's *Decameron*, which would have scandalized such radical gospellers as Latimer, Becon, and Crowley.[36] Although the gospellers tended to lose favor at court after Seymour's fall, Cecil continued to promote their interests while at the same time he ensured the continuity of humanistic scholarship.

Seymour's secretaries Thomas Smith and William Cecil were the most important scholars living in his household. Cecil's wife addressed the Duchess of Somerset as her patroness in a manuscript dedication signed "Your Graces in service Mildred Cicill" (MS Royal 17 B. XVIII, fol. 2ᵛ). Smith and Cecil directed the publication of propaganda on Seymour's behalf (see Appendix III) and channeled public discussion. Both had been members of the reformist circle led by Hugh Latimer at St. John's College during the 1530s. It was at Cambridge that they acquired reputations as eminent Greek scholars. Smith had risen to become Regius Professor of Civil Law and Vice Chancellor of the University. The Privy Council named both secretaries to the censorship committee established in 1549. As Seymour loyalists, both Smith and Cecil went to the Tower with their patron after his fall.[37]

Cecil played a major role in Seymour's patronage activities. As his private secretary, Cecil administered all requests for support. His loyalty, tact, and administrative

[35] *Annae, Margaritae, Ianae, Sororum Virginum, Heroidum Anglarum* [*sic*] *In mortem Divae Margaritae Valesiae, Navarrorum Reginae, Heçatodistichon*, ed. N. Denisot (Paris, 1550; French trans., ed. N. Denisot [Paris, 1551]).

[36] B.L. MSS Add. 35322-35323. The binder decorated both volumes with the motto from Seymour's 1547 seal: "Foy Pour Debvoir" (B.L. Add. Seal XC.35).

[37] See Conyers Read, *Mr. Secretary Cecil and Queen Elizabeth* (1955), pp. 41, 46-47.

ability won him unprecedented respect. Although he remained in contact with Seymour after his fall from power, Cecil first displayed his flair for survival by moving out of Seymour's household into the inner circle of Dudley's council. In order to advance in station, a Tudor gentleman required a friend at court. From the time he entered Seymour's service until his death in 1598, Cecil's influence was indispensable to those seeking crown patronage. Justus Jonas, who supplied the original Latin text for Cranmer's *Catechism*, sent Cecil a request from Germany for his royal bounty. Cecil obtained preferments for Protestant immigrants. In thanking Cecil for his kindness at court, the Hebrew scholar Immanuel Tremellius addressed Cecil as "patronus meus humanissimus" ("my most kind patron"). (The Bishop of Ely had written to Cecil in order to recommend Tremellius for a Carlisle prebendary.) Polydore Vergil requested a warrant for his royal gift of 300 crowns. Churchmen channeled requests for preferment through Cecil. With an intimacy dating back to their service in Seymour's household, William Turner congratulated Cecil on his escape from the court intrigues that destroyed Seymour. He concluded a letter of complaint over emoluments from his Wells deanery with the friendly salutation "fare well. i pray you commend me unto your bedfelow." Cecil used his influence on behalf of his old school, St. John's College. He served as a conduit for university scholars seeking appointments and favor at court. On the basis of Walter Haddon's recommendation, he took the Cambridge graduate Thomas Gardiner into his household. Cecil was at the center of efforts by the fellows of Magdalen College, Oxford, to obtain letters patent from Seymour in order to replace Dr. Oglethorpe with Walter Haddon as president of the college.[38]

[38] MS Lansdowne 2, fols. 44^r, 52^r, 97^r, 101^r, 116^{r-v}, 135^r, 139^v, 145^r, 151^r, 157^r, 185^r, 201^r, 218^r; MS Lansdowne 3, fols. 7^r-12^r, 15^r.

Cecil's extensive correspondence documents the unbroken continuity of Seymour's patronage policy. Tremellius's epithet shows that by 1551 Cecil was regarded as a patron in his own right. Ralph Robinson's translation of More's *Utopia* offers a typical example of how a Tudor writer secured support from a Tudor patron. Robinson and George Tadlowe, who procured the translation, were both guildsmen and citizens of London. In dedicating the text to Cecil, the translator reduces the complexity of More's satire. Losing sight of the work's structure as an unresolved debate over the problem of royal counsel and reform of the commonwealth, Robinson offers the book to Cecil as an unambiguous guide to statecraft. He implies that Cecil, "a man . . . profoundely learned" (✠5^r), offers the kind of counsel that Hythlodaeus despaired of finding at court. This dedication constitutes an introductory request for support. Although Cecil had not commissioned the project, a written request for employment followed the printed dedication. Cecil did take Robinson into his service, for a second letter addressed to *"patronus suus Unicus"* ("his singular patron") requested an increase in salary. Robinson later sent Latin verses in manuscript as the traditional New Year gift to his master (MS Lansdowne 2, fols. 129^r, 131^r).

As the most successful professional writer of the mid-century, John Bale offers a better example than Ralph Robinson of how an author organized a campaign for patronage. He designed *Summarium* as a homecoming gift to his sovereign in gratitude for the "free permission" (*"Edwardi sexti suffragium liberum"*) granted for the return of the Henrician exiles (3P4^v). Last-minute revisions stress the imminence of his return during the year 1548 at the age of fifty-three. Bale says that the work was in press as he prepared to leave Wesel (4Q4^r). Both variants of *Summarium* bear the publication date of 31 July 1548. Bale's giving to himself of the place of honor in *Summarium* ex-

emplifies the self-exaltation of the Tudor author in search
of reward. Placement of his autobiography at the very end
brings the volume full circle as an appeal to the Seymour
regime for patronage.

Bale's flattery of Edward VI as the inspiration for the
current revival of arts and letters would have seemed des-
tined to win support at a time when the government was
rewarding returned exiles and underwriting Protestant authors. His dedication to the king constitutes a request for
financial aid. The title-page woodcut shows Bale giving
Summarium to the king in his presence chamber. This
woodcut and a smaller variant illustrate Bale's return to his
homeland under a godly ruler (Figures 5-6). The careful
shaping of the beginning and ending of *Summarium* to focus on Bale's homecoming suggests that it was dated for
publication at the time of his actual return. At the end of
his Marian exile, Bale would similarly style *Catalogus* as a
text in celebration of his homecoming under Elizabeth and
as a request for royal patronage.

Why did Seymour deny Bale crown assistance? Although
the dedication in Leland's *Laboryouse Journey* reiterated his
appeal for royal patronage, Bale never addressed a direct
request to Seymour. Only the Duchess of Richmond offered support by lodging him in her London house. Despite Seymour's willingness to protect Bale from Gardiner's attacks, Bale's attack on Paget in Askew's *Examinations*
certainly would have embarrassed the government. Paget
was well positioned to block his appeals for patronage.

Not until 1551 did Bale succeed in winning appointments as Rector of the Church of St. Mary in Bishopstoke,
Hampshire,[39] and nonresident Vicar of the Church of St.

[39] *Registra Stephani Gardiner et Johannis Poynet Episcoporum Wintonen-
sium*, ed. H. Chitty and H. E. Malden (Canterbury and York Society,
vol. 37; Oxford, 1930), p. 133.

Peter and St. Paul in Swaffham, Norfolk. Soon afterward he dedicated his *Expostulation* to Dudley. The Bishopstoke appointment, which was in the gift of the Bishop of Winchester, made Bale household chaplain to John Ponet. Ponet held the manor at Bishopstoke as successor to Gardiner as Bishop of Winchester. During the Marian exile, Ponet wrote to Bale as "Youre assuerid old friend. Jo. Ponit Wint." and deferred to the older man as his literary mentor: "My frush book is ready and loo I send you one, to reade as a tryfell, and not as any wit. but you your judgment I wolde gladly have of it. practyse hath taught yow what falts should be shoned [polished]" (B.L. MS Add. 29546, fol. 25^r). Adjacent to the manor of the Duchess of Richmond, the Swaffham preferment belonged to the Duke of Norfolk. Prior to his scheduled execution, he petitioned Henry VIII to settle his estates on Prince Edward. After his father's death, King Edward accepted the offer. Bale therefore received the Swaffham appointment from the crown at a time when Dudley controlled royal patronage. It was through the intervention of the radical courtier John Philpot that Bale achieved his greatest success. According to Bale, he received his Ossory bishopric after Philpot arranged a 15 August 1552 interview with the king in Southampton during a royal progress (*Vocacyon*, B7^v-8^r). Unlike Dean Swift, he regarded his Irish appointment as an advancement.

THE LEGEND OF PROTECTOR SOMERSET

Seymour's career as a Protestant patron and man of letters continued even after his fall from power. Such loyalists as Thomas Becon, Miles Coverdale, and Robert Crowley still spoke out on his behalf. Although Seymour's public career had been marked by a general reluctance to commit his thoughts to writing, he broke silence during his two imprisonments in the Tower of London. His writings dramatize the inner spiritual life and dilemmas of conscience of the Reformation intellectual. He used two books that he edited, a meditation that he wrote by hand the night before his death, and the speech that he delivered from the scaffold on Tower Hill in order to idealize his conduct. These statements have great value as the only direct evidence concerning Seymour's thought other than his letters to Gardiner. Through these works, the fallen duke searches for spiritual consolation in an ancient tradition going back to Boethius's *De consolatione philosophiae*, Boccaccio's *De casibus virorum illustrorum*, and the medieval *ars moriendi*. In Seymour's Tower writings, we may trace a structure of actions through which he dramatized the final events of his life leading to its last act. Like More, Essex, Raleigh, and Charles I, he regarded his death as a performance scene.

As a devotional exercise during his first imprisonment, Seymour translated a letter from Calvin "to the saide Duke, in the time of hys trouble." Whitchurch published it on 5 April 1550 as *An Epistle both of Godly Consolacion and also of Advertisement*. In his threatening, apocalyptic preface, Seymour adopts the voice of the Protestant preacher in urging the rebels to repent. His account of the sermons and tracts that followed the 1549 risings demonstrates his familiarity with the art of propaganda: "[God] hath nowe in these last daies, reysed up many godly preachers, who cease not daylye to publish (as it were) gods proclamation in thys behalfe. . . . He hath provided many godly exhortacions and treatyses dayly to come forth . . ." (A2r-v).

Seymour sought consolation through meditation on the mutability of human life and worldly things. After his release from prison, he edited Coverdale's translation of Otto Werdmueller's *A Spyrytuall and Moost Precyouse Pearle* at "oure house at Somerset place, the .vi. day of May.

Anno. 1550" (A7^v). According to his introduction, Seymour commissioned publication because of the "greate conforte" that Coverdale's manuscript had given during "oure greate trouble":

> And hereupon we have requyred hym of whom we had the copye of thys boke the rather at our request and commendacyon, to set thys boke forth and in prynte, that not onelye we or one or two more, but all that be afflycted maye take profyt and consolacyon if they wyll. . . . (A7^{r-v})

By portraying himself as a man who spent his imprisonment in prayer and reading devotional works, Seymour achieves greater success than any other Tudor politician except More at creating a public image of piety. Appended prayers composed by Thomas Becon contribute to this image. Guided by Werdmueller's consolatory wisdom, Seymour relieves the inward "gryefe of . . . [his own] mynde" by meditation on death and the afterlife. He adopts the traditional Christian stoicism of the man swept downward by Fortune's wheel:

> . . . knowynge certeynely, that suche is the uncerteintye of the world and all humayne thynges, that no man standeth so sure, but the tempeste of afflyccion and adversyte may overtake hym, and if the grace of god do not syngularly helpe him, caste hym donne [down] and make hym fall. . . . (A7^v)

Similar mutability themes flourished at court. The king had dedicated his translation of a collection of scriptural commonplaces to his uncle with the admonition that the Bible is the sole source of constancy in a world characterized by "la vanité du monde, la mutabilité du temps, et le changement de toutes choses mondaines . . ." (B.L. MS

Add. 9000, fol. 1^{r-v}). As language exercises, neither this nor a related collection in the king's hand entitled "A lencontre les abus du monde" (B.L. MS Add. 5464) shows evidence of original thought. They do document an effort by his uncle and tutors to inculcate pietistic ideals at court. The courtier William Thomas issued a *de contemptu mundi* treatise under the title *The Vanitee of this World* (1549). After his master's fall, the Duchess of Suffolk wrote to console Cecil over "the assaultes of froward fortun." Such a departure from "the commen enfection of feyned frendship" was an unusual show of loyalty in the precarious world of the Tudor courtier (MS Lansdowne 2, fol. 58^r). Every courtier must have feared and expected the turn of Fortune's wheel. Seymour would have recognized in his final imprisonment circumstances similar in kind to those described in the king's final soliloquy in Shakespeare's *Richard II* (V.v.1-66). Even Princess Elizabeth wrote the following verses on a wall during her imprisonment at Woodstock:

Oh fortune, thy wresting wavering state
Hath fraught with cares my troubled wit,
Whose witness this present prison late
Could bear, where once was joy's loan quit.
Thou causedst the guilty to be loosed
From bands where innocents were inclosed,
And caused the guiltless to be reserved,
And freed those that death hath well deserved.
But all herein can be nothing wrought,
So God send to my foes all they have thought.[40]

Condemned prisoners and their counselors used the *ars moriendi* in preparing for death. The only English Prot-

[40] Queen Elizabeth I, *Poems*, ed. L. Bradner (Providence, R.I., 1964), p. 3.

estant handbook available during the Reformation was Luke Shepherd's *A Holesome Preservatyve against Desperation* (c. 1548). Although *The Sycke Mannes Salve* remained in manuscript until 1561, Becon seems to have written it during his service to Seymour. Both Shepherd and Becon divide the drama of death into the three traditional areas of Christian combat against the flesh, the world, and the devil (Ephesians 6:10-12). According to this pattern, the man about to die should meditate on the brevity and vanity of this world before coping with the terror of the devil's final assault. Seymour knew the death meditations in the prayer book and the sermon against fear of death in the *Book of Homilies*. The ritualistic etiquette of the scaffold included confession of sin, begging of forgiveness from the monarch and council, a declaration of the justness of the trial and sentence, confession of faith, and final words including the Lord's Prayer, Creed, and Psalm 51. Beheading took place during recitation of the last words of Christ on the cross: "O Lord, into thy hands I commend my spirit." In the case of More and Raleigh, the studied rhetoric of the occasion included macabre badinage with the headsman and assembled dignitaries.[41]

The night before his death on 22 January 1551/2, Seymour dramatized his spiritual distress by writing a short gospelling cento on the vellum flyleaf of an illuminated manuscript calendar (Figure 16).[42] The volume is appropriate for a military commander, for it contains the tide

---

[41] Beach Langston, "Essex and the Art of Dying," *HLQ*, 13 (1950), 112-13; see Beaty, *The Craft of Dying*, pp. 108-20.

[42] B.L. MS Stowe 1066, fol. 1ʳ. The inside back cover bears the name "Katerine Hartford Caterine Seamour." Daughter of Henry Grey, fourth Duke of Suffolk, and sister to Lady Jane Grey, Catherine Grey married Edward Seymour, Earl of Hertford and son of the Duke of Somerset. She evidently inherited the book from her father-in-law.

tables necessary for Channel crossings and expeditions to Scotland. The tiny size (77 × 96 mm.) of this aristocratic pocket book, with its elegant crimson velvet cover, precludes an entry longer than the following holograph inscription:

> fere of the lord
> is the bgenning [*sic*] of
> wisdume
>
> put thi trust in
> the lord with all
> thine hart
>
> be not wise in thyne
> owne conseyte but
> fere the lord and
> fle frome evele
> > frome the toware
> > the day before my dethe
> > 1551
> > E. Somerset.

Seymour's texts (Psalms 4:5 and 111:10, Proverbs 9:10, Ecclesiastes 5:7, Matthew 6:13, Luke 11:4, and Romans 12:16) dramatize the final struggle against despair and fear of death warned against in Shepherd's *Preservative* and Becon's *Salve*. In the manner of the Protestant exile familiar from Bale's writings, he turns away from this world. Psalm 4:5 and Romans 12:16 in particular allude to divine deliverance from false accusers and acceptance of vindication as God's prerogative. Having testified his faith and come to terms with a sentence that he considers unjust, Seymour welcomes death as a release from a corrupt world. As a death meditation, Seymour's inscription resembles the "psalm-like prayer" that More the prisoner wove into the marginalia of his prayer book.[43]

Seymour imitated the manner of a Protestant martyr in his final performance. Despite a Privy Council order, "Tower hill was covered with a great multitude" (*Annales*, 3E3ʳ). Both the directive and its violation attest to Seymour's popularity, for the authorities generally staged executions as public spectacles and warnings to potential malefactors. Foxe supplies a firsthand account of the execution "by a certain noble personage," which tallies with the eyewitness description by John Stow. Although Stow supplies no text for Seymour's speech, he confirms all other circumstances given by Foxe. Instead of the witty delivery of More or Raleigh, Seymour adopts the homiletic voice of Calvin's *Epistle*. Repeatedly exhorting his audience with the preacher's salutation " 'dearly beloved friends,' " he assumes the apostolic role of the true Christian who returned to " 'the form and order of the primitive church.' " Begging for silence in order to die in tranquillity, his final words self-consciously dramatize his death as that of a Protestant saint:

> For albeit the spirit be willing and ready, the flesh is frail and wavering, and, through your quietness, I shall be much more quieter. . . . Moreover, I desire you all to bear me witness, that I die here in the faith of Jesus Christ; desiring you to help me with your prayers, that I may persevere constant in the same unto my life's end.

According to Foxe's witness, the duke died "like a meek lamb" and "without any trouble of mind (as it appeared)" (*A & M*, VI, 293, 295).

Contemporary sources disagree over the exact manner of

[43] *Thomas More's Prayer Book*, ed. Louis L. Martz and Richard S. Sylvester (New Haven, 1969), pp. xxxvi-xxxviii.

Seymour's death. A courtly account accords with the known circumstances of the execution more closely than the Foxe version. Seymour's quieting of the turbulent crowd bears out his character as a general and his Tower meditations on the vanity of this world:

> . . . the Duke expressinge great constancy often desirede the people to remayne quiett that hee might quietly ende his life, ffor said hee I have often looked death in the face in greate adventures in the feilde, hee is nowe noe stranger unto mee. And among all the vayne mockeryes in the worlde, I repent of nothinge more, than in esteeminge life more deare than I should. I have adventured [incurred] the hate of great persons, soo much the more dangerous, because unjust. . . ."

His last words reflect an effort to steel himself for death. The courtier's comment that the beheading "cutt off his confused cogitacons and cares" confirms the fears of death that Seymour recorded in his calendar.[44]

During his lifetime, reformers revered this master of public appearances for dismantling the Tudor terror. Partisans continued to idealize him as "a myrrour off true innocencye and Christen pacience" after his death.[45] For Becon, Crowley, and Foxe, Seymour's execution was only one sign of divine retribution leading to Edward's death. Before he died, however, an alternative tradition began to attack him as an avaricious politician who proudly commissioned lavish building projects. According to MS Harley 2194, Edward VI criticized Seymour's demolition of

[44] B.L. MS Harley 2194, fol. 20ʳ. Prepared in collaboration with Jennifer Loach of Somerville College, Oxford, my forthcoming edition transcribes this unpublished manuscript account of Seymour's trial and execution, with its comment on life at the court of Edward VI.

[45] Thomas Becon, *A Confortable Epistle* [sic] (Wesel?, 1554), A3ʳ.

churches in order to erect Somerset House as an act of impiety that drew "open dislike from men and much secret revenge from God." Nevertheless, the king contended that his uncle had "advanced th[e] Honour of the Realme" and deserved to live for he "had done nothinge, or if hee had it was very small . . ." (fol. 20^r-v). Citing Seymour as the most advanced thinker of his time, Foxe treated his death as the first of many martyrdoms to come. For the Augustan antiquarian William Cole, the policy of toleration could only be wrong: "He is always called by the *Dissenters*, *The good Duke of Somerset*. We see for what Reason" (B.L. MS Add. 5809, fol. 103^r). His main flaw may well have been his aspiration for a place that rivaled the king's. The history of figures like Wolsey shows that such men inevitably had their fall. Seymour's own writings betray that he was not altogether surprised by the turn of Fortune's wheel.

CHAPTER 3
Vox Populi, Vox Dei

. . . s. Paule would have such language spoken to the people in the churche, as they might understande and have profite by hearyng the same. . . .

Preface to the *Book of Common Prayer* (1549)

THOMAS CRANMER AND HIS BOOKS

In his portrait by Gerlach Flicke (20 July 1546), the massive figure of Thomas Cranmer poses in his Lambeth study as a scholar among his books.[1] A copy of St. Augustine's *De fide et operibus* lies on the table before him as he looks up from the epistles of St. Paul. A third book bears an extremely faint title that appears to read "Erasm[i] [t]estam[en]tum." Yet rather than withdrawing from the world into contemplative scholarship, he is surrounded by the attributes of public office: his signet ring, archiepiscopal robes, and a royal letter on the table addressed "Too . . . my Lorde tharbusshope of Canterbury. . . ." In fact the entire portrait symbolizes Cranmer's ecclesiastical authority, which derives from his books as well as royal appointment. The scriptural texts embody Cranmer's return *ad fontes* as the source of truth. Like the Bishop of Hippo, a favorite authority, the English scholar codified doctrine

[1] London, National Portrait Gallery, No. 535.

[122]

and ritual for his church. Flicke based the design on the 1520 Holbein portrait of William Warham, who as Cranmer's predecessor occupied the see of Canterbury from 1503 until his death in August 1532.[2] With his Latin breviary open at the litany of the saints, the world-weary and contemplative Warham is overshadowed by his jeweled crucifix and miter. If one interprets the paintings, in effect, as a diptych, they personify the transition away from medieval beliefs on the eve of Henry VIII's death.

The succession of Edward VI marked the beginning of a new stage in Cranmer's career. Thus the archbishop proclaims the radical phase of the English Reformation in the title of the collection of authorized sermons that he edited under the new regime: *Certayne Sermons, or Homelies, appoynted by the kynges Majestie, to be declared and redde, by all persones* [parsons], *Vicars, or Curates, every Sondaye in their churches, where they have Cure.* The title announces Cranmer's concern for religious instruction in the vernacular. These homilies form part of the new English service which consists technically of reading and hearing the Word in the form of Bible readings, sermons, and the common prayers, sacraments, rites, and ceremonies drawn from the scriptures. The derivation of "sermon" from the Medieval Latin *sermo* ("word") corresponds to the origin of "homily" in ὁμιλία ("conversation, instruction"). The ultimate derivation of "homily" from ὅμιλος ("crowd, mob, multitude") reflects the demotic language and outdoor circumstances under which Jesus, Paul, and the apostles preached. Through the Vulgate translation, the *sermo humilis* ("humble style") had become associated with divine revelation. By analogy with the Incarnation, Cranmer's plain

[2] National Portrait Gallery, No. 2094.

style paradoxically unites highest and lowest in a style that corresponds to its subject matter.[3]

The *Book of Homilies* belongs to the self-contained collection of devotional works that Cranmer issued as a guide to Christian living. English Protestantism is by its very nature a book-centered and literalistic faith. The Royal Injunctions and an act of Parliament ordered the Great Bible, *Book of Homilies*, *Book of Common Prayer*, and Erasmus's *Paraphrases* into use in every parish church. Authorized lay reading of the English Bible and promulgation of an English service based upon it arrived with revolutionary impact after more than a millennium of Vulgate Latin. The prayer book exhorts the congregation to participate actively in hearing the scriptures, joining in communal prayer, and celebrating the communal feast of the Lord's Supper. Thus one may regard Cranmer's books as scripts for a spiritual drama performed Sunday after Sunday in every English church. Anglican ritual stresses proper interpretation of the Word by the individual, who may be both hearer and reader. People could purchase copies of these books at prices set by the Privy Council, or they could read the copies chained in each parish church.[4]

---

[3] Erich Auerbach describes the *sermo humilis* as the style appropriate "to set forth an enormously difficult paradox as though it were something self-evident and not to be doubted" in *Literary Language and Its Public in Late Latin Antiquity and in the Middle Ages*, trans. R. Manheim (1965), pp. 32-33 et seq. Quotations follow the second edition of the *Book of Homilies* (31 July 1547).

[4] Traditional scholarship has ignored Cranmer's book-making art. Most studies approach the texts as material sources concerning theological doctrine, ecclesiastical history, and philological analysis. A long and intricate debate lives on about the precise nature of Cranmer's views on the eucharist, how they evolved, and how they relate to positions on transubstantiation, Real Presence, and Spiritual Presence held by English and Continental theologians. Peter Brooks clearly summarizes the controversy and suggests

Vox Populi, Vox Dei

Cranmer's texts embody a premise fundamental to Protestant literary tradition: that the Bible is a book of the laity which is a valid model for imitation in both secular and divine literature. Republication of the homilies and 1552 prayer book in basically the same form under Elizabeth

---

a solution in *Thomas Cranmer's Doctrine of the Eucharist: An Essay in Historical Development* (1965). Although most historians ignore the books or quote from them out of context, A. G. Dickens documents the importance of the history of publication and popular reaction to these texts (*English Reformation*, pp. 183-96, 258-68, 301-307, 339-43 et seq.). C. S. Lewis calls for literary judgment of Reformation prose, including Cranmer's texts (*Sixteenth Century*, p. 157). In analyzing the prayer book in particular, both he and Stella Brook stress questions of diction, phraseology, and prose style. Finding that Cranmer submerges original literary qualities in the "corporate anonymity" of "committee" authorship, Lewis concludes that at best he writes stolid, utilitarian, comprehensible prose: "Cranmer's only concern is to state an agreed doctrine with the least possibility of misunderstanding" (op. cit., pp. 194-95). In *The Language of the Book of Common Prayer* (1965), Brook discusses problems of vocabulary, accidence, syntax, grammar, orthography, and etymology. For purposes of convenience, such anonymous documents as the prayer book and *Book of Homilies* are attributed to Cranmer as their chief architect.

Recent studies have recognized the rhetorical art concealed within the "corporate anonymity" of these books. They concentrate on the autonomous status of these texts as literary wholes and the problem of Erasmian influence on Cranmer's thought. James McConica demonstrates the continuity of Edwardian reform with the *via media* of Erasmian humanism; this influence transcended the radical break that Cranmer made with traditional religious practice (chap. 8). Especially valuable is his account of the patronage and publication of the English translation of Erasmus's *Paraphrases*. Because Cranmer based the 1547 Injunctions on Cromwell's 1536 Injunctions, Elton argues that little in the Edwardian reform program was truly original (p. 339). But see John Yost's analysis of Cromwell's "distinctively Protestant approach . . . to the problem of superstitious practices and their remedy" ("Protestant Reformers," p. 190). According to Yost, Cromwell focused less on theological doctrine than on such practices as Bible reading, vernacular preaching, confession, and veneration of saints and images. Most other studies fail to stress Cranmer's Protestant revision

enables one to read these texts as a summary of the world view of Sidney and Spenser, Shakespeare and Donne. Their phrases entered into the popular consciousness through the services that the English people attended week after week, year after year. Thus Ulysses' speech on order and degree repeats commonplaces from the homily on obedience (*Troilus and Cressida*, I.iii.75-137). As late as 1682, Dryden echoes Cranmer's insistence that the Bible is a book "easy and plain for the understandyng":

> And that the *Scriptures*, though not *every where*
> Free from Corruption, or intire, or clear,
> Are uncorrupt, sufficient, clear, intire,
> In *all* things which our needfull *Faith* require.
> (*Religio Laici or A Laymans Faith*, ll.297-300)

Cranmer shifted the center of worship away from the altar to the pulpit and lectern. If one approaches his texts from the vantage point of the parishioner, one is struck by the centrality of the Word. The Bible and the pattern of life that it describes are omnipresent. They define the subject matter, literary form, and homiletic goal of the new

---

of Erasmian ideals. John Booty, E. J. Devereux, and John N. Wall, Jr., analyze the interrelationship between Cranmer's texts as Erasmian vehicles of lay education and church reform. In "Publication of the English *Paraphrases*," Devereux examines the revolutionary publishing history of a work that had to be translated, edited, and produced on a truly massive scale. Wall and Booty view these texts in their social context as vehicles for the fulfillment of the Erasmian ideal of Christian society. In "The 'Book of Homilies' of 1547 and the Continuity of English Humanism in the Sixteenth Century," *Anglican Theological Review*, 58 (1976), 75-87, Wall points out the text's comprehensive pattern of the "life of active charity in imitation of Christ which Erasmus called his *philosophia Christi*." Booty identifies the need to "visualize" the participation of the laity in the new service as a felt experience. See the commentary and notes to his edition of *The Book of Common Prayer 1559* (Charlottesville, Va., 1976) and his forthcoming essay "Church and Commonwealth in the Reign of

service. The government required every English subject
"to heare and be at" the Sunday service, which stressed
scriptural readings and the exegesis in the authorized homily. During the course of a year, the regular churchgoer
would hear almost all of the Bible read in the order prescribed by the prayer book calendar. The order of services
omits portions of the Old Testament thought to be unedi-
fying as well as most of Revelation. Communication at the
Lord's Supper, on the other hand, was required only once
each year (the 1552 prayer book stipulates three times).
Cranmer and his followers wanted weekly communion, and
the laws reflect popular resistance to that. Gone forever was
the supremacy of the medieval mass, which had been celebrated out of the sight of the people in a language they
could not understand.

The English Bible was the central text, and the Reformation public encountered it in a variety of adaptations.
The common thread running through the sixty editions
published under Edward VI was the Erasmian doctrine
that individuals should read and interpret the scriptures for
themselves. Translations of *Paraclesis* appeared in several
editions. Printers and editors popularized Bible study by
augmenting their editions with forms of apparatus that were
new to English Bible printing. Their desire to supplement
a reliable text with a variety of scholarly aids to popular
understanding anticipated the Geneva Bible (1560), which
became the edition preferred by Elizabethans seeking an
accurate English translation. Although the Great Bible offered few interpretative aids other than Cranmer's preface,
most popular editions contained ancillary materials. Maps,
concordances, tables, illustrations, and indices invited the
reader to apply the Bible in light of his own experience.

King Edward VI." For bibliography, see *NCBEL*, I, cols. 1890-91, 1893-
96.

Prologues, prefaces, and annotations carried forward the precedent set by Tyndale's polemical readings. The popular tradition of Edwardian illustrated Bibles is an anomaly in the publication history of authorized editions. In the King James Version of 1611, woodcuts disappeared altogether.[5]

John Day was the most innovative and industrious popularizer of the Bible, particularly through the creative modes of annotation that he and his editors devised. They are far less intrusive than those of Tyndale or Bale. In the preface to his 1548 New Testament, he explains the removal of notes from the margins to the end of each chapter "that thou mayste the better fynde the thynges noted." Use of this location also permits an editor to tailor the length of his commentary to the requirements of the text. Day's commentary on Romans expounds the doctrine of justification by faith. His exposition of Revelation frequently refers the reader to his original source in such notes as the following: "Loke more of thys, in the Image of both the churches, gathered by John Bale." Day's 1549 folio Bible carries over this Revelation commentary intact. Because reading should involve a strenuous process of individual perception, true understanding destroys the validity of all external aids, including his own apparatus. The woodcut

---

[5] Volume 1 of the revised *STC* is the indispensable source for the study of the Tudor Bible. A. W. Pollard assembles the materials for its history in *Records of the English Bible* (Oxford, 1911). For a sound account, see S. L. Greenslade, "English Versions of the Bible, 1525-1611," in *The Cambridge History of the Bible: The West from the Reformation to the Present Day* (Cambridge, 1963), ed. S. L. Greenslade, pp. 141-74. A. S. Herbert's revision of T. H. Darlow and H. F. Moule, *Historical Catalogue of Printed Editions of the English Bible 1525-1961* (1968), must be used with caution and checked against the original texts. For a well-illustrated monograph that requires revision, see James Strachan, *Early Bible Illustrations: A Short Study Based on Some Fifteenth and Early Sixteenth Century Printed Texts* (Cambridge, 1957). See *NCBEL*, I, cols. 1829-41.

of each evangelist and the series of twenty large woodcuts for Revelation might seem to contradict Day's emphasis on reading and understanding (see Figures 9-10). Nevertheless, if one interprets the former in conjunction with its companion prologue for each gospel, the illustrations serve to break down whatever barrier may exist between reader and text. The prologues argue that the authority of the evangelists comes from their independent status as human witnesses to Christ's ministry rather than from church tradition. Prefatory lives and woodcuts such as the illustration for the gospel of Luke enable the reader to "se the authoritie of the man, and of what credence and reverence his writynge is worthy of. . . ." Just as each evangelist "wrote of his own experience," the woodcuts assist the reader in relating the gospels to his own life. In compliance with Day's emphasis on lay education, mnemonic couplets convert each Revelation image into a textual emblem.

Day's editions record his special concern for the common reader. The innovation of publishing the Bible and Apocrypha in six octavo parts (1549-1551) addresses "the commoditie of these pore" by enabling them to purchase separate sections. Day's preface to the Pentateuch (1551) explains that folio Bibles are too costly for the poor "to whose chiefe comforte and consolacyon, the holy goste hathe caused them to be wrytten" (A1ᵛ). After he completed his octavo series, he published the entire Bible for the third time as a single folio under the general editorship of Edmund Becke. Becke also comments that cost reduces Bible circulation because people have been discouraged by "the pryce of late tyme . . . from bying of the same" (1551; *3ᵛ). This use of large and small formats shows that Day cultivated a clientele of upper- and lower-class readers. The opportunity to expand his market and reduce the strain on his presses by printing smaller texts must have appealed to so shrewd a businessman.

Day conceives of the Bible in Erasmian terms as a storehouse of sacred literature in which the reader should find what "he deliteth most in" (Pentateuch, C2ᵛ). Becke also explains that all Englishmen should enjoy "Gods boke." Magistrates in particular should read it "as they have bene used heretofore to do in Cronicles & Canterbury tales." It should supplant "al blasphemyes, swearing, carding, dysing . . . & dissolute lyvyng" (✱4ᵛ). Becke's conventional simile from apologies for poetry compares the diligent reader to the honeybee who makes "by natural craft the swete hony" of "pure and cleare understandying." Thus he designed his concordance as an aid to the novice reader who lacks experience in approaching the Bible as literature: "In the whiche also we may fynde (the which helpeth grea[t]ly the study of the Readers) the opening of certayn Hebrew tropes, translacions, symilitudes, and maners of speakynges (which we call Phrases) conteyned in the Byble" (2A1ʳ).

Erasmus had foreseen the need for a popular guide to the scriptures in *Enchiridion militis Christiani* (1518); evidently he intended his *Paraphrases* to satisfy that need. The Royal Injunctions ordered every parish church to purchase the first volume of the *Paraphrases* as a companion to the Great Bible text. Clergymen were required "diligentely [to] study the same, conferryng the one with the other" (b4ʳ). Seymour and Cranmer inherited the Erasmus translation from the previous reign. Edited by Nicholas Udall under the patronage of Catherine Parr, the first volume (31 January 1548) is doctrinally orthodox (McConica, pp. 240-46). According to Udall, paraphrase embodies Cranmer's program of Bible reading as a means of lay education:

. . . a plain settyng forth of a texte or sentence open, clere, plain, and familiar, whiche otherwyse should per-

chaunce seem bare, unfruictefull, hard straunge, rough
obscure, and derke to bee understanded of any that wer
. . . unlearned. . . . (B7^r)

Despite the prestige that Princess Mary lent to the project,
Stephen Gardiner opposed it because of his fundamental
opposition to lay reading of the Bible in any form. He
perceived more clearly than Cranmer the regressive nature
of the threat to orthodoxy inherent in lay interpretation.
Gardiner argued that even a completely orthodox text may
be misread so as to undermine authority (*A & M*, VI, 45,
47). The second volume of *Paraphrases* that Miles Coverdale edited under Edward (16 August 1549) better war-
rants Gardiner's charges. Working under the patronage of
the Duchesses of Somerset and Suffolk, Coverdale conferred a stridently polemical tone on the work, particularly
through the addition of Tyndale's prologue to Romans and
the inclusion of Leo Jud's violently antipapal commentary
on Revelation. Erasmus himself refused to comment on
Revelation because of suspicions about its canonical authority. The addition of the Tyndale prologue and Jud
commentary is hardly compatible with the Erasmian middle way (but see McConica, p. 246).

The *Book of Homilies* (31 July 1547) provided Cranmer's vehicle for formal religious instruction, both through
private Bible interpretation and participation in the public
church service. In theory, the Bible explicates itself and
all readers can understand its meaning. Yet divergent
opinions and the proliferation of aids to popular understanding illustrate a fundamental problem in interpretation. The very act of supplanting the authority of the Roman church with the subjective experience of individual
faith necessitates reestablishment of some form of authority
in order to avoid pluralism of belief. The early dissent of
John Champneys and Henry Hart illustrates this problem.

Cranmer hoped that the authorized homilies, supplementing unrestricted Bible reading, would guide the study of the scriptures and formulate uniform doctrine. Belief that one understands the Bible is predicated on faith. In acknowledging this tautology in the initial homily on Bible reading, Cranmer exhorts the reader to "expounde it no further, then you can plainly understande it" (B2ᵛ). In principle, the Bible is "easy and plain for the understandyng" (*BCP*, p. 4). Yet some "obscure mysteries" can only be understood by the learned. The more ignorant reader understands passages "spoken more plainly and familiarly." In creating a document that can be understood by the learned as well as the ignorant, Cranmer assumes a double nature in his audience. This complexity parallels that of the Elizabethan stage, with its heterogeneous audience. The congregation of the outdoor wooden pulpit in the churchyard of St. Paul's Cathedral, popularly known as Paul's Cross, corresponded to the audience that Cranmer envisioned for the homilies. It included a cross-section of London society as well as provincials passing through the City. Peasants, aristocrats, and learned clerics listened together, with the king himself in occasional attendance. The universality of this audience made Paul's Cross and the *Book of Homilies* the most powerful channels for government propaganda.[6]

Cranmer exhorts the laity to play an active role in interpreting both Bible and homilies. The scriptures should enable the reader to rediscover the universality of Adamic sin "as it were in a glass." They permit the kind of self-knowledge that is tantamount to knowing God. The drama of salvation must be played out within each soul:

[6] Millar Maclure, *The Paul's Cross Sermons: 1534-1642* (Toronto, 1958), pp. 4-10.

And in readyng of Gods woorde, he moste proffiteth not alwaies, . . . that is moste ready in turnyng of the boke, or in saiyng of it without the boke, but he that is moste turned into it, that is most inspired with the holy ghost moste in his harte and life, altered and transformed into that thyng, whiche he readeth. . . . (B1^v)

By its very nature faith is personal. Cranmer's homily on faith leaves responsibility for conforming to the new doctrine with the individual: "every man must examine himself diligently, to know whether he have the same true lively faithe in hys harte unfaynedly or not . . ." (G2^r). Inner faith demands a form of spiritual exegesis because only the individual can read his own beliefs.

Just as the priest reads the homilies in the prayer book context, Cranmer sets faith in a communal context. His sermon on good works turns away from the concern with inner devotional life that characterized the first four homilies on Bible reading, sin, salvation, and faith. By expounding the Erasmian ideal of "the life of active charity" in the world,[7] this homily advocates action in the public, social world. Good works differ from faith in being subject to external authority and discipline. Although one's deeds play no direct role in justification, in an apparent paradox true faith must result in good works: "Faith may not be naked without good workes: for then it is no true faith: and when it is adjoyned to workes yet it is above the workes" (H3^r). Cranmer veers away from the Erasmian *via media* in his impassioned attack on such Catholic works as pilgrimages, sale of pardons, and veneration of images

---

[7] Wall, " 'Book of Homilies,' " p. 77. Wall attributes four homilies to Cranmer (on Bible study, salvation, faith, and good works) and one each to Harpesfeld (on original sin), Bonner (on charity), Becon (against whoredom and adultery), and Latimer (against strife and contention).

and relics. Such practices substitute the outward "appar-
aunce" of human inventions for inner faith (K1ᵛ). The
seven remaining homilies redefine good works in terms of
social action. According to the sixth homily, true charity
consists not in almsgiving but in conformity to Christ's
commandments to love God and one's neighbor. The last
three homilies define the place of the individual within the
structure of society. The sermon on "Obedience to Ruler
and Magistrates" discusses the analogy between the ideal
Christian commonwealth and the harmony of the universe.
This homily defends religious reform under the royal supremacy. The last two sermons apply the ten commandments to contemporary life in their condemnation of sins
that upset the ideal social order. Adultery, whoredom, and
fornication attack the foundation of society in the individual family and are made especially grievous vices by the
Protestant attack on celibacy and idealization of married
love.

Cranmer completed his cycle of sacred texts with the
first *Book of Common Prayer*, which went into use throughout England on 9 June 1549 (Whitsunday). There is little
doubt that the volume substantially represents Cranmer's
thinking on the liturgy.[8] Issuance of the English liturgy
in a single book breaks sharply with the bewildering pro-
fusion of sacerdotal texts in the old Latin rite. The survival
of the different uses of Salisbury, York, and Hereford had
compounded the confusion.[9] Cranmer built into the prayer

---

[8] On the book's construction, see *BCP 1559*, ed. Booty, pp. 349-59. Cranmer aligned the 1552 prayer book with the more radical reforms urged by
such theologians as Nicholas Ridley, John Hooper, Martin Bucer, and
Peter Martyr Vermigli. Unless otherwise noted, reference is to the 1552
prayer book.

[9] On Cranmer's Latin sources, see F. E. Brightman, *The English Rite*
(1915; 2 vols.).

book the same tension between freedom and authority that he addressed in his homilies on salvation, faith, and works. Although the Act of Uniformity demanded conformity, Cranmer's studied ambiguity placed the widest possible limits on individual interpretation. His epilogue defends the text as preserving individual responsibility for interpretation. Bucer, Ridley, Knox, and Hooper attacked the liturgy for retaining old superstitions. The low standing of Bonner and Gardiner with the radicals made their acceptance a mixed blessing. The Devonshire rebels compounded the turmoil by demanding the return of the Latin rite. After Dudley's coup, the radicals forced Cranmer to revise the liturgy. The English mass, vestments, prayers for the dead, private confession, and extreme unction were eliminated. The "Black Rubric" denied that kneeling at communion implied the Real Presence of Christ. The order for burning Latin service books in the second Act of Uniformity (1552) denied any possibility of compromise.

The new prayer book provided a guide to worship for both clergy and laity. Cranmer designed it with the practical needs of the congregation in mind. Rhetorical considerations must govern any service that depends on the ability of the congregation to hear, understand, and respond to the Word. The laity had been passive listeners at the late medieval service, with its hieratic language and elaborate polyphony. Cranmer's preface insists that as a vehicle of spiritual instruction, the service must be intelligible. Medieval communicants who "heard with theyr eares" had been denied edification in "their hartes, spirite, and minde" (*BCP*, p. 3). The rubrics insist on the audibility of the service. Those for matins instruct the priest to turn toward the congregation and read in the choir "distinctly with a loud voice, that the people maye heare." In churches retaining singing, lessons were to be sung "in a playne tune after the maner of distincte readyng" (p. 22). Removal of rood screens would have ensured the audibility of readings in the chancel. The second prayer book went one step further, however, in directing the priest to turn toward the people and stand in the part of the church where they could hear him most clearly (p. 347). The union in common prayer of clergy and laity permits a communal dialogue between God and humanity. This colloquy replaces the medieval distinction between priest as actor and congregation as audience.

Cranmer's denial of any inherent power of salvation in the sacraments forces the individual communicant into a more active role. The medieval laity witnessed the Latin mass as a vivid, dramatic spectacle. At the elevation of the host, the priest reenacted Christ's sacrifice at an altar where "the body of the Savior was visibly suspended on the cross."[10] Reliance on the sacrament as an external instrument of salvation encouraged popular belief in such intermediary aids as pardons and saints' images. The old rite had almost necessarily relied on such visual elements as processions, elaborate vestments, and candles in order to accommodate ineffable mysteries to human intellect.[11]

The new rite invites active lay participation. Placement of a communion table in "the body of the churche, or in the chauncell" (p. 377) altered the axis of worship. In medieval cruciform churches, the nave had been laid out from east to west with the transept running north to south. At its traditional location at the eastern end of the church,

---

[10] O. B. Hardison, *Christian Rite and Christian Drama in the Middle Ages* (Baltimore, 1965), pp. 64-65.

[11] On this point, see Josipovici: "It is a small though crucial step from the belief that there can be no salvation except through the sacraments of the Church to the belief that merely to partake of the sacraments is to ensure salvation" (*World and the Book*, p. 41).

the altar paralleled the transept. Stone altars and roods were now demolished at the order of the bishops and Privy Council. At the elevation of the host, the priest had turned symbolically toward the east, the site of Golgotha, with his back toward the people; it is from the east that the "Son of Man" is to come on the Last Day. Cranmer's stipulation that the priest stand at the north side of the communion table makes him face the surrounding congregation. Priests wear no vestments except for a simple surplice.[12] The elimination of all instruments except a white tablecloth and the administration of the sacrament in both kinds (bread and wine) stress the nature of the eucharist as a communal meal. Eliminating the word "mass," the second prayer book uses the terms "Lordes Supper" and "Holye Communion" as interchangeable phrases. The priest prepares the elements without prayer or such ceremonies as the elevation of the host, bell-ringing, or display of the sacrament to the people. Indeed, the consecration derives from congregational use rather than any magical transformation of the bread and wine.

The ritual of the Lord's Supper gathers individuals together into a community. Derivation of communion from κοινωνία ("fellowship") implies the "mutual participation of the faithful in Christ which constitutes their communion with one another."[13] Unlike the 1549 rite, in which the people received the sacrament by mouth from the priest, placement of the bread in the hands of communicants em-

[12] The austere, black-garbed portrait of Hugh Latimer (National Portrait Gallery, No. 295) depicts the conventional, everyday attire of the Reformation preacher that the Puritans and nonconformist sects would preserve in later centuries. In an equally somber portrait, Nicholas Ridley wears the simple surplice dictated by the prayer book (N.P.G., No. 296). Ridley and Latimer hold what appear to be New Testaments.

[13] Booty, "Church and Commonwealth," pp. 11, 14.

phasizes their ability to feed themselves. No power inheres in the elements: ". . . yf any of the bread or wine remayne, the Curate shal have it to hys owne use" (p. 392). Communion embodies an act of faith based upon a direct relation between the individual and God rather than any intermediate agency of priest or sacrament: "For neither the absolucion of the priest, can any thing avayle them [the unrepentent], nor the receivyng of this holy sacrament doth any thing but increase their damnacion" (p. 217). True communication rests upon the faith of individual believers. Although individual faith cannot guarantee salvation, it fulfills a necessary precondition. The sole test of the individual acknowledgment of sin that each parishioner contributes to the general confession prior to communion is his inner self-knowledge: ". . . and every man to be satisfied with his owne conscience, not judgyng other mennes myndes or consciences . . ." (p. 217).

THE PROTESTANT PLAIN STYLE

The English Bible and the texts that Cranmer built upon it exerted a major influence on the emergence of the Protestant plain style. Like the books themselves, this style fuses Erasmian theory with reformist religious practices. In *Dialogus, cui titulus Ciceronianus* (Basel, 1528), Erasmus had already opened an attack on slavish imitation of the ornate periodic style of classical Latin. John Jewel's *Oratio contra Rhetoricam* (1548) was the first native contribution to the campaign for greater simplicity. A lecturer in rhetoric at Corpus Christi College, Oxford, Jewel spoke for his age in contrasting Ciceronian eloquence with simple expression that avoids verbal ornament.[14] Humanists like

[14] Hoyt H. Hudson, "Jewel's Oration against Rhetoric: A Translation," *The Quarterly Journal of Speech*, 14 (1928), 374-92. The Edwardian con-

John Cheke and his students, Roger Ascham and Thomas Wilson, called for clarity in English prose. Wilson's *Arte of Rhetorique*, a handbook "for the use of all suche as are studious of eloquence," judges writing according to a standard of "plainness and aptness." Ascham defines suitable English style in the preface to *Toxophilus* (1545): "He that wyll wryte well in any tongue, muste folowe thys councel of Aristotle, to speake as the common people do, to thinke as wise men do" (a1ʳ). In *The Hurt of Sedicion*, Cheke employs an Attic manner standing between Ciceronian aureation and the refined plainness of Cranmer.

Early Protestants imitated the English Bible. In contrast to Elizabethan mannerism, mid-Tudor reformers used biblical English as their chosen medium, having inherited the tradition of vernacular prose that had developed by the end of the fifteenth century.[15] In *The Obedience of a Christian Man*, William Tyndale defended English as a more accurate medium than Latin for the translation of Hebrew and Greek. On the basis of structural parallels between English and the biblical tongues, he fixed London English of the early Tudor period as the language of Bible translation:

> For the greke tonge agreeth moare with the english then with the latyne. And the propirties of the hebrue tonge agreth a thousande tymes moare with the english then with the latyne. The maner of speakynge is both one so that in a thousande places thou neadest not but to translate it in to the english worde for worde when thou must seke a compasse in the latyne, and yet shalt have moch

---

text argues against C. S. Lewis's suggestion that the oration is ironic (*Sixteenth Century*, pp. 306-307).

[15] George Williamson, *The Senecan Amble: A Study in Prose Form from Bacon to Collier* (Chicago, 1951), p. 27.

worke to translate it wel faveredly, so that it have the same grace and swetnesse, sence and pure understandinge with it in the latyne, as it hath in the hebrue. (B7ᵛ)

Assimilation of Tyndale's work into later translations associated his language with the scriptures just as medieval Christians identified Jerome's Vulgate Latin with the Bible. Tyndale's diction is the foundation of the King James Bible. If the Authorized Version of 1611 now seems archaic, it is because Tyndale's colloquial idiom has atrophied due to the normal process of linguistic change.[16]

The universality of Cranmer's audience dictated his search for a plain style. His insistence on simplicity in the form, diction, and enunciation of the church service lessens the distinction between priest and people. Didactic considerations dictate that the new rite be read "in suche a language and ordre, as is moste easy and plain for the understandyng, bothe of the readers and hearers" (BCP, p. 4). Cranmer shows concern for the understanding of the young: ". . . my words be so plain, that the least child . . . in the town may understand them." The service should be comprehensible to all the people: ". . . my chief study be to speak so plainly that all men may understand every thing what I say. . . ."[17] He countered Gardiner's defense of Latin by reference to the needs of the laity whom Gardiner wished to supply with images and spectacular devotional forms: ". . . and that so sincerely & plainly, without doubts, ambiguities, or vain questions, that the very simple and unlearned people, may easily understand the same, and be edified thereby."[18]

---

[16] Charles Butterworth, *The Literary Lineage of the King James Bible: 1340-1611* (Philadelphia, 1941), p. 233 et seq.

[17] *Works*, ed. J. E. Cox (Cambridge, 1844-46; 2 vols.), I, 108, 140.

[18] *Aunswere unto Stephen Gardiner* (1580), D6ʳ.

Although Cranmer offers little theoretical explanation for his choice of the *sermo humilis*, Nicholas Udall in his preface to Tome I of Erasmus's *Paraphrases* voices a detailed defense of Protestant plainness. Because his other writings exhibit a wide range of manners, plain style is by no means Udall's usual mode. As a didactic vehicle that can teach the broadest possible audience, unadorned English represents a practical vernacular application of Jewel's theory:

> For divinitie, lyke as it loveth no cloking, but loveth to be simple and playn so doth it not refuse eloquence, if the same come without injurie or violacion of the truth. . . . Albeit in this English paraphrase the translatours have of purpose studied rather to write a plain stile, then to use their elegancie of speche. . . . partely because there was a special regarde to be had to the rude and unlettred people, who perchaunce through default of atteigning to the high stile, should also thereby have been defrauded of the profite and fruicte of understanding the sence, which thing that they might doe, was the onely pourpose why it was first translated. . . . For as the learned are hable enough to helpe themselfes without any translacions et al. (B6^v)

The other contributors agree with Udall on the political purpose of the plain style. John Old defends Erasmian simplicity in his prologue to the paraphrase on Ephesians:

> For althoughe curious soughte termes of Rhetoricall Englishe, in thys translacion woulde better please the delicate eares and fyne wyttes of men fynely broughte up in trickynge of termes and tongues, yet in asmuche as these translated Paraphrases are set forth for the informacion and playne teaching of the Kynges majesties

playne Englyshe subjectes that understande none other but theyr owne native barayne tongue, I thoughte it rather better to seke the edification of the playne unlearned by playne termyng of wordes, than by tedious circumlocucion to make a Paraphrase upon a Paraphrase, and by that meanes . . . to leave the simple vulgare people untaught or never the better. . . . (II, ¶2ʳ)

Hugh Latimer fully explored the possibilities of Protestant plainness. As the greatest preacher in the first generation of English reformers, he fashioned a mode of pulpit oratory that earned for him the apostolic epithet of the "faythful messenger of god."[19] Latimer employs a popular style more colloquial than that of either Cranmer or Udall. It features homely diction and figures of speech as well as picturesque imagery. One scholar traces his controlled colloquial speech to the preaching of the medieval friars.[20] Latimer adopts an archaic manner in order to imitate the plain-speaking Englishman of the *Piers Plowman* tradition. During the fifteenth and early sixteenth centuries, the Lollards had affected the archaic dialect of the West Midlands because of its association with Wyclif and Langland.[21]

The "Sermon on the Plowers" (18 January 1548) exemplifies Latimer's plain delivery to the heterogeneous congregation at Paul's Cross. In this analysis of the Protestant ministry, the simple gospel conceit of the Bible as seed, the preacher as plowman, and the people as the sown fields of the Lord (Luke 8:4-15) unites the clergy with the

[19] From the dedication to Catherine Bertie (formerly Brandon) by Augustine Bernher, editor of Latimer's *Twenty-Seven Sermons* (1562; 2 pts.), ii, ¶1ʳ. Bernher describes himself as one-time "servaunt" to Latimer.

[20] Maclure, *Paul's Cross Sermons*, pp. 147-48.

[21] R. L. Kelly, "Hugh Latimer as Piers Plowman," *SEL*, 17 (1977), 14-15.

1. The Saints in Glory. Voragine's *Golden Legend* (1483).

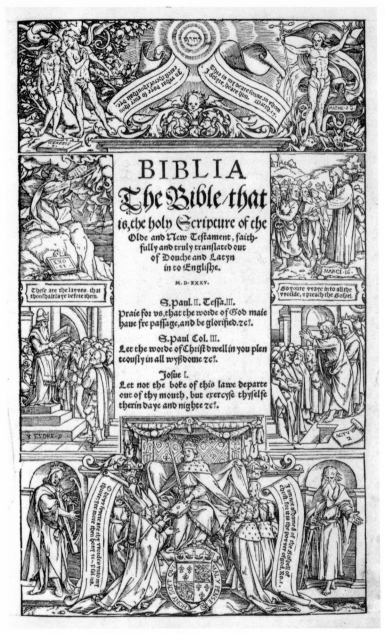

2. Holbein Title Page. Coverdale Bible (1535).

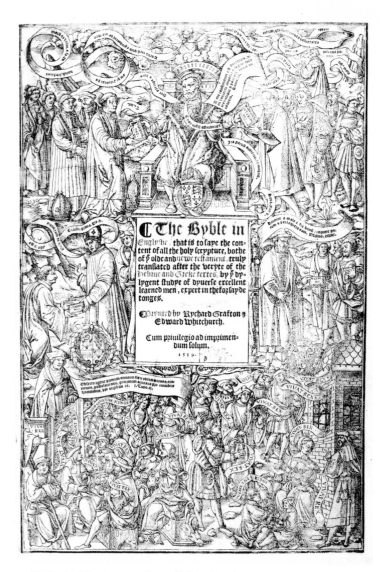

3. Holbein Title Page. Great Bible (1539).

of both churches.

¶ The proude paynted churche of the pope/ or synnefull Synagoge of Satan.

Apoca.17.

¶ I sawe a woman sytt vpon a rose co loured Beast/ full of names of blasphe mye/ decked wyth golde/ precious stone/ and pearles/ with whome the kynges of the earthe com mitted whoredome/ and the inhabi ters of the earthe are droken wyth the wyne of her fornycacyon.

The Images

¶ The poore persecuted churche of Chry ste/ or immaculate spouse of the lambe.

Apoca.12.

¶ The Dragon was wrothe with the woman which fledde into the wyldere nesse/ and went and made warre with the remnaunte of her sede which kepe the com maundemente of God and haue the testymonye of Jesus Chryst.

4. The Images of Both Churches: The Woman Clothed with the Sun and the Whore of Babylon. Bale's *Image of Both Churches* (c. 1545).

ILLVSTRIVM
MAIORIS BRITANNIAE

SCRIPTORVM, HOC EST, ANGLIAE, CAMBRIAE,
ac Scotiæ Summariũ, in quaſdam centurias diuiſum, cum di-
uerſitate doctrinarũ atq; annorũ recta ſupputatione per
omnes ætates a Iapheto ſanctiſsimi Noah filio, ad
annum domini. M. D. XLVIII.

AVTORE IOANNE BALAEO S. DVOLCA.

EXCVDEBATVR PRAESENS OPVS, ANNO A NATIVI-
tate unicæ illius pro peccatis uictimæ, patri in crucem oblatæ, quadrageſimo octa
uo ſupra milleſimum & quingenteſimum, pridie Calendas Auguſti.

5. John Bale Giving His Book to Edward VI. *Illustrium maioris Britanniae scriptorum summarium* (1548).

Figura Ioannis Wicleui doctoris Anglie

7. John Wyclif. *Illustrium maioris Britanniae scrip-*
torum summarium (1548).

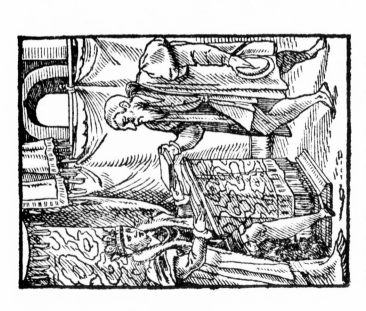

6. John Bale Giving His Book to Edward VI.
Illustrium maioris Britanniae scriptorum summa-
rium (1548).

8. The Execution of Anne Askew. Crowley's *Confutation of Nicolas Shaxton* (1548).

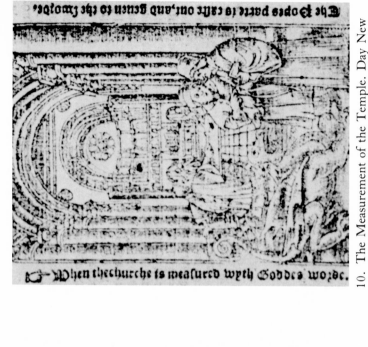

10. The Measurement of the Temple. Day New Testament (1548). Copyright photograph by courtesy of the British and Foreign Bible Society's Library, London.

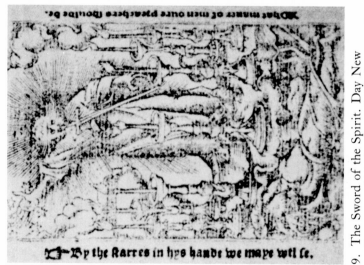

9. The Sword of the Spirit. Day New Testament (1548). Copyright photograph by courtesy of the British and Foreign Bible Society's Library, London.

¶ The beginning and endynge of all po=
pery, oz popiſhe kyngedome.

And then ſhall that wicked be vtte=
red, whom the lozd ſhal cōſume with
the ſpirite of his mouth, and ſhal de=
ſtroy with the apperaunce of his cō=
mynge, euen him whoſe comminge is
after the workinge of Sathan.

11. The Day of the Lord. Lynne's *Beginning and Endynge of All
Popery* (c. 1548).

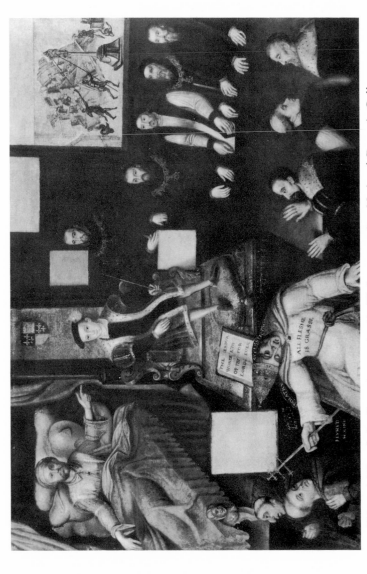

12. Edward VI and the Pope (c. 1548–49). Unknown artist. National Portrait Gallery.

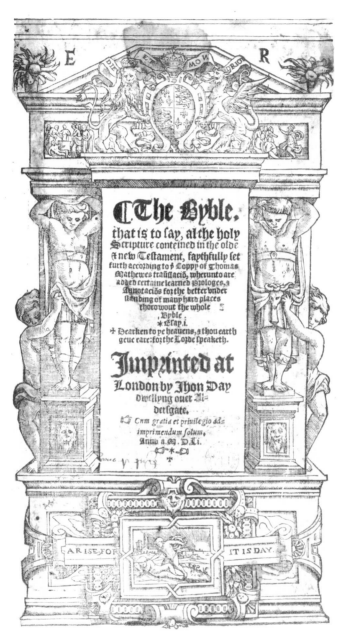

13. Arise for It Is Day. Third Day Bible (1551).

¶ **Philargyrie**
of greate Britayne

i. ꞇimoth.vi,

**The rote of al mischife ꝑ euer dyd spring
Is carefull Couetise, a gredy Gathering**

14. The Great Giant Philargyrie. Crowley's *Philargyrie of Greate Britayne* (1551).

15. Edmund Becke Giving
His Revision to Edward
VI. Third Day Bible
(1551).

16. Inscribed Death
Meditation by
Edward Seymour.
MS Stowe 1066
(21 January
1552).

17. Hugh Latimer Preaching before Edward VI. Foxe's *Actes and Monuments* (1563).

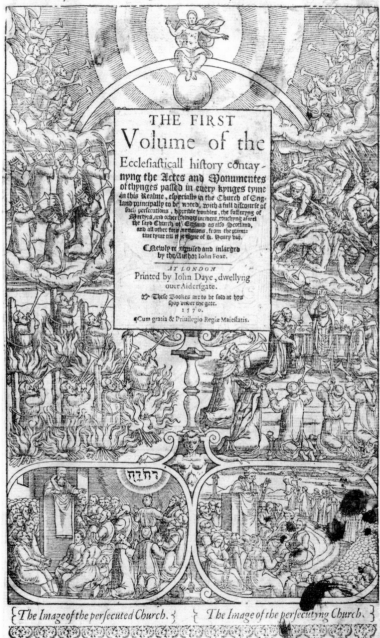

18. The Images of Both Churches. *Actes and Monuments* (1570).

¶ The ninth booke containyng the
Actes and thynges done in the reigne of kyng
Edvvard the 6.
(*⁎*)

Burning of images.

The Temple well purged.

The ship of the Romish Church.

Shoppe ouer your trinkets and be packing ye Papistes.

The Papistes packing away their pastryue.

Euery plaunt which my heuenly father hath not planted, shall be pluckte vp. Mat. 15.

The Commnion Table.

King Edward delivering the Bible to the Prelates.

King Edward the vj.

AFter the death of kyng Henry succeded kyng Edward his sonne, beyng of the age of ix. yeares. He began hys reigne, the 28. day of January, and reigned vj. yeres, vij. moneths, and viij. dayes; and deceased. an. 1553. the 6. day of July. Of whose excellent vertues, & singular graces wrought in him by the gift of God, although nothing can be said enough to his commendation: yet because the renowned fame of such a worthy Prince shall not vtterly passe our story without some gratefull remembraunce, I thought in fewe wordes to touch some little portion of his prayse, taken out of great heapes of matter, which might bee inferred. For to stand vppon all that might be sard of him, it would be to long: and yet to say nothing, it were to much vnkynd. If kynges and Princes which haue wisely and vertuously gouerned, haue found in all ages writers to solemnise and celebrate their Actes and memory, such as neuer knew them nor were subiect vnto them, how much then are we Englishe men bound, not to forget our ductie to kyng Edward, a Prince although but tender in yeares, yet for hys sage and mature rypenes in witte and all princely ornamentes, as I see but few to whom he map not bee equall, so agayne I see not many, to whom he may not iustly be preferred.

And here to vse the example of Plutarch in comparyng kynges and rulers, the Latines with the Grekes together: if I should seeke with whom to match this noble Edward, I finde not with whom to make my AAAa.j. match

Commendation of kyng Edward.

19. The Reign of Edward VI. *Actes and Monuments* (1570).

laity as common laborers in the Reformation plowland. He defines the relationship thus:

> They have great labors and therefore they ought to have good livings, that they may commodiously feed their flock; for the preaching of the Word of God unto the people is called meat. Scripture calleth it meat, not strawberries, that come but once a year, and tarry not long but are soon gone. But it is meat; it is no dainties. The people must have meat that must be familiar and continual and daily given unto them to feed upon. Many make a strawberry of it, ministering it but once a year; but such do not the office of good prelates.[22]

Latimer drives home his theme—that ministers must be paid well in order to fulfill their pastoral duties rather than seek nonresident benefices—by use of the vivid metaphor of preaching as "meat" but not "strawberries." His memorable domestic terminology develops the alimentary imagery central to the sermon as a whole. Latimer's "meat" is the Protestant gospel sermon that continual preaching renders "familiar and continual." His familiar style is conducive to this end. By means of persuasive imagery compatible with an audience made up of laymen of all classes, he contrasts the lax preacher who starves his unwitting congregation on an intermittent diet of "strawberries" and "dainties" with the true pastor who nourishes his parishioners with "meat."

Although Stephen Gardiner made no specific comment concerning style, one may assume that his hostility to scriptural translation extended to the Protestant affectation of plain "biblical" English. His vocal opposition to the English Bible, *Paraphrases*, and *Book of Homilies* recapitulated

[22] *Selected Sermons*, ed. A. G. Chester (Charlottesville, Va., 1968), p. 32.

More's attack on Tyndale's call to "lat the laye man have the worde of God in his mother tonge . . ." (*Obedience*, B6ʳ). Fundamental to his argument is the same phenomenon of linguistic change upon which Erasmus and Tyndale built their defense of the vernacular. Gardiner questioned the sufficiency of the Bible as a layman's book because its text had been corrupted by the process of change inherent to all languages, oral and scribal traditions, and book printing:

> For, albeit the authority of the Scripture dependeth not upon man, yet the ministration of the letter, which is writing and speaking, is exercised, and hath been from the beginning delivered, through man's hand, and taught by man's mouth; which men the Scripture calleth holy men; and that is, contrary to liars. (*A & M*, VI, 40)

Fundamental to the controversy over language and style are all the limitations of human intellect consequent upon the Fall. Tyndale and Cranmer, More and Gardiner all sought the truth in the mutable world of change and decay.

ICONOCLASM AND ART

The difficulties of determining the correct language for religious discourse carried over into the Reformation debate concerning religious images; Edwardian iconoclasm offered a clear analogy to the search for a simple prose style. After an outbreak of image-smashing at Portsmouth within his own diocese, Gardiner contrasted Cranmer's vernacular texts with traditional devotional images. He defended the latter in a letter of 3 May 1547 to Captain Edward Vaughan, the local military commander. Gardiner's letter, which Vaughan passed on to Seymour, distorts

Gregory's qualified acceptance of the image as an appropriate "book" for illiterate laymen:

> And if we (a few that can read), because we can read
> . . . shall pull away the books of the rest, and would have
> our letters only in estimation, and blind all them, shall
> not they have just cause to mistrust what is meant? And
> if the cross be a truth, and if it be true that Christ
> suffered, why may we not have a writing thereof, such
> as all can read, that is to say, an image? (*A & M*, VI,
> 27)

Seymour attacked the patristic defense because of the practical problem of distinguishing between the true and false use of images. The Bible, declared Seymour, does not admit to the same kind of abuse:

> We cannot see but that images may be counted marvellous books, to whom we have kneeled, whom we have kissed, upon whom we have rubbed our beads and handkerchiefs, unto whom we have lighted candles, of whom we have asked pardon and help: which thing hath seldom been seen done to the gospel of God, or the very true Bible. For who kisseth that . . . or who kneeleth unto it, or setteth a candle before it? and yet it seeth or heareth, as well as the images or pictures either of St. John, or our Lady, or Christ. Indeed images be great letters; yet as big as they be, we have seen many which have read them amiss. (*A & M*, V, 29)

In what form could Protestants accept images? The iconoclastic provisions of the Royal Injunctions voiced Seymour's distinction between true and false images. Reissuance of Cromwell's orders followed spontaneous outbursts of iconoclasm and mob violence that greeted the new reign in London, Portsmouth, and other towns. These edicts stipulated that only those images "devysed by mennes phantasies" must be destroyed. As forms of "idolatrye," such images substitute devotional objects for the reading, preaching, or practice of gospel teaching. Edwardian mobs attacked such cult objects as relics, images of the Madonna and Child, crucifixes, statues of saints, and doom paintings as idols. The injunctions defined permissible Protestant images, on the other hand, as objects of

> . . . remembraunce, whereby, men may be admonished, of the holy lifes and conversacion of theim, that the sayde Images do represent: whiche Images, if they do abuse for any other intent, they commit Ydolatrye in the same, to the great daungier of their soules. (a3ᵛ)

The reformers contrasted "fantasies" invented by the imagination with recollection of archetypal truths through the memory. The injunctions embody Protestant suspicions of the productive imagination. According to Calvin, *phantasia* ("imagination") should be the lowest human faculty (*Institutes*, I.xv.6-7). But as a consequence of the Fall, the imagination, with its false images and associations, has supplanted the higher faculties of the reason, intellect, and will as the basis for human judgment and action. Thus Cranmer's homily on good works attacks idolatrous "images and phantasyes" (I1ʳ). In association with the higher faculties, the memory can reunite one with truth through spiritual understanding. Under the influence of Augustine's Neoplatonic doctrine of memory (*Retractiones* I. 8. 2), Cranmer identifies true images with the recovery of what mankind has forgotten as a consequence of the Fall. The second prayer book defines holy communion as an act of "remembraunce" (p. 389). So also, the efficacy of images inheres not in the objects but in their use.

Juxtaposition in the injunctions of the edicts on images

with the provisions concerning Bible reading clarifies the nature of Reformation iconoclasm. The Protestants returned to the patristic use of images as handmaids to biblical understanding. John Stow interpreted as iconoclastic acts the destruction of the monastic cloister at St. Paul's Cathedral and demolition of other London churches in order to provide stone for Somerset House. He described the "dance of death, commonly called the dance of Pauls," at the cloister as an image "painted upon boord" (*Annales*, 3D3^{r-v}; *Survay* [1603], H7^v). In many churches religious paintings were whitewashed and covered with inscriptions of the ten commandments and other biblical texts. Although some decapitated saints' images survived, much stained glass, statuary, and monumental brass was destroyed.[23] In conjunction with an upper limit of two candles, a bare cross or open Bible replaced the crucifix or host on the high altar in commemoration of Christ as the "very true light of the worlde" (*Injunctions*, a3^v). In contrast to the multitude of colorful images and votive candles in elaborately decorated medieval sanctuaries, the barren appearance of Edwardian churches broken only by wall texts encouraged introspective memory and the intellectual operations of Protestant faith (see Figure 10). John Bale records local resistance to these edicts in his attack on a Hampshire recusant for "the craftie conveyaunce of certen ymages in hope of a change" (*Expostulation*, C2^r).

Woodcut images also came under attack. Very few indulgenced pictures escaped disfigurement. Many copies of *The Golden Legend* display systematic defacement that conforms to Reformation iconoclasm. Except for the loss of leaves due to heavy use by early Tudor readers, most of the damage to the Denchworth copy stems from Edward-

[23] Phillips, *Reformation of Images*, pp. 88-97, and plates 24a, 24b et al.

ian iconoclasts.[24] Defacement of the conclusion parallels the 1548 attack on the mass. The Christmas edict issued in 1549 by the Dudley Privy Council mandated further attack.[25] A mid-Tudor secretary hand revised Caxton's incipit: "Here begynneth the noble historye of thexposicion of the masse." With the striking out of the word "noble," the altered title reads "Here begynneth the most abomynall historye of thexposicion of the popyshe masse moste to be aborryd of all Cristianes." The running headlines for the section carry similar alterations. The surviving text has been badly damaged by crude crosshatching and the tearing out of scattered leaves. A defaced reference to the apostolic succession carries the marginal gloss "horrendum" in a second hand (2i4^r-8^v). The expurgator crossed out the entire passage on the feast of Corpus Christi with its illus-

[24] The iconoclasts also tended to damage the text of illustrated indulgences. Their general defacement of text rather than picture shows that they objected to the substitution of images for the Bible as "laymen's books" rather than to religious pictures in themselves. For printed indulgences that escaped the iconoclasts because they had been inserted into devotional manuscripts, see Bodl. MS Bodley 850, fol. 109^r; MS Bodley 939, frontispiece; and MS Rawlinson, D. 403, fols. 1^v and 2^v (STC 14077c.7, c.8A, c.22, and c.13). See above, Chapter 1 at notes 6 and 7. Conclusions about the Denchworth copy of The Golden Legend derive from comparison with B.L. C.11.d.8. In the latter copy, leaf B4 was torn out and later replaced. B5^r was stricken out by hand in order to delete references to St. Thomas Becket and an illustration of the martyrdom that portrays Becket adoring a statue of the Virgin on the high altar. Although the defacement of this woodcut probably followed Cromwell's Injunctions and the 1539 desecration of the Becket shrine at Canterbury Cathedral, the special hostility toward the mass ties most of the damage to Edward's reign. The word "pope" was stricken from this and other copies in accordance with the 1542 order that Cranmer obtained from Convocation. Removal of woodcuts from Bodl. Douce 270 parallels the damage to the Denchworth Caxton.

[25] P. L. Hughes and J. F. Larkin, eds., Tudor Royal Proclamations (New Haven, 1964-69; 3 vols.), I, no. 353. Hereafter cited as Proclamations.

tration of two monks carrying the host in the festival procession (d6^v-8^r; Hodnett, no. 245). The tearing out of other leaves could reflect the work of the same iconoclasts. The loss of woodcuts for the Nativity and Epiphany (a4^v, a8^r; Hodnett, Figs. 5-6) may reflect the radical Protestant conviction that artistic emphasis on those events undermines Christ's preachings, which constitute gospel truth. During the Middle Ages those happenings had undergone apocryphal expansion and elaboration. Reformers attacked medieval carols and mystery plays on the same ground. The missing woodcut for the story of St. Helena depicted her legendary discovery of the cross at Calvary (x6^r).

The Golden Legend epitomizes medieval substitution of nonscriptural stories and traditions for the Bible as a layman's book. Cranmer includes such collections in his attack on Catholic service books in the preface to the prayer book:

> But these many yeares passed this Godly and decent ordre of the auncient fathers, hath bee[n] so altered, broken, and neglected, by planting in uncertain stories, Legendes, Respondes, Verses, vaine repeticions, Commemoracions, and Synodalles, that commonly when any boke of the Bible was begon: before three or foure Chapiters were read out, all the rest were unread. (p. 3)

Cranmer's elimination of nonbiblical saints' observances extended to the patron saint of England. Foxe's amusing anecdote about the Garter celebration at Greenwich Palace on St. George's Day, 23 April 1550, clarifies this shift. The tale also contributes to the king's reputation as a witty boy:

> . . . when he was come from the sermon into the presence-chamber . . . he said . . . "My lords, I pray you,

what saint is St. George, that we here so honour him?"
. . . the lord treasurer . . . gave answer, and said, "If
it please your majesty, I did never read in any history
of St. George, but only in 'Legenda Aurea,' where it is
thus set down: That St. George out with his sword, and
ran the dragon through with his spear." The king, when
he could not a great while speak for laughing, at length
said, "I pray you, my lord, and what did he with his
sword the while? (*A & M*, VI, 351-52)

A manuscript revision of the Garter Statutes ordained by
Edward VI deletes all references to St. George and describes his image on the Garter badge as that of an "armed
knight" (MSS Royal 18 A. I-IV). Queen Mary returned
the saint to the statutes. The St. George's Day celebration
was one of the few forms of pre-Reformation pageantry to
survive into Elizabethan England. Although William Nelson notes that no "Renaissance humanist could have thought
the legendary life of St. George a respectable literary
model,"[26] Spenser chose the nationalistic legend as the vehicle for the Reformation allegory of the "Legende of Holinesse." His narrative harmonizes Protestant materials with
what the radical reformers regarded as idolatrous sources.

By means of calendar symbolism, Cranmer exploited the
iconoclastic movement as an emblem for the entire process
of church reform. According to John Stow, the iconoclastic
edicts took effect during the year 1548 in conjunction with
Cranmer's piecemeal institution of elements of the new
English service. The introduction of changes on appropri-

[26] *The Poetry of Spenser: A Study* (New York, 1963), p. 150. On the
Protestant reforms in the Order of the Garter, see Roy Strong, *The Cult
of Elizabeth* (1977), p. 166. In *Astraea: The Imperial Theme in the Sixteenth
Century* (1975), Frances Yates notes the element of paradox involved in
Elizabeth's retention of the image of this saint in the ritual of a Protestant
court (pp. 108-109).

ate feast days presented iconoclasm as a positive rather than a negative process. In effect, the demolition of the false church paralleled a retrograde movement toward the primitive church of the apostles. In a dedication to Princess Elizabeth, Walter Lynne speaks of that year as the *annus mirabilis*: "the tyme of Christes raygne & kyngedome, wherein the Gospel is the rule of the princely powers, and mercy is more estemed then sacrifyce [the mass]. . . ."[27] Cranmer's symbolic calendar presents 1548 as the first year of the true English church. By preaching the Circumcision Day sermon at Paul's Cross (1 January), Hugh Latimer broke his silence of eight years. The day celebrates the transition from Old Law to New Law at the advent of Christ. On Candlemas the bearing of candles "was left off throughout the whole Citie of London." The "use of giving ashes" was omitted on Ash Wednesday. The bearing of palms was left out on Palm Sunday "and not used as afore." The English service, which had been in experimental use at court, was introduced in various London parishes on Easter. Congregations could receive communion in both kinds and choose to hear "the Communion and Confession in English." The institution of the revised service at St. Paul's Cathedral on Whitsunday (Pentecost) coincided with the celebration of the birth of the church at the descent of the Holy Spirit upon the apostles. The demolition of the collegiate churches of Barking Chapel and St. Martin's le Grand as well as the London parish churches of St. Nicholas in the Shambles, St. Ewine's within Newgate, and Strand Church without Temple Bar proceeded during Whitsuntide. Under the superintendence of John Thynne, Somerset House was erected on the site of the last-named church and adjacent properties. Thus the

---

[27] Luther, *A Frutefull Exposition of the Kyngdom of Christ*, trans. Lynne (1548), A2ʳ.

first Palladian structure in England supplanted Gothic art
and architecture. Gardiner became the butt of antipapal
irony by preaching his recantation sermon at court on St.
Peter's Day (29 June). Introduction of the new service
throughout England on Whitsunday 1549 mirrored the
symbolic calendar of Cranmer's *annus mirabilis*. In a similar fashion Cranmer's 1549 commission against the Anabaptists, who affirmed "that Christ tooke no flesh of the
virgin Mary," met at the Lady Chapel in St. Paul's on the
last Saturday in Easter week. The 1551 burning of George
van Paris, the Dutch Arian, on the fourth Friday after
Easter (24 April) made a macabre play upon the new symbolism of the Anglican liturgy. The gospel readings for
that week all affirm the resurrection and the operation of
the Holy Spirit.[28]

The revival of woodcut art in Bibles and other books
offers another corollary to Reformation iconoclasm. Despite the received opinion that book illustration languishes
after 1535 (Hodnett, p. vi), publications by Crowley, Bale,
Lynne, and Day contain some of the finest Tudor woodcuts
(see Appendix II). Unlike suppressed religious images,
these printed emblems appeal to an audience of lay readers.
Protestant images represent the Word visibly. Because of
the primacy of the Bible, few Reformation pictures are
divorced from text in the form of a book, quotation, motto,
or book image. The literalism of Protestant imagery presupposes a radical disjunction between the planes of nature
and grace. In subordinating pictures to specific biblical
texts, these woodcuts anticipate the fashion for emblematic
texts associated with Geoffrey Whitney's *A Choice of Emblemes and Other Devises* (1586) and the seventeenth-cen-

[28] *Annales*, 3D3ʳ⁻ᵛ, 3E1ᵛ, 3E2ʳ.

tury collections of George Wither and Francis Quarles.[29] The emblem-poems of George Herbert reflect the same tendency. The selectivity of damage to indulgenced pictures proves that English Protestantism lacks an inherent hostility toward art. Protestants do suspect mimetic forms that substitute artifice and decoration for divine revelation. They deny the aesthetic validity of images that distort truth as they see it. Thus Guyon and the Palmer may dismantle artifice that degrades nature in Acrasia's Bower of Bliss, but *The Faerie Queene* as a whole displays the natural art of universal harmony inherent in God's providential design.[30] So also the manneristic elegance of Pandaemonium gives way to the natural beauty and order of the Garden of Eden:

> . . . which not nice [refined] art
> In beds and curious knots, but nature boon
> Poured forth profuse on hill and dale and plain . . .
> (*PL*, IV.241-43)

Many Reformation woodcuts symbolize Protestant epistemological theories that derive from the premise that God, as a consequence of the Fall, manifests himself through the Logos and leaves Christ as the sole intercessor between himself and man. Because God is invisible and universally immanent, pictures should not represent him in forms that are spatially and temporally limited. According to Calvin and such English followers as Hooper, incorporeal forms

[29] In *English Emblem Books* (1948), Rosemary Freeman notes that Edward VI owned a 1549 Italian translation of Alciati's *Emblematum Liber* (p. 47).

[30] See *FQ*, I.x.53-61; II.xii.42-87; III.vi; VI.x.8-17. On Art and Nature in *The Faerie Queene*, see C. S. Lewis, *The Allegory of Love* (Oxford, 1936), pp. 326-30.

such as clouds, smoke, or flame should represent God.[31] Thus divine representation in the form of the Tetragrammaton (the Hebrew consonants for the deity whose name is too sacred to pronounce) as the sun or a clouded sun became a favorite device of English Protestant art (see Figures 2, 11, and 18). In addition to the proliferation of images of the Word in the form of a book, this principle may account for the loss of the Trinitarian frontispiece from most copies of Caxton's *Golden Legend* (Figure 1). The use of blinding light or visible darkness as divine manifestations derives from the synthesis of Christian theology and Neoplatonic philosophy effected by the Johannine gospel, the epistles of St. Paul, and the "Johannine" Revelation. The writings of Augustine, the Pseudo-Dionysius, and such English mystics as Richard Rolle, Juliana of Norwich, and the anonymous author of *The Cloud of Unknowing* passed on the doctrine that one may perceive the deity only in negative terms through inspired spiritual vision. In the first three books of *Paradise Lost*, Milton plays upon this tradition of visual epistemology.

Protestant dialectic distinguishes between particular images and the truth that they imitate. Because only the Word can synthesize the human and divine, biblical woodcuts embody the verticality of Protestant spiritual experience (see Figure 3). According to Cranmer's exegetical theory, individual interpretation should apprehend truth rather than impose subjective readings on the Bible. Protestant religious images represent the inner experience of faith rather than autonomous devotional objects. The broad visual analogies of Reformation woodcuts should assist the reader in perceiving the providential pattern in the mutable world. Like Cranmer's homilies and communion ritual, the effi-

---

[31] *Institutes*, I, 98, as cited in Phillips, *Reformation of Images*, p. 83.

cacy of woodcuts inheres in their proper use. Their function mirrors Tyndale's definition of pulpit *exempla* as

> . . . worldly similitudes which we make ether when we preach ether [or] when we expound the scripture. The similitudes prove no thinge, but are made to expresse moare playnely that which is contayned in the scripture & to leade the [e] in the spirituall understondinge of the text. (*Obedience*, S1ʳ)

In applying sacred texts to his own experience, each individual should understand that they illuminate his life through revelation that is complete in itself and antecedent to his own experience. Catholic images broke down this duality by manifesting the divine by means of tangible material objects. Medieval artifacts could acquire sacramental status. The old believer gained assurance of salvation through the worldly experience of relics, rosaries, and devotional objects. Popular attitudes of the late Middle Ages had identified Catholic images as the repositories of the truth that they represented.[32]

The problem of discriminating between true and false images furnishes the comprehensive pattern of English Reformation literature. The Protestant eradication of external, worldly authorities made the search for the true image of both the church and oneself an arduous and dangerous process that every believer had to resolve for himself. Tyndale's attack on the "hipocrisie of outward works" pinpoints the difficult nature of the task (*Whole Workes*, G4ᵛ). John Bale designed the *Image of Both Churches* as a resolution of the problem. His title suggests the final met-

---

[32] Erich Auerbach, " 'Figura,' " in *Scenes from the Drama of European Literature: Six Essays*, trans. Ralph Manheim (New York, 1959), pp. 45, 49-60, passim; Keith Thomas, *Religion and the Decline of Magic* (1971), pp. 27, 30-31, 76.

amorphosis of the Gregorian concept of the image as the layman's book. The terminal woodcuts contrast the two churches as the Whore of Babylon and the Woman Clothed with the Sun (Revelation 12:1), who, like the Tetragrammaton, appears in a heavenly sunburst (Figure 4). Woodcuts derived from Dürer and Cranach fill the text with images of the Word in the form of a book.

Protestant epistemology grappled with a world where competing churches made apparently equal claims to spiritual authority, in which even the concerned layman and theologian could easily fall into error. This uncertainty leads the Red Cross Knight into despair, unlike the medieval Everyman who could address the peril of his soul through the implementation of unitary truth by means of good works. A major contrast between sixteenth-century thought and that of the seventeenth century is the tendency of the Reformation Protestant to accept external doctrinal formulations of the established Church of England. The passage of time brought increasingly fine subjective and sectarian distinctions into what the Edwardian perceived as a dualistic problem capable of comparatively simple resolution. Protestantism supplanted the external mediation of the Roman church with the inner experience of faith, but left the individual especially prone to doubt and skepticism. The chasm between God and man can be bridged only through grace. Faith may free the individual from the penalty of sin and justify salvation, but the fallen world offers the human intellect no certainty of being saved. The only resolution of this paradoxical circle of doubt and fear comes through the Bible and the phenomenological experience of the quest for truth.

A tradition of religious warfare and conflict between truth and falsehood is a corollary to this epistemological problem. The Pauline Armor of God (Ephesians 6:10-17) and the martial imagery of Revelation underlie the pattern. Luther's great hymn "Ein' feste Burg" expresses the militancy of the early Protestant, who felt a need to seek shelter in the castle of his faith against the hostile deceptions of a diabolical world. Although this problem manifests itself in complex multiplicity, the Protestant resolves it through simple fideism. The "easy and plain" formulations of the homilies and prayer book repeatedly refer the act of faith to the "conscience" or concealed, inner knowledge that enables the individual to discriminate between right and wrong.

The familiar medieval pattern of the seven deadly sins gives way to the intricate dissimulations and false appearances of Catholic characters named Hypocrisy in many Reformation works. The comical application of the medieval *topos* in *Doctor Faustus* (II.ii; scene 6) cannot approach the impact of the Protestant drama of salvation in Faustus's last scene, with its despairing recognition of the enormity of sin. Although the Red Cross Knight sees through the falsity of the pageant of the seven deadly sins (*FQ*, I.iv.18-37), he falls prey to despair after his defeat by Orgoglio. Bunyan's Christian suffers similar defeat by Giant Despair. Juventus, a character from an Edwardian youth drama, confuses Catholic Vices with Protestant Virtues. Without the truth of the Bible, Crowley's ideal king cannot spring into action against the giant Philargyrie (a deceptively alluring image of avarice). Discrimination between true and false symbols permeates *John Bon and Mast Person* and Luke Shepherd's Skeltonic satires. In Baldwin's *Beware the Cat*, people drop their public disguises of truthfulness and religious conformity behind closed doors in the presence of their house cats. All of Bale's plays, dialogues, and tracts turn upon this elementary conflict. John Day imitates Bale's title in the legend that he added to the title page of Foxe's *Actes and Monuments* (1570): "The Image of the persecuted Church. The Image of the persecutyng Church" (Figure 18).

English Protestant literature builds upon this conflict. *The Faerie Queene* begins with the Red Cross Knight's quest for true faith. The competing claims of Una, whose "blacke stole" cloaks her heavenly light, and the gorgeously costumed Duessa personify the Reformation dilemma. The knight could originally heed Una's admonition to "add faith unto your force" in battle against Error. But Spenser's Protestant Everyman cannot distinguish between Una and the false image of truth conjured by Archimago ("source of images"). The Catholic antagonist receives the epithet "Hypocrisie" in the title to Canto I. Archimago can only defeat the knight during the latter's sleep, when the imagination has the greatest power to deceive the reason. The description of the false Una sounds suspiciously like an image of the Virgin Mary:

> Now when that ydle dreame was to him brought,
>   Unto that Elfin knight he bad him fly,
>   Where he slept soundly void of evill thought,
>   And with false shewes abuse his fantasy,
>   In sort as he him schooled privily:
>   And that new creature borne without her dew,
>   Full of the makers guile, with usage sly
>   He taught to imitate that Lady trew,
> Whose semblance she did carrie under feigned hew.
>   (*FQ*, I.i.46)

In his search for true religion, John Donne's speaker in "Satire III" doubts that he will ever recover truth within the material objects of this world. But he identifies the increasingly difficult process of the quest with the object of desire:

To adore, or scorne an image, or protest,
May all be bad; doubt wisely; in strange way
To stand inquiring right, is not to stray;
To sleepe, or runne wrong, is.

(ll. 76-79)[33]

Donne's Holy Sonnets recount the Christian warfare against "the world, the flesh, the devill" (Sonnet 6). Sonnet 18 resolves the Reformation dilemma by fideistic paradox.

With the return to increasingly ritualistic and imagistic practices under Archbishop Laud, the iconoclastic conflict became the property of seventeenth-century Puritans and sectarians.[34] In *Paradise Lost*, the shrinelike splendor of Pandaemonium disguises the real despair of the damned behind a façade that parodies the image of Solomon's Temple (I.710-98). The Temple is a Reformation commonplace for the true church (Figure 10). Milton's Satan shares Archimago's ability to change appearances at will as well as Mephistophilis's capacity for logic-chopping portrayed by Marlowe. Not even Archangel Uriel penetrates Satan's disguise as the "stripling cherub" whose true identity is known to God alone:

For neither man nor angel can discern
Hypocrisy, the only evil that walks
Invisible, except to God alone,
By his permissive will through heaven and earth . . .

(III.636, 682-85)

It comes as no surprise then to find that Satan tempts Eve through a dream like the one used by Archimago against the Red Cross Knight:

[33] *Poems*, ed. H.J.C. Grierson (Oxford, 1912; 2 vols.).
[34] Phillips, *Reformation of Images*, pp. 157-200, passim.

Assaying by his devilish art to reach
The organs of her fancy . . .
(IV.801-2)

Complicated paradoxes characterize the English Protestant tradition. Because of the Reformation, the orthodox believer found himself caught between true and false images, predestination and free will, election and reprobation, permission and control, and private faith and public worship. Despite the impossibility of resolving these dilemmas, the process of the spiritual quest is plain and simple. The doctrines of justification by faith and imputed grace should lodge immense power and immense responsibility within the individual. For Milton as for Cranmer, ultimate victory in the fallen world may be won only in the inner temple of the heart (1 Corinthians 3:17):

What will they then
But force the spirit of grace it self, and bind
His consort liberty; what, but unbuild
His living temples, built by faith to stand,
Their own faith not another's: for on earth
Who against faith and conscience can be heard
Infallible? Yet many will presume:
Whence heavy persecution shall arise
On all who in the worship persevere
Of spirit and truth; the rest, far greater part,
Will deem in outward rites and specious forms
Religions satisfied. . . .

(XII.524-35)

CHAPTER 4
The King and the Kingdom

. . . it now evidently appereth your Majestie to be the faythful Josias, in whose tyme the booke of the lawe is found out in the house of the Lorde . . . and a covenaunt made with the Lorde that they shal walke after the Lord & shal kepe his commaundements. . . .

Nicholas Udall, Preface to Erasmus's *Paraphrases*, Tome I

IMAGES OF THE KING

"Woe unto thee, O land, when thy king is a child" (Eccles. 10:16) cried Dr. John Story during Parliamentary debate over the introduction of Protestant reforms.[1] One of the greatest threats to political stability in Tudor England had materialized when Prince Edward succeeded his father at the age of nine years. In order to buttress their own authority, the Protestant lords who controlled the king constructed a royalist myth that has survived into present times. Searching the Bible for guidance, the reformers discovered ample precedent for governance by a pious youth. They acclaimed their monarch as the New Josiah, the boy king who rediscovered the book of the Law, restored the temple, and returned Israel to pure faith (2 Kings 22-23). Edward was also Solomon, who surpassed his father David in building the temple. In Seymour Edward found an able

---

[1] *House of Commons Journal*, I (1547-1628), 5, as quoted in A. G. Chester, *Hugh Latimer: Apostle to the English* (Philadelphia, 1954), p. 179.

Nehemiah, the architect who oversaw construction of the temple.[2] Unlike the fearful symbolism of apocalyptic warfare, erection of the temple offers a positive image for the English Reformation. Upon such precedents, the reformers built a cult of Protestant kingship that associated Edward VI with the ideal ruler, the just and pious king of longstanding millennial tradition. By reputation Edward fulfilled the Augustinian ideal of the just and humble ruler. Life at court was so organized as to dramatize this ideal of the wise boy of saintly piety, the worldly embodiment of divine providence and revelation. Emblematic portraits of the young king, armed with Bible and sword, appeared in defense of the new regime in such disparate forms as coronation pageantry, pulpit sermon, court masque and poetry, book illustration, and popular literature.

The English debated the authority of a minor king. Hugh Latimer, Seymour's chief pulpit spokesman, replied to Story by preaching on the text "Blessed is the land where there is a noble king" (Eccles. 10:17). In glossing *Piers Plowman*, Crowley explains away "V[a]e terre, ubi puer Rex est," the Vulgate translation of Story's text, as a reference to a "childish king" who is lazy, foolish, or incompetent, not to chronological age.[3] Crowley elsewhere compares the boy to his great medieval namesake:

> Kyng Edward the .iii. did Wicklife defend
> Wherbi he did florish in Oxford longe while
> But Richard the .ii. King did something bend
> To papistis bi whom Wicklife was in exile.

---

[2] From the dedication by Jean Veron, translator of Heinrich Bullinger, *An Holsume Antidotus agaynst the Anabaptistes* (1548), A5ᵛ-8ᵛ.

[3] Latimer, *Sermons*, p. 77. Crowley's gloss reads: "Omnium doctissimorum suffragio, dicuntur, h[a]ec de lassinus, fatuis, aut ineptis principibus, non de etate tenellis. Quasi dicat, ubi rex puerilis est" (A3ᵛ).

Despite Edward VI's status as a minor, Crowley sees his reign as a return to the imperial greatness of Edward III, the last monarch to allow free circulation of the English Bible. In line with Bale's *Image*, Crowley asserts that the Age of Locusts began during the reign of the weak king Richard II: "When Satan was suffrid to ren without staie" (*True Copye*, A1ᵛ). According to Bale's *Expostulation*, the controversy extended to the everyday conversation and gossip of his Hampshire parishioners. He attacks his Catholic antagonist for the argument that Protestant lords were exploiting the king as a figurehead:

> Alas poore chyld (sayd he) unknowne is it to hym, what actes are made now a dayes. But whan he cometh of age, he wyll se an other rule, and hange up an hondred of suche heretyke knaves. Meanynge the preachers of our tyme. . . . (B1ʳ)

Bale's retort suggests that the Latimer-Crowley defense became a conventional argument: "And though all these chyldysh wayes be detestable in a kynge yet is not the chyldehode of youthe in him to be reproved" (B2ᵛ). Bale had earlier quoted Latimer's biblical text ("Beata ter[r]a cuius rex nobilis est") in defense of royal authority (*Answer*, B2ʳ).

The problem of authority is inherent in the reigns of any minor kings. During the sixteenth century, the disastrous reigns of Henry VI and Edward V automatically came to mind. The problem was magnified in this case by Henry VIII's efforts to preserve the Tudor dynasty. By illegitimizing and disinheriting his daughters, he encouraged the possibility of an "elected" successor. Although he had left Seymour and the Protestant faction in control at court by the time of his death, Henry tried to rule from beyond the grave through his will. It delegated power to a regency council composed largely of Henry's privy councilors. The absence of any powerful conservative except Thomas Wriothesley, Lord Chancellor, ensured the Protestant character of Edward's government. Through his sister Jane, Seymour alone among the executors could claim kinship to Edward. On 31 January 1547 the executors followed precedent by naming the king's uncle lord protector. The king endorsed this decision by signed commission and delegated authority to Seymour until his eighteenth year, thus allowing his uncle to ignore the Privy Council and rule effectively as king.[4] The real contest was over Seymour's authority as his nephew's chief councilor. In correspondence with Seymour, Gardiner adroitly applied the Tudor principle of obedience to royal authority against the reformers: "When our sovereign lord cometh to his perfect age (which God grant), I doubt not but God will reveal that which shall be necessary for the governing of his people in religion" (A & M, VI, 38).

The doctrine of royal supremacy solved the reformers' problem. They argued that God lodged transcendent powers in the king's office that were distinct from the king's person.[5] Even from exile, Tyndale and Bale had upheld the absolute supremacy of Henry VIII and looked to the monarch as the sole source of legitimate reform. Under Edward, the *Book of Homilies* counseled obedience to the king unless he contradicts the word of God; the homily on obedience does mandate passive resistance to an ungodly ruler. No Edwardian Protestant dissented from the Cromwellian goal of reform through the ideal king who works through his bishops and magistrates. Seymour retained the assumption of the king's unshakeable authority as head of church and state. It was only after Edward's death that a

[4] Hoak, *King's Council*, pp. 114-16, 178-79, 261-62, and passim.

[5] See Ernst Kantorowicz, *The King's Two Bodies: A Study in Medieval Political Theology* (Princeton, 1957), p. 9 et seq.

few radicals began to call for active resistance to Mary Tudor. In advocating tyrannicide in his 1556 treatise, Ponet anticipates the rejection of royal supremacy during the Puritan Revolution.

Coronation spectacle furnished the first public defense of the new regime by dramatizing the heavenly origin of Edward's authority.[6] An ambitious cosmological tableau on a double scaffold near Cheapside apotheosized Edward as a providential agent; its heraldic allegory combined the arms of Henry VIII and the king's mother, Jane Seymour. Containing "an element or heaven, with the sunn, starrs, and clowdes very naturally," the upper level represented the timeless plane of divine grace. After descending from the heavens above to the lower level of the temporal world, a phoenix mated with a gilded and crowned lion on a mount covered with Tudor roses. An imperial crown borne downward by two angels marked the offspring of this union, a young lion, as God's deputy on earth. The phoenix, a traditional emblem for Christ and the resurrection, served as the Seymour family crest. Thus Edward Seymour incorporated a phoenix issuing from flames into his seal as protector (B.L. Add. Seal CV. 83). An epigram "On Q. Jane who had a Phoenix for her Crest & died in Childbed of K. Edward" (Bodl. MS Eng. poet. e. 14, fol. 97ᵛ) combines lamentation on the late queen with compliment to her son:

> Phoenix Jane dies, a Phoenix borne, wee're sad
> That no one age two Phoenixes e're had.

The prominent role of the Bible in the pageantry symbolized the divine authority of Protestant kingship. A boy

---

[6] For discussion of the Edwardian adaptation of pageantry designed to honor Henry VI, see Sidney Anglo, *Spectacle, Pageantry, and Early Tudor Policy* (Oxford, 1969), pp. 283-93.

playing Edward VI sat enthroned on the lower story. Enacted by four children, the kingly virtues of Regality, Justice, Truth, and Mercy provided pillars of the throne. Armed with its sword, Justice was a traditional attribute of royal authority; the figure of the Sword and the Bible recurs again and again in Edwardian iconography. An interpolated speech by "auncyent Trewth" transformed the pageant of Faith, Truth, and Justice at the great conduit in Fleet Street into Reformation allegory. As a figure for the pure belief of the primitive church, Truth stepped forward to address the king in Messianic terms. Truth prophesies that the Edwardian *renovatio* will suppress "hethen rites and detestable idolatrye" left intact by the incomplete reforms of Henry VIII: "Then shall England, committed to your gard, rejoyce in God, which hath geven her nation, after old David, a yonge kynge Salomon."[7]

Seymour joined Cranmer in placing the crown on Edward's head. This modification of the coronation ritual denied that the king's temporal authority is in any way subordinate to ecclesiastical control. Ever since Pope Leo III crowned Charlemagne in 800, coronation rituals had asserted the spiritual authority of the church over temporal power. In accordance with Reformation principles, Edward was the first king installed in an English rite. Eliminating those sections acknowledging the elective origins of the monarchy, Seymour revised the Medieval Latin ritual in order to emphasize royal supremacy.[8] Declaring that the ritual in itself lacked "direct force or necessity," Cranmer's

[7] Edward VI, *Literary Remains*, ed. J. G. Nichols (1857; Roxburghe Club, 2 vols.), I, cclxxxvi, ccxci.

[8] *Acts*, ed. Dasent, II, 29-33. Nichols transcribes a later manuscript of the coronation ritual in *Remains*, I, cclxxviii-cccv. See Anglo, *Spectacle*, pp. 294-95. MS 123 of the Society of Antiquaries, London, contains an abstract for the ceremony.

coronation sermon proclaimed divine election of the monarch. His biblical precedent would capture the imagination of the reformers:

> Your majesty is God's vice-gerent and Christ's vicar within your own dominions, and to see, with your predecessor Josiah, God truly worshipped, and idolatry destroyed, the tyranny of the bishops of Rome banished from your subjects, and images removed. These acts be signs of a second Josiah, who reformed the church of God in his days. You are to reward virtue, to revenge sin, to justify the innocent, to relieve the poor, to procure peace, to repress violence, and to execute justice throughout your realms.[9]

Edward's reputed conduct at his coronation contributed to his pietistic reputation. According to John Bale, the king ordered the display of the Bible as an emblem of spiritual authority. The lack of manuscript support for his account suggests that he invented this story in order to foster the myth of Edward's precocious wit and wisdom. Living in exile, Bale could not have attended the ceremony. He reports that at the presentation of the three swords representing his kingdoms of England, France, and Ireland, the king complained that one sword was missing. When attendant lords marveled, Edward explained that he meant the Bible, "the sword of the spirit," which should be borne far ahead of the other swords. He directed that the Bible be carried "with the greatest reverence" at the head of the procession. On the precedent of historians like Tacitus, Eusebius, and Einhard, Bale invented such sententious dialogue as the following: "Without that sword we are

---

[9] Cranmer, *Works*, II, 127. For contemporary examples of the Josiah *topos*, see *Remains*, ed. Nichols, I, xcvi, cxl, cxlix, cxcviii, cciii-ccv, ccxxxiv, ccxxxvii, ccli.

nothing, we can do nothing, and we have no power. . . .
Whoever rules without that should be called neither minister nor king."[10] Despite the historical inaccuracy of this
anecdote, it is in keeping with the pious iconography of
the reign. Later scholarship has transmitted as fact this
myth of the bearing of the Bible at Edward's coronation.[11]

COURTLY ART AND ENTERTAINMENT

Although the traditional entertainments of lute song and
dancing, interludes and pageants flourished at the court of
Edward VI, many forms of courtly art underwent adaptation in order to define and confirm the course of the Reformation. Quite typical is *De Regno Christi* (MS Royal 8
B. VII), a New Year gift that Martin Bucer presented to
the king. Ignoring traditional questions of court etiquette,
this Protestant courtesy book looks to Edward for fulfillment of reform. Under the supervision of the chamberlain, courtiers constantly attended the Tudor heir. Their
number included gentlemen of the bedchamber and privy
chamber, esquires of the body, musicians, physicians, and
pages. Chaplains and choristers served under the Dean of
the Chapel Royal. Edward's court was unique in offering

[10] In *Catalogus* (I, 673-74), Bale attributes the following speech to
"sanctissimus rex": "Respondit, esse sacrorum Bibliorum volumen. Ille
liber, inquit, gladius spiritus est, & gladius his omnibus longe anteferen-
dus. . . . Sine illo gladio nihil sumus, nihil possumus, nihil potestatis
habemus. . . . Sine illo qui regit, nec Dei minister, nec rex appellandus
est." According to Bale, the king acted upon his words: "Cum vero haec
& his similia dixisset plura, iussit sacrorum Bibliorum volumen cum max-
ima veneratione ante se ferri."

[11] William Camden, *Remaines of a Greater Worke Concerning Britaine*
(1605), 2G3ʳ; John Strype, *Ecclesiastical Memorials* (1721; 3 vols.), II,
22; David Daiches, *The King James Version of the English Bible* (Chicago,
1941), p. 46.

positions to so many radical Protestant writers and scholars. His retinue included such poets, translators, and pamphleteers as Miles Coverdale, Thomas Sternhold, Ann Cooke, Philip Gerrard, Edward Underhill, and John Philpot. Works of courtly piety furnish a unique record of the intellectual revolution of the time.

The royal court was the center of Tudor government and society. Even during a minority, the king was at the center of the court and was the ultimate source of advancement and reward. The avenue to power lay through conrol of the king. Seymour retained personal control over all access to the royal court, appointing Michael Stanhope, his brother-in-law, as his deputy in matters concerning the governorship of the king's person. Protestant tutors and preachers dominated court life during the protectorship. During movements of the itinerant court, Seymour stayed on the queen's side of royal palaces. When the king was at Whitehall or Hampton Court, however, Seymour stayed at his own residence at Syon, Sheen, or Somerset House. With Whitehall, Greenwich, and Hampton Court as the favorite residences, Edward would sometimes lodge at St. James, Windsor, and Oatlands. Not until the Dudley regency did the king go on formal summer progresses. These holidays anticipated the annual excursions that Queen Elizabeth would use as an element of statecraft. Dudley exploited ceremonial pomp as an important anchor of kingship. During state visits, Edward's carefully controlled display of languages and courtly skills fostered the myth of his precocious learning and wisdom.

The princesses maintained independent establishments, but as unmarried claimants to the throne they were watched closely. Elizabeth lived at Sudley Castle in the charge of Catherine Parr. Edward's senior by four years, Elizabeth continued her education under William Grindal and Roger

Ascham. Publication of her translation of Margaret of Navarre's *Godly Medytacyon of the Christen Sowle* cast her in the role of a learnedly pious princess. The title-page woodcut showing Christ's appearance to the kneeling princess lends her royal authority to the progress of reform. With Bible in hand, she assumes the conventional apostolic pose. As the only queen in the land, Catherine Parr now served the ambitions of Thomas Seymour by marrying the king's younger uncle. After Catherine Parr's death in childbirth in September 1548, Seymour began to court Elizabeth. Once again he threatened to marry close to the throne. After Seymour's execution on a charge of high treason, Latimer lodged an obscure charge that he had attempted to smuggle letters out of the Tower of London urging both princesses to "make some stur against the Lord Protector, and revenge his death" (*Annales*, 3D3^v). Following her removal to Hatfield House, Seymour's former retainer John Harington joined Elizabeth's household.

The resistance of Princess Mary threatened the Protestant ascendancy. Her household sheltered Roman clergy and such loyalists as Henry Parker, Baron Morley. Unlike his mistress, the Erastian Morley quietly conformed to new practices and devoted himself to noncontroversial projects like his verse translation of Petrarch's *Trionfi*. He did cultivate Edward Seymour by means of a manuscript commentary on Ecclesiastes. The dedication praises Seymour "as well for the wittie defence of us alle frome our foreyne enymies as for thadvauncement of godde[s] veritie, all vayne supersticion and Romysshe errour troden under ffoote" (MS Royal 17 D. XIII, fol. 1^{r-v}). Parker was not a timeserver, for his manuscript only attacks nondoctrinal abuses. A full generation older than her brother, Mary had a potent claim to regency following Seymour's fall. Faced by a threat from conservative councilors to replace him with the older princess, Dudley created the fiction that Edward could exercise personal rule.[12] Mary encouraged the conservatives through her refusal to come to court. Spurred on by an attempt by the Imperial navy to carry her off to the Continent, Dudley demanded Mary's submission and arrested her chaplains and other members of her retinue. By late 1551, both princesses had been summoned to court.

Continuation of the king's education was the most powerful influence on the royal household. Erasmus, More, and Machiavelli agreed that the appointment of the ideal tutor offered the best hope for good government in hereditary monarchies. Continuing in the tradition established by Catherine Parr (see McConica, pp. 215-17), royal schooling put into practice the theories of Erasmus's *Institutio Principis Christiani* (1516). Edward's studies therefore parallel the remarkable program of princely education devised by Ponocrates, the humanistic tutor in *Gargantua and Pantagruel* (I. 23-24). The appointment of Protestant tutors placed Edward and all potential claimants to the throne except Princess Mary under the influence of zealous reformers. The king studied the classics with John Cheke, Anthony Cooke, and Richard Cox. The Huguenot Jean Belmaine taught him French. Edward's holograph exercise books (Bodl. MSS Bodl. 899 and Autogr. e. 2) disprove, however, the extravagant claims to precocity advanced by royal apologists and their modern successors.[13] Although they reflect Cheke's tendency to choose classical platitudes concerning moral and political wisdom, the Latin and Greek phrases that the young king copied were vehicles for grammatical instruction and document no original thought.

[12] Hoak, *King's Council*, pp. 29-30, 118-24, 135, 154-55, 264-65.

[13] W. K. Jordan, *Edward VI*, II, 21-22, 408-11. *The Chronicle and Political Papers of King Edward VI*, ed. W. K. Jordan (Ithaca, N.Y., 1966), pp. 69-73, 89-94, and passim, hereafter cited as *Journal*.

Sermons were spectacular performances at the New Jerusalem of Edward's court. Seymour included Hugh Latimer, Nicholas Ridley, and his own retainer Thomas Becon among court preachers. The Chapel Royal at Whitehall
was the stage for the most dramatic confrontation over royal
authority during the reign. In response to Stephen Gardiner's continual criticism, Seymour ordered the bishop to
preach before the king as a test of obedience. Gardiner
received orders to affirm royal authority to institute religious "innovations." William Cecil attempted to manage
Gardiner's delivery on behalf of Seymour. When Gardiner
refused to comply with a request for an advance draft,
Cecil produced an outline and suggested topics for the sermon. Gardiner's continued resistance brought a summons
into Seymour's presence in the gallery of Somerset House.
During these negotiations, Cecil supplied contrived evidence of Edward's formulation of policy. Gardiner claimed,
for example, that "the said Master Cecil brought me papers of the king's majesty's hand, showing me how the
king's highness used to note every notable sentence . . ."
(*A & M*, VI, 67-68).

Gardiner preached under unusually close scrutiny, for
Nicholas Udall joined him in the pulpit on 29 June 1548.
Udall took down the sermon in shorthand for "a noble
personage of this realm," evidently Seymour. In the absence of a manuscript text, Foxe transcribed Udall's summary. Gardiner acknowledged royal authority over such
nondoctrinal practices as images and ceremonies. But with
Edward in attendance, he criticized preaching by royal license, public attacks on the mass, and violation of vows of
clerical celibacy. He must have known that his endorse-
ment could damn the new liturgy in the eyes of the radicals. During an Erastian age, Gardiner's delivery was remarkable for its frank subjectivity. He described his text

as a declaration of "conscience" and "the plain truth as it lieth in my mind." Foxe asks the reader to compare Gardiner's points of agreement with his actions during Mary's reign in order to "see how variable he was, how inconstant and contrary to himself, [and] how perjured . . ." (A & M, VI, 255-57). Foxe's insistence on constancy contradicts the reformist demand for liberty of conscience. One must credit Gardiner with consistency and courage during his lonely opposition. His sermon stands in contrast to the famous silence of Hugh Latimer. Unlike Seymour, who had reasoned with the bishop, Dudley's council later baited its prisoner. When Gardiner wrote to complain about "want of bookes to relieve my minde," the councilors "laughed very merrily thereat, saying, hee had a pleasant head."[14]

As Seymour's favorite preacher, Latimer helped to create the homiletic atmosphere at court. During 1548 and 1549, he preached the Friday sermons during Lent. Because his sermons were so popular that congregations filled the Chapel Royal to capacity, a wooden pulpit was erected in the privy gardens at Whitehall in order to accommodate the crowd. John Day's engraving of the scene (Figure 17) portrays the king listening at a casement window with Seymour at his side (A & M [1563], p. 1353). Bibles in the hands of Latimer and the woman sitting at his feet typify the evangelical piety of the Reformation court. In contrast to the popular style that he employed at Paul's Cross, Latimer tailored his preaching to his courtly audience. Paraphrasing the Augustinian dictum that the preacher adapt his delivery to his listeners (De doctrina Christiana, IV. 2 and 9), he obeyed his own advice to the preacher: "If he preach before a king, let his matter be concerning the office of a king . . . and so forth in other matters, as time

[14] Annales, 3D3ᵛ, 3D5ᵛ; also see A & M, VI, 67-69, 81-84, 87-93, 198, 246, and Remains, ed. Nichols, I, cviii.

and audience shall require" (*Sermons*, p. 53). Decorum prevented reuse of the homely imagery and diction that he employed in his "Sermon on the Plowers." Such metaphors as the following must have entertained the boy king:

> Faith is a noble duchess. She hath ever her gentleman-usher going before her, the confessing of sins. She hath a train after her, the fruits of good works, the walking in the commandments of God. He that believeth will not be idle; he will walk; he will do his business. Have ever the gentleman-usher with you. So if ye will try faith, remember this rule; consider whether the train be waiting upon her. (p. 137)

As court preacher, Latimer fulfilled a special role akin to that of a royal tutor. Focusing on the public and private duties of kingship, his 1549 Lenten sermons function as a Reformation courtesy book. In the tradition of the *speculum principis*, they define the office of the king with reference to the various estates. The sermons exemplify the problem of counsel central to the minority:

> But who shall see this "too much" [royal extravagance] or tell the King of this "too much"? Think you, any of the King's privy chamber? No, for fear of loss of favor. Shall any of his sworn chaplains? No, they be of the closet and keep close such matters. But the King himself must see this "too much". . . . (p. 65)

In order to instruct Edward in his dual authority over church and state, Latimer conflates sword imagery from the coronation ceremony with the Pauline definition of "sword of the Spirit, which is the word of God" (Ephesians 6:17):

> For in this world God hath two swords; the one is a temporal sword, the other a spiritual. The temporal sword

resteth in the hands of kings, magistrates, and rulers under him, whereunto all subjects, as well the clergy as the laity, be subject and punishable for any offense contrary to the same book. The spiritual sword is in the hands of the ministers and preachers; whereunto all kings, magistrates, and rulers ought to be obedient, that is, to hear and follow so long as the ministers sit in Christ's chair, that is, speaking out of Christ's book. The king correcteth transgressors with the temporal sword and the preacher also, if he be an offender. But the preacher cannot correct the king, if he be a transgressor of God's word, with the temporal sword; but he must correct and reprove him with the spiritual sword. . . . (p. 51)

This familiar figure of the Sword and the Book became the hallmark of the reign.

Just as the Young Josiah renewed God's covenant with his chosen people, Latimer's ideal preacher filled the role of an Old Testament prophet. Latimer's spiritual authority was such that he could play Nathan to England's David. He directed at the king and his uncle the explosive precedents of Henry VI and his protector, Humphrey, Duke of Gloucester (pp. 78-79). According to Foxe, Latimer fulfilled his chosen function: ". . . if England ever had a prophet, he might seem to be one" (*A & M*, VII, 463-64). In contrast to the temporal assertions of the papacy, the Protestant preacher exercises admonitory authority over the king. Although Latimer affirmed the clerical duty to instruct the king, he argued that the royal office unites temporal authority over both church and state. As the encyclopedic text for all men, be they king, cleric, or commoner, the Bible represents the source of royal authority: "In this book is contained doctrine for all estates, even for kings. A king may herein learn how to guide himself.

. . . He shall have the book with him. . . . He must read the book of God . . ." (pp. 70-71, 84). With examples ranging from David to Ahab, 1 and 2 Kings were considered a God-given courtesy book for monarchs. In the millennial kingdom, all distinctions between king, subject, and clergy dissolve in obedience to the Word: "The poorest plowman is in Christ equal with the greatest prince that is" (p. 149).

Latimer's message is clear. The health of the commonwealth depends upon the king, who must choose between faith, "the noble duchess," and the regal vices of pride, extravagance, and licentiousness. In dramatizing Edward's capacity to abuse the state, the 1549 sermons articulate the problem of counsel raised by works ranging from *Utopia* to *1 Henry IV*. They create a picture of precarious life at a court beset by danger and intrigue. Latimer scarcely veils his criticism of the profligacy of Henry VIII when he comes to define the limits of permissible court entertainment:

"And when the king is set in the seat of his kingdom . . . ," what shall he do? Shall he dance and dally, banquet, hawk, and hunt? No, forsooth, sir. . . . What must he do then? He must be a student; he must write God's book himself, not thinking, because he is a king, he hath license to do what he will, as these worldly flatterers [courtiers] are wont to say. . . . And yet a king may take his pastime in hawking or hunting or suchlike pleasures. But he must use them for recreation, when he is weary of weighty affairs. . . . And this is called pastime with good company. (p. 79)

Allusion to "Pastime with good company," a song composed by Henry VIII, points to the previous reign when, as Ascham complained, "Gods Bible was banished the Court, and *Morte Arthure* received into the Princes chamber."[15] Latimer's advocacy of authorized Bible translation cites as a precedent Josiah's rediscovery of the book of the law contained in Deuteronomy:

> Where shall he [the king] have a copy of this book? Of the Levites. And why? Because it shall be a true copy, not falsified. Moses left the book in an old chest, and the Levites had it in keeping. . . . It had lain hid many years, and the Jews knew not of it. (p. 80)

Allusion to the dynastic chaos created by Henry VIII's marriages lodges Latimer's criticism very close to the king. "Polygamous" David set a bad example for the Tudor Solomon who inherited the kingdom "by the advice and will of his father." Conveniently overlooking the indiscretions of Solomon's age, Latimer argues that Edward must live in chastity with a "godly wife" and procreate for the sake of the kingdom. As Edward's Adonijah, the recently executed Thomas Seymour is cast in the role of an impious scapegoat in stark contrast to his godly wife:

> I have heard say when that good queen that is gone had ordained in her house daily prayer both before noon and after noon, the Admiral gets him out of the way, like a mole digging in the earth. He shall be Lot's wife to me as long as I live. He was a covetous man, an horrible covetous man. I would there were no more in England! He was an ambitious man. I would there were no mo in England! He was a seditious man, a contemner of common prayer. I would there were no mo in England! He is gone. I would he had left none behind him! (pp. 127-28)

[15] *The Scholemaster* (1570), I3ᵛ.

The king's younger uncle had died on 20 March 1549, one month before this Good Friday attack. At the same time that he praises Catherine Parr, Latimer exculpates the protector from responsibility for his brother's death.

Music and poetry were very important at the royal academy, for the king inherited his father's taste and talent for music. Thomas Tallis remained in the Chapel Royal, and the King's Musick employed seventeen musicians. Edward reaffirmed his father's Erasmian taste for the singing of biblical verse in popular ballad measures. According to George Puttenham, Henry VIII appointed Thomas Sternhold Groom of the Privy Chamber in reward for his English Psalms.[16] The Edwardian editions of the poems of Sternhold and Christopher Tye record a consistent effort to create a public image of royal piety. Advancing to the office of Groom of the Wardrobe after Henry VIII's death, Sternhold attributed progress on his Psalm paraphrases to the urging of his young patron. According to tradition, Tye served as music preceptor to Edward VI.[17] A member of the Chapel Royal, Tye creates an idealized image of the king as a Davidic singer of songs in the dedication to his metrical *Actes of the Apostles* (1553):

> That suche good thinges, youre grace might move
>   Your lute when ye assaye:
> In stede of songes, of wanton love
>   These stories then to playe.   (A3ᵛ)

Traditional scholarship has interpreted the testimony of Sternhold, Tye, and various radical Protestants as evidence of an effort to wean courtiers away from secular love song (see below, Chapter 5). In actual fact, Edward's journal

[16] *Essays*, ed. Smith, II, 17.

[17] Thomas Warton, *The History of English Poetry* (1774-81; 3 vols. and vol. 4 unfinished), III, 190-91.

records his pleasure in traditional madrigals and lute music (pp. 73, 92, 94). The manuscript miscellanies of the Protestant courtiers Sir George Blage and John Harington prove that courtly love lyrics remained fashionable. Latin verses that the king received from Nicholas Denisot conform to the mythographic traditions of courtly allegory (MS Royal 12 A. VII, fols. 9^r-15^v).

Despite Latimer's praise for that court where "kings be no banqueters, no players, and they spend not the time in hawking and hunting" (*Sermons*, p. 77), Edward and his courtiers played themselves in masques and interludes. Choristers and gentlemen of the court performed in extravagant spectacles. The world of actors and spectators merged in the Renaissance masque, for when the king performed within a play the court provided both the subject matter and the audience for the drama.[18] Like Queen Elizabeth, Edward performed in allegorical masques. Although *Jacob and Esau* is the only extant court drama from his reign, the manuscript records of the office of the Master of the Revels document performances at court.[19]

The Reformation court dramatized itself by means of antipapal polemics. Recurrence among stage properties of both papal insignia and royal crowns and regalia suggests that political allegories were popular at court. Edward joined the masquers with some frequency. Dramatic inversions symbolized the temporary dissolution of hierarchal distinctions during the Christmas revels. Thus the king played a priest in a play that required costumes for "ffryers," "Cardynalles hattes for players," and "Crownes & Crosse for

[18] Dale B.J. Randall, *Jonson's Gypsies Unmasked: Background and Theme of "The Gypsies Metamorphos'd"* (Durham, N.C., 1975), pp. 11-12.

[19] Folger Shakespeare Library, MSS Loseley. Ed. Albert Feuillerat in *Documents Relating to the Revels at Court in the Time of King Edward VI and Queen Mary* (Louvain, 1914).

the poope." According to John Bale, Edward wrote an antipapal interlude entitled "De meretrice Babylonica" ("The Whore of Babylon"; *Catalogus*, I, 674). A related biblical interlude about the Tower of Babylon, which was performed at Hampton Court during the first Christmas of the reign, dramatized a similar figure for the Roman church. The same apocalyptic conflict was enacted in a Shrovetide entertainment that required costumes for priests, hermits, and a seven-headed dragon. Although it was performed three months before the introduction of the new prayer book on Whitsunday 1549, the play required "Albes Surplyces and heade clothes" that evidently referred to planned changes in vestments.

Dudley returned to more traditional courtly spectacles and increased expenditures for revels after Seymour's fall; entertaining masques, triumphs, and tournaments overshadowed the polemical interludes of the protectorate. Latimer would have disapproved of the masque of Cupid, Venus, and Mars. In appointing George Ferrers Master of the King's Pastimes during Christmas 1552/3, Dudley revived an office that had fallen into disuse and sanctioned elaborate revelry during the twelve-day festivities. Ferrers's title suited his status as a gentleman better than the traditional epithet: Lord of Misrule. Ferrers, who later contributed to the *Mirror for Magistrates* (1559), drew its editor William Baldwin and Thomas Chaloner, another contributor, into the celebrations. Baldwin wrote a "playe of the state of Ierland" for performance at court. Disputations reputed to include speeches by Edward ("auditi concii") fitted the academic tenor of the court (*Catalogus*, I, 674). In a return to the rhetorical manner of the interludes that John Heywood wrote before the break with Rome, performance of a dialogue between Riches and Youth evidently referred to the reign of the boy king; Chaloner may have written the piece. Heywood wrote at least one play for Edward's court.[20]

Radical gospellers perceived the Mark of the Beast in the Dudley revels. Robert Crowley attributed to them a central role in the downfall of Seymour, who was beheaded shortly after Epiphany on 22 January 1552:

> In this meane while, the younge kynge was entised to passe time in maskeyng & mumminge. And to that ende there was piked oute a sorte of misrulers to devyse straunge spectacles in the courte, in the tyme of Christmas to cause the yonge kynge to forgette, yea rather to hate, hys good uncle, who had purged the courte of all such outrage, and enured the kynge unto the exercyse of vertuouse learninge, and hearynge of sermons. This was the high waye, firste to make an ende of the kynges uncle, and after of the kyng hymselfe.[21]

Grafton's *Chronicle* (1569) picked up Crowley's accusation and passed it on to modern times. Although Sidney Anglo questions the reputed need to distract the king from the proceedings against Seymour, he suggests that Dudley used revelry to counter public rumors that Edward opposed his uncle's death sentence. Indeed Ferrers performed in a pageant in Cheapside on the tenth day of Christmas. The Revels accounts list among the dramatic properties for this macabre celebration stocks, a pillory, the paraphernalia of torture, an axe, and a headsman's block. Although no re-

---

[20] *Documents*, ed. Feuillerat, pp. 5-6, 26, 33, 39, 47, 60, 93-94, 96, 134, 142, 145, 256, 288. Hereafter cited as Feuillerat. See Alfred Harbage, *Annals of the English Drama*, rev. Samuel Schoenbaum (1964), pp. 30-33.

[21] Thomas Lanquet, *An Epitome of Cronicles* (1559), 4E3[r]. Continued to the reign of Queen Elizabeth by Crowley, whose additions cover the reigns of Edward VI and Mary. Hereafter cited as Crowley, *Epitome*.

cord survives of Ferrers's performance, Anglo explains its topical significance: "It was surely no coincidence that the very next item of public entertainment at Tower Hill, after this merry pastime devised by Northumberland and the Council, was the beheading of the Duke of Somerset."[22]

Dudley's heavyhandedness contrasts starkly with his predecessor's skillful manipulation of public opinion. Surely he must bear much of the responsibility for his reputation as "one of the bad men of Tudor history" (but see Elton, p. 353). Public rumors about court revelry and the dramatization of Seymour's beheading shortly before his actual death could only inflame the populace. All contemporary accounts record a popular outcry against the execution (see *Annales*, 3E3r). Such spectacle created a difficult problem for royal apologists like Crowley and Grafton. What had become of the godly ruler who regarded sermons and Bible reading as the only permissible form of entertainment? They had to rationalize their idealized image of Edward as a just and pious king with his acceptance of his uncle's execution. Either they genuinely believed their charges against Dudley or they used him as a surrogate for the king whom they could not attack. Crowley's retrospective account exonerates Edward from personal responsibility and interprets his death as a providential punishment to a people that refused to give up sin:

> The sommer folowyng, the kyng wente in progresse into the weste countreye, wherein his yonge affections were fedde by them that were about him, not withoute great daunger of his lyfe, by outragious ridyng in haukyng and huntyng. Towardes wynter he retourned to London, & from thens he went to Grenewich, wher was prepared

[22] Anglo, *Spectacle*, pp. 304, 307-308. See *Documents*, ed. Feuillerat, pp. 72, 81.

matter of pastyme, a fort counterfaited, riding at the tylte, and goodly pastimes at Christmas, tyll the kyng had gotten a cough that brought hym to his ende. (*Epitome*, 4E3ᵛ)

In actual fact, Edward was his father's son. Long before Dudley made his final moves against Seymour, the king's journal recorded his enjoyment of the traditional courtly skills of dancing, archery, hawking, hunting, and riding. He may have favored Sternhold's Psalm-singing, but he could also play the lute. He liked bull-baiting, banqueting, bear-baiting, jousting, and mock combats. Although the sickly boy could not match his father's physical vigor in his prime, such entries as that for 31 March 1551 record his own participation in these pastimes: "A challenge made by me that I, with sixteen of my chamber, should run at base, shoot, and run at ring with any seventeen of my servants, gentlemen in the court."[23] Edward's invention of a "combat to be foughte with Wylliam Somer," the royal jester, undermines the stereotyped view of the king as a sober youth (Feuillerat, p. 73). Yet one need not assume that these enthusiasms contradict Edward's pious reputation. He discovered no inherent improbability in the use of physical combat as the occasion for reenacting the Reformation conflict between the Lutherans and the papacy:

All these fought two to two at barriers in the hall. Then came in two appareled like Almains [Germans]: the Earl of Ormonde and Jacques Granado; and two came in like friars; but the Almains would not suffer them to pass till they had fought. The friars were Mr. Drury and Thomas Cobham. (*Journal*, p. 105)

[23] *Journal*, pp. 31-36, 57, 61-63, 73, 75, 92, 100-101, and passim.

[183]

W. K. Jordan concludes that the king lacked "personal warmth" and "boyish affection" on the basis of his journal's failure to record either effort to save his uncle or grief at his death (pp. xxiii and 107, n. 19). Yet MS Harley 2194 contradicts Jordan's negative evidence. The courtly witness states:

> Upon the death of the Duke albeit the King gave noe token of any ill distempered passion, as takeinge it not agreeable to Ma[jes]tie openly to declare himselfe, and albeit the Lords had laboured with much variety of sports, to dispell any dampy thoughts, which the remembraunce of his Unckle might rayse, yet upon speech of him hee would often sigh and lett fall teares, sometymes holdinge opinion that his Unckle had done nothinge . . . and where then said hee was the good nature of a Nephew? Where was the clemency of a Prince? (fol. 20^r)

This document verifies the moralistic interpretation of Dudley's motives advanced by Crowley. G. R. Elton rightly corrects efforts to draw elaborate inferences about the king's thoughts and feelings from the skeletal entries in his diary. Nevertheless MS Harley 2194 suggests that the real Edward is an unexpectedly intricate figure standing somewhere between the Reformation myth of the ideal Christian king and Elton's "boy tyrant" (p. 372).

ROYAL ICONOGRAPHY

Royal iconography filled the vacuum left by outbursts of Edwardian iconoclasm. Images of the king and royal heraldry inherited the veneration that statues of the Virgin and Child, saints' images, and other cult objects had acquired by the late Middle Ages. The king's coat of arms replaced the crucifix on the rood screens of churches. The woodcut allegory of Edward's reign that John Day inserted into the second edition of Foxe's *Actes and Monuments* (p. 1483) portrays this iconographic shift (Figure 19). The top panel juxtaposes the pulling down of a statue from the wall of a church with the inset at the lower left showing "King Edward delivering the Bible to the Prelates." This inset derives from Holbein's title-page woodcut for the Coverdale Bible (Figure 2). The stark simplicity of the right-hand inset symbolizes the Edwardian church service with its "Communion Table." In a variation of Day's Latimer woodcut (Figure 17), gospel preaching to a Bible-reading congregation supplants the allegedly idolatrous images depicted above. In reply to Gardiner's defense of the image as a layman's book, Seymour argued that only royal emblems deserve homage: "the king's majesty's images, arms, and ensigns, should be honoured and worshipped after the decent order and invention of human laws and ceremonies . . ." (*A & M*, VI, 28). In order to avoid idolatry, Seymour interprets the royal image as a temporal mirror of truth revealed in the Bible. This Edwardian cult of kingship would be revived in the "sacred" images of Queen Elizabeth (Yates, pp. 42-59).

In the text-centered Protestant kingdom, the Bible inevitably served as an emblem of royal authority. The prominence of the Bible at court conformed to Latimer's sermons and the counsel of such humanistic documents as Gargantua's letter to Pantagruel (II.8). The manuscript of the Wyclif Bible from which Robert Crowley derived his published prologue was highly prized, for the discovery of this manuscript in 1550 among the books in the privy chamber was taken to confirm the providential hand behind Edward's reign (above, pp. 99-100). The legends on the first vellum insert identify the text with the newly found "book of the law" that prompted Josiah's sweeping reli-

gious reforms (2 Kings 22:8). Edward VI owned two copies of Leo Jud's *Biblia Sacrosancta* (Zurich), the elaborate
bindings of which were probably commissioned by suitors
for royal favor. It is impossible at this distance to determine whether these Latin Bibles were personal household
copies read by the king or ceremonial objects in the royal
library. Although most monarchs took little interest in them,
books did occupy a special place in Edward's schooling.
We know that he read pietistic works; for example, he
borrowed Anne Stanhope's copy of Edward Courtney's
translation of Aonio Paleario's treatise on the passion. The
devout king noted in the margin: "Faith is dede if it/be
without workes/your loving neveu EDWARD" (C.U.L.
MS Nn. 4. 43, fol. 4ᵛ).

Edward inherited the 1543 folio copy of *Biblia Sacrosancta* (B.L. C.23.e.11) from his father. The rich gold
embroidery on the red velvet binding features the monogram "HR." The illuminated title page, which would have
been extremely rare by the mid-century, converts this copy
into a Tudor court text. Gilding covers the printed word
"BIBLIA" and a pasted-on illumination of the Tudor arms
conceals a printed device. The illuminator included Tudor
roses and other heraldic devices in the ornamental borders.
Painted heraldry decorates the book's edges. The extremely
fine gold tooling on the green velvet covers of the 1544
octavo copy of the Jud Bible (B.L. C.23.a.9) is much
rarer than the folio's gold embroidery, which was standard
on velvet covers. It bears the royal seal and the monogram
"E.VI." The intermingling of biblical texts with royal emblems lends divine authority to Edward's temporal rule.
The covers bear the following texts: "ESTO FIDELIS
USQUE AD MORTEM ET DABO TIBI CORONAM
VITAE. APOC. 2" and "FIDEM SERVAVI QUOD
SUPEREST REPOSITA EST MIHI CORONA IUS-

TITIAE: 2 TIM. 4" (Revelation 2:10 and 2 Timothy 4:7-8). The carved and gilded edges carry crowns and a Bible, the Tudor rose and portcullis, Edward's monogram, and the royal motto "Dieu et mon Droict [*sic*]." They also bear the following texts: "DOMINUS LUX MEA ET SALUS MEA QUEM TIMEBO," "VERITAS LIBERABIT BONITAS REGNABIT," and "IN PRINCIPIO ERAT VERBUM ET VERBUM ERAT APUD DEO" (Psalm 27:1, John 8:32, and John 1:1).

John Day's 1551 folio edition of Becke's revision provides the best example of the use of the printed Bible as a royal emblem. Day commissioned the title-page woodcut for this edition (Figure 13). The illustration symbolizes divine revelation through the agency of the crown; at the same time it contains a rebus on Day's name, trade, and faith. The upper compartment contains the royal arms supported by the British griffin and crowned lion. The two small side compartments, which portray the raising of Lazarus and the Resurrection, link the royal monogram and heraldry to God's word. At the bottom, Day's motto "ARISE, FOR IT IS DAY" and his device, which depicts one naked man waking another at the sun's rising, continue the symbolism of resurrection and revelation. Like Donne's "Goodfriday, 1613. Riding Westward," the woodcut alludes to the conceit of Christ as the rising sun. To the elect Christian reader, the emblematic motto and device identify the text as the source of salvation by means of allusion to 1 Thessalonians 5:5: "For you are all sons of light and sons of the day; we are not of the night or of darkness." Day sold books at the sign of the Resurrection. The walled city in the background probably represents the New Jerusalem. Day's insertion of a separately printed additional sheet converts this Bible into an emblematic argument for obedience to royal authority. This large woodcut (*STC* 7507)

[187]

contains the royal arms flanked by the initials ".E. .R." The wood block was carved at the time of the Norfolk and Devonshire rebellions, for the scroll at the top reads ".1549. .VIVAT. .REX. .1549." The insert carries the printed texts: "O Lord for thy mercyes sake, save the Kyng" and "Feare God, and honour the Kynge." Two side columns bear the printer's initials.

Some Bible editions associated the image of Edward VI with Christ the King—for example, Richard Jugge's 1552 quarto edition of Tyndale's New Testament. The woodcut portrait of the king supplants a medallion portrait of Christ on the title page of Jugge's 1548 sixteenmo edition. An inscribed garter encircles the royal portrait in the manner of the king's great seal. The traditional homage "Vivat Rex" links royal authority to the heavenly kingdom through a couplet paraphrase of the parable of the pearl of great price (Matthew 13:45-46):

> The pearle which Christ commaunded to be boughte
> Is here to be founde, not elles to be sought.

Jugge's quarto contains the Tyndale text that Dudley's Privy Council authorized late in the reign.

Conventional portraits of Edward bearing Bible and Sword represent the union of spiritual and temporal authority in the king. The symbolism of the sword and the book derives from the ancient *topos* of *sapientia et fortitudo*, which goes back to the Homeric conflict between the physical courage of Achilles and the prudential wisdom of Odysseus. Virgil unites the two aspects of leadership in the imperial figure of Aeneas (*Aeneid*, VI. 853). Edwardian iconography inherits a Christianized form of this tradition. St. Augustine redefined the ideal ruler as the "rex iustus et pius" who governs his kingdom according to the Christian principles of justice and mercy (see *De civitate dei*, V.

24). According to Augustine, the wise king governs by means of the Bible. Such emperors as Constantine, Justinian, and Charlemagne modeled themselves on this ideal of the wise Christian ruler. The ideal furnishes the intellectual context of Christian heroism and chivalry as they are defined in such disparate works as *Beowulf*, the *Ruodlieb*, the *Chanson de Roland*, and *The Faerie Queene*.[24] During the medieval conflicts with the papacy, this theme was identified with the millennial yearnings for imperial *renovatio* and Davidic kingship.

Roy Strong suggests that this definitive image of the Tudor monarch is an iconographic variant of the Renaissance emblem of "Ex utroque Caesar," the Emperor bearing sword and book which allude to his power in peace and war.[25] Strong's interpretation loses sight of native and biblical sources for the emblem. Images of the king holding either scepter or sword could be seen everywhere in seals, coins, manuscript illuminations, and woodcuts. In correspondence with Gardiner, Seymour clarified the symbolism of the great seal: "the king's image is on both the sides; on the one side, as in war, the chief captain; on the other side, as in peace, the liege sovereign: In harness, with his sword drawn, to defend his subjects . . ." (*A & M*, VI, 29). According to Seymour, Gardiner's confusion of the royal image with that of St. George exemplifies the danger of misinterpretation implicit in the retention of religious images. The great seal portrays the enthroned king under his statecloth holding his scepter and orb. The royal arms are encircled with

---

[24] See Ernst R. Curtius, *European Literature and the Latin Middle Ages*, trans. W. R. Trask (1953), pp. 167-82.

[25] *Holbein and Henry VIII* (1967), pp. 14-15. Elizabeth H. Hageman contributes the best study of the *topos* in "John Foxe's Henry VIII as *Justitia*," *Sixteenth Century Journal*, 10, i (1979), 35-44.

garters inscribed with the king's formal title: "EDWAR-
DUS SEXTUS DEI GRATIA ANGLIAE, FRAN-
CIAE, ET HIBERNIAE REX, FIDEI DEFENSOR,
ET IN TERRA ECCLESIAE ANGLICANAE ET
HIBERNICAE SUPREMUM CAPUT." Edward thus
followed the same style as his father. Mary omitted the
claim to supremacy. Sensitive to the caesaropapal implications of headship, Elizabeth would eventually control the
church as *gubernator* ("governor") rather than *caput* ("head").
The counterseal depicts the king on horseback brandishing
a sword.[26] Every subject would have recognized the seal
images on such coins of the realm as gold sovereigns and
half-sovereigns as well as silver crowns and half-crowns.[27]
The half-length figure of Edward VI on the coronation
medal adapts the equestrian pose of the great seal and bears
the king's formal title in Hebrew and Greek on the reverse.

The Pauline concept of "the sword of the Spirit, which
is the word of God." (Ephesians 6:17) underlies the Reformation *topos* of the Sword and the Book. Dürer's diptych
of the Four Apostles (1526), which identifies Paul as the
Protestant saint, is perhaps the best example of this theme.
Dominating the painting are Paul and John, who represent
the bases of Lutheran theology: the Johannine gospel, Pauline epistles (notably Romans), and Revelation. As a Reformation allegory, the portrait depicts the victory of Paul
over Peter, who retreats into the background with the keys
of Catholic tradition. Paul carries a staff that looks very
much like a sword. Dürer conflates iconography of the

---

[26] B.L. Add. Charter 6017. See A. B. and A. Wyon, *The Great Seals
of England* (1887), pp. 72-73, plate XX, nos. 105-106.

[27] Herbert Grueber, *Handbook of the Coins of Great Britain and Ireland
in the British Museum*, rev. J.P.C. Kent et al. (1970), nos. 449, 450, 452,
454 et al.

Evangelists derived from medieval manuscript illumination with the symbolism of the four humors. The melan-
cholic temperament of white-robed Paul accords with the
intellectuality of Protestant theology. John, the sanguine
visionary, shares the foreground as he peaceably reads the
Word. Paul crowds choleric Mark into the background of
the right-hand panel, as aged and phlegmatic Peter studies
the gospels held by John on the other side. Paul and John
represent the active and contemplative sides of Protestant
faith.[28] Endemic woodcuts of the Pauline image of the Word
as the "two-edged sword" issuing from the mouth of Christ
(Hebrews 4:12, and Revelation 1:16, 19:15) fill Protestant
Bibles and editions of Bale's *Image* (Figure 9). The emblem descends from Dürer's series of Revelation engravings.

Holbein's 1535 woodcut (Figure 2) assimilates Lutheran iconography. Figures of harp-playing David and
sword-bearing Paul that represent the Old and New Testaments flank Henry VIII, who is armed with the Sword
and the Book. The three figures personify the Reformation
ideal of evangelical kingship at the moment of transition
from Old Law to New Law. Appearing in a burst of heavenly light, the Tetragrammaton at the top symbolizes the
direct revelation of the Word to the sovereign, who passes
it on to the people through his prelates. The incarnation
of Christ as the Logos brings release from the original sin
of Adam and Eve. Royal permission for the English Bible
corresponds to Moses' reception of the Ten Commandments, Esdras' preaching of the Old Law, and Jesus' gospel preaching, which are portrayed in side panels. As the
transmitter of the scriptures as opposed to church traditions, the king replaces the pope as the supreme spiritual

[28] Munich, Alte Pinakothek. See Erwin Panofsky, *Albrecht Dürer* (1945;
2 vols., rev. ed.), I, 234-35; II, no. 43, figs. 294-95.

authority on earth. The many keys in the portrait of Christ and his disciples repudiate the papal claim to apostolic succession and exemplify the communal and spiritual nature of Protestant apostleship. Holbein's Great Bible border offers a more nationalistic variation of the same Lutheran themes (Figure 3).

Anthony Scoloker's edition of Luther's *Sermon uppon the Twent[i]eth Chapter of Johan of absolution and the true use of the keyes* (Ipswich, 1548) clarifies the meaning of this symbolism. In his woodcut frontispiece, two "mynysters of the Church" mark the elect with keys at the time of the Second Coming. Labeled as Catholics by their false keys and crosses, the reprobate spectators cannot enter the millennial kingdom. The translator Richard Argentine denies papal claims to Petrine supremacy and "the auctoritie of the keies of heaven" by identifying the latter with the "holye woorde frelie . . . geven" by the Young Josiah:

> . . . the which is the very true key wherby to enter into the Kingdome of heaven ande the nexte waye to obteyne the mightie ande stronge stwearde [sword] for ever to beate downe the devell and hys derelie beloved antechriste.

The papal keys symbolize idolatrous "tradicions and not Cryst onelye" (A2^v).

Allusions to the Sword and the Book abound in the pictorial symbolism of Reformation books and sermons. The figure receives verbal statement in Hurlestone's *Newes*, Turner's *Preservative*, Latimer's Friday sermons, and Bale's apocryphal account of Edward's coronation. According to Cranmer's homily on Bible reading, the scriptures are "sharper then any two edged sworde" (B1^r). Day flanks his woodcut of the Measurement of the Temple (Figure 10) with the couplet "When the churche is measured wyth

Goddes worde, / The Popes parte is caste out, and geven to the sworde." In dedicating his 1550 folio Bible to the king, Miles Coverdale distinguishes between Edward's weapons of the "worde of god" and the "temporall swearde" (✠ 3ʳ). According to Bernardino Ochino, "the sworde of the spirite, that is the worde of god" is the king's chief weapon in conflict with the papacy (*Tragoedie*, 2C2ᵛ; see 2C5ʳ). For William Baldwin, Protestant ministers are the "true and faythful prechers whiche holde the sweard of the spirit, able to confound therewith what so ever doctrine of man . . ." (*Canticles*, e3ʳ). With such armament, Crowley's ideal King moves into action at the conclusion of *Philargyrie of Greate Britayne*:

> Wyth that the Kynge
> For feare gan sprynge
> Unto the Bible boke
> And by and by
> Ryght reverently
> That swerde in hand he toke
> (ll. 1379-84)[29]

Portraits of Edward VI conflate the Reformation *topos* of the Sword and the Book with the conventional image from the king's great seal. Walter Lynne illustrated Cranmer's *Catechism* with a fine woodcut of the king with his sword of justice conferring the Bible on the bishops at his right hand (A1ᵛ). In imitation of Holbein's 1535 woodcut, the artist carved the magistrates kneeling at the left and set the royal arms into the base of the picture. John Day combined this conventional type-scene with the imagery of the dedication portrait in the historiated initial E that he commissioned for his 1551 folio edition of Becke's version of

---

[29] Ed. John N. King, *ELR*, 10 (1980), 46-75.

the Bible (Figure 15; compare Figures 2, 5-6). Day reused the same initial at the beginning of Foxe's account of Edward's reign in the first edition of *Actes and Monuments* (p. 684). Showing the king among his councilors, the capital furnished the germ for the compartment entitled "King Edward delivering the Bible to the Prelates" in the allegorical woodcut that replaced it in the second edition (Figure 19).

An open Bible is at the center of an allegorical painting of the English Reformation (Figure 12). The anonymous work was probably painted under court auspices, for it descends from the royal portrait series and contains identifiable portraits of members of the Privy Council. The relaxation of Edward's figure contrasts with the stiff formality of his public portraits. By pointing at his son from his deathbed, Henry VIII endorses the progress of reform. Seymour stands at the king's side in a position more exalted than that of the seven seated councilors including Dudley, Cranmer, Cuthbert Tunstall, and John, Lord Russell. A window in the upper right corner reveals iconoclasts smashing images and toppling a statue of the Virgin and Child. Roy Strong rightly interprets the scene as an apotheosis of the new regime. But in discovering a "note of irony" in Henry's approval, he ignores a major theme of Protestant apologetics written under both Henry and Edward.[30] Irony there may be, but it was a conventional element in reformist propaganda of the time. Seymour and Cranmer wrapped their reforms in Henry's authority. The probable allusion to Rome as the Fallen Babylon in the smoldering ruins of the inset pinpoints 21 February 1548

[30] National Portrait Gallery, No. 4165. "Edward VI and the Pope: A Tudor Anti-Papal Allegory and Its Setting," *Journal of the Warburg and Courtauld Institutes*, 23 (1960), 311-13.

as the *terminus a quo* for the work. Seymour's fall on 10 October 1549 gives the *terminus ad quem*.

The scene symbolizes the victory of the English Bible over the nonscriptural practices of the papacy. With its inscription "THE WORDE OF THE LORDE ENDURETH FOR EVER," the Bible embodies the immutability of divine revelation. The text on the pope's alb, "ALL FLESHE IS GRASSE" (Isaiah 40:6), links him to the mutability of the material world. The tiara toppling from his head carries bands reading "IDOLATRY" and "SUPERSTICION." Diametrically across from the open window, the flight of two tonsured friars dramatizes the expulsion of Roman practices. The vertical axis of the painting runs from the royal arms above the throne through the Bible to the fallen pope. Thus scriptural truth upholds royal government as it crushes down the old religion. The three startled councilors, including the tonsured Tunstall, who are on the same level as the pope, apparently represent members of the conservative faction that the Protestants defeated at court.

The victory of crown and gospel over tiara was a familiar theme in Tudor iconography. Strong cites three variations of this motif among pictures in Henry VIII's collection. John Day incorporated many variations into the editions of Foxe's martyrology. The initial C in the dedication depicts a crowned Queen Elizabeth seated on her throne with sword and orb. Flanked by three attendants, she surmounts the toppled pope, who is entwined with a serpent in the border beneath her feet. A large woodcut in the 1570 edition depicts Henry VIII treading on Clement VII as he holds his sword in one hand and confers the Bible on Cranmer with the other (p. 1201). Clement's death in 1534 links this scene to the actions of the Reformation Parliament. Such tableaux invert the medieval ascendancy of ecclesiastical authority over temporal power (see Yates, pp. 57-58). They contradict such woodcuts as the portrayal of Pope Alexander III treading on the neck of Emperor Frederick Barbarossa (*A & M* [1563], p. 40). At the end of the first volume of the 1570 edition, Day includes a formal series of twelve large woodcuts entitled "The Image of the true Catholicke Church of Christ," with the subtitle "The proud primacie of Popes paynted out in Tables. . . ." The first woodcut shows a crowned Roman emperor, seated on his throne and holding a sword, persecuting "good Bishops" and other primitive Christians. The embracing of Christian bishops by Emperor Constantine, who wears the same imperial regalia, demonstrates the proper subordination of ecclesiastical authority. The following scenes portray the progressive deterioration of the relationship between the two powers: emperors kissing the feet of popes; Pope Celestinus IV crowning Emperor Henry VI with his feet; Henry IV going to Canossa in order to surrender his crown to the pope; King John giving the crown to the papal legate Pandulphus; the disgrace of Frederick I for holding the papal stirrup on the wrong side; a pope riding on horseback led by an emperor with kings going before; and a pope carried in a procession led by kings and emperors. Stage scenes featuring the pope stepping on kings and emperors as his footstool demonstrate the influence of this motif on Elizabethan drama. Marlowe dramatizes the Reformation conflict thus in the Vatican scene in *Doctor Faustus*. Tamburlaine's ascension to his throne on the back of Bajazeth maintains the idolatrous implications of the typescene. As the Scourge of God, Tamburlaine is a variant of the papal Antichrist.

The title-page woodcut of Walter Lynne's *The Beginning and Endynge of All Popery* (c. 1548) recapitulates the allegory of Edward VI and the Pope (Figure 11). The Tetragrammaton replaces the king and royal arms. As the embodiment of "the spirit of his mouth," a dove flies down the single ray of light that pierces the opaque clouds veiling the heavens. Symbolic of the Holy Spirit, this image portrays the Logos (John 1:32) as the sole means of reuniting the planes of nature and grace. The dove similarly appears over the king's head as an emblem for royal inspiration in the pen drawing of Edward that illuminates the initial E of a royal charter (Bodl. MS Morrell 5). In Lynne's woodcut foreshortening emphasizes the figure of the pope, who loses his tiara and falls from his richly caparisoned donkey beneath the power of the dove. With its procession of mitered bishops, tonsured friars, and other palm-bearing clerics, the tableau parodies the simplicity of Christ's donkey ride into Jerusalem on Palm Sunday. These associations suggest a connection with Cranmer's ban on the use of palms on Palm Sunday 1548. A great gulf separates this ritualistic procession from the hilled city in the upper left, the Heavenly Jerusalem. Identified with the Fallen Babylon or the Augustinian City of Man, the complicated detail of papal vanity contradicts the plain simplicity of the Word. The scene sets forth the prophecy of the Day of the Lord: "And then shall that wicked be uttered [*sic*], whom the lord shal consume with the sprete of his mouth, and shal destroy with the apperaunce of his comynge, even him whose comming is after the workinge of Sathan" (2 Thessalonians 2:8-9). Lynne designed the illustration to fit this text as an autonomous biblical emblem. His dedication applies the millenarian text to the *renovatio mundi* under Edward VI, who will "use the sword to . . . [him] committed" in order to clear away vestigial Catholic practices (A3ᵛ).

Lynne translated his text from Andreas Osiander's German rendition of *Vaticinia de summis pontificibus*, an apocryphal work attributed to Joachim de Fiore (c. 1135-1202).[31] Summoned to an interview with Richard Lionheart because of his reputation as a prophet, Joachim made the famous statement that Antichrist had already been born in Rome ("Romae iam diu fuisse natum"). As the first to equate the pope with Antichrist, Joachim, along with the pseudepigraphous prophecies attributed to him, was the favorite authority during the Reformation. During the late Middle Ages and Renaissance, he came to be associated with the prophecies of Merlin and the Sybilline oracles as well as with Imperial claims against the papacy. He revolutionized the interpretation of Revelation by reading it as a continuous description of human history that is divided into the Old Testament era of the Father, the New Testament era of Christ, and the last era of the Holy Spirit. The beginning of the last era (c. 1260) would coincide with the temporal ascendancy of Antichrist.

What is new to Joachim's reading is the radical historicity of the last age, during which victory over Antichrist should be fulfilled in the temporal world. Joachimist prophecies attached great importance to determining the exact point at which history turned into prophecy. The Last Emperor would govern then in an age of prosperity and peace. Joachimist sources lie behind the Protestant shift toward a more optimistic interpretation of Revelation as a prophecy of a millennial kingdom that would be fulfilled in this world by a renewal of the pure faith of the primitive church.[32] Among English reformers, John Bale was

[31] *Eyn Wunderliche Weyssagung von dem Babstumb wie es yhm biss an das endt der welt* (Nuremberg, 1527).

[32] See Marjorie Reeves, *The Influence of Prophecy in the Later Middle Ages: A Study in Joachimism* (Oxford, 1969), pp. 6-7, 84, 96, 105-107, 453-62, 501-502, and passim, and her "Joachimist Influences on the Idea of a Last World Emperor," in *Joachim of Fiore in Christian Thought,* ed.

most influenced by Joachimist traditions. *The Image of Both Churches*, for example, applies the Joachimist interpretation of Revelation to ecclesiastical history. In an entry for A.D. 1191 in *Actes of Englysh Votaryes*, Bale directs against the monks a passage entitled "Antichrist detected, by Joachim Abbas":

> . . . he [Richard] axed [asked] hym of Antichrist, what tyme and in what place he shulde chefely apere. Antichrist (sayth he) is already borne in the cytie of Rome, and wyll set hym selfe yet hyghar in the seat Apostolycke. I thought (sayd the king) that he shuld have bene borne in Antyoche or in Babylon. . . . Not so (sayth Joachim) . . . and him shall God destroye with the sprete of hys mouth, and lyghte of his commynge. (ii, 04^v-5^r)

Bale alludes to the Joachimist application of 2 Thessalonians that influenced Lynne's emblematic woodcut. The Joachimist extracts that Bale appended to his life of Sir John Oldcastle set the suffering of the Lollard martyr in an apocalyptic context (see Firth, p. 49).

Osiander transformed *Joachini abbatis Vaticinia circa Apostolicos viros & Eccle[siam]. Roman[or]um* (Bologna, 1515) into a Reformation emblem book. He discovered copies in the library of the Carthusian monastery and Ratsbibliothek in Nuremberg. The Latin text consists of an annotated series of woodcuts descended from the much finer illuminations in medieval manuscripts (see MS Harley 1340). He adapted a set of even cruder woodcuts copied from the

---

D. C. West (New York, 1975; 2 vols.), II, 511-58; Ernest L. Tuveson, *Millennium and Utopia: A Study in the Background of the Idea of Progress* (Berkeley and Los Angeles, 1949), pp. 19-20; R. Freyhan, "Joachism and the English Apocalypse," *Journal of the Warburg and Courtauld Institutes*, 18 (1955), 212; and Norman Cohn, *The Pursuit of the Millennium* (1957), p. 15.

Bologna edition by adding an antipapal commentary.[33] Lynne's patron Thomas Cranmer had married Osiander's daughter and remained in close contact with German reformers. Perhaps Cranmer supplied Osiander's text to Lynne or requested its translation. Because Lynne's artist cut his blocks exactly as he saw the German woodcuts, the fifteen printed illustrations from the longer *Vaticinia* series contain identical poses that are consistently reversed. Lynne commissioned his title-page woodcut as an addition to the series.

Lynne dedicated the text to Edward VI and Seymour with the argument that the antiquity and conventionality of the *Vaticinia* series lend it authority lacking in Catholic devotional images. Because they had been preserved in "auncient libraries" for more than three hundred years, the prophetic pictures date back to the beginning of the Age of the Holy Spirit. They claim spiritual authority derived directly from the apostolic church. According to Lynne's preface, the "fathers of auncient tyme" employed esoteric symbolism in order to protect their knowledge about the late medieval papacy until God ordained that the truth be declared in "wrytynge and wordes." By its very nature, therefore, *Beginning and Endynge* is considered to be a providential text. The illustrations are incomplete reflections of divine archetypes. Lynne's exposition and biblical texts complete their meaning and

> . . . prove the thinges that they represente, to be true, so that these figures may appeare rather to be the figures of some Apocalipsis or revelacion, then the invencion of any man. (A3^{r-v})

The woodcut sequence prophesies the rise and fall of papal power by means of royal iconography, beast im-

[33] Roland Bainton, *Studies on the Reformation* (1963), pp. 62-66.

agery, and scriptural allusions. With a scepter representing usurped political power, the pope initially vanquishes the crowned eagle of imperial Rome and threatens the monarchs represented by other birds. Although he claims spiritual authority, the pope receives the keys to the earthly kingdom, "that is, power and might," from Satan in a parody of divine revelation (E2^v). In a similar parody of the Revelation image of the Word as the sword from Christ's mouth, the pope attacks the *agnus dei* with a sword issuing from his mouth (compare Figure 9). The figure of the pope standing on the imperial crown beside a sword-bearing wolf inverts the imagery of the painting of Edward VI and the Pope. In a complicated inversion of the gospel imagery of Christ as both Good Shepherd and Lamb of God, the wolf is a traditional symbol for corrupt pastors who attack the flock they are sworn to protect.[34] Pictures of the pope's closed book reverse the Revelation image of the unsealed book. Eventually the unicorn, an emblem of British royalty, thrusts the tiara from the pope's head. Temporal power, by which Satan conferred papal authority, supplies the sole means of reasserting legitimate government.

Lynne inserted the Day of the Lord woodcut into his amended issue of Bernardino Ochino's *A Tragoedie or Dialoge of the Unjuste Usurped Primacie of the Bishop of Rome, and of all the just abolishyng of the same* (1549). By setting the identical biblical text in the compartment, Lynne links the later work to *The Beginning and Endynge of All Popery*. According to his dedication to the *Tragoedie*, Ochino intends to portray "the beginnynge of thys theyr Papacie, and howe it encreased" (A2^r) prior to the papal defeat by Edward VI. Like all of Lynne's publications, the book

[34] See Chaucer, *General Prologue*, ll. 512-13; Spenser, *The Shepheardes Calender*, May, l. 127; and Milton, "Lycidas," ll. 114-15, 128.

appeared under Cranmer auspices. The archbishop's chaplain John Ponet translated Ochino's lost Latin manuscript. It is the only fictional work of the time to include Cranmer as a literary character. Appearing in the same scene with Henry VIII and Papista, a personification of the Catholic clergy, Cranmer cites the Day of the Lord prophecy (2 Thessalonians 2:8-9) and other apocalyptic texts in support of Joachim's assertion that Antichrist had already appeared in Rome (dialogue 8).

Born in Siena in 1487, Ochino had gained a reputation as Italy's foremost preacher. A member of the strict order of the Observant Franciscans, he transferred to the more austere Capuchins and became their vicar-general. After fleeing to Geneva in 1542, he proceeded to England in 1547.[35] As one of the Protestant exiles who came to England at Cranmer's invitation, Ochino received a nonresident prebendary at Canterbury Cathedral and resided in Lambeth Palace at the time that he completed *Tragoedie*. His co-residents included Latimer, Ponet, and Continental theologians involved in preparation of the prayer book. He received a crown annuity of one hundred marks. The dedication copy of *Tragoedie* that Ochino presented to the king (B.L. C.37.e.23; second issue) carries the inscription "Gwalter Lynne" in a sixteenth-century hand on the inside back cover.[36]

---

[35] Unlike that of his fellow Edwardian immigrant Peter Martyr Vermigli, Ochino's flight caused scandal throughout Italy. His apostasy followed increasingly evangelical sermons that apparently preached the doctrine of justification by faith. See Philip McNair, *Peter Martyr in Italy* (Oxford, 1967), pp. xxi, 32-39, 277-83.

[36] The tooling of the intact, original leather covers is not by the royal binder. Gold tooling at the four corners and the Tudor rose ensigned with a crown are superimposed on the original blind tooling. Lynne probably had a text from his own book stock redecorated as a dedication copy for Edward VI.

As an apotheosis of Seymour's protectorship, the original issue of *Tragoedie* emerges from the same courtly tradition as the painting of Edward VI and the Pope. The dedication that Edward VI shares with his uncle praises the king as the fulfillment of Joachimist prophecies of the fall of Antichrist. Christ's prophecy praises Seymour's imminent election as a providential agent:

> . . . and he [Edward] shal have a Christian protectour, whom I will use as a meane, and instrumente, and very fyt messenger betwyxte me and the kinge to performe thys my purpose. . . . (Y1^r)

The book was in press when Seymour was deposed on 10 October 1549. After his fall Lynne canceled three leaves containing references to "the Lorde Protectour." The new typesetting refers instead to the Privy Council ([–]2, Y1, 2B4). A copy at the British Library (C.25.e.31) contains the rare cancel leaves; references to Seymour in other editions are crossed out by hand. Lynne used his Day of the Lord woodcut to fill a page that the new typesetting left blank (Y1^v).

Lynne did not add the woodcut as mere filler. He could easily have had the printer carry over a few lines of type as a decorative pyramid of text. The illustration would not influence book sales because the reader has to search for its location. He included it because the woodcut fortuitously fits the specific context of the cancellation. It introduces dialogue 8 in which Henry VIII, at the direct inspiration of God's messenger Archangel Gabriel, decides to reform abuses and suppress the religious houses (Y2^r). 2 Thessalonians 2 could apply equally well to the dissolution of the monasteries and the accession of Edward VI. Medieval and Renaissance iconography linked the dove of the Holy Spirit to Gabriel in representations of the Annunciation (Luke

1:26-38). Christ's allusion to the Annunciation in dialogue 7 (X4ᵛ) treats the English Reformation as the renewal of Christ's worldly mission. In a curious involution of traditional iconography, Henry VIII replaces the Virgin Mary as a temporal intercessor between God and his people.

Although Lynne could not have conceived of his densely discursive argument as drama, his title *Tragoedie* has led some critics to classify the work as a play or closet drama.[37] The title instead links the papal fall to Boccaccian *de casibus* tragedy. Ochino divides the work into nine dialogues featuring a variety of biblical, historical, and allegorical figures; he imposes on his materials the same formal pattern that Shakespeare would employ in the history plays. The papal rise via Fortune is paralleled by an equally well-shaped fall. In the pyramidal structure of this *de casibus* narrative, Christ's prophecy of the advent of Edward VI is the geometric climax; the royal triumph complements the tragedy of the papal fall. Ochino thus employs the same comedic pattern as Dante's *Commedia*, for temporal tragedy functions as part of the universal providential comedy.

Particular dialogues function as exemplary scenes in the tragic tale. Set in Rome, the first six dialogues represent the rise of the papacy as a spiritual and temporal power. In dialogue 1, Lucifer describes to Beelzebub his invention of the papacy as his only means of combating Christ's kingdom on earth. Receiving his primacy from Satan rather than Christ in a parody of the apostolic succession, the pope creates an infernal church that leads communicants to hell rather than heaven. Although Dante gained a reputation among reformers as a crypto-Protestant for placing particular popes in the *Inferno*, Luther made the generic identification between the Vatican and hell. Ochino's lit-

[37] Samuel Schoenbaum, *Annals of English Drama: 975-1700: A Second Supplement to the Revised Edition* (Evanston, Ill., 1970), entry for 1549.

erary device became a commonplace of English Protestant tradition through such works as Donne's *Ignatius His Conclave* and Milton's *Paradise Lost* (note the "secret conclave" in Pandaemonium, I.752-98). As the single historical figure in the early dialogues, Boniface III typifies later popes in asserting the claim to primacy that led to the Byzantine Schism (dialogue 2). Conflict between the People of Rome and the Church of Rome personifies the stratification of the medieval church hierarchy (dialogue 3). Among the Roman characters, Man's Judgment would have been the most offensive figure to Ochino's iconoclastic audience. In "fantasizing" biblical sanction for papal claims, the character personifies the replacement of divine will by human invention.

The final dialogues transcend the Roman scenes by setting the English Reformation within the universal context of providential history. In the heavenly setting of dialogue 7, Christ reveals that he has used the pope "as an instrument and servaunt for the larger setting forth of goddes glory" (X3^v). The Protestant doctrine of nonresistance to tyrants, which sees the bad king as the unknowing agent of God, is a corollary to this predestinarian argument. The dramatization of Marlowe's Tamburlaine and Milton's Satan as providential agents is a later variant of this pattern. Like the doctrine of *felix culpa*, the tragedy of the papacy should demonstrate God's ability to bring good out of evil. As an elect "instrument," Henry VIII perceives heavenly inspiration through Gabriel in the form of "a thought entred into oure head, which we bee perswaded commeth of god" (Y2^r). His convocation of bishops, who ponder his doubts about papal authority in their "myndes," exemplifies the intellectual nature of Protestant faith (dialogue 8). In this idealized dialogue of royal counsel, Cranmer unites the

Utopian vision of the perfect commonwealth with Protestant theology.

Prophecy turns into current history in the final dialogue. This conclusion is unique in depicting a reigning Tudor monarch speaking *in propria persona*. Literary convention dictated the generalized representation of living rulers by means of biblical, historical, or allegorical types.[38] Juxtaposition with the words of Christ places Edward's speeches within the providential context of sacred history. His leadership marks the English as an elect nation (Y1v), in contrast to Ochino's personified People of Rome. The Young Josiah attacks the papal Antichrist by means of the conventional weaponry of Edwardian iconography:

> And to dryve him out of the heartes of men it is not nedefull to use sword, nor violence; the sworde of the spirite, that is the worde of god, is sufficient, wherby Christe overcame and conquered his enemy Sathan in the desert. (2C2v)

When the Christian monarch rules by means of the Sword and the Book, the way to the millennial kingdom lies through the court of the temporal king.

[38] Such figures include Henry VIII as either Magnificence or King John in plays by Skelton and Bale, the ideal King in Crowley's *Philargyrie of Greate Britayne*, Mary as Nemesis in *Respublica*, and Elizabeth in *Godly Queen Hester*.

PART II

LITERATURE DURING THE ENGLISH REFORMATION

CHAPTER 5
Poetry and Prophecy

"Ghostly Psalms" and "Bawdy Ballads"

In *An Apology for Poetry*, Sir Philip Sidney defined scriptural poetry as the highest kind of verse:

> The chiefe [poets] both in antiquitie and excellencie were they that did imitate the inconceivable excellencies of GOD. Such were *David* in his Psalmes, *Salomon* in his song of Songs, in his Ecclesiastes, and Proverbs, *Moses* and *Debora* in theyr Hymnes, and the writer of *Job*; which, beside other, the learned *Emanuell Tremelius* and *Franciscus Junius* doe entitle the poeticall part of the Scripture. . . . and this Poesie must be used, by whosoever will follow *S. James* his counsell, in singing Psalmes when they are merry: and I knowe is used with the fruite of comfort by some, when, in sorrowfull pangs of their death-bringing sinnes, they find the consolation of the never-leaving goodnesse.[1]

Although Sidney lamented the scarcity of early Tudor literature, the gospellers had produced metrical versions of most of these books of biblical poetry under Edward VI. Robert Crowley published many of them at his Holborn bookshop. The reformers paraphrased the scriptures for

[1] *Essays*, ed. Smith, I, 158.

publication in collections that generally employed a single, native verse form. They used such staples of popular culture as ballad measure, fourteener couplets, or poulter's measure. The dedications of Thomas Sternhold and Christopher Tye document the fluidity of elite and popular auspices during the Reformation. Their popular ballads and plain style appealed to the king at the same time that they were read by a broad popular audience. The gospellers rejected the imported forms that Wyatt and Surrey introduced at court: the sonnet, ottava rima, and terza rima. When Sidney paraphrased the Psalms in collaboration with his sister Mary, Countess of Pembroke, however, he did so as a sophisticated exercise in varied verse forms that circulated within a narrow coterie.[2] By the end of the sixteenth century, the verse of Tudor courtiers had diverged from its homely origins.

Popular native traditions and conventions constitute both the norm for Reformation poetry and the immediate background for Elizabethan verse. Despite radical differences in style, diction, metrics, and stanza forms, Sidney and the gospellers held in common a Protestant conception of poetry. In contrast to some later Puritans, the mid-century reformers embraced poetry as a powerful vehicle that combines aesthetic pleasure with didactic instruction. Crowley, for example, intended his *Psalter* to move his audience "to delyte in the readynge and hearynge" of poetry (✠✠ 1ᵛ). Sidney repeated this Horatian commonplace in defining "right Poets" as "they which most properly do imitate to teach and delight, and to imitate borrow nothing of what is, hath been, or shall be."[3] Although judgment by Sid-

---

[2] *Poems*, ed. W. A. Ringler, Jr. (Oxford, 1962), pp. 507-508; Hallett Smith, "English Metrical Psalms in the Sixteenth Century and their Literary Significance," *HLQ*, 9 (1946), 268-70.

[3] *Essays*, ed. Smith, I, 159.

ney's standards would define the greater part of Edwardian
poetry as mere versification rather than right poetry (that
is, fiction), Crowley, Baldwin, Luke Shepherd, and a variety of their contemporaries wrote mimetic fiction in addition to scriptural paraphrases.

Court taste was far more eclectic under Edward VI than
during the age of Queen Elizabeth. Italianate and native
modes coexisted in the poetry of the Reformation court.
Not until the 1580s did a gulf widen between the native
tradition of the gospellers and the courtly art of Sidney and
his peers. During the reign of Edward VI, homely traditional verse was written, read, and sung at court and among
all classes of English society. Old-fashioned biblical, moralistic, satirical, and prophetic poetry had greater public
appeal than the Petrarchan love songs of the courtiers.

Gospelling poetry represents a practical application of
ideas that were current in *Paraclesis* and in Protestant biblical commentaries by Bullinger, Jud, and Calvin. The
radical reformers crusaded to purify poetry as one avenue
toward complete reformation. In attempting to cleanse
church and state by applying the scriptures directly to contemporary conditions, they were forerunners of Elizabethan Puritanism. Erasmus inspired the movement with his
call for creation of a body of popular scriptural poetry in
the vernacular so that even the lowliest peasant could sing
Bible songs. In order to encourage universal understanding of the Bible, *Paraclesis* advocates versification of the
scriptures:

> Me thynke it is more unsemely, or rather more folysshe
> maner, that unlerned men & women do mumble up
> theyr Psalmes & Pater noster in Latyn after the maner
> & lykenes of popyngayes, that is to say, nothyng under-
> standyng what it is that they do saye. I beynge of the

same oppynyon & mynde, whiche saynte Hierome was
of, wolde rejoyce so moche the more . . . [if] the
ploughman holdynge the plough dyd synge somwhat of
the mystycall Psalmes in his owne mother tonge. Yea
and yf the wever, syttyng at his worke, dyd synge somwhat of the gospell, for his solace & conforte in his
labours. . . .[4]

The metrical paraphrase of the Pentateuch by William
Samuel, "servaunt to the Duke of Somerset hys grace," is
a good example of the new standard of Protestant taste. In
dedicating *The Abridgemente of Goddes Statutes in Myter*
(1551) to Anne Stanhope, Samuel applies *Paraclesis* to the
current state of English literature:

> My mynd is that I wold have my contrey people able in
> a smale some to syng the hole contents of the byble, &
> where as in tymes past the musicians or mynstrells, were
> wont to syng fained myracles, saints lives, & Robin hode,
> in stede thereof to sing, undoutyd truthes, canonycall
> scryptures, and Gods doynges. . . . Also thys my doyngs
> I trust shall cause the scrypturs, to be often read, as the
> man that hearyth a parte of a story in the scryptures, &
> doth not knowe the hole: thys may move the hole to be
> red. . . . (A2[r-v])

Because they identified poetry with truth, the gospellers
subordinated poetic form and diction to biblical content.
In contrast to the tradition of amplification and accretion
in medieval religious verse, Protestant biblical poetry relied on close literalistic paraphrase of specific texts. The
development of elaborate forms of medieval allegory and
iconography had permitted the inclusion of apocryphal ma-

---

[4] *An Exhortacyon to the Study of the Gospell*, trans. William Roy (1540;
2nd ed.), G2[r-v].

terial in the vast corpus of religious anthems, lyrics, carols, and mystery plays. Foxe therefore criticized Catholics for opposing the singing of gospel verse in church when "they them selves have doone the same before, much more worthy of rebuke, whiche . . . have intermixed their own senses with the wordes of the lord . . ." (*A & M* [1563], p. 1134). The reformers on the other hand reduced divine poetry to a form of exegesis that is either incorporated into the text itself or left to the reader. Densely scriptural thought and style therefore characterizes the verse of such poets as Becon, Bale, Sternhold, and Samuel. They stud their poems with profuse quotations, allusions, and marginal references to scriptural texts. The verse drama of Becon's *Newe Dialog betwene thangell of God, & the Shepherdes in the Felde* (c. 1547), for example, departs from the medieval mystery plays in consisting wholly of close paraphrase of biblical texts.

Hugh Latimer joined Samuel in lumping the traditional folk art of the Robin Hood ballads together with medieval religious verse:

> It is no laughing matter, my friends; it is a weeping matter, a heavy matter; a heavy matter, under the pretense for gathering for Robin Hood, a traitor and a thief, to put out a preacher, to have his office less esteemed, to prefer Robin Hood before the ministration of God's word. (*Sermons*, p. 105)

Latimer's attack, voiced in his sixth Lenten sermon (12 April 1549), forms part of the general Reformation assault on the ballads and popular celebrations associated with Robin Hood's Day (1 May). Robin Hood and *Bevis of Hampton* came under special attack because of their continuing popularity. In *The Scholemaster*, Ascham similarly attacked "certaine bookes of Chevalrie" and the "open mans slaughter, and bold bawdrye" of *Le Morte d'Arthur*.[5]

The plain style and verse forms adopted by the gospellers come from the very same tradition of popular art that they attacked. They employed parody, or the transference of conventions from one genre to another, in order to adapt biblical content to their audience. Similar accommodation of secular techniques to divine purposes had been widespread on the Continent during the previous century. Adaptations of popular airs to profane love songs had also been fashionable at Henry VIII's court. Recognition of the technique of parody, which had not yet acquired exclusively derogatory associations, clarifies the Reformation vogue for ballad measure and the traditional minstrel form of tailed rhyme. Bishop Percy records the analogous "adaptation of solemn church music" in Scotland for satirical purposes:

> . . . at the time of the Reformation, ridiculous and baudy songs were composed by the rabble to the tunes of the most favourite hymns in the Latin service. *Greene sleeves and pudding pies* (designed to ridicule the popish clergy) is said to have been one of these metamorphosed hymns: *Maggy Lauder* was another: *John Anderson my jo* was a third.[6]

The plainness of gospelling verse derives from the same tradition as the *sermo humilis* employed by St. Jerome and

---

[5] I2^r. The reformers adopted charges familiar from medieval works like *Dives and Pauper* and *Piers Plowman*. See R. P. Adams, "Bold Bawdry and Open Manslaughter: The English New Humanist Attack on the Medieval Romance," *HLQ*, 23 (1959), 33-48.

[6] *Reliques*, II, ii, preface to Ballad 2. See Rosamund Tuve, "Sacred 'Parody' of Love Poetry, and Herbert," *Studies in the Renaissance*, 8 (1961), 250-51, 254-55.

Thomas Cranmer. L. B. Campbell attempts to locate the origins of English divine poetry in Savonarola's effort to supplant the profane songs of the Medici with his *Laudi Spirituali*, as well as in the metrical Psalms that Clément Marot wrote for the court of François Ier.[7] Yet she ignores patristic sources read by Crowley and his contemporaries. The antecedents of the gospelling movement instead go back at least as far as the fourth-century hymns of St. Ambrose, who parodied secular lyrics in order to keep the attention of his Milan congregation. St. Augustine explained that the Fathers introduced the singing of Psalms and hymns "lest the people waste away through the tedium of grief."[8] The simplicity of Ambrosian meter (iambic dimeter) made it especially popular. Marot's Psalms, on the other hand, were complex courtly exercises in the manner later practiced by Sidney. During the Carolingian *renovatio*, a school of Medieval Latin poets adapted Virgilian diction and hexameter verse to Christian purposes.[9]

This impulse to create a Christian alternative to pagan poetry reappeared in the earliest surviving English vernacular verse. According to Bede, the Anglo-Saxon maker Caedmon parodied the conventions and meter of Old English heroic verse in his Bible songs (*Historia ecclesiastica gentis Anglorum*, IV. 24). During the Reformation, the English still accepted the traditional attribution to Caedmon of the alliterative *Genesis* and *Exodus*. Through their studies in medieval English and Latin sources, Leland, Bale, Foxe, and Crowley discovered Anglo-Saxon prece-

---

[7] *Divine Poetry*, pp. 12, 37-38.

[8] "tunc hymni et psalmi ut canerentur . . . ne populus maeroris taedio contabesceret, institutum est" (*Confessionum*, IX. 7).

[9] F.J.E. Raby, *A History of Christian-Latin Poetry from the Beginnings to the Close of the Middle Ages* (Oxford, 1927), pp. 32-35, 154-201, passim.

dents for Protestant poetry. Bale, for example, commends Caedmon for producing "psalm-like songs" that were filled with "sweet feeling." He also praises Alfred the Great as the ideal king, poet, and priest for translating the Psalms into Anglo-Saxon verse.[10]

Only a handful of traditional religious poems survive from Edward's reign. The versified *Life of Christ* by the conservative curate Robert Parkyn exemplifies the kind of verse that the gospellers deplored. Parkyn's extensive paraphrase of the gospels, which was intended for public reading in church, is superficially similar to Protestant poetry. Yet he continues to incorporate legendary and apocryphal materials as well as the exegeses of patristic and medieval commentators.[11] According to the author's own account, *The Assault of the Sacrament of the Altar* (1554) was "written in the yere of oure Lorde 1549. By Myles Huggarde, and dedicated to the Quenes most excellent majestie, beyng then ladie Marie." Crowley's attack on Hogarde and the general tenor of Edward's reign prevented publication at that time. Hogarde's puzzling allegory resists interpretation until the arrival of an old man who explains such allegorical figures as the Ark, Manna, Egypt, Pharaoh, and Moses as references to the Church, the sacrament, sin, the devil, and Christ (A3^r-B1^v). The superior knowledge of this priestly figure personifies conservative opposition to the Protestant doctrine of the priesthood of all believers.

---

[10] "Ex inhabitante ergo Dei spiritu, Cedmonus instar psalmorum protulit cantica quaedam, suavi compunctione plenissima . . ." (*Catalogus*, I, 76). Concerning Alfred, see *Summarium*, R1^r-2^r, and *Catalogus*, I, 125-26. Bruce Mitchell of St. Edmund Hall, Oxford, argues that the Anglo-Saxon Psalms are too crude to have been Alfred's work.

[11] Bodl. MS Eng. poet. e. 59 (composed between 1548 and 1554). See Dickens, *Reformation*, p. 21 et seq., and "Robert Parkyn's Life of Christ," *Bodleian Library Record*, 4 (1952), 67-76.

The lost original of Hogarde's ballad "The Abuse of the Blessed Sacrament" (c. 1548) survives only because Crowley quoted it *in extenso* in the *Confutation* that he directed against the author. The silence imposed on the Catholics is the subject of "Little John Nobody" (composed c. 1550), a popular ballad with a refrain lamenting that its narrator is "little John Nobody, that durst not speak."[12] The ballads in a Marian miscellany (Bodl. MS Ashmole 48), however, document the survival of old oral traditions that the Protestants could not suppress.

Gospelling poetry flourished in aristocratic circles. Thomas Sternhold dedicated his metrical Psalms to his royal patron. According to Sternhold, Edward VI preferred to hear these songs within the privy chamber instead of the carols and love lyrics favored at his father's court:

> Seyng furdre that youre tender and godlye zeale doeth more delyght in the holy songes of veritie than in any fayned rymes of vanitie, I am encouraged to travayle furdre in the sayed boke of psalmes, trustyng that as your grace taketh pleasure to hear them song sumtimes of me, so ye wil also delight not onely to see & read them your selfe, but also to commaund them to be song to you of others, that as ye have the Psalme it selfe in youre mynde, so ye may judge myne endevoure by your eare.[13]

Although Coverdale's *Goostly Psalmes* (c. 1535) and Becon's *Davids Harpe* (1542) had appeared surreptitiously under Henry VIII, Sternhold's version initiated the Edwardian vogue for paraphrasing the scriptures in ballad measure. The fad first took hold at court, where Sternhold

[12] Percy, *Reliques*, II, ii, Ballad 3.
[13] *Certayne Psalmes* [19] *Chosen out of the Psalter* (c. 1549), A3ʳ.

sang his Psalms many years before publication. Christopher Tye, acknowledging that he produced his metrical *Actes of the Apostles* in imitation of Sternhold, states that he and other courtiers versified Psalms and the books of Kings to Edward's "delyte" (A2^v). Even the Catholic courtier and priest William Forrest used ballad measure in the "godlye Psalmes" that he dedicated to Seymour "Insteade of balades dissonaunte and light." Forrest's posthumous praise of Sternhold speaks of the high esteem in which he was held at court (MS Royal 17 A. XXI, fol. 1^{r-v}). William Hunnis, another member of the Chapel Royal, issued *Certayne Psalmes Drawen into English Meter* (1550) with a dedication to Sir William Herbert, later Earl of Pembroke. Crowley's collaborator Francis Seager dedicated *Certayne Psalmes Select out of the Psalter of David* (1553) to Francis Russell, son of the Earl of Bedford. Crowley published *Certaine Psalmes in Number 21, with 102 Proverbs* (1550) by his patroness Lady Fane.[14] Bale recorded manuscript versions of the Psalms by Seymour's retainer John Mardeley and by Anthony Cope, Chamberlain to Catherine Parr (*Summarium*, 3N1^v; *Index*, p. 232). William Samuel turned the Pentateuch into fourteener couplets (a variant of ballad measure) during service to Seymour.

The effort to publish Protestant poetry also emanated from the court. The popularity of biblical poetry in the Sternhold tradition documents the catholicity of aristocratic taste under Edward VI. Appearing in more than five hundred editions during the next century, the "old version" of the Psalms by Sternhold and Hopkins became the most familiar collection of English verse during the sixteenth and seventeenth centuries. Sternhold soon gained a

[14] Andrew Maunsell lists this lost octavo in *Catalogue of English Printed Bookes* (1595; 2 pts.), i, fol. 85^r.

reputation as a Protestant authority. Shortly after Whitchurch first published *Certayne Psalmes*, John Case chose the following title for a manuscript that he edited: *Certayne Chapters of the Proverbes of Salomon Drawen into Metre by Thomas Sterneholde* (1549-50). Case must have made the attribution in part because it would help book sales:

> The copye of thys boke was delivered me by a frende of myne beynge sometyme servaunte unto maister Thomas Sterneholde, whereby it is to be conjectured, that the same were putte in metre by hym, yet not so perfectly perused, by reason of sodaine deathe, as perchaunce he would have done, if he hadde longer lyved. (A2ᵛ)

The court connection would have helped to advertise the text. John Hall claimed these ballads as his own work on the title page of *Certayne Chapters Taken out of the Proverbes of Salomon* (1550). The inclusion of Surrey's paraphrases of Ecclesiastes 1-3 and Psalm 88 in the Case edition establishes a concrete link between the Whitchurch press and aristocratic circles, for Case must have had either direct or indirect access to copies of the poems in a courtly miscellany (B.L. MS Add. 36529).[15] Publication of Bale's version of Psalm 13 as part of Princess Elizabeth's translation of *Godly Medytacyon* lent her royal authority to this kind of poetry.

Both as poet and bookseller, Robert Crowley was at the center of the gospelling movement. At roughly the same time that Whitchurch published the first Sternhold edition, Crowley issued his complete *Psalter* (20 September 1549) in ballad measure. The text anticipates the extraordinary success of *The Whole Book of Psalms*. Even though Stern-

---

[15] Ruth Hughey, *John Harington of Stepney* (Columbus, Ohio, 1971), p. 21. Hereafter cited as *Harington*.

hold swamped Crowley's psalter, the two poets simultane-
ously chose fourteeners as their medium (each couplet contains a ballad stanza). Although one cannot determine the
order in which the Sternhold and Crowley versions appeared, comparison of texts and sources shows that Crowley made his translation independently of all other versions
of the English Psalms.

Crowley's publication of biblical poetry by William
Samuel and Lady Fane links him to the Seymour circle.
Crowley shared the insistence of Pore Shakerlaye, one of
his authors, that the Bible should be heard as popular song.
Although Shakerlaye feared comparison with Surrey's paraphrases of Ecclesiastes, he proceeded with his own version
"how be it not so fynely as many other can." Despite its
crudity, Shakerlaye's short measure is a musical form: "the
chapters be devidyed so, that thou mayste syng, or cause
them to be songe to anye instrument, and but that there
are manye beter therin then I, I wold have set notes to
every one of them."[16] Crowley's publication of Shakerlaye's text on behalf of John Case, who had recently published Surrey's Ecclesiastes, is another proof of the general
continuity between aristocratic and popular poetry during
Edward's reign.

By stating most fully the critical attitudes that inform
many other selections of gospelling verse, Crowley's *Psalter* functions as a manifesto on the nature and purpose of
Protestant poetry. The text exemplifies divine poetry of the
time through its purpose of moving the reader "to delyte
in the readynge and hearynge of these Psalmes, wherin
lyeth hyd the most precious treasure of the christian religion" (✠✠ 1ᵛ-2ʳ). Such poetry should be a means of sanctification because of its identification with prophecy. Crow-

---

[16] *The Knoledge of Good and Ivyle, Other Wyse Calyd Ecclesiastes* (1551),
A1ᵛ-2ᵛ.

ley would have read that King David was both poet and priest in Heinrich Bullinger's preface to the *Biblia Sacrosancta* (β4ᵛ). Crowley himself described "Holye David" as "boeth propheth [*sic*] and kinge" in *One and Thyrtie Epigrammes* (D1ʳ). Sidney similarly conceived of the poet as a prophet: "And may not I presume a little further, to shew the reasonableness of this word *Vates*? And say that the holy *Davids* Psalmes are a divine Poem? . . . his handeling his prophecy . . . is meerely poetical."[17] These prophetic associations confer both a public and private aspect upon the *Psalter*. In the course of congregational song, individuals were expected to apply the texts to their own personal circumstances.

Unlike the other gospellers, who paraphrased selections from the English Bible, Crowley made his own translation. His primary goal was to translate the Psalms accurately into intelligible English verse: "And so far as my knowledge woulde serve me: I have made open and playne, that whiche in other translations, is obscure & harde. Trustynge some better learned, wyll hereat take occasion to adde more lyght" (✠✠ 2ʳ). Although he knew no Hebrew and ignored the Vulgate, Crowley, like any educated man, realized the shortcomings of Coverdale's revision of Tyndale's translation. In working exclusively from the *Biblia Sacrosancta*, the Latin translation of the Bible from the original Greek and Hebrew texts by Leo Jud and his Swiss colleagues, he chose the most accurate translation then available (✠✠ 2ʳ).

Crowley planned the *Psalter* as a popular collection of sacred poetry. Although it is difficult to conceive of his mechanically iambic fourteeners as popular verse, their very simplicity and regularity would have appealed to the popular Tudor taste for poetry with an insistent rhyme and

---

[17] *Essays*, ed. Smith, I, 154-55.

emphatic beat. Lacking Shakerlaye's modesty about his talents as a musician, Crowley included a simple tune in four parts, the earliest music for the English metrical Psalms;[18] the tune has direct links to the Gregorian reciting tones of the Medieval Latin Sarum tradition. Printing in red and black links the volume visually to the manuscript and printed psalters of the Sarum use. This example of two-color is almost unique in Reformation book production.

Crowley's simple, vertical, note-for-note block harmony is closely linked to Cranmer's liturgical reforms (see Appendix IV). He manifestly intended his Psalms to be sung as part of the new English service, for he concludes the volume with an appendix containing "all the canticles that are usually songe in the church"; translated into fourteeners, these verses are to be sung to the same music as the Psalms (✠•✠ 1ᵛ, 2T2ʳ-2U4ᵛ). The Royal Injunctions of 14 April 1548 ordered the limitation of church song to scriptural texts in English instead of Latin "Anthemes off our lady or other saynts." Cranmer rejected the rich tradition of Latin hymnody that had evolved by the end of the Middle Ages when, on the eve of the Reformation, elaborately polyphonic song had become the preserve of the clergy and choir who sang in procession behind the rood screen in a language incomprehensible to the laity. Crowley followed Cranmer's stipulation that only one note be allotted to each syllable so that the Psalms would be sung simply and with full understanding.[19] The *Psalter* therefore functions as a musical analogue to Edwardian icono-

---

[18] ✠•✠ 2ᵛ-3ʳ. Crowley's tune is printed in *Grove's Dictionary of Music and Musicians*, 5th ed., ed. E. Blom (1954), VI, 958.

[19] Henry Bradshaw and Christopher Wordsworth, eds., *Statutes of Lincoln Cathedral*, II (1897), 592, as quoted in Gustave Reese, *Music in the Renaissance* (1954), pp. 795-96. Ann Scott of Bates College generously advised on musicology.

clasm. Although singing all one hundred fifty Psalms to the same tune would now seem unbearably tedious, simply to sing them in English verse would have been a refreshing novelty during Edward's reign. The plainness of Crowley's music reflects the intellectuality of early Protestant tradition and its suspicion of sensational art forms.

According to Crowley such song could only confer "more delyte of the mynde" (✠ 1ʳ). This concept of taking spiritual rather than corporeal pleasure in psalm-singing derived from Calvin, who approved of church song on the authority of "these wordes of Paule, I will syng in Spirite, I will syng also in mynde." Giving warning lest "oure eares be not more hedefully bente to the note, than our myndes to the spiritual sense of the wordes," Calvin noted with approval Athanasius' recommendation "that the reder shoulde sounde hys wordes with so small a booming of hys voice, that it should be liker to one that readeth than to one that singeth."[20] Crowley's *Psalter* returns to the apostolic and patristic practice of congregational singing of the Psalms and canticles in the vernacular. Opposition to vernacular church song outraged John Foxe, who complained that the Catholics "have so wrasted and depraved the same [biblical song], that the thyng which the lord hath set forthe for publique and generall petitions, they have turned to a private request" (*A & M* [1563], p. 1134). Although Tye and Seager followed Crowley by including music in their editions, a standard tune did not appear in Sternhold and Hopkins until the Anglo-Genevan psalter (1556). By 1562 John Day had printed sixty-five tunes in *The Whole Book of Psalmes*.[21]

[20] *Institution of Christian Religion*, trans. Thomas Norton (1561), 2G5ᵛ.

[21] For an overview of the relationship between music and poetry during the English Reformation, see John Stevens, *Music & Poetry in the Early Tudor Court* (1961), pp. 74-97.

A tradition going back to the Restoration declares that Sternhold versified the Psalms as part of a campaign to supplant secular lyrics favored at court:

> . . . he became so scandaliz'd at the amorous and obscene Songs used in the Court, that he forsooth turn'd into English meeter 51 of *Davids Psalms*, and caused musical notes to be set to them, thinking thereby that the Courtiers would sing them instead of their sonnets, but did not, only some few excepted.[22]

Because they accept Anthony à Wood's account as evidence of a court-based attack on traditional love songs, many critics argue that Reformation poetry emerged in opposition to profane love poetry of the time.[23] Nevertheless, Hallett Smith observes that Sternhold's dedication speaks of Edward's fondness for biblical ballads without reference to an effort to wean courtiers away from bawdy poetry. The king's diary records his lute playing in the context of festivities where Bible songs would have been inappropriate. Christopher Tye denies that he attacks the "ynkhorne termes" and "pleasaunt style" of courtly poetry; such aureation is simply unsuitable to the plain truth of the scriptures (*Actes*, A3ʳ). Although Tye defined a standard that embraced love poetry and gospelling verse as distinct Reformation genres, Wood applied the anachronistic limits of neoclassical decorum to the eclectic taste of the Edwardian court.

The complexity of courtly tradition encompassed secular love lyrics as well as satires that mocked the same lyrics as foolish objects. John of Salisbury had satirized the love songs of courtier poets as early as the twelfth century,[24] but his condemnation of courtly folly anticipated Tye's distinc-

---

[22] *Athen. Oxon.* (1691), I, col. 62.

[23] See Campbell, *Divine Poetry*, pp. 41-42.

[24] Heiserman, *Skelton and Satire*, p. 28.

tion between the right and wrong use of verse. Wyatt's attack on courtiers who honor "Venus and Bacchus all their life long" in "Mine Own John Poyntz" (l. 23)[25] complemented his Petrarchan love songs. Both Boccaccio and Chaucer followed the bawdy *fabliaux* of the *Decameron* and *Canterbury Tales* with retractions that were dictated as much by rhetorical convention as by any notion of personal confession. Seymour possessed an illuminated manuscript of the *Decameron* at the same time that he housed gospellers like Thomas Becon. Although in *Davids Harpe* Becon advocated the cultivation of divine poetry and the suppression of secular literature, one cannot infer that he therefore determined his patron's taste.

Although love poetry was acceptable at the Reformation court, printed editions did attack such verse. In dedicating his *Canticles or Balades of Salomon* (1549) to Edward VI, William Baldwin justified his paraphrases with the argument that such

> . . . songes myght once drive out of office the baudy balades of lecherous love that commonly are indited and song of idle courtyers in princes and noble mens houses. They are not fine ynough sum will answer: wel than woulde I wish that such fine felowes would becum course ynough for such course matters. (A3ᵛ)

Yet Baldwin participated in court revels that included *Cupid, Venus, and Mars,* a masque on a traditional theme of profane love (above, p. 180); he included a ribald tale about an adulterous wife and her lover in *Beware the Cat.* Baldwin's serious concern with moralistic verse is not incompatible with occasional bawdry. This would also be the case in *The Faerie Queene,* which encompasses the Protestant

[25] *Collected Poems,* ed. Joost Dalder (1975).

piety of the "Legende of Holinesse" as well as the ribald *fabliau* of Paridel and Hellenore (III.ix-x). A sophisticated humanistic scholar like Baldwin evidently felt comfortable in adapting his works to the rhetorical expectations of different audiences. His dedication to *Canticles* should be read as an advertisement to the devout Protestant clientele that bought such works rather than as a serious critique of court depravity.

Hallett Smith suggests that a confusion of Sternhold and John Hall may account for Anthony à Wood's misjudgment of Reformation court taste. In the preface to his 1550 Proverbs, which disputed Sternhold's claim to authorship, Hall vilified love songs that circulated in the

> . . . court of Venus, or other bokes of lecherous Ballades, the whych have bene a greate occasion to provoke men to the desyre of synne, where as in these workes thou shalt learne to fle from evyl company, from dronckenes & dronkardes, from covetousnes & slouthfulnes, from wrathe and envy, from whoredom & all the subtyle behaviours of whores. . . . (A5ᵛ)

The five Wyatt poems of *The Court of Venus* (c. 1538) mark the first publication from the manuscript miscellanies of the courtly makers. Republication of the text as *A Boke of Ballettes* (c. 1549) and the moralistic arguments of the gospellers prove that such verse flourished during the Reformation. Courtly love poetry remained in continuous fashion between the 1530s and publication of *Songs and Sonnets* in 1557. The third edition of *The Court of Venus* appeared c. 1563. The badly fragmented state of these editions suggests great popularity, which would explain the bitterness of Hall's attack. In a curious historical accident, the text also included *The Pilgrim's Tale*, an anticlerical allegory popular with the radicals. Because of the inclusion of this apocryphal tale, John Bale attributed *The Court of Venus* to Chaucer (*Summarium*, 3D2ʳ).

In a commonplace book dating from the mid-century, Hall parodied two Wyatt lyrics from *The Court of Venus*. He follows Reformation practice in defining parody as the substitution of a new text for a known lyric tune. The sober Hall cannot perceive the genre's potential for burlesque and satire; thus his imitation of "My Lute, Awake" begins

> My lute awake and prayse the lord,
> My heart and handes therto accord:
> Agreing as we have begon,
> To syng out of gods holy worde.
> And so procede tyll we have done.

Hall's "Dittie of the Pen Inveiying Against Usury and False Dealing" adapts the invocation of the thwarted lover in "My Pen, Take Pain a Little Space" to a complaint against the time.[26]

Hall's unsophisticated literalism leads him into serious misreading of Wyatt. The courtly habit of experimentation with varied *personae* eludes him. Although the invocation of "My Lute, Awake" voices the traditional Petrarchan complaint against the cruel mistress, the poem as a whole mocks the game of love with its conventional lute songs. Wyatt's conclusion adapts the elegiac themes of mutability and *de contemptu mundi* to an attack on the mistress. The speaker's vision of the lady's distress in old age may best be read as a critique of the art of courtly love:

---

[26] *The Court of Virtue (1565)*, ed. R. A. Fraser (1961), pp. 169-72, 191-200. Fraser reconstructs *The Court of Venus* (Durham, N.C., 1955) from the three black-letter fragments.

Perchance thee lie withered and old
The winter night that are so cold,
Plaining in vain unto the moon:
Thy wishes then dare not be told.
Care then who list, for I have done.

And then may chance thee to repent
The time that thou hast lost and spent
To cause thy lovers sigh and swoon.
Then shalt thou know beauty but lent,
And wish and want as I have done.

(ll. 26-35)

Although Wyatt's speaker in "They flee from me, that sometime did me seek" avoids the outright hostility of "My Lute, Awake," his melancholy disillusionment reflects an inability to comprehend the faithlessness of his lady:

It was no dream: I lay broad waking.
But all is turned thorough my gentleness
Into a strange fashion of forsaking,
And I have leave to go of her goodness,
And she also to use newfangleness.
But since that I so kindly am served,
I would fain know what she hath deserved.

(ll. 15-21)

The fine ironies of these poems and the ideal of fidelity that they assume are closer to Hall's ideological position than he could ever realize.

The Pleasaunt Playne and Pythye Patheway Leadynge to a Vertues and Honest Lyfe (c. 1552) matches Hall's parodies in its misunderstanding of courtly art. Printed by Nicholas Hill for publication by John Case, the poem has been attributed to Hill's printing assistant Urban Lynyng. Readers would recognize the conventional springtime opening as an imitation of Chaucer's *General Prologue* (ll. 1-18):

"It chaunced that on the eleventh daye, / Of the flory-shynge Moneth, of lustye Maye. . . ." The encounter between the young speaker and a "fayre aged man" derives from medieval debates between Youth and Age. This background sets this prudential warning against the dangers of lust within the context of philosophical complaints against the mutability and corruption of the material world. Unlike Hall and most other gospellers, Lynyng transcends verse complaint and biblical paraphrase by achieving manifest fiction. One cannot reduce the poem to a simple argument for the Protestant ideal of married love.

Lynyng embodies his delicately implicit burlesque of courtly love in a narrative conveying far more humane and subtle morality than the ranting of Hall and Becon; his exemplary technique instead resembles the fourteenth-century moral tales of Robert Mannyng's *Handlyng Synne*. The poem as a whole imitates *The Miller's Tale*, and Lynyng's domestic comedy approximates the spirit of Chaucer's burlesque of courtly love better than the jeremiads of the preacher-poets. The old man's comic account of his youth as a parish clerk who spilled his "holie water bucket" out of lust recaptures the temper of Absolon's courtship in Chaucer's tale. Attracted by his love songs and "minstrelsie," all the "maydes in the parish" gave him the nickname Lusty Lewis. Lynyng's failure to articulate overt anticlerical satire is rare in published Reformation poetry—yet his very ability to distinguish between Chaucer's burlesque and realistic advocacy of lust suggests one reason that early Protestants found the *Canterbury Tales* to their taste. Toward the end of the century, this distinction escaped Sidney when he overlooked Chaucer's major work in favor of *Troilus and Criseyde*.[27]

[27] *Essays*, ed. Smith, I, 196. In *Renaissance Chaucer*, Alice Miskimin neglects both the Chaucer apocrypha and the question of how sixteenth-

The gulf between the clerk's lowly rank and his hyperbolic courtly diction renders his condition absurd. Spurned by fair Grace, "that in bewtie did excell," Lusty Lewis suffers "the crueltie, of cruell Cupido" (C3ᵛ-4ʳ). After many rejections, he sings the following "Ballet" as a final appeal to the sullen village girl:

> Oh my love Grace,
> Your bewtyfull face,
> Hathe perced so my brest,
> Youre countenaunce mylde,
> With youre tonge so wel fylde,
> Is causer of all myne unrest,
>
> Not Troylus of Troye,
> By Cresside hys joye,
> In love was ever so set on fyre,
> Neyther Piramus the younge,
> By the love of Thisby so stronge,
> Or burnte in suche hote desyre,
>
> Neyther Hercules the myghtye,
> By Dianiras bewtye,
> Was at any tyme so overcome,
> Neyther Sampson the stronge,
> With love was so wronge,
> Of Dallida the wicked woman
>
> Neyther that wofull Dido,
> Eneas loved so,
> As I do nowe love you hartely,
> For in good faythe,
> Yt wyll be my deathe,
> Excepte ye extende your mercy.
>
> (E1ʳ)

---

and seventeenth-century editors, authors, and readers interpreted Chaucer texts.

In sinking beneath its allusions to tragic love affairs and the deceits of treacherous ladies, this "ballet" burlesques both the speaker and his song as effectively as John Littlewit's puppet version of Hero and Leander in Jonson's *Bartholomew Fair* (V.iv.112-351). Although his diction is more refined, Lynyng's comic use of language resembles the Chaucerianism of William Dunbar's "In secreit place this hyndir nycht." Grace's stubborn silence typifies the Protestant domestic comedy: "At last hir father bad me good nyghte, / So did hir mother and her syster full ryghte." In a Reformation variant of a popular theme in medieval antifeminist satire, Lusty Lewis eventually marries a "good huswyfe" who is only "indifferente fayre." Grace, on the other hand, reveals her true nature as an "yll hyswyfe" in marriage to a "servynge man." Her marriage is marked by "nothynge but chydynge and stryfe, / Brawlynge and fyghtynge all her longe lyfe." Because of her husband's prodigality, they eventually descend into a life of beggary and "wanderynge" (E1ᵛ). The tale closes on a prudential note familiar from the epigrams of Heywood and Crowley. In contrast to the antifeminist tradition that rose out of the monastic and celibate ideals of the medieval church, Lynyng's moral tale dramatizes the Protestant ideal of married love familiar from the prayer book.

POETS ON TOWER HILL

Reformation courtiers preserved the aristocratic tradition of elite poetry. Schooled in the writings of Quintilian and Cicero, they versified ancient themes of erotic love, secular morality, and religious devotion. When they fell out of favor or faced from a prison cell the prospect of execution, courtiers often turned to poetry for consolation. Their acquaintance with classical rhetoric and Petrarchan love conventions accustomed them to the adoption of *personae* and arguments that need not represent personal feeling. Only Protestant extremists like John Hall charged that all non-scriptural literature contradicted divine revelation; such reformers as Crowley and Baldwin rejected that position. John Bale, for example, praised Wyatt as Chaucer's peer because "he taught the British nobility to compose the most elegant kinds of songs."[28] Both Wyatt and Surrey had written moralistic verse and biblical paraphrases in addition to Italianate love poetry.

Prior to Tottel's publication of *Songs and Sonnets*, Protestant courtiers preserved the most important manuscripts containing love poetry by Wyatt and Surrey. Sir George Blage, who belonged to Puttenham's "new company of courtly makers," compiled a miscellany that is a valuable mirror of court taste during the two decades prior to his death in 1551 (Dublin, Trinity College, MS D. 2. 7). The Blage manuscript records the continuing popularity of Henrician love songs into the age of Sternhold. John Harington the elder compiled a collection containing poems by Wyatt and Surrey as well as Edwardian love lyrics (Arundel Castle, MS Arundel). He also owned a collection containing poems and corrections in Wyatt's own hand (B.L. MS Egerton 2711) and another early miscellany (B.L. MS Add. 36529).[29] At the court of Anne Boleyn, the Devonshire Manuscript (B.L. MS Add. 17492) had circulated between the Protestant Duchess of Richmond and other ladies.

At one time or other almost every Reformation courtier poet found himself in the Tower of London. When *in extremis* they tended to abandon love poetry, and turned to

[28] "Nam es preceptore (ut Lelandus habet) Britannica nobilitas in omni rhithmorum genere carmina nitidissime componere didicit" (*Summarium*, 3N1ᵛ).

[29] *Harington*, pp. 16, 21.

the Bible for consolation. Athanasius supplied a precedent for self-examination through the versification of biblical paradigms: "Whosoever take this booke [the Psalms] in his hande, he reputeth & thinketh all the wordes he readeth (except the wordes of prophecy) to be as his very owne wordes spoken in his own person."[30] Courtiers had for a long time versified the Psalms and wisdom literature as occasional poetry divorced from doctrinal considerations. Their handling of the scriptures during periods of personal distress, especially when they faced death at the headsman's block, led to the emergence of a recognizable mid-Tudor genre of the prison paraphrase. Protestant courtiers adopted the medieval convention of meditation on Psalms 6, 32, 38, 51, 102, 130, and 143 as an act of contrition, a pattern established by St. Augustine when he had copies of these Penitential Psalms hung around his bed where he could read them as he lay dying. During his final imprisonment, Surrey turned Psalms involving themes of mutability, betrayal, and divine providence into poulter's measure; his Ecclesiastes apparently dates from the same period.[31] Unlike Surrey, Wyatt used ottava rima and terza rima in the *VII. Penytentiall Psalmes* that appeared posthumously in 1549. References to betrayal and danger of death relate them to his imprisonment of 1536 or 1541. By adapting Aretino's *Parafrasi* (1534) in his prologues, Wyatt invites the reader to interpret his Psalms as a *de remedia amoris*.[32]

In a manner similar to Wyatt's, Sir Thomas Smith paraphrased Psalms into hexameter couplets as a means of exploring his predicament when he was imprisoned following Seymour's fall (MS Royal 17 A. XVII). Instead of the

---

[30] Matthew Parker, *The Whole Psalter Translated into English Metre* (c. 1567), C1ᵛ.

[31] *Poems*, ed. Emrys Jones (Oxford, 1964), nos. 36-37, 43-50 and notes.

[32] Smith, "Psalms," p. 262.

Penitential Psalms, Smith made a personal selection of texts
that pray for deliverance from tribulation and personal
enemies (Psalms 102, 141, 142, 119, 85, 30, 40, 70, 54,
144, 145; Vulgate numbering). The order in which he
arranged these songs of lamentation enables the reader to
trace the course of his imprisonment from despondency
and prayer for deliverance to hymns of thanksgiving for
salvation. The apparently incongruous choice of ballad
measure for the original poems that the learned classicist
placed at the end of the manuscript may be explained by
the endemic influence of Sternhold's measure. Hobbling
verses from the third ballad (fol. 27^r) treat his dilemma
far more explicitly than the Psalm translations:

This day made men Duke, Marquis, Earle, or Baron
Yet maie the ax, stand next the dore.
Everie thing is not ended, as it is begone
God will have the strok, either after or before.

Is there any thing in this world suer or fast
That death or Injurie can not break
Look but on this yeare, and yeares before past
And wey Gods judgement, and his fearfull wreak.

His patron was imprisoned at the same time that Smith
versified Psalms "in the Tower of London . . . to pas the
tyme there. 1549." (fol. 1^r). Seymour wove verses from
Psalms into the quasi-metrical cento that he inscribed in
his pocket calendar the night before his death (Figure 16;
see above, Chapter 2 at n. 42). Later during the reign of
Queen Mary, Robert Dudley made a vengeful paraphrase
of Psalm 93 out of the Vulgate text. Imprisoned at the
same time, his brother John Dudley, the eldest son of
the Duke of Northumberland, made a similar version of
Psalm 54. Smith had already chosen this text for his Tower

collection. Both Dudley compositions went into the Arundel Manuscript of John Harington, who shared their imprisonment in the Tower.[33]

The gospellers would have objected to the subjective
character of aristocratic paraphrases and to the use of verse
forms lacking in popular appeal. Thus personal confession
did not enter into their prison paraphrases, for they intended their exemplary verses to console the Protestant
reading public. Thomas Becon, for example, published
metrical versions of Psalms 103 and 112 under Queen
Mary "for a thanksgeving unto God immediatly after hys
deliveraunce out of pryson whose emprysonmente began
the .16. daye of August the yeare of oure Lorde 1553, and
ended the .22. of Marche then nexte ensuynge" (*Confortable Epistle*, D5^v-7^v).

As the best mirror of the composition and taste of the
Reformation courtier, the miscellany composed by John
Harington the elder is a major document concerning the
evolution of Tudor poetry. He began the collection c. 1550-
60, and dates of composition for particular poems range
from the last years of Henry VIII until shortly before
Harington's death in 1582. The poems transcribed in a
mid-Tudor secretary hand (Hand A) comprise a coherent
anthology of verse by Harington and his contemporaries.
Although the miscellany contains recensions that are later
than MS Egerton 2711 and MS Add. 17492, its texts are
more authoritative than those in Tottel's *Songs and Sonnets*.
Inheriting the manuscript from his father, Sir John Harington (1561-1612) continued the collection at the end of
the century.[34]

---

[33] *Arundel-Harington Manuscript of Tudor Poetry*, ed. R. Hughey (Columbus, Ohio, 1960; 2 vols.), nos. 289-90. Hereafter cited as *AH*.

[34] See *AH*, introduction and notes, for a description of contents. Ruth

A royal favorite under Henry VIII and Queen Elizabeth, the elder Harington first served the latter during Edward's reign. As a retainer of Thomas Seymour, he was on the periphery of the royal court at that time, but he went to prison in the Tower of London after the younger Seymour fell in early 1549. After her accession, Elizabeth rewarded such figures as Harington, William Cecil, and Nicholas Bacon who had remained loyal to her as princess; they did so at the risk of personal danger when she faced possible execution during her sister's reign. Prior to the establishment of her household at Hatfield, Harington would have known the princess when she lived in the household of Thomas Seymour as the charge of Catherine Parr. Imprisoned for a second time during the aftermath of Wyatt's Rebellion (18 January 1554–c. January 1555), Harington attended the princess during her own imprisonment (18 March–19 May 1554). As the queen's godson, the younger Harington had an unshakeable place as a court wit, which was not seriously endangered by Elizabeth's reputed show of displeasure over his translation of a ribald canto from Ariosto's *Orlando Furioso*.

Harington's Edwardian poems record the continuing fashion for courtly love poetry. He addressed Petrarchan lyrics to Isabella Markham, his future wife, when she attended Princess Elizabeth at Hatfield House (*Harington*, II A 12-14, 19). These poems adapt the paradoxical conventions of baited hooks and Cupid's arrows that Wyatt imported. For example, "To Isabella Markham" dramatizes the condition of the weeping and distraught lover who begs requital from his disdainful lady. In praising six ladies-in-waiting to the princess, Harington turns the kind

---

Hughey edits the complete poems of Harington the elder from *AH*, other manuscripts, and printed texts, with an introductory biography, in *Harington*, pp. 3-81, 85-134.

of elaborate compliment that would become a staple of Elizabethan verse:

> To Markhams, modest mynde
> that Phenixe bird most rare
> So have the godes assynde
> with Gryselde to compare
> Oh, happie twyse is hee
> whome Jove shall do the grace
> to lynck in unytie
> that blissful to enbrace.
> (*Harington*, II A 15, ll. 25-32)

Idealization of chaste love by means of allusion to the patience of "Gryselde" scarcely supports the attacks on court verse made by Hall and Becon. Two other poems in the MS Arundel complement the Markham lyrics in their praise of the Protestant ideal of married love, thus resembling Spenser's *Epithalamion* far more than the Petrarchan complaints of Wyatt and Surrey (*AH*, nos. 269, 283).

Harington collected verse written by his companions in the Tower and other associates, especially ethical poems lamenting the vagaries of Fortune occasioned by the factional intrigues of the time. Their *de casibus* themes correspond to the prevailing mood of the Edwardian court. For example, iambic dimeter lines written by Thomas Seymour seem to have formed part of the conventional death preparation recommended by the *ars moriendi*. According to Bishop Percy, he wrote the verses the "Week before he was beheaded, 1549." Unlike his elder brother, who would shape his deathbed meditation according to scriptural formulas and the Protestant ideals of penitence and martyrdom, Thomas Seymour unrepentantly looks forward to vindication; his bitter complaint anticipates Raleigh's "The Lie." The younger Seymour concludes:

[237]

Then deathe Haste the
thow shalt me gayne
Immortallye
with Hym to raigne

Who send the Kinge
Lyke yeares as Noye
in governing
His Realme in joye

And after this
ffrayle Lyf suche grace
as in His blysse
I may have place
(*AH*, No. 291, ll. 17-28)

These poets all lament their slippery hold on Fortune's wheel. John Astley, a member of Princess Elizabeth's retinue who was implicated in the downfall of Thomas Seymour, wrote an elegy on the mutability of the material world (*AH*, no. 296). George Blage celebrated the death of Thomas Wriothesley (d. 1550) with a sarcastic epitaph. His forceful invective bitterly summarizes the career during which the onetime Lord Chancellor "creapt full highe" in pride "ffrom vyle estate, of base and low degree," only to fall downward into the grave and toward hell (*AH*, no. 295). Harington's poems in the Blage Manuscript, including one holograph text, show that their miscellanies circulated within a coterie that included both Harington and Blage (*Harington*, II A 1-3, and notes). Harington's mock appeal to Gardiner for clemency during his second imprisonment vents similar rage:

A Leven [eleven] months full and longer space
I have endured your deavellishe dryftes
whylest you have sought bothe man and place

[238]

and sett your snares with all your shyftes
the fawtlesse foote to wrapp with wyle
in any guylt by any guyle
and now you see it will not be
how can you thus for shame agree
to kepe hym bownd you ought sett free

(Harington, II A 7, ll. 10-18)

The biting epithets in this poem echo Harington's earlier imputation of perjury on the part of his patron's enemies, who "sought thy free foote in suttle wyles to have snared" *(Harington*, II A 30). They reflect the prayer that God "shuld pluck our feete out of the net" offered by Thomas Smith, whom Harington had come to know in the Tower during his first imprisonment (MS Royal 17 A. XVII, fol. 20^r). After Gardiner's death in 1555, Harington wrote a mock epitaph full of the same ranting rhetoric as Blage's Wriothesley poem.

On a more philosophical level, Harington meditated on the meaning of friendship during his first imprisonment. In dedicating Cicero's *Booke of Freendeship* (1550) to the Duchess of Suffolk, he explains his translation in Boethian terms: "Wherby I tried prisonment of the body, to be the libertee of spirite: adversitee of fortune: the touche stone of freendship, exempcion from the world, to be a contempt of vanitees: and in the ende quietnes of mind, the occasion of study" *(Harington*, p. 137). Praising Thomas Seymour for true friendship and hospitality, Harington's earlier eulogy to his lost patron grieves a death that violates Nature, Reason, and the Laws *(Harington*, II A 10). A related poem mourns the younger Seymour's death in terms that parallel the Duchess of Suffolk's complaint to Cecil against "the commen enfection of feyned frendship" (MS Lansdowne 2, fol. 58^r):

None can deeme righte, whoe Faithfull freendes do rest
whilste they doe Rule, and Raigne in great degree
For than bothe faste, and fained freendes are preste
Whose faithes seeme bothe, of one effect to bee
                    (*Harington*, II A 4, ll. 1-4)

For Harington, the touchstone of true friendship is loyalty
that survives when "welthe unwynde and fortune flee."

Like all of Harington's Tower meditations, "Yf Ryght
be rakt and over Roon" yearns for the quiet life of contemplative withdrawal in contrast to the "Ryches," "Rewll,"
and "Power" that destroy justice and threaten life at court
(*Harington*, II A 1). Harington may also have written "Erst
in Arcadia's londe," a pastoral elegy on Thomas Seymour
that was printed as "The Hospitable Oake" in an eighteenth-century edition of Haringtoniana. Although they are
alien to gospelling poetry, the classical conventions of the
piece were familiar to the humanistic scholars at Edward's
court. The author idealizes the late Lord Admiral's virtues
as a patron by means of an allegorical fable of a friendly
oak tree that shelters nesting birds, sheep, and other helpless creatures. The speaker mocks as sophistical the arguments of those enemies who envy the reputation of the tree
that "did shadowe too much grounde":

> With much despight they aim its overthrow,
>   And sorrie jestes its wonted giftes deride,
> How 'snaring birdlimes made of mistletoe;
>   Nor trust their flocks to shelter 'neath its side;
> It drops chill venom on our ewes, they cry,
> And subtle serpent at its root doth lie.

Despite their success in toppling the tree, Jove himself
announces the apotheosis of his favorite:

> On high Olympus next mine tree I'll place,

Heavn's still unscann'd by sich ungrateful rase.[35]

Harington's moralistic poems develop traditional themes from the Wyatt satires that he read in MS Egerton 2711 and copied into MS Arundel (*AH*, nos. 103, 141, 142). Imprisonment in 1536 or 1541 had occasioned the verse epistles in which Wyatt disassociates himself and his friends John Poyntz and Francis Brian from his censure of life at court. Brian's translation of Antonio Guevara's *Dispraise of the Life of a Courtier* (1548) documents the survival during the Reformation of the satirical tradition of attack on the court. Wyatt's satires resemble his version of the Penitential Psalms (*AH*, nos. 154-67) as vehicles for channeling strong personal feelings concerning the fragility of royal favor and life at court. Harington's praise of the "quyet lief" of rural retirement, with its pleasures of "the contented mynd" (*Harington*, II A 1), derives from the same tradition as the solitary conclusion to Wyatt's "Mine own John Poyntz":

> But here I am in Kent and Christendom
> Among the Muses where I read and rhyme,
> Where if thou list, my Poyntz, for to come,
> Thou shalt be judge how I do spend my time.
>
> (ll. 100-103)

Richard Tottel's *Songs and Sonnets* (1557) is, justifiably, the most famous Tudor verse miscellany. Generally it is approached as an anthology of Henrician court poetry. Nevertheless Wyatt and Surrey contributed less than half of the collection.[36] The volume does represent the first ma-

---

[35] *Harington*, II B 5, ll. 25-30, 35-36. See *Nugae Antiquae*, ed. Henry Harington (1769-75; 2 vols.), I, 93-94. Hughey conjectures that the text may derive from missing folios 189-91 of MS Arundel (*AH*, I, 23).

[36] *Tottel's Miscellany* (1557-1587), ed. Hyder Rollins (Cambridge, Mass., 1965; 2 vols., rev. ed.).

jor published response to the forms and styles of the Continental Renaissance; it juxtaposes foreign modes and techniques, however, with the conventions of native English poetry. Although Sidney knew the work as "the Earle of Surries *Liricks*,"[37] his lavish praise refers to a text that contains verse by Nicholas Grimald, Thomas Vaux, John Heywood, Thomas Norton, and William Gray. They wrote many of their poems during the reign of Edward VI. Even though their pieces may not all be dated with precision, publication within four years of Edward's death enables one to read many poems attributed to Grimald and "Uncertain Authors" as a collection of Reformation courtier poetry. Moral and didactic themes dominate the Edwardian stratum of the miscellany. Humanistic scholarship and classical mythology influence the mid-century poems more than the Italianate models of Wyatt and Surrey affect the same poems.

With forty poems in the first edition, Nicholas Grimald is the major contributor after Wyatt and Surrey. Grimald lectured in rhetoric at Oxford University and eventually became chaplain to Nicholas Ridley. The presence of his verse might seem anomalous in a court anthology, but university scholars came into their own during Edward's reign when they dominated appointments to civil positions at court. *Congratulatorium carmen*, the lost manuscript collection of Latin verse that he presented to Seymour in celebration of his release from the Tower on 6 February 1550, attests to his loyalty to the fallen politician (*Index*, p. 302). He had earlier written an epitaph on Sir James Wilford (no. 156), a close associate of Seymour. Five encomia that he wrote to the Seymour daughters went into Tottel (nos. 139, 142-45). The inclusion of these New Year gifts, the traditional

[37] *Essays*, ed. Smith, I, 196.

acknowledgment of a protégé, suggests that the verses were written after Edward's accession but prior to Grimald's appointment as a preacher in Eccles, Staffordshire c. 1552-53.[38] Grimald's links to the Seymours, the dedicatory poem that he contributed to Turner's *Preservative*, and his important clerical appointments document his contemporary stature as a Reformation courtier. His later reputation as an apostate must have been based on hearsay, because his friend John Bale praises his Christian faith (*Catalogus*, I, 701).

Grimald's neoclassical poems exemplify the taste of the Reformation humanist. In imitation of Theodore Beza's *Poemata* (Paris, 1548), Grimald composed love poems and elegies under Edward; as Calvin's chaplain and continuator of Marot's French psalter, Beza was a sanctioned neoclassical model for the Protestant poet. The complaints in "The Lover to His Dear" and "The Lover Asketh Pardon" (nos. 129-30) incorporate static classical allusions and *exempla* rather than Petrarchan conventions. Their brittle neoclassicism could scarcely offend the Protestant extremists. Even when Grimald makes a rare biblical allusion to Solomonic wisdom in "Of Mirth" (no. 138), it matches the measured elegance of his other poems rather than the popular style of the gospellers. He did, however, share Robert Crowley's interest in fourteenth-century alliterative verse. The unique text of the Middle English *Alisaunder of Macedoine*, which Grimald copied into his notebook (Bodl. MS Greaves 60; c. 1551), influenced his occasional use of archaic diction and phraseology.[39] His versification of a Stoic simile for the golden mean in "Marcus Catoes Com-

---

[38] L. R. Merrill, ed., *The Life and Poems of Nicholas Grimald* (New Haven, 1925), p. 423.

[39] T. Turville-Petre, "Nicholas Grimald and *Alexander A*," *ELR*, 6 (1976), 180-86.

parison of Mans Life with Yron" (no. 135) advocates moderation in terms familiar from such prudential works as *Catonis disticha* and Baldwin's *Treatise*; the epigrammatic couplets of "Prayse of Measure-Kepyng" (no. 150) restate the same doctrine in a form that anticipates the heroic couplets of Ben Jonson and the Augustans. "Marcus Tullius Ciceroes Death" (no. 166) versifies similar ideals from Beza's *Mors Ciceronis*. The blank verse in this poem and "The Death of Zoroas" (no. 165) continues in the same tradition as Surrey's metrical experiments. Harington's translation of *The Booke of Freendeship* and the Suffolk-Cecil correspondence show that the truisms in Grimald's "Of Frendship" (no. 154) were in fashion at the Edwardian court.

Thomas, second Baron Vaux, shared Grimald's fondness for moralization and stringing out loose trains of similes. He contributed two poems to *Songs and Sonnets* (nos. 211-12), and thirteen others appeared in *The Paradise of Dainty Devices* (1576).[40] After fleeing court in 1536, the Catholic lord lived in the safety of rural retirement until his death of the plague in 1556. In the rough-hewn, forceful style of mid-Tudor verse, Vaux's meditative poems dwell on the ancient topics of mutability and the fickleness of Fortune. He is not known to have written any purely erotic verse. "The Aged Lover Renounceth Love" and "He Renounceth all the Affectes of Love" should be read as philosophical discourses on contempt for the world and the vanity of human wishes. The last-named poem develops the conceit of entrapment by "inward hidden hooks":

As to the fishe, sometyme it doeth befall,
That with the baite, doeth swallowe hooke and all.

[40] Ed. Hyder Rollins (Cambridge, Mass., 1927).

This stock idea mirrors Wyatt's:

> Farewell Love, and all thy laws for ever!
> Thy baited hooks shall tangle me no more.

Vaux, however, never achieves the bitter scorn of the courtly lover's *De consolatione philosophiae* in the Wyatt poem. Scattered poems by Edwardian courtiers went into Tottel's *Miscellany*. Cheke may have written "Totus Mundus in Maligno Positus" (no. 284), a mutability complaint stemming from an ancient tradition represented by poems ranging from the twelfth-century *De contemptu mundi* by Bernard of Cluny to Donne's *Anniversaries*. Its concluding prayer exemplifies the poet's imitation of native English plain style:

> In thee we trust, and in no wight:
> Save us as chickens under the hen.
> Our crokednesse thou canst make right,
> Glory to thee for aye. Amen.

William Gray's antifeminist epitaph (no. 255) blames his wife for "the shortnyng of his life." The Marian editor of *Songs and Sonnets* omitted the last sixteen stanzas of the ballad because of its vigorous antipapal satire and advocacy of the English Bible as the guide to life. Gray probably wrote the original version under Edward VI because he appended it to a New Year gift to Seymour (MS Sloane 1207, fols. 9ʳ-10ʳ). Seymour's amanuensis Thomas Norton contributed another antifeminist satire and a *de casibus* poem that articulates themes of Fortune and contempt for the world (nos. 257, 289). The iambic pentameter of "Against Women either Good or Badde" may reflect the tendency toward metrical regularity that Norton and Sackville furthered in *Gorboduc* (1561). Norton's contribution of a dedicatory poem to Turner's *Preservative* and translation of Calvin's *Institutes* attest to his Reformation zeal.

In addition to John Heywood, Thomas Churchyard was the only contributor to Tottel's edition who was a professional author. According to Churchyard's own account, the earliest verse from his long career as a hack poet and balladeer dates back to the reign of Edward VI:

> The bookes that I can call to memorie alreadie Printed: are these that followes. First in King Edwards daies, a book named *Davie Dicars dreame*, which one *Camell* wrote against, whome I openly confuted. *Shores Wife* I penned at that season. Another booke in those daies called the *Mirror of Man*.[41]

Even during the liberty of Edward's reign, printed Protestant poetry lacked the immunity that Harington and Blage sought in their private miscellanies. Seymour's intervention in Churchyard's behalf when he was harassed by the Privy Council must refer to the controversial ballad *Davy Dycars Dreame* (c. 1551) rather than the conventional morality of his other poems (above, p. 106). These early poems cater to the Reformation demand for native moralistic verse. *A Myrrour for Man* (c. 1552), for example, voices devotional commonplaces concerning the ages of man.

Churchyard's later reputation loses sight of his popularity with Tudor contemporaries. After selecting *Shore's Wife* for inclusion in the second edition of *The Mirror for Magistrates* (1563), William Baldwin recorded the pleasure of his genteel audience in the epilogue to the tale:

> This was so well lyked, that all together exhorted me instantly, to procure Maister Churchyarde to undertake

---

[41] *Churchyards Challenge* (1593), *1^v.

and to penne as manye moe of the remaynder as myght by any meanes be attaynted at his handes.[42]

Churchyard found this *de casibus* tragedy ready-made in the version of Thomas More's *History of King Richard III* handed on by Hall's chronicle. The fall of the mistress of Edward IV is a particular example of the "myserable state of thys worlde" envisioned by *A Myrrour for Man*, and the proverbs and moral *exempla* of Churchyard's rhyme royal stanzas emphasize the futility and corruption of the material world. The penitent withdrawal from court of the tragic heroine recalls the aphorisms of Wyatt, Harington, and Vaux:

> The setled minde is free from Fortunes power,
> Thye nede not feare who looke not up aloft,
> But they that clyme are carefull every hower,
> For when they fall they light not very softe. . . .
>
> (ll. 239-42)

As one of the most popular pieces in *The Mirror for Magistrates*, Churchyard's poem was imitated in many ballads and plays during the 1590s fashion for *Shore's Wife*.[43]

Churchyard's earliest ballads reflect the Reformation vogue for *Piers Plowman* triggered by Crowley's editions, for he bases the millennial vision of a perfect commonwealth in *Davy Dycars Dreame* on Langland's prophecy of the poor ditcher's death by starvation. Churchyard derives his prophecy of a reforming Christian king directly from Crowley's printed text:

---

[42] Ed. L. B. Campbell (Cambridge, 1938), hereafter cited as *Mirror*.

[43] Barbara Brown, "Sir Thomas More and Thomas Churchyard's *Shore's Wife*," *YES*, 2 (1972), 47; Samuel Pratt, "Jane Shore and the Elizabethans: Some Facts and Speculations," *TSLL*, 11 (1970), 1303.

When truth doth tread the strets and liers lurke
   in den,
And Rex doth raigne and rule the rost, and weedes
   out wicked men:
Then baelful [*sic*] barnes be blyth that here in
   England wonne,
Your strife shall stynt I undertake, your dredfull
   dayes ar done.

(A1^{r-v})

These couplets graft native alliterative technique onto the
newer imported tradition of rhymed poetry. In *Westerne
Wyll*, William Waterman acknowledges Langland's influence on *Davy Dycars Dreame* and the ensuing debate that
it inspired:

This Diker sems a thryving ladde, brought up in pieres
   scole
The plowman stoute, of whom I thynke ye have often
   harde. . . .
And for your lesson, lo by Christ I lyke it well
And such a lyke I wiene, doth Pierce the ploughman
   tell.

(C4^{v}, G1^{r})

These ballads by Churchyard and Waterman form part
of a flyting in which various speakers debate questions of
ethics, religion, politics, and learning. *The Contention bettwyxte Churchyeard and Camell, upon David Dycers Dreame.
Newlye Imprinted* (1560) gathers up the separate parts of
the extended series that Churchyard, Waterman, Thomas
Camel, Geoffrey Chappell, and Richard Beard originally
issued as broadsides (c. 1552).[44] Despite Churchyard's ref-

---

[44] Citations from the flyting including those by Churchyard and Waterman, above, follow the 1560 reprint.

erences to difficulties with the Privy Council, these ballads lack the urgency of the commonwealth complaints by Crowley, Becon, and Latimer. The medieval genre of the flyting is in fact based upon the collaboration of the partic…ipants. It survived into the sixteenth century in the *débat* between Dunbar and Kennedy, Skelton's replies to Sir Christopher Garnesche, and William Gray's 1530s exchange with Thomas Smith (not Sir Thomas Smith).[45] The wit combat in the *Contention* entertains the reader at the same time that it advertises the beginning of Churchyard's career as a popular, professional poet. Churchyard's "Playn and Fynall Confutacion of Camells Corlyke Oblatracion" also announces the entry of the bookseller William Griffith into the London book trade.

The speech by the fictional observer in Waterman's *Westerne Wyll* attests to the conventionality of this Edwardian flyting. The speaker witnesses a bookseller duping three illiterate mariners from Maldon (Wilkin, Wat, and Herman) into buying the ballad series:

> To Poules they hied as place most fytte, for newes in
> their device
> Amonge the printers gan they searche, and busilye en-
> quire
> For thinges that might for Noveltie, at hom be had in
> price
> The printer sayd he thought he had, to pleasen theyr
> desyre
> And drewe them here into his shoppe, and gan unfolde
> then light
> A rolle of Rithimes, wher of the fyrst, the dickers dreame
> it hyght

---

[45] *Summarium*, 3S3ᵛ; Heiserman, *Skelton and Satire*, pp. 283-85.

Then folowed aunswere to this dreame, to Davie dickers
  whan
A solempne processe at a blusshe, be quoted here &
  there
With [Latin] matter in thee margent set, wheron to gase
  they gan
But they ne wist for ought I knewe, but hebrue that it
  were
A Replication was the next, whiche well I understoode
For that I founde no worde ther in, but it was Englyshe
  good.

(C3^v)

This unique comic vignette dramatizes the hawking of
wares among the crowded bookstalls at St. Paul's churchyard. The attacks on Camel, the ostensible target of the
series, defend the native tradition of English language and
literature. The debate over the plain style evidently reached
down to the lower classes, for Churchyard's riddles, puns,
proverbs, and alliteration mock the false sophistication of
the "good laten" in Camel's classical allusions and marginal
glosses. His burlesque of Camel's learning echoes the familiar charges of the gospellers:

Your knowledge is great, your judgment is good
The most of your study hath ben of Robyn hood.
And Bevys of Hampton, and syr Launcelot de lake,
Hath taught you full oft, your verses to make.

(A2^v)

Camel in turn attacks Churchyard for using "chorles termes"
and "uncouth speeche" (E2^v). In his "Supplication unto
Mast Camell," Geoffrey Chappell imitates Somerset dialect in order to construct the simple *persona* of the plain-

speaking countryman similar to that of Davy Diker, the three Essex mariners, or Piers Plowman.

John Heywood entered the controversy over language as the only Reformation Catholic to see his books circulate without impediment. After achieving favor as a minstrel and dramatist under Henry VIII, he remained at court under both Edward and Mary. The prudential wisdom of his witty proverbs and epigrams resembles the native art of Churchyard and his collaborators. Heywood would not drop his guise of impartiality until *An Hundred Epigrammes* (1556). He assumes that the epigram is a close relative of satire in his piece about an illiterate layman who could not learn the Lord's Prayer:

A man of the countrey shriven in Lent late
(Accordyng to thinjunction) his curate
Bad him, the *Pater noster* in englishe saie,
Iche can it not maister (quoth he) by my faie. . . .
And yet master vickar by gods sacrament,
Cha [I] jumbled about it ever sens last lent.
And some of it ich had in the clensyng weeke,
But now, whan ich should say it, all is to seeke.
Well (quoth the priest) if your wit be so far decayde,
Say the *Pater noster*, ye have alway sayde [in Latin]
  Nay by the Masse (sware he) if you will have all tolde,
Cha so grated on the new, cha forgot tholde.[46]

Unlike the rustic speech in *Contention*, which idealizes the speakers as Protestant truth-tellers, Heywood's dialect mocks the countryman who personifies the Protestant ideals of vernacular education and the priesthood of all believers.

[46] *"Works" and Miscellaneous Short Poems*, ed. B. A. Milligan (Urbana, Ill., 1956), p. 126.

The political content of Heywood's epigrams is slight by comparison with *The Spider and the Flie* (1556). Ever since the dissolution of the abbeys, he had worked in manuscript on this attack on the Reformation. Only after the reconciliation with Rome was it safe to drop his allegorical veil and identify Queen Mary as the maid who ends the protracted conflict between the Protestant spider and the Catholic fly by killing off the predator and sweeping England's house clean of cobwebs and debris.

LUKE SHEPHERD AND THE WORLD UPSIDE DOWN

The verse satires of Luke Shepherd bring forward Protestant plain speakers similar to Davy Diker and the three Essex mariners. Shepherd, more than any of his contemporaries, recognizes the power of verbal wit and linguistic play as vehicles for satirizing old beliefs. Among Reformation artists, he shares with William Baldwin an ability to stimulate laughter as well as indignation. Shepherd's poems succeed where those of so many reformers fail because of his refusal to reduce composition to artless scriptural paraphrase. Yet the verse Psalms that Bale ascribes to him attest to his credentials as a gospeller (*Index*, p. 283). Shepherd skillfully mixes traditional devices of structure, diction, and character in order to construct satires that attack such particular historical objects as celibacy, the mass, and incompetent clergy.[47] A major concern of all of his poems is a defense of the *sermo humilis* and a corresponding attack on decadent church Latin by means

[47] This discussion follows Heiserman, *Skelton and Satire*, pp. 298-305, in its terminology and assumption that the essence of satire (from *satura*, meaning "a bowl of mixed fruits") lies in its deliberate mixture of diverse literary conventions, techniques, and devices in order to attack a discernible historical object.

of such varied devices of language as macaronic verse, word torrents, puns, monologue, dialogue, and obscene word-play. The obscurity of some of his dramatic monologues shows a Rabelaisian willingness to direct his ironies against the reader as well as external satirical objects. Deliberate obscurity was a convention of Tudor satire that was prompted by genuine need in this case, for Shepherd repeatedly voices fears that Gospel faith will not endure and that the Roman mass will return to England. His verse embodies the real danger and anxiety experienced by the Reformation Protestant.

Shepherd the man remains a shadowy figure. In providing all but one attribution for Shepherd's nine anonymous works,[48] John Bale gives the Latinized name "Lucas Opilio" for a poet born in Colchester, Essex (*Catalogus*, II, 109). He translates the name into English as "Lucas Shepeherd" (*Index*, p. 283).[49] In all probability the author was "mr. Luke, my very frende, off Colemane strete visissyone [physician]," of whom the courtier Edward Underhill speaks. Underhill credits his friend with *John Bon and Mast Person* and many other "proper bokes agaynst the papistes" for which he was jailed in Fleet Prison. Underhill defended Shepherd and his publisher, John Day, by appearing before the Lord Mayor and handing him a copy of *John Bon* with the comment: "ther is many off them in the courte." Sir John Gresham's response that "it was bothe pythye and mery" suggests that Shepherd's poems set a

---

[48] Circa 1548. Friedrich Germann attributes *Pathose* to Shepherd on the basis of style in *Luke Shepherd, ein Satirendichter der englischen Reformationszeit* (Augsburg, 1911), pp. 72-73. Germann appends editions of *Upcheringe*, a fragment of *Philogamus*, and an abridgement of *Pathose*.

[49] Arthur F. Kinney of the University of Massachusetts at Amherst suggests that Bale may translate a pseudonym made up of elements suggesting Christ, the Good Shepherd, and the evangelist Luke.

standard of Reformation wit that could appeal to both elite and popular audiences.[50] According to Strype, the "Book took much at the Court, and the Courtiers wore it in their pockets" (*Eccl. Mem.*, II, 116). Broad acceptance of this homely satire by courtiers, City of London authorities, and London readers illustrates the eclecticism of Reformation taste.

Shepherd's art emerges out of the native tradition of English verse satire that includes works by Langland and Dunbar, Skelton and Crowley. Bale labels him a "most facetious poet who, in poems and verses that were not inferior to Skelton, elegantly issued works in his native tongue that were full of jokes and wit."[51] Shepherd is the only imitator to master the idiosyncratic form of skeltonics; he shares Skelton's fondness for run-on rhyme leashes, short lines of irregular length and measure, vigorous colloquial diction, alliteration, puns, macaronic diction, copious verse catalogues, and scatological and sexual innuendo. Because Bale always translated titles and incipits into Latin, his Shepherd attributions were forgotten. Some of the satires were thus absorbed into the Skelton canon. Francis Douce, for example, assigned *A Pore Helpe* to Skelton on the flyleaf of his copy (Bodl. Douce H 100). The Bodleian Library catalogue credits its unique copy of *Doctour Doubble*

---

[50] J. G. Nichols, ed., *Narratives of the Days of the Reformation, Chiefly Drawn from the Manuscripts of John Foxe* (1859; Camden Soc., o.s. 77), pp. 171-72. According to his autobiography, Underhill was himself imprisoned under Mary for writing an anti-Catholic ballad (pp. 134-35). See above, Chapter 2 at n. 19.

[51] ". . . poeta valde facetus erat, qui in poematibus ac rhythmis Skeltono non inferior, in patrio sermone eleganter edidit, honestis iocis ac salibus plenos" (*Catalogus*, II, 109). Despite Skelton's hostility to the Lutherans, the reformers approved of his verse because they read *Colyn Cloute* in the Lollard tradition of *The Plowman's Tale*.

Ale (Arch. Af. 83) to Skelton. C. H. Hartshorne attributed the same poem to Skelton on the basis of style.[52]

Reformation readers appreciated Skeltonic art, for twenty-one Skelton editions appeared c. 1545-63. John Bale called him a "poetical prophet" ("vates pierius") who "saw many evils in the clergy, which he sometimes carped at in lively colors, which are jeering but not obscene";[53] he applauded Skelton's violation of clerical celibacy. By identifying the author as a classical English poet, Churchyard's dedication to John Stow's collected edition of *Pithy Pleasaunt and Profitable Workes* (1568) sets Skelton up as a defender of native artistry against the recent fashion for Italianate poetry:

> Peers plowman was full plaine,
>> And Chausers spreet was great:
> Earle Surry had a goodly vayne,
>> Lord Vaus the marke did beat.
> And Phaer did hit the pricke,
>> In things he did translate:
> And Edwards had a special gift,
>> And divers men of late
> Hath helpt our Englishe toung,
>> That first was baes [base] and brute
> Ohe shall I leave out Skeltons name,
>> The blossome of my frute. . . .
>
> ([-]3^r-v)

Shepherd joined in the defense of native literary tradition against foreign influences that he identified with Catholic Italy. The hyperbolic rhetoric of *Philogamus* mocks an enemy poet who, under the influence of the "Muses nyne," has a dream vision that inspires him to write "Newe Po-

---

[52] *Ancient Metrical Tales* (1829), p. xxiii.

[53] "In clero pleraque videbat mala, que nonnunquam vivis carpebat coloribus, atque scommatibus non obscoenis" (*Index*, p. 253).

etry" (A2ʳ). The nativists lost the contest, however, for Skelton's collected works were to go out of print from 1568 until 1736. By the 1580s watershed, neoclassical standards of decorum had led to the denigration of Skeltonic art. For George Puttenham, Skelton is "a sharpe Satirist, but with more rayling and scoffery then became a Poet Lawreat: such among the Greekes were called *Pantomimi*, with us Buffons [*sic*], altogether applying their wits to Scurrillities & other ridiculous matters."[54] It was early antiquarian interest that led to the editions of *The Tunnyng of Elynour Rummyng* in 1624 and 1718.

Experimentation with varied modes of argument and devices of language distinguishes Shepherd from all other gospelling poets except Crowley. Instead of writing drearily explicit controversial attacks, the poet dramatizes error through a variety of different *personae*. The unambiguous statement and devout piety of Shepherd's manual on dying, *A Godly Preservatyve against Disperacion*, is a useful foil to his satires, which restate many of the same arguments in deliberately confusing, veiled, parodic, and ironic forms. The Pauline imagery of the armor of God runs through this prose collection of biblical tags. According to the terminal prayer, the Christian reader should receive a "swerd and buckeler" that protects "agaynst al the assaultes of the devyl" at "the houre of death" (A2ᵛ, E7ʳ).

The epigraph of *A Pore Helpe* identifies it as a parody of the serious argument in *Preservative*:

> The bukler and defence
> Of mother holy kyrke,
> And weapen to drive hence
> Al that against her wircke.[55]

[54] *Essays*, ed. Smith, II, 65.

[55] The two Bodl. copies of the first edition preserve a better state of the text than the uncorrected C.U.L. copy of the second edition.

Unlike the literalistic paraphrases of the gospellers, the mimetic fiction of this text forces the reader to determine that the verbal abuse that it hurls against the Protestants personifies Catholic error. Like all of Shepherd's dramatic monologues, the poem invites the naive reader to mistake irony for truth. In the manner of Rabelais or Swift, Shepherd demands the strenuous participation of any reader who wishes to avoid misinterpretation. Thus he implicitly raises the epistemological problem inherent in Protestant faith. Because skeltonics characterize flawed speakers rather than the author, the apparent courage and learning of the old believer serve as an inadequate disguise for his real folly. The jingling rhythm and metrical chaos of Shepherd's prosody furnish a symptom of the speaker's moral decay. The self-portrait of the unregenerate speaker reveals him as the butt of the satire at the same time that he serves as its narrator. Reformation satires by other poets use unambiguous speakers.

Shepherd portrays the Reformation as a battle of books. The narrator of *A Pore Helpe*, for example, personifies the bookishness of contemporary turmoil through his preference for portases (portable Latin breviaries) rather than the English Bible or Erasmus's *Paraphrases* (A3^r). The long catalogues of Protestant and Catholic authors in satires like *Pathose* (B2^v-3^v) contribute to this motif of literary warfare. The ostensible defense of the old learning in *A Pore Helpe* ridicules Catholic norms:

> Against our lerninges olde
> Or images of golde
> Which nowe be bought and solde
> And were the lay mannes boke
> Where on they ought to loke.
>
> (A4^r)

In his horror at popular religious discussion "in plays /

In Taverns and hye wayes" where "al is done in ryme" (A5ʳ⁻ᵛ), the speaker associates Protestant literature with heresy and Lollardry. Although he cites Stephen Gardiner and Miles Hogarde as examples of clerkly learning, the absurdly spun-out, punning variations on their names undercut their authority:

> He hath ben a pardoner
> And also a garddener
> He hath ben a vitaylar
> A Lordly hospitelar.
> A noble teacher
> And so so a preacher. . . .
> And also mayster huggarde
> Doth shewe him selfe no sluggard
> Nor yet no drunkin drunkarde.
>
> (A7ʳ)

The speaker's implicit refutation of his own arguments is most obvious when he sinks into the rhymed doggerel and formless nonsense verse that typify the conclusions of Shepherd's satires.

John Bon and Mast Person is the only satire to dramatize one of the illiterate laymen who are apparently vilified in Shepherd's other works. In this dialogue between a simple plowman and a priest, John Bon explicitly states the Protestant thesis implicit in the monologues. Shepherd sets their encounter on the eve of Corpus Christi, the traditional celebration of transubstantiation and the mass when festivities included the procession of the Blessed Sacrament and performances of the mystery cycles. Day and Seres may have timed publication to coincide with Cranmer's disestablishment of the feast in 1548. Shepherd evidently wrote the work in collaboration with his publishers because the rhyme royal epigraph interprets the title-page woodcut; Day and Seres would have supplied the illustration. The verse directly addresses the priests who bear the host in the Corpus Christi procession as "poore fooles" who are led into "Idolatrye" by man-made traditions.[56] The emblematic title page sets the text against the background of the current iconoclastic controversy, during which analogous woodcuts of the procession of the Blessed Sacrament were pulled out and defaced in copies of *The Golden Legend* (above, p. 148 and n. 24). The Spanish ambassador's account of a court masque that ridiculed the bearing of the host by a procession of costumed priests and bishops underscores the topicality of this satire.[57]

John Bon's rustic dialect labels him as a plain speaker coming out of the *Piers Plowman* tradition; his name is a Protestant lay variation of the conventional epithet for a priest: "Sir John." In order to discredit the Catholic defense, Shepherd relies on John Bon's unpretentious speech and the priest's inarticulate failure to deflect the laborer's simple but only superficially naive questions about the mass. The questions asked by the "playne man" (A1ᵛ) illustrate Protestant epistemological concern with knowledge and proof in contrast to his opponent's argument from precedent and tradition. The plowman's common-sense rationalism prevents him from believing in transubstantiation because he cannot taste or see it:

> Yea but mast parson thynk ye it were ryght
> That if I desired you to make my blake oxe whight
> And you saye it is done, and styl is blacke in syght
> Ye myght me deme a foole for to beleve so lyght.
>
> (A4ʳ)

---

[56] Hodnett, no. 1472, previously used in Pynson's *Rule of Seynt Benet* (1516). Pynson's block imitates Caxton's 1486 illustration of the Blessed Sacrament (Hodnett, no. 333).

[57] Jordan, *Edward VI*, II, 99.

The conclusion circles back to the epigraph in its plain-spoken attack on clerical folly.

Shepherd transcends such simple dialogue with a complex pattern of thesis, antithesis, and synthesis in the three parts of *The Comparison betwene the Antipus and Antigraphe: Antipus, Antigraphium*, and *Apologia Antipi*. These obscurely dark texts may best be approached as a flyting of the kind written by Churchyard and his collaborators. Originally published as a broadside ballad, *Antipus* consists of twenty fourteener couplets stating paradoxes concerning transubstantiation. The Latin epigraph gives the learned reader a key to the puzzling poem: "Nam horum contraria verissima sunt" ("For the contraries of these things are truest"). It builds up to an attack upon the priests and a man named Leighton who "wyll neades his maker make." Wordplay on "antipapus" ("antipapist") gives Shepherd his title. *Antigraphium* (from ἀντιγραφή, "a written reply") personifies the English recusant, who attacks the gospellers and states a rhyme-by-rhyme reply to Antipus's paradoxes. The rhyme royal defense of Antipus in *Apologia Antipi* includes among its objects of attack the "false latine" of Antigraphium's defense of medieval oral and apocryphal traditions: "Nam ea audite verissima sunt" ("For hear those things that are truest").

Shepherd inherited the accumulation of obscure pseudo-allegories, esoteric allusions, and animal names as a confusing satirical device. Similar conventions are used in Skelton's *Speke, Parrot* as well as the medieval prophecies of Geoffrey of Monmouth and John of Bridlington. This literary tradition argues against identification of real persons whose names may be concealed within the puns, riddles, and anagrams of *Apologia Antipi*:

> A Mason, a Smyth, and a Paynter fyne
> Wyth a Mugge, and a Gray, and a Perkens grosse

Be fooes to Antipus, at whom thei repine,
And hym wyth great anger, thei turne and thei tosse.

(B1ᵛ)

Cathleen Wheat's ingenious identifications ignore the satirical art of these poems by reducing them to constituent elements in the 1548 pamphlet attack on transubstantiation and the mass.[58] The efforts of the "commentator" on Pope's *Dunciad* demonstrate the inevitable failure of literalistic interpretation of such involuted references. Wheat's conjecture that *Apologia Antipi* may attack Sir John Mason is unlikely on the face of it. Mason was a prominent Protestant and a member of the Edwardian Privy Council, who later became Chancellor of Oxford University. The main attraction of the name Mason is its potential for being spun out into puns on the stonemasonry that went into two biblical prototypes for papal Rome: the city of Babylon and the Tower of Babel. The babbling diction of these poems reveals Shepherd's concern with the process rather than the content of particular kinds of speech. In this flyting the confusing medley of words and voices personifies Reformation controversy as a whole rather than specific doctrinal arguments.

Doctor Doubble Ale is Shepherd's only work of narrative fiction. Like John Bon, the lower-class speaker typifies the Protestant ideal of lay rationalism. His "gentill tale" about a curate who prefers the alehouse to pastoral duties satirizes clerical ignorance. Juxtaposition of the speaker's commentary with his quotation of a long and rambling drunken monologue by the priest furnishes implicit dialogue. The "reading and sobrietie / and judgement in the veritie" of the "cobblers boy," who has the same unlearned origins as the speaker, give him a better claim to moral wisdom than this priest ("A man of learning great"; A4ʳ⁻ᵛ). Such pro-

---

[58] "Luke Shepherd's *Antipi Amicus*," *PQ*, 30 (1951), 58-68.

letarian figures emerge out of the Lollard tradition of lay dissent. The dialogue between the shoemaker and priest by the cobbler-poet Hans Sachs derives from a related German tradition. In a similar fashion, the ironies of Shepherd's *Upcheringe of the Messe* lament the attack on church tradition by artisans and laborers:

> Yet plowmen smythes & cartars
> With such as be their hartars
> Will enterprise to taxe
> Thes auncyent mens actes
> And holy fathers factes.
>
> (A2^r)

Topical allusions invite the reader to identify the work with the current moment of the Reformation. The English would recognize in Doctor Double Ale the inversion of provisions in the Royal Injunctions:

> . . . Ecclesiasticall persons, shall in no wise, at any unlaufull tyme, nor for any other cause, then for their honest necessitie, haunte or resorte to any Tavernes, or Alehouses. . . . they shal not geve them selfes to drynckyng or ryot, spending their tyme ydlely, by day or by night, at dise, cardes, or tables plaiyng, or any other unlaufull game. . . . (b1^{r-v})

Shepherd's artistry results from his skillful patterning of such mundane materials by means of ancient satirical devices. The ironic confession of the drunken priest is reminiscent of the medieval type-scene of the tavern sermon found in works like Chaucer's *Pardoner's Tale*. Such confession resembles the tavern scenes in *Piers Plowman* (B. V. 304-91) and Skelton's *Tunnyng of Elynour Rummyng*. This *in taberna* scene derives from *Confessio Goliae* and other goliardic poems by the wandering scholars of the

twelfth century. Goliardic verse was a live influence on
Reformation literature. The inscription on the title page of
Rhithmi vetustissimi (MS Bodl. 538) by William Patten (see
below, Appendix III at n. 2) attests to a Protestant scholar's reception of the first printed edition of *Apocalypsis Goliae*. John Bale cites many manuscript copies in the chambers of John Leland and Nicholas Grimald, at the king's
library, Oxford libraries, and in other collections (*Index*,
pp. 107-10).

Traditional anticlericalism links English Reformation
literature to the goliardic poets, *Piers Plowman*, and Wyclifite Lollardry. Despite the doctrinal orthodoxy of goliardic attacks on avarice, simony, and clerical laxity, Bale
interpreted the violent satire of *Apocalypsis Goliae* as a Reformation prophecy in *Rhithmi vetustissimi*. Crowley's preface to *Piers Plowman* notes a goliardic passage on kings
and princes that "secretly in latine verses . . . rebuketh
their cruelnes and tyranny":

> Than greved hym a Goliardes, a gloton of wordes
> And to the angell on hygh, answered after
> > *Dum Rex a regere, dicatur nomen habere,*
> > *Nomen habet sine re, nisi studet iura tenere.*
> Than gan all the commons crye, in verses of laten
> To the kynges counsel, construe who so would.
> > *Precepta regis, sunt nobis vincula legis.*
> > (A3ʳ; B. Prol. 139-45)

The stringing out of internal and terminal rhymes on -re
and -is in the quoted Latin verses illustrates the "word
gluttony" of Langland's goliard. Rhyme leashes resembling Shepherd's skeltonics are found in the *aaaa* rhymes
of Bale's edition of *Rhithmi vetustissimi*:

> Sed visa scripserat ille mysteria
> Septem ecclesiis quae sunt in Asia,

[263]

Tu scribes eadem, forma sed alia,
Septem ecclesiis quae sunt in Anglia.

(A5ʳ)

The disorganized jumble and disconnected phrases of
Doctor Double Ale's mock Latin pinpoint Church Latin
as an object of satire. Shepherd's burlesque dramatizes
clerical corruption through the deliberate lapse of logical
connections. Implicit throughout is the contrast to the plain
speech of the Protestant lay narrator. The priest's macaronic speech disguises obscene blasphemy and folly with
the appearance of wisdom and esoteric learning. His pa-
thetically drunken attempt to defend the old service personifies clerical abuses through a scurrilous parody of the
mass that is far more effective than direct pamphlet attacks. Except for the parody of "hoc est corpus meum,"
his words are not a strict burlesque of the liturgy. They
come out of the tradition of learned Latin known to physicians such as Rabelais and Shepherd:

Hys latin wyll utter
and turne and tosse him
wyth tu non possum
Loquere latinum
this alum finum
Is bonus then vinum
Ego volo quare
Cum tu drinkare . . .
Iuro per deum
Hoc est lifum meum
quia drinkum stalum
Non facere malum. . . .

(A8ʳ)[59]

[59] ". . . with 'you are not able / to speak Latin / this excellent ale / is

Shepherd employs ironic confession and nonsensical Latin as basic satirical devices in two related monologues by personifications of the pope or Roman clergy. These satires dramatize the disestablishment of the Roman rite during Cranmer's *annus mirabilis* of 1548. The attack on "Maister Evangelium," a personification of the gospeller, by the speaker in *The Upcheringe of the Messe* unwittingly proves the Protestant charge that the mass lacks scriptural authority. Both *Upcheringe* and *Pathose, or an Inward Passion of the Pope for the Losse of hys Daughter the Masse* incorporate funeral elegies for Mistress Missa. This scurrilous personification of the mass derives from the priest's words "ite, missa est" ("go, you are released").[60] Her hellish descent as the granddaughter of Pluto, illegitimate daughter of the pope, and niece of Mohammed (*Pathose*, A3ᵛ, B6ʳ) parodies the genealogical praise recommended by epideictic rhetoric. Shepherd's device had become a convention of Protestant satire by the time that Spenser described Duessa as

. . . the sole daughter of an Emperour,
He that the wide West under his rule has,
And high hath set his throne, where *Tiberis* doth pass.
(*FQ*, I.ii.22)

Una, on the other hand, is the daughter of the ruler of the East, the "most mighty king of *Eden* faire" (I.xii.26). As

---

better than wine / For that reason, I / Want to drink with you / . . . I swear by God / This is my life: / To drink stale [ale], / Not to do evil. . . .' "

[60] In *Duessa as Theological Satire* (Columbus, Mo., 1970), D. Douglas Waters omits Shepherd's poems from his catalogue of examples of the Mistress Missa *topos*. In reducing Protestant satire and allegory to literalistic paraphrase of eucharistic controversy, Waters ignores artistic techniques, genres, and conventions of English Reformation literature.

a literary analogue of the iconographic conflict between Edward VI and the pope, the expulsion of Mistress Missa became a familiar gospelling figure in 1548 dialogues (below, Chapter 6, sect. 2).

Upcheringe carries Bale's identification of the Whore of Babylon with the Church of Rome one step further by presenting Mistress Missa in the biblical role of a harlot. Shepherd's pun "Winchester goslynge" alludes to the cant term for prostitute ("Winchester goose") derived from the location of brothels in the Southwark estate of the Bishop of Winchester. Because the area lay immediately beyond the jurisdiction of the Lord Mayor of London, the Globe Theater would be erected in the same neighborhood. Abusing the mass as a harlot ("Naye some wyl cal hir whore"), the punning invective vilifies Gardiner as Bishop of Winchester and defender of images as laymen's books (A3^r-4^v). Bale makes the same equation in his attack on "the stews of both kinds at Rome . . . of Winchester's rents in England" (*Image*, p. 518). The coarse obscenity of this dirge for Mistress Missa exemplifies Reformation attitudes toward the mass in a manner similar to Spenser's stripping of Duessa in order to reveal her as a loathsome harlot (*FQ*, I.viii.46-49):

> A good mestres missa
> Shal ye go from us thissa?
> Wel yet I muste ye kyssa
> Alacke for payne I pyssa
> To se the mone here Issa
> Because ye muste departe
> It greveth many an herte
> That ye should from them start
> But what then tushe a farte.
>
> (A8^r)

The incomprehensibility of medieval church music, with its "mery piping / And Besy chauntyng," is for Shepherd a major object of satirical attack. The mock dirge in *Up-cheringe* dissolves into a macaronic burlesque of the requiem mass that imitates Skelton's elegy on the death of Jane Scrope's pet sparrow in *Philip Sparrow*.[61] In contrast to Skelton's use of tags from the mass to shape the moral disorder of the girl into gentle comedy, Shepherd violently ridicules the Latin rite:

> Requiem eternam
> Lest penam sempiternam
> For vitam supernam
> And umbram infernam
> For veram lucernam . . .
> But trudge ad ultra mare
> And after habitare
> In regno plutonico
> Et Eus acronyco
> Cum cetu babilonico
> Et cantu diabolico. . . .
>   (A8[r-v])[62]

Mockery of the *Placebo* (A8[r]) also imitates *Philip Sparrow*. Shepherd's allusion to "Laetabundus exultet," a medieval carol sequence, echoes *Colin Clout* as it mocks Latin hymnody:

> Wherefore nowe totus mundus
> That round is and rotundus

[61] See Ian Gordon, "Skelton's 'Philip Sparrow' and the Roman Service Book," *MLR*, 29 (1934), 389-96.

[62] " '[Give me?] eternal rest / Lest everlasting pain / For heavenly life / And infernal shade / For the true lantern / . . . But trudge beyond the sea / And afterwards [to] live / In the realm of Pluto / And timeless [?] Dawn / With the Babylonian whale / And a diabolical song. . . .' "

Be mery and Jocundus
And sing the letabundus
With al the whole chorus
That here hath ben before us.

(A5ᵛ-6ʳ)

Although the papal dirge in *Pathose* functions as a sequel
to the illness and death of Mistress Missa in *Upcheringe*,
its satire assumes a more sweeping historical perspective.
The pope's placement of his daughter's death in the context
of a continuous series of reverses since the loss of Thomas
More and John Fisher (his "knightes of England") personifies the English Reformation. Despite disapproval of
More's veneration as a Catholic martyr, Bale is far more
generous than Shepherd in praising his unrivaled learning
and prose style (*Summarium*, 314ʳ⁻ᵛ). Mistress Missa's personified cortege consists of prohibited practices: pilgrimages, confession, voluntary works, and monastic orders.
Reading like a bookseller's list of Reformation authors, the
Rabelaisian catalogue of Protestant and Catholic theologians symbolizes the book warfare of the time (A2ᵛ-3ᵛ). Goliardic "word gluttony" pervades Shepherd's use of authorities as diction in an erudite litany of names; he treats
words and names as subject matter throughout his poems.
In the manner of *Upcheringe*, the pope's mock anthem burlesques the service of extreme unction:

Tu quum defungeris
Sacro que ungeris
Oleo papali.

(B7ʳ)[63]

Shepherd boasts of his anonymity and the extraordinary

[63] " 'That when you die / You will be anointed / With the sacred papal
oil.' "

obscurity of *Philogamus* in its conclusion: "Quod Phylogamus, Alias .J. Whatcall Ye Hym." The shifting paradoxes of his monologue impede determination of the speaker's stance. Deriving his name from φιλογυνία ("love of
woman"), the verbal ironies of this personification of the
celibate clergy articulate the Protestant ideal of married
love. The speaker is a Reformation refraction of the conventional figure of the lustful priest found in the *Decameron, Canterbury Tales*, and other medieval works. His dual
violation of the vow of celibacy and the Protestant ideal of
chaste wedded love expected of both layman and priest (see
Spenser's "Legend of Britomartis, Or Of Chastitie") en-
hances the complexity of the satire. The obscene language
and thought of the priest attack the celibate ideal at the
same time that they construct a negative argument for the
wholesome sexuality possible within marriage. The skillful
goliardic imitation entitled "A Latten Clubbe, or Hurle
Batte" directs a double-edged attack against both Church
Latin and immoral clergy. Its convolutions exemplify
Shepherd's procedure in all of his satires—the incomprehensibility is typical and deliberate:

> Sed Amicti Nebride
> Quod non estis Nupti
> Eo plus Corrupti
> Castum profitentes
> Non custodientis . . .
> Incestui cedentes
> Lupi Existentes
> Lupam subsequentes
> Priapo servientes
> In Deum statuentes
> Ipsum quo Colentes
> Vulvas Indagantes

[269]

Illecebras Amantes
Velut Scortatores . . .
Lupinis Vestibus
Caudis and Testibus
Dediti Incestibus
Viperarum Genus. . . .
(B1ʳ⁻ᵛ)[64]

[64] " 'Dressed in the fawn-skin [of Bacchus] / Because you are not married / By that fact are you more corrupt, / Professing chastity / Not guarding it / . . . Giving in to incest / Living as wolves / Chasing after whores / Serving Priapus / Setting up in God / The same where you worship [?] / Seeking the pudenda / Loving seductresses / Like prostitutes / . . . In wolves' clothing / With Penis and Testicles / Given over to incestuous ones / Generation of vipers. . . .' " The transferred sense of *cauda* ("tail") follows Horace, *Satires*, I.ii.45, II.vii.49. Michael J. Curley of the University of Puget Sound very generously advised on Shepherd's Latin and contributed most of the translation in notes 59, 62-64.

CHAPTER 6
Reformation Drama and Dialogue

THE REFORMED STAGE

In the prologue to *Tamburlaine*, Christopher Marlowe distances himself "from jigging veins of rhyming mother wits / And such conceits as clownage keeps in pay." From Marlowe's time onward, scholars have seen in the blank verse drama of the Elizabethan stage a sharp departure from previous theatrical practice. Sidney began this tradition by exempting *Gorboduc* alone from his attack, in *An Apology for Poetry*, on early Tudor plays, which are "not without cause cried out against." Most modern critics have continued in this tradition by interpreting the Reformation as a destructive movement that exerted a negative influence on the development of pre-Shakespearean drama—arguing, for example, that Protestant antipathy toward art retarded movement toward a Renaissance in drama. L. B. Campbell and Murray Roston declare typically that Tudor biblical drama attempted to supplant secular theater with a Christian stage.[1] Glynne Wickham asserts flatly that the Reformation conflicts with all forms of neoclassical drama.[2] It is true that Reformation dramatists were preoccupied with the great public issues of the day. No records survive of mid-Tudor Protestant plays that enacted purely roman-

[1] *Divine Poetry and Drama*, pp. 149-50; *Biblical Drama in England: From the Middle Ages to the Present Day* (1968), p. 53.

[2] *Early English Stages, 1300 to 1660* (1959-80; 3 vols.), II, 1, 35.

tic or tragic themes. Nevertheless, comedy and satire were well suited to the stage representation of the Protestant concern for individual and communal regeneration. The nativist drama of the middle sixteenth century represents a lively and important phase in the development of later stage tradition. It passed on, in particular, the themes and conventions of the early moral interlude in a form suitable for adaptation by the Elizabethan dramatists. The present study therefore aims to document the canon of Reformation drama, its inheritance of generic and technical aspects of medieval tradition, and the varieties of its theatrical art.

The late Elizabethan attack on earlier Tudor drama paralleled the contemporary attack on native English verse. Such critics as Marlowe and Sidney concerned themselves largely with diction and style, and modern criticism has inherited their strictures. The anachronistic application of neoclassical standards of decorum has led to the assumption that Renaissance drama springs, either directly or indirectly, from neoclassical and Italianate influences. Yet examination of native English tradition shows that the biblical drama of the Reformation developed organically from the medieval religious stage.[3] In *Christian Rite and Christian Drama*, O. B. Hardison argues that the myth of the Renaissance return to the classical golden age obscures the medieval origins of Elizabethan drama. Recent studies indicate that later dramatists incorporated traditional medieval forms that had undergone adaptation during the Reformation. David Bevington demonstrates that the achievement of Marlowe and his contemporaries springs from their synthesis of new secular subjects with traditional doubling patterns and the psychomachia form of the me-

[3] E. K. Chambers, *The Mediaeval Stage* (Oxford, 1903; 2 vols.), II, 216-17.

dieval morality play and Tudor moral interlude.[4] Shakespeare adapts the art of the medieval moralities to blank verse tragedy; Jonson's comedies preserve the old morality structure.[5]

The structures of the Tudor moral interlude lived on, for a new Reformation Everyman continued to fight out the old psychomachia before Elizabethan audiences. He differed from his late medieval predecessors by agonizing over subjective problems of knowledge and faith rather than external works in the world. Protestant epistemological concerns underlie the providential design of Marlowe's plays as well as Shakespeare's tragedies and comedies.[6] For example, *Doctor Faustus*, the last avowedly religious drama in Renaissance England, dramatizes the same dilemmas of nature and grace that Cranmer had discussed in the *Book of Homilies*. Reformation drama accommodated a complex variety of forms. A major reason for critical inattention to the Edwardian drama is the survival of relatively few plays. Stage records show that the great bulk of Reformation plays has been lost (above, Chapter 4, n. 20). This contrasts with the well-preserved and fully edited remains of medieval and Elizabethan drama.

[4] *"Mankind"* to Marlowe, pp. 1-7 et seq.

[5] In *Shakespeare and the Allegory of Evil* (New York, 1958), Bernard Spivack traces the emergence of such problematic hero villains as Iago and Richard III from the psychomachia tradition of the morality play. Alan Dessen parallels this argument in *Jonson's Moral Comedy* (Evanston, Ill., 1971). But see Harriett Hawkins's attack on the discovery of "some abstract moral order operating in tragedy and comedy alike," which substitutes "moral criteria for dramatic criteria in its evaluation of characters" in *Likenesses of Truth in Elizabethan and Restoration Drama* (Oxford, 1972), p. ix et seq.

[6] Wilbur Sanders, *The Dramatist and the Received Idea* (Cambridge, 1968), chaps. 5-6, 10-14; R. G. Hunter, *Shakespeare and the Mystery of God's Judgments* (Athens, Ga., 1976).

The Protestant lords of Edward VI's reign encouraged dramatic production both at court and throughout the land, for the repeal act freed the stage as well as the press. Protestant ideas and stage conventions penetrated almost every extant Reformation play, even though technical differences distinguished between production within aristocratic circles and that under popular auspices. The lost drama *Old Custom* (c. 1547-49) presented the Reformation as an outwitting of "Old Blind Custom," a personification of the Roman clergy, by a Protestant scholar and gentleman.[7] John Dudley's ownership of "a play called old custome" attests to its courtly auspices.[8] The piece reflects the Reformation commonplace used in the title of the Elizabethan allegory *New Custom* (c. 1570) and in the gospellers' endemic attacks on the "old customes" of the medieval church (see Peter Moone, *Short Treatyse*, A3r). The offering for acting of *Impatient Poverty* and *Lusty Juventus* suggests an effort to place topical plays in the hands of itinerant troupes for performance before popular audiences. Seymour's patronage of the Lord Protector's Men documents his involvement in such an attempt, for the earliest notice of this troupe of traveling players records a violation of Henrician controls. On 12 January 1545 the Court of Aldermen of the City of London ordered that "certeyn comen pleyers of enterludys belongyng (as they seyd) to the Erle of hertford" comply with the 1544 proclamation limiting performances to aristocratic households.[9] Seymour evidently

---

[7] Albert Feuillerat, "An Unknown Protestant Morality Play," *MLR*, 9 (1914), 94-96; C. R. Baskervill, "On Two Old Plays," *MP*, 14 (1916), 16.

[8] Cited in an inventory dated 31 January 1550 (Bodl. MS Add. C. 94, fol. 13).

[9] E. J. Miller and E. K. Chambers, eds., "Dramatic Records of the City of London: The Repertories, Journals, and Letter Books," *Malone Society Collections*, II, 3 (1931), 291.

continued the patronage practiced by Cromwell and Cranmer in the 1530s. Similar companies acted under the protection of Dudley and the Duchess of Suffolk.[10] Staging at least one production at Cambridge University, Seymour's Men performed frequently in the provinces under Edward VI. The troupe disbanded or went under the protection of another patron after Seymour's execution.[11]

Taking only a short step from pulpit to stage, actors declaimed the same ideas that congregations heard every Sunday. For the only time in English theater history, clergymen were the driving force behind the drama. The following clerics wrote plays: Bale, Becon, Foxe, Baldwin, Udall, and Grimald. Udall wrote *Ralph Roister Doister* at the same time that he edited Erasmus's *Paraphrases* and translated Vermigli's *Discourse Concerning the Sacrament* (1550). In *De Regno Christi* Martin Bucer fuses the Erasmian call for biblical drama with Protestant theology, thus anticipating Sidney's argument that drama's great strength is its capacity to move and inspire. In rejecting neoclassical canons, Bucer reduces the distinction between comedy and tragedy to the simple difference between representation of everyday happenings as opposed to extraordinary actions "such as excite greater wonder." His finding that the Bible abounds in actions that "happen contrary to expectation and which Aristotle calls 'reversals of fortune' " effects a synthesis of the *Poetics* and *Paraclesis*. In associating tragedy with *de casibus* tradition, Bucer makes

[10] John T. Murray, *English Dramatic Companies: 1558-1642* (1910; 2 vols.), II, 71-73, 91.

[11] Ibid., II, 68; G. C. Moore-Smith, ed., "The Academic Drama at Cambridge: Extracts from College Records," *Malone Society Collections*, II, 2 (1923), 151. For mention of " 'one Myles, one of my lord of Summersettes players,' " see E. K. Chambers, *The Elizabethan Stage* (Oxford, 1923; 4 vols.), II, 330.

Milton's distinction that Adam is the best "godlike and heroic" figure. [12]

The theories of Bucer and Bale clarify the Reformation vogue for comedy as the embodiment of God's providential design. *Nice Wanton* is unique among Reformation plays in imitating the tragic pattern of despair and damnation. [13] Bale distinguishes between the two genres in terms of the apocalyptic pattern of salvation and damnation, thus differentiating characters into the comic elect or the tragic reprobate. All of his plays reenact the archetypal pattern of *King Johan*, which draws its structure from Kirchmeyer's *Pammachius*. Inherent in Bale's eschatological framework is the assumption that the Reformation provides an essentially comic resolution to the otherwise tragic course of human history, a resolution that looks forward to the final victory over Antichrist at the time of the Last Judgment. Although the misery of King John (a figure for Henry VIII as a reforming monarch) may appear tragic from our human perspective, from the standpoint of divine providence individual suffering is subsumed in the fulfillment of divine will. Bale later expanded his dramatic scheme into the full-scale reading of apocalyptic history in the *Image of Both Churches*.

Bale's comedic vision of the Reformation conflict is made perfectly clear in two accounts of his own dramatic productions given in his autobiographical writings. He designed his 1551 Bishopstoke production of *A Comedy Concernynge Thre Lawes*, a "boke [that] was imprynted about .vi. yeares ago, and hath bene abroad ever sens," as a reflection of the Edwardian reforms. Bale's dramatization

---

[12] Cited from Wickham's translation of the chapter "De honestis ludis" ("Concerning the Respectability of Plays"), in *Stages*, II, 1, Appendix C.

[13] J.M.R. Margeson, *The Origins of English Tragedy* (Oxford, 1967), pp. 40-41.

of himself as "Baleus prolocutor" in this and other plays confused the boundary between the world and the stage. A Catholic opponent wittily tried to neutralize Bale's dramatic authority by tampering with the text and inducing a servant in Bale's household who belonged to the cast to insert an added speech: "Moreover he requyred hym, in hys own stought name to do a lewde massage [*sic*], whych was to call the compiler of that Comedie, both heretike and knave, concludynge that it was a boke of most perniciouse heresie" (*Expostulation*, C3ʳ). Although Irish priests later welcomed Edward's death by drinking in taverns "with Gaudeamus in dolio," Bale's "celebration" of the event with a performance of his trilogy implied that Mary's accession was a temporary setback in the apocalyptic conflict. Such performance shows that Bale, as Bishop of Ossory, interpreted the production as a counterpart to *de casibus* tragedy by demonstrating the comedic pattern of divine providence. Performance by "yonge men . . . at the market crosse with organe plainges and songes" was met by the "small contentacion of the prestes and other papistes there" (*Vocacyon*, C6ʳ, C8ᵛ).

Contrary to later sterotypes about the Puritans, early evangelicals approved of drama. Foxe called it a divinely inspired form: "players, printers, preachers . . . be set up of God, as a triple bulwark against the triple crown of the pope, to bring him down . . ." (*A & M*, VI, 57). Except for Foxe's use of Latin, his apocalyptic comedy *Christus Triumphans* (Basel, 1556) is a gospelling play. The "tragedies" in *Actes and Monuments* follow the *de casibus* pattern. Biblical drama in the gospelling manner flourished until near the end of Elizabeth's reign.[14] Not until the

---

[14] Louis B. Wright, "The Scriptures and the Elizabethan Stage," *MP*, 26 (1928), 47-56.

opening of the first public theater in 1576 did radical Protestants begin to attack the stage, not out of principle but because of the corrupting social effects of the commercial theater.[15] Only in the period leading to the Puritan closure of the theater in 1642 did evangelical opinion crystallize into the kind of unthinking opposition that Jonson parodied in Zeal-of-the-Land Busy's attendance at the puppet show in *Bartholomew Fair*. Nevertheless an anonymous attack on the stage provoked Lewis Wager to reply in the prologue of the Edwardian interlude *Mary Magdalene*:

> Doth not our facultie learnedly extoll vertue?
> Doth it not teache God to be praised above all things?
> What facultie doth vice more earnestly subdue?
> Doth it not teache true obedience to the kynge?
> What godly sentences to the mynde doth it brynge?
> I saie, there was neuer thyng invented
> More worthe for man's solace to be frequented.
>
> (ll. 31-37)[16]

As one of the earliest documents for the Tudor controversy over the stage, Wager's defense implies the moralistic theory that Sidney systematized in his *Apology*.

Wager's defense of the stage attests to opposition to Reformation drama. In an age that prized "plain and easy" statement adapted to an unlearned audience, it was by no means a natural decision to cast advanced ideas in dramatic nor even fictional form. Like Luke Shepherd's satiric inversions, dramatic irony makes strenuous demands upon a sometimes confused audience. One cannot deny that controversial prose dominates Reformation composition. The-

[15] William A. Ringler, Jr., "The First Phase of the Elizabethan Attack on the Stage, 1558-1579," *HLQ*, 5 (1942), 391-418.

[16] *The Life and Repentaunce of Marie Magdalene*, ed. F. I. Carpenter (Chicago, 1902).

ological treatises and artless paraphrases of theological argument suited the unambiguous statement of Protestant ideas. Yet an impulse toward entertaining fiction resulted in the creation of dialogues and interludes. *Mary Magdalene* promises on its title page a work "Not only Godlie, Learned and Fruitefull, But Also Well Furnished with Pleasaunt Myrth and Pastime, Very Delectable For Those Which Shall Heare or Reade the Same." Despite dour stereotypes about Protestant art, the first regular English comedies date from Edward VI's reign. *Roister Doister* and *Gammer Gurton's Needle* stand in gentle contrast to the flood of violent pamphlet attacks on the mass and traditional doctrine.

Scriptural themes are the hallmark of Edwardian drama. Gospelling playwrights shape their material according to two basic structures: dramatization of individual Bible stories and incorporation of diverse biblical texts into dialogue, character, and action. Extensive paraphrases are important in both formats. Even such ostensibly secular plays as *Nice Wanton* and *Lusty Juventus* turn out to be reworkings of stories such as the parable of the Prodigal Son. Becon's retelling of the Nativity story by means of a biblical cento is an extreme example of both techniques. As Tyndalean analogues to pulpit *exempla*, these materials acquire topical relevance through application to contemporary life. When the Messenger in *Lusty Juventus* comments on an "order to bring up youth, Ecclesiasticus doth write," the author actually inserts a citation into dialogue. As a book emblem analogous to Reformation woodcuts, the New Testament that Juventus receives from Good Counsel symbolizes lay Bible education. Becon so thickly glosses the margins of *New Dialog* with biblical citations that the printed text resembles a Protestant Bible commentary. The gospellers grafted their scriptural style and thought onto the traditional forms of the mystery play and moral interlude.

[279]

Unlike the Reformation plays, the old mysteries mingled Bible texts with apocryphal and contemporary materials. On the rare occasions when they quoted from the Bible, medieval dramatists used Vulgate Latin that would have baffled lay members of the audience.

The major topic of the Reformation stage is the education of youth. For Bucer and Wager, moral and spiritual instruction is a guiding principle that transcends the simple use of tag phrases from the Bible. Thus Juventus wavers between Catholic Vices and Protestant Virtues who offer radically different lessons during the course of his spiritual education. Cranmer's *Catechism*, the confirmation rite in the prayer book, and the orders to parents and clergy in the Royal Injunctions attest to the governmental concern with the upbringing of youth. Generational conflict between youth and age is a corollary theme. The harshness of tension between parent and child as well as brothers and sisters may confuse the modern reader. But just as Donne uses the transition from one generation to the next as a metaphor for religious reform in "Satire III," the gospellers treat the youth as a Reformation Everyman who is torn between the "young" faith of the Protestant and the "old" carnal corruption of the Catholic.

Conflict between the generations personifies the Reformation by means of an application of the Pauline admonition to "put off the old man" (see Romans 6:6, Ephesians 4:22, and Colossians 3:9). In the prologue to Romans, Tyndale states that faith "killeth the olde Adam, and maketh us altogether new in the hart . . ." (*Whole Workes*, H1ᵛ). The Reformation *topos* of the transition from Old Law to New Law underlies these themes. In the process of conversion, a youth may personify an old believer of any age. The gospellers saw the Reformation not as something radically new but as a return to "infantile" faith that had atrophied under the papacy. Becon's nativity play, for example, dramatizes the rebirth of Protestant faith. The Red Cross Knight would later assist Una, a figure for truth, in rescuing her Adamic parents from the "eternall bondage" of sin and error (*FQ*, I.xii.4-5; see I.i.5). Wager attributes Mary Magdalene's fallen condition to parental indulgence as well as childish disobedience.

Lust as the chief failing of youth was exploited by the gospellers in order to heighten the dramatic realism and interest of their plays. Although Bucer would have disapproved on the ground that the plays would be "defiled by impious and disgusting interchanges of buffoonery, even if some pleasure is given by refinements of wit and learning," the gospellers successfully mixed instruction with entertainment through their comic handling of corruption. The Vice always plays the comic lead.[17] Shepherd's satires parallel Reformation drama in ribaldry.

Sexual frankness was compatible with scriptural materials to the gospellers, for their plays dramatize negative arguments for the prayer book doctrine that marriage purifies heterosexual love. The witty figure of Dame Christian Custance in *Roister Doister* is the only positive embodiment of Protestant marriage ideals in a comic character; her widowed matronliness contrasts with the conventional dramatization of callow stage youths. These Reformation principles underlie Spenser's idealization of married love in *Epithalamion* and the "Legend of Chastitie," as well as Milton's paeon to the "naked majesty" of Adam and Eve (*PL*, IV.290 et seq.).[18] The link between domestic comedy and Protestant attitudes toward love may help to explain the conventional marriage scenes that conclude Shake-

[17] F. P. Wilson, *The English Drama: 1485-1585*, ed. G. K. Hunter (Oxford, 1969), p. 59.

[18] See William and Malleville Haller, "The Puritan Art of Love," *HLQ*, 5 (1942), 235-72, and William Haller, " 'Hail Wedded Love,' " *ELH*, 13 (1946), 79-97.

speare's comedies. The Protestant ideal of married love is both the literal means and the symbolic image of the reforming of human society. The contrasting denial of love by the medieval celibate ideal explains Reformation fascination with the unnatural lusts and sodomy imputed to the priesthood in works by Luther, Tyndale, Bale, Shepherd, and Baldwin. Milton similarly delights in the doubly incestuous lineage of Sin and Death as the offspring of Satan (*PL*, II.727-814).

By costuming the old morality Vices in clerical vestments and giving them oaths and blasphemies to recite, the gospellers transform the moral interlude from ethical allegory into a vehicle for polemics against the Roman church. The crude puns and jests of the Catholic Vices, an inheritance from such medieval forebears as Titivillus, counterbalance the didacticism of Reformation drama. Thus Juventus's seduction by the harlot Abominable Living personifies his backsliding. In a parody of courtly love, the naive youth cautiously arranges a "secret" assignation only to find Hypocrisy deflating his "romantic" efforts:

> What and it were known? It is no deadly sin;
> As for my part I do not greatly care,
> So that they find not your proper buttocks bare.
> (ll. 849-51)[19]

Infidelity's sole response to Mary Magdalene's remorse is the leering remark:

> Prick of conscience, quod she? It pricketh you not
> so sore
> As the yong man with the flaxen beard dyd, I thinke.
> (ll. 1050-51)[20]

---

[19] J.A.B. Somerset, ed., *Four Tudor Interludes* (1974).

[20] In *Biblical Drama* Roston misinterprets the symbolic purpose of Prot-

Allusion to *Prick of Conscience* (ascribed to Richard Rolle) redoubles Wager's innuendo.

Hypocrisy's words to the contrary, fornication becomes a composite symbol for the seven deadly sins. In an age when Bale identified the Whore of Babylon with the Church of Rome, dramatic bawdry symbolized the "spiritual fornication" of Roman ritualism (Revelation 19:2).[21] Similarly, Spenser associates loose sexuality with spiritual error in Duessa's seduction of the Red Cross Knight (*FQ*, I.vii.6-7). Nevertheless, Bucer's warning articulates a problem inherent in the dramatization of evil. Despite authors' manifest disapproval of their villains, fascinated audiences tend to sympathize with attractively rendered vice. Paradoxical response to such figures as Doctor Faustus, Richard III, Volpone, Bosola, and Milton's Satan attests to the intensity of this reaction. In a retrospective account of his youthful attendance at a moral interlude, R. Willis documents this inherent difficulty in *Mount Tabor* (1639). Having forgotten the strict morality, he remembers only the exciting action.[22]

Protestant drama analyzed the Reformation conflict by mirroring biblical archetypes in contemporary life. Although Jerusalem is the historical setting of *Mary Magdalene*, the heroine's clothing and manner mark her as a fallen woman who could have strolled the stews of Southwark. In Grimald's *Archipropheta*, John the Baptist preaches to Herod, Annas, and Caiaphas in the manner of the Protestant preacher. Biblical names are important in some sec-

---

estant ribaldry: "For a play so moral in its intent, there is an extraordinary amount of hugging and kissing on the stage itself, and the scene of 'debauchery' ends with the singing of a merry song" (p. 69).

[21] *Duessa as Theological Satire*, passim.

[22] Bevington analyzes Willis's record in *"Mankind" to Marlowe*, pp. 13-15.

ular plays. The names Dalilah and Ismael distinguish reprobate children from their elect brother Barnabas in the
domestic tragedy of *Nice Wanton*. Just as blind Milton
would perceive Samson in himself, the Reformation audience saw Dalilah as a seductress who enervates true faith.
Ismael recreates the fall from grace of Abraham's elder
son, by the bondwoman Hagar, after the birth of his elect
son Isaac. As the namesake of the disciple of Paul and one
of the first Christian missionaries, Barnabas bears the mark
of the Protestant saint. In a curious hybrid, the neglectful
mother of the children receives the name of Socrates' proverbially shrewish wife Xantippe.

Symbolic names provide a key to the meaning in other
plays. Although they leave little room for dynamic growth
and change, these generic type-names differ from full-blown
personifications in their application to otherwise realistic
characters. Type-names are a familiar device in moralistic
works like *Piers Plowman*, Jonson's comedies, and Restoration comedy. Reformation type-characters represent a
transitional stage between medieval personifications and
Jonsonian humors characters. Thus Juventus comes out of
the morality tradition of *Mankind*, *Everyman*, and the
Henrician interlude *Youth*. The fidelity of Christian Custance (Constance) stands in pointed contrast to the moral
disarray of Ralph Roister Doister.

THE BANISHMENT OF "MISTRESS MISSA"

Dialogue might seem better suited than drama to the purposes of Reformation controversy. More's dialogues against
Luther and Tyndale show that the form adapts well to
polemical attack. Perhaps it could have satisfied the need
fulfilled by Protestant drama. The staging of a few dialogues and the dramatization of allegorical conceits from

dialogues suggest that some Edwardian authors even conceived of the form in dramatic or semidramatic terms. With John Heywood still living at court, *The Play of the Wether*, *The Foure PP*, and his other dialogues provided ample English precedent. Nevertheless, the Protestant dialogues follow More rather than Heywood in marshaling thinly fictionalized pamphlet arguments. Because Catholic interlocutors never articulate convincing arguments, the form is used for purposes of polemical attack rather than disinterested discussion. Protestant drama fulfills the purposes of debate and discussion much better than dialogue. In contrast to the straightforward doctrinal formulations of pamphlets and dialogues, Reformation interludes dramatize the complexity of human behavior. In bringing to life both sides of the religious controversy, such plays as *Lusty Juventus*, *Jacob and Esau*, *Nice Wanton*, and *Mary Magdalene* forcefully embody the central epistemological problem of the Reformation Protestant. Caught between opposing and attractive forces, Juventus's relationship to the Vice figures is indeed ambiguous, and he experiences genuine difficulty in resolving problems of faith and knowledge of good and evil.

English Reformation dialogues emerge out of the popular tradition of German Lutheranism as well as the controversy between More and Tyndale. Because Erasmian humanism had undergone the same metamorphosis in Germany that it experienced at the hands of Tyndale and his followers, English Protestant dialogues represent an indirect and simplified offshoot of the academic tradition of Renaissance humanism. Rediscovery of Plato and Lucian permitted the humanistic revival of the dialogue as a vehicle for philosophical discussion and satire. Unlike the dominant medieval tradition represented by Justin Martyr's dialogue with the Jew Trypho and Augustine's *Contra*

Academicos, the humanistic dialogue permitted discussion of a wide range of issues through sophisticated debate and intellectual analysis. The form could be adapted to refutation or to the unresolved statement of problems and arguments. In such works as *Moriae Encomium* and *Utopia*, Erasmus and More exploit the potential for irony of Lucianic satire in order to conceal authorial opinion behind a web of arguments by historical and fictional interlocutors.[23] Raphael Hythlodaeus and *persona* More leave so many points unresolved in their debate over royal counsel that More wishes for "another chance . . . to talk them over more fully." His polemical dialogues, on the other hand, aim at one-sided refutation of nascent Protestant doctrine. Even though Thomas Starkey's *Dialogue between Reginald Pole & Thomas Lupset* (written c. 1533-35) is more evenly balanced, Pole is led toward Lupset's conclusions. Starkey uses the speakers as mouthpieces for his program of social reform.[24]

English imitations of the popular dialogues of Lutheran Germany avoid irony in favor of explicit doctrinal statement. The nominal fiction of these Reformation allegories continues to furnish readers with some entertainment. The favored forms for Lutheran dialogues are debates between fathers and sons, laymen and clerics, and trials of personified ideas.[25] Proximity to Protestant Germany made Ipswich a likely place for Anthony Scoloker to translate and print Hans Sachs's dialogue between the shoemaker and

[23] See Hanna H. Grey, "Renaissance Humanism: The Pursuit of Eloquence," in *Renaissance Essays*, ed. P. O. Kristeller and P. J. Wiener (New York, 1968), pp. 214-15.

[24] Ed. Kathleen Burton (1948).

[25] C. H. Herford, *Studies in the Literary Relations between England and Germany in the Sixteenth Century* (Cambridge, 1886), pp. 28-29.

priest.[26] The anonymous *Dyalogue or Disputacion bytwene a Gentylman and a Prest Concernynge the Supper of the Lord* (1548) attests to the same German influence as *John Bon and Mast Person.* The *Dyalogue*'s reputed publication under the pseudonymous imprint of Hans Hitprick suggests the possibility of authorship by William Turner, whose *Rescuynge of the Romishe Foxe* (Bonn, 1545) attacked Gardiner with its false colophon "winchester, by me Hanse hit prik." At their meeting on the road to London during Parliament time, a gentleman succeeds in converting a cleric from the "north partese of England" through the recitation of biblical texts.

A spate of Mistress Missa dialogues circulated during the thick of the 1548 debate on the mass; they appear to reflect courtly auspices. After his recent return from Germany, Turner conflated the Lutheran device of the allegorical trial with Luke Shepherd's Mistress Missa conceit in *A New Dialogue Wherein is Conteyned the Examination of the Masse.* His characters derive from native dramatic tradition and German Reformation drama. Turner's names label the advocates for the defense, Porphyry (a doctor of canon law) and Sir Philip Philargiry (a doctor of divinity), as scholastic enemies of the new faith. He takes Porphyry from Kirchmeyer's *Pammachius* or Bale's lost translation. As a figure for avarice, Philargiry ("love of silver") probably comes from the allegorical trial in *Nigramansir*, a lost interlude by John Skelton.[27] The humanistic education of Palemon, the judge, and of the Masters of Arts from Oxford and Cambridge who serve as prosecutors denies medieval scholastic and sacerdotal traditions. Palemon accepts their credentials with the gospelling argument: "Must they

---

[26] *A Goodly Dysputatyon betwene a Christen Shomaker and a Popysshe Parson* (1548).

[27] Warton, *History of English Poetry*, II, 360-63.

now be unlearned, because they are no priestes?" (B4ᵛ-5ʳ). The prosecution's citation of gospel texts embodies Protestant rejection of the apocryphal tradition of unwritten verities represented by the defense. The introduction into evidence of Master Knowledge's quotation from the Greek New Testament strikingly personifies the fundamental literalism of the Reformation return *ad fontes*: "I take to wytnes both Erasmus translation and the Greke Ε'κῖνος ὑμᾶς διδάξι πάντα καὶ ὑπομνέσι ὑμᾶσ πάντα οσα εἶπον ὑμῖν that is to saye, he shall teache you all thynges and put you in remembraunce of al thinges whatsoever I have sayd unto you" (D4ʳ⁻ᵛ; see John 14:26). Both the name of the prosecutor and the text that he cites personify the epistemological problem of Protestant faith.

William Punt imitates Turner's trial format in *A New Dialoge Called the Endightment agaynste Mother Messe*. A tailor with that name worked on a 1550 Shrovetide play at court that required costumes for a king and a seven-headed dragon (Feuillerat, p. 39). His involvement in antipapal polemics and the radical tradition of artisan-authors make it far more likely that he wrote the work than the William Punt whom Foxe attacked as a "great writer of devilish and erroneous books" (*A & M*, VIII, 384). During the Marian exile, Bale referred to a William Punt as "one of our number" ("ex horum numero"; *Catalogus*, I, 741-42). Sere's publication of two more editions of the dialogue within three weeks of the initial publication on 17 December 1548 attests to the popular reception of the work. Punt models his spokesmen, who include Sergeant Wisdom and the prosecutors Verity and Knowledge, on Turner's personifications of lay rationalism. The empaneling of the twelve apostles as the jury by the presiding judge, the Word of God, offers a more sensational version of Turner's formula.

Publication of *A Breife Recantacion of Maystres Missa*, a truncation of the trial figure of Turner and Punt under the initials J. M., suggests authorship by Seymour's retainer John Mardeley. Poor laymen could readily afford this lurid chapbook confession by the Roman harlot. A scurrilous genealogy traces her descent as the eldest daughter of the pope and Dame Avaritia, as well as her parentage of many offspring (masses for the dead and other rites) fathered by the pope and College of Cardinals. Her incestuous liaisons identify her as a Protestant variant of the Whore of Babylon and spiritual forebear of Spenser's Duessa. Her fecundity as a mother figure parallels that of Spenser's Error (a prototype of Duessa in her double aspect as fearsome dragon and loathsome hag), with her famished brood of a "thousand yong ones" (*FQ*, I.i.14-15, 25). Creeping in and out of the womb of the mother upon whom they feed, the monstrous offspring of Milton's Sin, sired by Death and grandchildren of Satan, emerge prolifically out of this indecent tradition of Reformation allegory (*PL*, II.795-800). As the most vivid allegory for the suppression of the mass, the conviction and banishment of Mistress Missa after her three-hundred-year sway in England anticipate the exile of another papal daughter, Duessa (*FQ*, I.ii.22).

The Protestant Everyman

Reformation plays fall into the two broad categories of elite drama and popular interlude. One may differentiate between the two groups on the basis of the auspices and circumstances of production, as well as the techniques and conventions of staging. Because of the omnipresence of the English Bible and Protestant ideology on the Reformation stage, any classification based upon subject matter or topical ideas would be limited in its results. Choristers, students, and courtiers performed the elite plays in churches, university colleges, aristocratic households, and at court. Itinerant troupes of four men and a boy enacted popular interludes in market squares, inn yards, and the halls of provincial lords and gentry. Because distinctions between elite and popular drama are not mutually exclusive, aristocratic plays adopted many of the elements and conventions of the popular interlude. Elite drama ranges from the purely catechetical church dialogue of Thomas Becon to the Latin plays and English comedies performed at the universities and royal court. Popular plays, on the other hand, fuse evangelical fervor with ribald humor in a manner puzzling to most readers today.

Although D. Douglas Waters ascribes "dramatic" method to the Mistress Missa dialogues,[28] the works lack dramatic structure and could not have been performed. The prolix wordiness of their tractlike speeches precludes representation with physical action, music, and spectacle. Lack of rhetorical shaping places the extensive prose arguments and scriptural paraphrases of these dialogues only one step away from nonmimetic sermons and pamphlets. Punt's auxiliary role in the court revels suggests, however, that costumed readers could have recited his dialogue. The direct address to his "gentle audience" (C3ʳ) supports this possibility. Punt's phrase may refer both to the apostolic jury within the work and to an audience of aristocratic auditors. In all probability, the epithet is a narrative relic of deferential salutations such as the Franklin's addresses to his gentle "sires" and "Lordynges" in the *Canterbury Tales*.

Thomas Becon, on the other hand, definitely composed *A New Dialog betwene thangell of God, & the Shepherdes in the Felde* (c. 1547) for performance. Affinities between the

[28] *Duessa as Theological Satire*, p. 7.

liturgy and the dialogue suggest that he had church production in mind. Because the writing of plays was a normal
duty of chaplains in large Tudor households, Becon's composition of the work during service to Seymour places him
in the company of such clerical playwrights as Skelton,
Medwall, Bale, and Udall.[29] The impersonation of characters by actors is the major innovation that separates Becon's work from other Reformation dialogues. The title
page tells the reader that the plot comes directly from Luke's
account of "the nativite and birthe of Jesus Christ." Only
the absence of physical movement by the characters during
performance prevents the piece from becoming completely
dramatic.

This work is an important transitional link between the
pamphlets and dialogues of the gospellers and fully dramatic Reformation plays. Becon's text, with its biblical
glosses, takes on the appearance of a Protestant tract. John
Day's note that the text is "swete and pleasante to reade"
shows that Becon, like Skelton in *The Bowge of Court*, addresses both reader and spectator. Becon's insertion of "The
Songe of thangels" suggests that a church choir, or the
choirboys and gentlemen of the Chapel Royal, recited the
dialogue. In moving from dialogue between a single angel
and a group of shepherds to twin choruses of angels and
shepherds, the piece lends itself to performance by two
half-choirs. The piece reads quickly, and its 1,328 dimeter
and octosyllabic lines could be recited in less than one hour.
Recitation could have taken place in churches, at court, or
in aristocratic households. Edifying discourses were sometimes presented at court between the courses of banquets
or on important state occasions.[30] Songs are characteristic

[29] Wickham, *Stages*, II, 1, 125.
[30] Bevington, *"Mankind" to Marlowe*, pp. 41-42; Feuillerat, p. 60.

of such boys' plays as *Roister Doister* and *Jacob and Esau*. The need for a sizeable choir of angels would have made popular presentation difficult if not impossible.

Stage directions announce the dramatic nature of the dialogue. Becon notes at the very beginning that "thangell speketh." Throughout the work "the Shepherds speake" responsively (A2ʳ, A5ᵛ et seq.). Similar directions appear frequently in medieval moralities and Tudor interludes. The manuscript of *Mankind*, for example, informs the reader that Titivillus directs his speeches to three different characters in quick succession: "loquitur ad newgyse . . . loquitur ad nowadays . . . loquitur ad nought."[31] Henry Medwall's *Fulgens and Lucrece* contains simple directions such as "Intrat A dicens" (1.1). Becon's *Dialog* is no less dramatized than John Heywood's *Wytty and Wytless*, a dialogue that implies no stage action and lacks stage directions altogether.[32]

Anthony Scoloker's translation of Hans Sachs's *Goodly Dysputatyon betwene a Christen Shomaker and a Popysshe Parson* is the only other Reformation dialogue to contain instructions similar to Becon's directions. In other mid-Tudor dialogues, authors present speech in the past tense and in a narrative rather than dramatic mode. Scoloker's translation begins when "the Shomaker comminge to the parsones house, speaketh to the parsons servaunt" (A2ʳ; quoted from the 2nd ed.). Sachs wrote one-act farces, comedies, Shrovetide plays, and tragedies for performance. Although the printed text of *Disputation zwischen einem Chorherren und Schuchmacher* (Nuremberg?, 1524) contains no references to dramatic performance, Scoloker's title page

---

[31] Ed. David Bevington in *The Macro Plays* (New York and Washington, 1972), ll. 477, 482, 486.

[32] See R. C. Johnson, "Stage Directions in the Tudor Interlude," *Theatre Notebook*, 26 (1971), 37.

refers to performance as it was "done within the famous Citie of Norembourgh." The work "done" refers to dramatic performance rather than prose composition in the same sense as does Bale's description of his enemy's attempt to interpolate a discrediting speech into his Hampshire production of *Three Laws*: "he requyred hym . . . to do a lewde massage [*sic*], whych was to call the compiler of that Comedie, both heretike and knave . . ." (*Expostulation*, C3ʳ).

Becon imitates the form of John Bale's anti-Catholic mystery plays. Bale's *Chefe Promyses of God*, for example, substitutes dialogues between God and a variety of biblical figures, including Adam, Noah, and Abraham, for fully dramatic action. Bale appears to have written his dramatic trilogy with church production in mind, because stage directions specify performance by "chorus cum organis." Although he could have had a portable organ at his disposal, Bale's reference to performance of the trilogy at the market cross in Ossory "with organe plainges and songes" suggests that the players acted at the porch of the cathedral church or at an adjacent square (*Vocacyon*, C8ᵛ). Along with Bale's performances, Becon's Protestant nativity play supported the effort by Seymour and Cranmer to supplant the mystery cycles. The traditional occasion for the performance of mystery plays disappeared when the feast of Corpus Christi was suppressed in 1548. At roughly the same time, references to transubstantiation and the seven sacraments were edited out of the Towneley cycle. Archbishop Robert Holgate ordered plays on the death, assumption, and coronation of the Virgin Mary stricken from the York cycle.[33]

Becon's *Dialog betwene thangell & the Shepherdes* breaks

[33] Harold C. Gardiner, *Mysteries' End: An Investigation of the Last Days of the Medieval Religious Stage* (New Haven, 1946), p. 61.

sharply with the conventions of the medieval cycles, except for its parody of two staple rhyme schemes from the mystery plays: *aaabcccb* and *ababcdcd*. The work's autonomy contradicts the cyclic context of the mysteries, with their festive performances on pageant wagons. Although his static, expository speeches would impede popular performance, Becon's ritualistic, catechetical manner suits performance in church. If Bale and Becon designed their Protestant mysteries for church production, they returned English biblical drama indoors to the site where it originated when the "*quem quaeretis*" performance was added to the Easter liturgy at Winchester (c. 970). Performance during Christmastide would complement efforts by reformers to eradicate Christmas carols and other nonscriptural forms of entertainment.

Comparison with the *Secunda Pastorum* of the Towneley cycle highlights the distinctively Protestant qualities of Becon's nativity play. The Wakefield Master accommodated sacred history to his unlearned audience by setting his realistic comedy on the wintry Yorkshire moors. The peasant comedy of Mak, Gill, and the three shepherds outbalances the fleeting nativity scene at the conclusion. Medieval iconography explains the inclusion of the apparently incongruous sheep-stealing episode as a homely parody of the birth of Christ, the Lamb of God.[34] The angel's Latin hymn to the shepherds constitutes the tiny scriptural core of the play: "Angelus cantat 'gloria in ex[c]elsis' " (l. 637). Aside from quotation of "[Ecce] virgo concipiet" (ll. 681-82), the prophecy of the Messiah in Isaiah 7:14, only two stanzas spoken by the angel and Mary have biblical support (ll. 638-46, 737-45). The poet dramatizes the radical

[34] William Manly, "Shepherds and Prophets: Religious Unity in the Towneley *Secunda Pastorum*," *PMLA*, 78 (1963), 151-55.

effect of the angel's message on the shepherds rather than the message itself. In the Towneley pageant, the Word inheres in the world rather than the Book. In the *Prima Pastorum* and other medieval nativity plays, the shepherds' inability to understand the angel's Latin functions as a comic convention.[35]

Becon's reversal of the medieval relationship between angel and shepherds dramatizes Protestant attitudes toward the scriptures. As a Protestant radical, he rejects the Vulgate and all comic additions to *Secunda Pastorum* in favor of the English Bible. Instead of apocryphal peasant comedy, Becon's biblical cento documents a scrupulous effort to transmit the gospel message. As an emblem for the Incarnation, the vertical axis of the Protestant nativity descends from God to man by means of the angel's vernacular news. By way of contrast, Coll, Gyb and Daw move horizontally from English moorland to the stable at Bethlehem. The Wakefield Master assumes that truth is immanent in the "legendary" story of Christ's birth. For the Reformation playwright, however, only the providential intervention of the Incarnation illuminates a dark and fallen world. Because of the stubbornness of medieval traditions of carol and folk art, later Puritans in England and New England attempted first to reduce and then ban all popular Christmas celebrations. In the sensuous conceits and allegory of "The Burning Babe," the Jesuit martyr Robert Southwell preserves pictorial imagery analogous to the religious art demolished by iconoclastic attack. In Milton's ode "On the Morning of Christ's Nativity" (composed 1629), however, the omission of traditional elements in the Christmas "legend" accords with the evangelical tra-

[35] *The Towneley Plays*, ed. G. England (1897; EETS, e.s. 71). See Roston, *Biblical Drama*, p. 41.

dition of Reformation art. In the haunting moment of still-
ness and silence, one perceives the timeless consequences
of the Incarnation when

> Nature that heard such sound
> . . . knew such harmony alone
> Could hold all heaven and earth in happier union.
>
> (ll. 101, 107-108)

Becon shapes his nativity drama as an archetype for the
English Reformation not through interpolation of authorial comment or extraneous material, but by means of pat-
terned selection of scriptural texts. Although he builds upon
Luke's narrative, his synoptic speeches draw texts from
various portions of the Old and New Testaments. The three
epigraphs conflate the story of Jesus' birth with the Protestant theology of original sin and imputed grace, predestination and election (Isaiah 9:6; 1 Timothy 1:15; 1 John
3:8). Calvin's interpretation of the shepherds as the elect
of God is the intellectual foundation of Becon's evangelical
work.[36] The dialogue dramatizes the Reformation as a time
of unimpeded lay Bible education. Unlike the comic peasants of *Secunda Pastorum*, Becon's shepherds engage in serious discourse with the angel concerning salvation. The
angel's answers to the questions of the ignorant shepherds
function as short homilies. The angel, who speaks in the
voice of the Protestant preacher, dominates the work; the
shepherds offer, on the other hand, a means of providing
some semblance of action in an otherwise static play without falling into the fictions of the mystery cycles. The contrast between Christ's ministry and the sterile formalism
of the Pharisees and Sadducees mirrors reformist attacks

---

[36] *A Harmony of the Gospels Matthew, Mark, and Luke*, trans. A. W.
Morrison, 3 vols. (Edinburgh, 1972) in Calvin, *Commentaries*, ed. D. W.
and T. F. Torrance, 12 vols. (Edinburgh, 1960-72), I, 75.

on Roman ritualism. Protestant doctrines concerning justification by faith, denial of purgatory, and the spiritual
nature of Christ's presence in the communion service run
through the angel's speeches (B8^r-C5^r). In contrast to the
misunderstandings of Coll, Gib, and Daw, two long shepherd speeches at the conclusion of Becon's dialogue dramatize their comprehension and the success of Protestant lay
education (C8^v-D1^v, D3^v-4^v). In discussing the angel's
message among themselves, the shepherds speak for the
first time in scriptural paraphrase. Their new understanding permits them to discourse wisely and locate the Bethlehem stable without further intervention from the divine.

Nicholas Grimald's *Archipropheta* is the best example of
a Reformation university play. His subtle fusion of classical form and biblical content contrasts with the nativism
of Becon's *Dialog*. Grimald's manuscript (MS Royal 12 A.
XLVI) dates from very near the beginning of Edward's
reign, during his tenure at Christ Church College, Oxford.[37] As a friend of Grimald resident in Wesel, John
Bale could have arranged Martin Gymnicus's 1548 publication of the text in Cologne.[38] Grimald's dedication to
Richard Cox, Almoner to Edward VI and Dean of Christ
Church, supports Boas's argument that he designed the
play for performance in the college hall before university
scholars. A learned clerical audience would appreciate its
sophisticated dramatization of religious problems.

The choice of John the Baptist as his hero suggests that
Grimald wrote the work as a Reformation play. Designa-

---

[37] In *University Drama in the Tudor Age* (Oxford, 1914), pp. 33-34,
F. S. Boas argues for composition in 1546 before Henry's death. Harbage, on the other hand, enters it for 1547 in *Annals*.

[38] Bale records a copy of the play at Oriel College, Oxford (*Index*, p.
301). He attributes to Grimald a text addressed "to his friend John Bale"
("Ad amicum Ioan. Baleum") in *Catalogus*, I, 701.

tion of the play as "tragoedia" parallels the generic ideas
of Bucer and Bale. Thus despite the particular tragedy of
the Evangelist's fall, Jehovah's explanation of the "hidden
victory" in the denouement enables the audience to perceive "comic" irony in the ensuing ministry of Christ.
Grimald's designation of *Christus redivivus* (Cologne, 1543)
as "comoedia tragica" shows that he thought along such
lines. The reformers saw John as the prototype for the
Protestant preacher, and commentators read an attack on
the Roman clergy into John's outbursts against the Hebrew
priesthood. According to Calvin, Pharisaic corruption justified the harshness of his preaching:

> Truly, if you compare the Pope and his foul clergy with
> the Sadducees and Pharisees, the kindest thing that you
> can say is that they should be tossed into the same bun-
> dle.[39]

Hugh Latimer preached the same comparison: "Now at
this time, I know of none more like them [the Pharisees]
than the hypocritical hollow-hearted papists. The name is
changed, but the thing remaineth."[40] The attacks on "new
religion" by Grimald's Pharisee, Philautus, associate Hebrew oral or traditional law with medieval devotion. The
Evangelist's simple message of baptism as a means of repentance and forgiveness of sins contradicts the stifling ritualism of the Pharisees' ablutions, confession, fasting, and
tithing. Grimald identifies these practices with justification
by good works by means of the Reformation *topos* of the
transition from Old Law to New Law.

Like Becon, Grimald adapted the mystery play to the
changed circumstances of the Reformation. His allusion in

[39] *Harmony*, I, 121.

[40] *Works*, ed. G. E. Corrie (Cambridge, 1844-45; Parker Soc., 2 vols.),
I, 287.

Christus redivivus to the Resurrection plays from the Hegge and Digby cycles, in addition to Plautus and the Bible, demonstrates his familiarity with native biblical drama.[41] This knowledge of the medieval cycles suggests that he deliberately chose to avoid the medieval tradition of centering Herod plays, like *Magnus Herodes* from the Towneley cycle, on Herod rather than John. The tradition of the ranting Herod found in the English mystery cycles derived from amplification of Matthew 2:16 in medieval commentaries and legends. Hamlet's reference to "out-Heroding Herod" (III.ii.14) shows that this tradition flourished throughout the Tudor age. The humanity of Grimald's Herod follows Josephus, however, rather than any medieval source. Herod's initial sympathy for John, his aborted conversion, vacillations over sentencing, and grief following the decapitation dramatize a state of religious confusion. The chorus views him as an example of religious backsliding (III.x). According to *De Regno Christi*, Bucer would have found the complexities of Herod's character to be a more profitable means of religious instruction than the comic stereotyping of the medieval stage: "when . . . even the crimes of the most abandoned of men [are shown], yet some dread of divine judgement and a horror of sin should appear in them: no exultant delight in crime or shameless insolence should be displayed."

By nature of its audience, Reformation court drama is more entertaining than Grimald's Latin play or Becon's catechetical dialogue. Edward VI's journal entries show that he, like the author of *Mount Tabor*, took great pleasure in the mixture of Protestant theology with dramatic spectacle.

---

[41] G. C. Taylor, "The *Christus Redivivus* of Nicholas Grimald and the Hegge Resurrection Plays," *PMLA*, 41 (1926), 840-59; Patricia Abel, "Grimald's *Christus Redivivus* and the Digby Resurrection Play," *MLN*, 70 (1955), 328-30.

Even a tragedy like *Nice Wanton* would have diverted the sober Protestant courtiers.[42] Although it was licensed for printing in 1560, alteration of the conventional epilogue in praise of the monarch shows that the original version of the play was performed at the Edwardian court by the choirboys. After bringing predestination theology to life by dramatizing the growth and education of three siblings, the young choristers of the Chapel Royal concluded in full chorus with a hymn in praise of God's mercy. When the Messenger defines the hero as a biblical example of faith ("Barnabas, [by interpretation / The son of comfort] . . ."), the Elizabethan printer updated the prologue by quoting Acts 4:37. Marked as a Protestant saint by his bookish habit of quoting scripture, Barnabas lectures Dalilah and Ismael when they cast away their textbooks and play truant. In refusing to discipline them, their mother Xantippe personifies the inability of the old religion to save individual souls. Barnabas, on the other hand, is old beyond his years and utters somber prudential wisdom. In a survival from the old psychomachia, Barnabas combats Iniquity, the Reformation reincarnation of the medieval Vice who seduces Dalilah and Ismael. By characterizing his hero in the generalized role of the Protestant Virtue rather than that of the wavering Mankind figure, the anonymous playwright loses the perennial battle to make good characters sympathetic. In moving from a reactive position between opposing forces, the hero becomes a proponent of the good in his own right. Barnabas's homilies sacrifice dramatic vitality for doctrinal orthodoxy. Despite the deterministic theology that appears to bar his reprobate relatives from salvation, Barnabas succeeds late in life in converting his

[42] Ed. Glynne Wickham in *English Moral Interludes* (1976).

mother and pox-ridden sister through last-minute repentance. The king's journal entries suggest that his Protestant
court might have found moral "comedy" in the conclusion
of this depressed application of the parable of the Prodigal
Son to a spiritually divided England.

Jacob and Esau is a much more lively boys' play. Although it was entered in the Stationers' register in 1557-
58, the interlude must have been written during Edward's
reign, for it is too radical for Mary's. Internal evidence
supports attribution of authorship to Nicholas Udall,[43] whose
position at court gave him a good vantage point for participation in court entertainment. The lost *"Tragoediam de
papatu"* that Bale attributes to Udall (*Summarium*, 3N1ᵛ)
could have been one of the antipapal masques that the king
played in. Although the Marian printer altered the concluding prayer of *Jacob and Esau* to address "the Quenes
majesty," he retained praise of the "counsailours" who
governed on Edward VI's behalf.

Udall's subtle design is less evangelical than that of the
popular interlude. Freed of the need to convert by virtue
of addressing an audience made up of the initiators of reform, he could enliven Protestant theology by means of a
comic retelling of the story of Jacob and Rebecca (Genesis
27). Although the prologue cites the scriptural texts chosen
by Calvin to support his doctrine of predestination (ll. 8-
14), the epilogue's emphasis on free will softens the play's
Calvinistic bias.[44] The cast even includes Terentian slaves.[45]

---

[43] Ed. John Crow and F. P. Wilson (Oxford, 1956; Malone Society
Reprints), vol. 96; see Leicester Bradner, "A Test for Udall's Authorship," *MLN*, 42 (1927), 378-80.

[44] Helen Thomas, *"Jacob and Esau*—'rigidly Calvinistic'?", *SEL*, 9 (1969),
199-213.

[45] Roston, *Biblical Drama*, p. 77.

The Edwardian *topos* of conflict between youth and age, father and son, and brothers and sisters underlies the use of Jacob's trickery as a figure for the Reformation.[46] As a former schoolmaster at the court of a student king, Udall had every reason to graft the theme of the education of youth onto the Bible story. Esau plays the reprobate as the disobedient elder brother, and the playwright austerely interprets his early-morning hunting as an entertainment fully as dissolute as the dicing and fornication of Ismael and Dalilah. His grave and colorless brother Jacob is yet another Barnabas, who shows the calculating self-interest that Tawney and others have associated with the emergence of the sainthood of the elect. As a sober speaker of "good sad wyse counsaile" (l. 198), Jacob joins Barnabas as an idealized Protestant Youth figure.

Jacob and Esau is a proclerical play. As such, the concluding prayer honors "the whole clergy" prior to king and councilors (l. 1824). In stepping forward to apply his deterministic message directly to the gathered court audience, the Poet signals the play's function as self-justification of government by Protestant councilors and prelates. Rebecca converts Isaac in the manner of a Protestant preacher and prophetic spokesman for God. Her memory of the birth of her two sons typifies England's spiritual division into two camps:

> I remember when I had you both conceived,
> A voyce thus saying from the Lord I received:
> Rebecca, in thy womb are now two nations,
> Of unlike natures and contrary fashions.

[46] Calvin, *Institutio Christianae Religionis*, 247-48, as quoted in G. Scheurweghs, "The Date of 'The History of Jacob and Esau,'" *English Studies*, 15 (1933), 218-19. See the topical reading of the play in Bevington, *Drama and Politics*, pp. 109-13.

The one shal be a mightier people elect:
And the elder to the yonger shall be subject.
I know this voice came not to me of nothing. . . .

                                        (ll. 226-32)

Prayers and hymns furnish the framework for the play.
After Rebecca contrasts man's innate depravity with the
inscrutable workings of providence, Isaac eventually imitates her belief in God's justice in one prayer of his own.
Rebecca calls for a "himne or psalme" (l. 860) in a
masquelike representation of the Reformation court where
Thomas Sternhold was the king's favorite. The presence
of two hymns argues for performance by the choristers of
the Chapel Royal, or of St. George's Chapel after Udall
received his appointment as Canon of Windsor. As the
doctrinal core of the play, these hymns exalt the new covenant theology by singing praise that implicitly identifies
the ruling faction with the wisdom of God:

> Of thine owne will thou didst Abraham electe,
> Promising him seede as sterres of the skie,
> And them as thy chosen people to protecte,
> That they might thy mercies praise and magnifie.
>   (ll. 1784-87)

Terentian comedy links *Jacob and Esau* to Udall's other
boys' play, *Ralph Roister Doister*, which shares with *Gammer Gurton's Needle* the claim to designation as the first
regular English comedy. Although Udall's skillful synthesis of classical and native elements has won *Roister Doister*
acclaim as a major forerunner of Elizabethan comedy, most
traditional scholarship has addressed questions of dating,
authorship, and sources.[47] In their rush to move from clas-

---

[47] For a survey of scholarship on the play, see A. W. Plumstead, "Satirical Parody in *Roister Doister*: A Reinterpretation," *SP*, 60 (1963), 141,

sical and medieval origins to the unquestionable genius of Shakespeare and Jonson, critics have ignored signs that identify the play as Reformation moral comedy. Sharing in the topicality of all good satire, the play furnishes a unique comic vantage point on the Tudor religious controversy. Udall's satirical stance distinguishes *Roister Doister* from the more occasional wit and comedy of *Jacob and Esau* and the popular interludes.

Because *Roister Doister* was printed early in Elizabeth's reign (c. 1566), Udall could not be identified as author nor could composition be placed in Edward's reign until the discovery of both versions of Roister Doister's courtship letter in Thomas Wilson's *The Rule of Reason* (January 1553; 3rd ed.), with an attribution to "an entrelude made by Nicholas Udal."[48] The comedy therefore joins the other Reformation plays in which conventional flattery to Edward VI was clumsily converted into praise of Elizabeth.[49] The presence of four songs, a "psalmodie," a burlesque of the requiem mass, and a peal of bells suggest that Udall wrote the play for choir boys. Edward VI's September 1552 visit to Windsor, where Udall could have written the play and overseen production as Canon of St. George's Chapel, was the most likely occasion for performance. Preservation of the unique copy of the edition at Eton College Library strengthens the Windsor associations of the play.

The seriousness of Udall's comedy epitomizes the moral earnestness of Edward's court. On the authority of Plautus

---

and William Edgerton, "The Date of *Roister Doister*," *PQ*, 44 (1965), 555-56.

[48] A. W. Reed, "Nicholas Udall and Thomas Wilson," *RES*, 1 (1925), 275-83; Edgerton, "Date," 55-56.

[49] Ed. Edmund Creeth in *Tudor Plays: An Anthology of Early English Drama* (New York, 1966), I.i.38, V.vi.46-59, and notes.

and Terence, he strikingly defends comic humor as an allegorical veil for truth:

> The wyse Poets long time heretofore,
> Under merrie Comedies secretes did declare,
> Wherein was contained very vertuous lore,
> With mysteries and forewarnings very rare.
> (Prol., ll. 15-18)

Contrary to the neoclassical designation of comedy as an inferior genre, Udall's notions echo the Protestant theory developed by Bucer, Bale, and Sidney concerning the "right use of Comedy."[50] The prologue assures the audience that the play eschews the ribald innuendoes typical of the popular Reformation interlude: "all scurilitie we utterly refuse." Matthew Merrygreek's parody of the Latin burial rite (III.iii.53-87) satisfies the dramatic norms of the court that entertained itself with papal pratfalls and Reformation combats. Udall's mockery of Latin tag phrases, bell ringing, liturgical paraphrases, prayers for the dead, and the crucifix transforms the homiletic attacks of Latimer and Cranmer into courtly comedy.[51]

Dame Christian Custance emerges as Udall's moral heroine in contrast to Roister Doister, the swaggering "roisterer" who upsets public order. Her given name designates this Protestant widow as an example of prudential gospelling wisdom. Her threat to enforce the 1547 law concerning vagabondage against Roister Doister supports the vision of the well-ordered commonwealth envisioned by the *Book of Homilies* (IV.iii.104-109, and note). The surname Custance links this "woman of honestie" to the heroine of *The Man of Law's Tale* as an example of patient Christian

---

[50] *Essays*, ed. Smith, I, 177.

[51] Edwin S. Miller, "Roister Doister's 'Funeralls,'" *SP*, 43 (1946), 51-58.

faith, in contrast to the fallen women of the Edwardian stage: Dalilah and Mary Magdalene. Udall had read Chaucer in Thynne's Protestant edition of 1542, for he cites him as a stylistic model for religious translation.[52]

Christian Custance shares with Rebecca, Udall's other heroine, complete faith in divine providence. Citing Susanna and Esther as examples of God's deliverance of helpless believers, she articulates the predestination theology in fashion at court (V.iii.7-14). In contrast to Roister Doister's witless depravity, Christian speaks for the author in recommending strict morality:

> O Lorde, howe necessarie it is nowe of dayes,
> That eche bodie live uprightly all maner wayes. . . .
>   (V.iii.1-2)

Although court drama associated Esther with Catherine of Aragon,[53] Christian's good conduct more probably reflects the Protestant piety of Catherine Parr, the king's foster mother. As a protégé who dedicated tome I of Erasmus's *Paraphrases* to Edward VI and the dowager queen, Udall had every reason to idealize the matronly faith of Henry VIII's widow.

Christian Custance has a dry sense of humor that leads her into an apparently incongruous alliance with Matthew Merrygreek in order to outwit his lovesick friend Roister Doister. Although Merrygreek fills the role of the medieval Vice (he is a friend of Tom Titivile, a Tudor descendant of Titivillus), his is a denatured villainy that poses no real threat. The alliance of the two wits to ridicule the witless Roister Doister has a Jonsonian quality that anticipates the mutual understanding between Face and Lovewit

---

[52] Dedication to Catherine Parr of the paraphrase of Luke in Erasmus's *Paraphrases*, I, ❡6ʳ.

[53] Bevington, *Drama and Politics*, p. 123.

in *The Alchemist*. The moral comedy of Udall and Jonson shares a common origin in both the medieval morality tradition and the conventions of Latin comedy. Unlike Jonson's characterization of Zeal-of-the-Land Busy as a stage buffoon, Udall's gentler comedy portrays Christian Custance sympathetically as a middle-class Protestant saint.

The heroine personifies the transformation of the medieval ideals of celibacy and courtly love into the hardheaded Protestant vision of married love, which exerted such a powerful influence on Spenser and Milton. Udall dramatizes this shift through the conflict between widow and roisterer over the nature of love. In spurning Roister Doister, Christian remains faithful to her betrothed Gawin Goodluck, the London merchant who returns toward the end of the play. Her choice of this rather drab but successful entrepreneur holds out the promise of bourgeois concord, domestic bliss, and material prosperity. Although *Roister Doister* is hardly "a parody of Chaucer's *Troilus and Criseyde*," the braggart's lovesickness and Merrygreek's absurd flattery of his friend as the sucessor to the Nine Worthies (I.ii.115-27) do support Plumstead's reading of the play as a "satirical parody of medieval chivalric heroes."[54] The go-between Dobinet Doughty testifies that his master applies the traditional methods of courtly love in the absurd manner of Chaucer's Absolon:

Then up to our lute at midnight, twangledome twang,
Then twang with our sonets, and twang with our
    dumps [sad tunes],
And heyhough from our heart, as heavie as lead
    lumpes. . . .

                (II.i.20-22)

[54] "Satirical Parody," pp. 142, 147-50.

The braggart's silly despair over rejection by the "un-kinde" widow ("I will go home and die") is the occasion for the mock requiem ministered by Merrygreek (III.iii.53-87). *Roister Doister*'s "Songs and Balades" contrast with the hymns and prayers of *Jacob and Esau*.

Even the most secular play of the time pays lip service to Reformation attitudes. Although *Gammer Gurton's Needle* was held back from the press until 1575, reference to the "kings name" (V.ii.236) links its composition by Mr. S., Master of Art, to the reign of Edward VI.[55] Writing it for undergraduate performance at Cambridge University near in time to Udall's composition of *Ralph Roister Doister* for younger schoolboys,[56] Mr. S. effects a similar fusion of the five-act structure and character types of neo-classical comedy with native traditions of language and humor. The plot spins out farcical amplification of the absurdly trivial loss of Gammer Gurton's needle under the presiding genius of the Diccon of Bedlam, a descendant of the medieval Vice, at the expense of a small crowd of un-lettered villagers.

The joint mockery of uneducated laymen and the priest, all of whom speak in Somerset dialect, documents the gulf between university wit and contemporary idealization of the laity in literary forms designed for popular consumption. An Edwardian audience would recognize in the ale-drinking, card-playing Doctor Rat an ignorant cleric similar to Doctor Double Ale and his kind, who matches the witless Hodge in gullibility and such blasphemous oaths as "Gods sacrament" and "Gods woundes." After deflating

---

[55] Ed. Creeth in *Tudor Plays*. On probable authorship by William Stevenson, see STC 23263 and Wilson, *English Drama*, p. 225.

[56] H. A. Wyatt, "The Staging of *Gammer Gurton's Needle*," in *Elizabethan Studies and Other Essays*, ed. E. J. West (Boulder, Colo., 1945), pp. 86-87.

the self-important curate through the beating administered by Dame Chat, Diccon mocks him as an unregenerate priest ("this Sir John for madness"). With equitable tolerance, the local magistrate Master Baily reimposes order and instructs the vengeful cleric in the kind of forbearance appropriate to his vocation:

> Wel Master Rat, you must both learne, and teach us to forgeve.
> Since Diccon hath confession made, and is so cleane shreve,
> If ye to me consent, to amend this heavie chaunce,
> I wil injoyne him here, some open kind of penaunce.
>
> (V.ii.256-59)

The denouement, with its rediscovery of Gammer's precious needle, derives from Diccon's comic punishment of kissing Hodge's breeches rather than the gallows urged by Doctor Rat.

Udall's banishment of "scurilitie" from *Roister Doister* contrasts the moral decorum of courtly drama with the coarse raillery and scatological humor of a university comedy like *Gammer Gurton's Needle*. It suggests an even greater distance between the diction and conventions of elite drama and the coarse puns, invective, and bawdry of the moral interludes performed by itinerant troupes. The less sophisticated form of these moralities reflects their popular origins. Showing little if any neoclassical influence, performance of popular interludes on outdoor platform stages similar to those of the mystery cycles conferred a theater-in-the-round effect unlike that of the *domus* used in the halls of colleges and aristocratic households. The Tudor interlude inherited its essential acting convention of the doubling of parts from the medieval morality. Thus four adult players and one boy could handle all roles in the popular plays;[57] the elite drama was more wasteful in its use of performers. The title page of *An Enterlude Called Lusty Juventus* stipulates: "Foure may play it easely . . . so that any one tak of those partes that be not in place at once." In the Reformation interlude, the alternation and suppression of roles by means of doubling leads to the juxtaposition of discourse with comedy rather than open conflict between Virtue and Vice. The pulpit tradition of the preacher-playwrights encouraged the expository tendency of the Protestant dramas. The only actor who must remain in the same character throughout the performance is the actor who plays the central Mankind figure. In place of any attempt at concealing doubling, the prominent costume changes involved in the disguising of Vice characters furnish a visual emblem for their hypocrisy. The more uniformly sober attire of the Protestant Virtues functions as an ironic complement to the colorful costumes of the Catholic Vices.

Every extant Reformation interlude personifies the religious controversy. The tolerant climate of Edward's reign that encouraged the influx of Continental theologians would also have permitted the importation and translation of the Huguenot play *La Vérité Cachée* (Neufchâtel, 1534). The fragmentary text of *Somebody and Others* (c. 1550) could have been translated at any point between the 1530s and the beginning of Elizabeth's reign.[58] The French drama-

---

[57] David Bevington, "Popular and Courtly Traditions on the Early Tudor Stage," in *Medieval Drama*, ed. N. Denny (1973; Stratford-upon-Avon Studies, vol. 16), pp. 91-108. On the pervasive influence of this pattern, see Bevington, *"Mankind" to Marlowe*.

[58] In his edition for *Malone Society Collections*, II, 3 (Oxford, 1931), 251-57, W. W. Greg assigns the text to Edward's reign on the basis of content. Also see Peter Houle's argument for possible dates of translation under Henry, Edward, and Elizabeth in "A Reconstruction of the English

tization of religious turmoil may be applied easily to the complex shifts and retrenchments of the English Reformation; indeed, it has a plot paralleling Crowley's analysis of the Reformation in *Philargyrie of Greate Britayne*. As the leading Catholic Vice, the acquisitive Minister, after complaining to Avarice that Lady Verity "wold have me chaunge my lyvyng," conspires with Sister Simony to bury his one-time mistress underground. In taking Verity's place, Sister Simony disguises herself in the clothing of a "faythful and holy precher." Stage doubling therefore mirrors the familiar Reformation tradition of narrative doubling represented by Bale's *Image*, the Mistress Missa dialogues, and Spenser's metamorphosis of Duessa into the Una-figure of Fidessa. Instead of preaching the gospel, Simony and Minister enrich themselves through traditional abuse of tithes, pardons, and indulgences. Despite this setback, Verity voices a "prophecy" of the return of true faith:

> The tyme is come that I dyd prophecy
> How that I shold be hyd many yeres
> And that many wold gyve theyr eares
> To lesynges and vanytes
> To fals, doctryne and tromperyes
> And do ye not se how
> The tyme is come very now
> Of the warnyng of Jesus Chryst
> Fro the Fals Prophetes of Antechryst.
> (ll. 125-33)

In contrast to the calm argument of *Somebody and Others*, the fragmentary text of *Love Feigned and Unfeigned* (c. 1547-49) articulates incendiary Anabaptist arguments for aboli-

---

Morality Fragment *Somebody and Others*," *PBSA*, 71 (1977), 259-77. Houle reconstructs the argument of the English interlude by comparison with the parallel text from *La Vérité Cachée*.

tion of private property ownership and leveling of social ranks.[59] In all probability it appeared following the abrogation of the Henrician controls on the stage. According to Holinshed, the leaders of the Norfolk rebellion used a similarly provocative play to stir up the mob; the stringent controls imposed after the 1549 risings would apply to any Anabaptist play.[60] *Impatient Poverty* (written c. 1550) resembles conservative counterattacks following the rebellions. Superficial adaptation for publication under Mary leaves untouched the basic thesis of this Reformation call for order and obedience.[61] The struggle of Peace and Envy for the soul of Impatient Poverty, a figure for the discontented commons, personifies Cranmer's ideal of the perfect commonwealth. Only Peace can recostume Impatient Poverty as Prosperity. Advocacy by Peace of Christian patience and her warnings against drinking, gambling, and loose women echo the moral admonitions of the *Book of Homilies*. Led on by Misrule and false Charity (the disguised form of Envy), Prosperity denies the orthodox hierarchy of order and degree and squanders his new-found wealth. In contrast to Seymour's opposition to enclosures and public sympathy for the poor commons, this interlude voices the traditional magisterial argument that the poor are to blame for their own misfortune.

The near-anonymity of the author of *Lusty Juventus* attests to the lowly estimation of the popular interlude; other than his name, nothing is known about the R. Wever who wrote the play. The concluding prayer for the king in the unique copy of the first edition (c. 1550) proves that Wever

[59] Ed. A. Esdaile, *Malone Society Collections* (Oxford, 1907), I, 1, 17-25.

[60] Bevington, *Drama and Politics*, p. 106.

[61] Ed. R. B. McKerrow, *Materialien zur Kunde des älteren Englishchen Dramas*, vol. 33 (Louvain, 1911), ll. 1038-39, 1053-55.

wrote the work under Edward VI. As a wavering Mankind figure, Juventus is a Reformation Everyman who must decide in his youth between the competing claims of traditional religion, on the one hand, and the plain gospel faith and stringent ethical demands of the reformers. Unlike the medieval Everyman, who finds in Good Works one loyal companion into the next world, Juventus fights a more lonely battle that can be won only through inner faith and imputed grace. As spiritual advisors rather than absolving companions, Good Counsel and Knowledge personify the epistemological problem of the Reformation conflict. They can advise Juventus, but he must guide himself according to biblical interpretation and the inner dictates of his own conscience. The names and costumes of the Devil and Hypocrisy identify them as Catholics.

The conflict arises out of Juventus's conventional predisposition toward lust and licentiousness. As figures for original sin, these vices lead him to indulge in idleness, dicing, and minstrelsy. His downward slide is checked only by Good Counsel's homiletic warnings against vanity ("there is no such passing the time appointed in the Scripture") and preachment of the gospel as the guide for life. Insights derived from his new avocations of "continual prayer" and Bible study lead Juventus into acquaintance with Knowledge, who speaks in paraphrases from the Psalms and gospels. Speaking in the voice of the Protestant preacher, Knowledge, in effect, delivers Cranmer's homily that faith must be declared by works as "fruits of the spirit." The Reformation *topos* of Youth and Age signals Juventus's conversion: "My elders never taught me so before." The old religion of his ignorant parents denied him the Bible as the sole means of instruction; however, Juventus's youthful schooling personifies the conversion experience of the new faith. After receiving a New Testament as a gift from Good

Counsel, the youth promises never to abandon his new friends.

The "filthy sodometry" of church tradition is the basic weapon in Hypocrisy's counterattack on behalf of the Devil, who personifies the papal Antichrist. Mocking Juventus (and by extension all Protestant faithful) as a "New Gospeller," the Devil and Hypocrisy conspire to separate him from Knowledge and Good Counsel by introducing him to the prostitute Abominable Living en route to a sermon. Juventus's liaison with the harlot personifies the "spiritual fornication" of the old religion. In this simple dramatization of Bale's image of the two churches, Hypocrisy sophistically reverses roles with Juventus and recites his gospel code and Ten Commandments back against him:

> Can you deny but it is your duty
> Unto your elders to be obedient? . . .
> Wilt thou set men to school
> When they be old?
> I may say to you secretly,
> The world was never merry
> Since children were so bold;
> Now every boy will be a teacher,
> The father a fool, and the child a preacher. . . .
> (ll. 643-44, 648-54)

Hypocrisy's mockery ironically reduplicates Latimer's charges that the superficial piety of the new faith can readily disguise the old believer. Despite Juventus's ensuing despair, his second rescue by the Protestant Virtues preaches that sincere repentance may earn the worst sinner Christ's mercy. Good Counsel articulates the scriptural core of the play by interpolating a paraphrase of Luke 15:11-32 into the dialogue:

[314]

The prodigal son, as in Luke we read,
Which in vicious living his goods doth waste,
As soon as his living he had remembered,
To confess his wretchedness he was not aghast;
Wherefore his father lovingly him embraced
And was right joyful, the text saith plain,
Because his son was returned again.

(ll. 1075-81)

In the manner of the "Christianized" Terence of Continental drama, both *Lusty Juventus* and *Nice Wanton* adapt the older form of the Prodigal Son plays to the changed circumstances of the Reformation.

Lewis Wager's *Life and Repentance of Mary Magdalene* (composed c. 1550) matches *Lusty Juventus* in both doctrinal exactitude and ribald humor. Although it went to press in 1566, Wager's defense of drama because it teaches "true obedience to the kynge" (prol., l. 34) and the play's gospelling manner place composition during Edward's reign. Unlike Wever, Wager mixes the personified abstractions of the moral interlude with realistic characters. Serious scenes involving biblical figures alternate with those featuring comic abstractions. The significant advance of the play is its use of allegorical episodes in order to provide entertaining background for the realistic action in the biblical scenes. The play's transitional form marks the beginning of a movement away from abstract morality drama toward the more concrete chronicles and romances of the Elizabethan stage.[62] In dramatizing Luke 7:36-8:4, Wager excludes the apocryphal embellishments found in *Legenda Aurea* and in medieval lives of Mary Magdalene, which invariably treat her story as an orthodox example of penitence and remorse. Wager's iconoclastic reworking of the episode into

---

[62] Bevington, *"Mankind" to Marlowe*, pp. 171-72, 174.

an example of justification by faith corresponds to the Edwardian attacks on *The Golden Legend*. Aside from the English Bible, his only other sources are the *Book of Homilies* and Erasmus's *Paraphrases*.

The play dramatizes the Reformation by means of the *topos* of the transfer from Old Law to New Law. Infidelity personifies the Old Law through his friendship with the Pharisees, who know him as "Moysaicall Justice." The name of their leader Simon recalls Simon Magus. Infidelity's lying admonition that he "would have them justified by the lawe [of Moses]" conceals his knowledge that "faith is the roote of all goodnesse" (ll. 22, 34). Wager integrates disguising and costume changes into the action by doubling the four Catholic Vices as hypocritical Virtues: Pride (Nobility and Honor); Cupiditas (Utility); Carnal Concupiscence (Pleasure); Infidelity (Legal Justice to priests and Pharisees; Prudence to publicans and people). Infidelity remarks on the implications of costuming for the morality argument:

> For every day I have a garment to weare,
> According to my worke and operation.
> Among the Pharisies I have a Pharisies gown;
> Among publicans and synners another I use.
>
> (ll. 920-23)

His Pharisee's gown is "bordered with the [ten] commandements" (l. 1523). Pride boasts *in propria persona* that he and his four fellows embody all of the traditional seven deadly sins (ll. 291-92). Infidelity signals the seduction of Mary Magdalene by recostuming her in the dress of a Southwark harlot. His identification of parental indulgence as the cause of her fall marks her as the type-character of the spoiled child, like Dalilah, Ismael, and Juventus:

Of parentes the tender and carnall sufferance,
Is to yong maidens a very pestilence.
It is a provocation and furtherance
Unto all lust and fleshly concupiscence.
(ll. 175-78)

Incessant discussion of the advent of the Messiah announces the millenarian theme of the play. As a figure for Antichrist, Infidelity turns the Pharisees and priests against Jesus. Christ's entry follows immediately upon the fall of Mary Magdalene, who has committed fornication with Malicious Judgment. Christ's victory over Infidelity personifies the advent of the New Law.[63] Unlike Everyman, who is abandoned by all but Good Deeds, Mary Magdalene retains Faith as her companion. Reentry of the repentant sinner initiates the dense paraphrase of Luke 7 that concludes the play. Wager takes the unique step of alluding to Luke not only through dialogue, but in a stage direction for the washing of Christ's feet: "Let *Marie* creepe under the table, abydyng there a certayne space behynd, and doe as it is specified in the Gospell" (following l. 1725). In accordance with Cranmer's reinterpretation of medieval *caritas*, the redefinition of good works by Love and Justification is the moral kernel of the play:

Love deserved not forgevenesse of sinnes in dede,
But as a fruite therof truely it did succede.
(ll. 2004-2005)

The gospelling convention of dramatizing original sin as stage licentiousness fuses *caritas* with erotic characters such as Carnal Concupiscence and Abominable Living. But Mary

---

[63] Roston notes in *Biblical Drama* that this is one of the last appearances of Christ on the British stage for 350 years (p. 69).

Magdalene exemplifies the Protestant Everyman of the Reformation stage in her ultimate comprehension of the Pauline teaching of spiritual love: "So faith, hope, love abide, these three; but the greatest of these is love" (1 Corinthians 13:13).

CHAPTER 7
Robert Crowley: A Tudor Gospeller

THE PROTESTANT PLOWMAN

Robert Crowley is mentioned in the history of English literature chiefly for editing *The Vision of Pierce Plowman*, the first printed edition of the medieval epic. Nevertheless, his prolific career as a radical poet deserves closer attention. By turns a pamphleteer, stationer, poet, and clergyman, Crowley cultivated an audience in London's growing middle class and among pious aristocrats for his biblical poetry, Protestant tracts and polemics, and editions of the riddling poem that William Langland had written in the archaic dialect of the fourteenth-century midlands. Although he eventually became a leader of the fledgling Puritan movement that emerged out of the Elizabethan vestiarian controversy, Crowley refused to participate in the attack on poetry and fiction that was often associated with the Puritan faction. He contributed to the Reformation defense of fiction that anticipated Sidney's *Apology for Poetry*. As a corollary to his radical Protestant zeal, Crowley wrote as a nativist poet. Instead of simply restating Langland's medieval ideal of the Christian commonwealth, however, Crowley adapted traditional literary conventions to the Reformation crisis. By exemplifying the popular native traditions of the mid-Tudor period, the conventionality of Crowley's verse is valuable to the literary historian because it represents a standard for Reformation poetry, which is one of the least known areas of English Renaissance literature. With enthusiasm and wit, Crowley turned out a body of verse that, for sheer bulk and variety, was extraordinary at a time when prolix theological tomes crowded most other texts out of the bookstalls near St. Paul's Cathedral.

From a Protestant vantage point, Crowley's poetic vision is essentially tragic. The biblical pattern of sin and fall and the corresponding need for regeneration unify all of his works, in which he applies the Old Testament pattern of cyclic apostasy to the English people. Unlike so many other radical poets of the time, Crowley transcends particular religious controversies to produce enduring art; his verse rises above the tractlike poems written by the other gospellers except Luke Shepherd. Because of the poetic manifesto in his *Psalter*, the little "satires" of his collection of epigrams, and the manifest fiction of *Philargyrie of Greate Britayne*, Crowley emerges as the most significant poet between Surrey and Gascoigne. His jeremiads may sometimes resemble the topical warnings of the Protestant preachers and such tract-poets as William Samuel and Peter Moone. In place of their explicit concern for contemporary events, however, Crowley substitutes utterances by biblical *personae*, details of diverse failures from the Old and New Testaments, type characters, and personifications derived from *Piers Plowman* and the Tudor moral interlude. He carefully blends these kaleidoscopic devices in order to express the recurrent cycle of spiritual victory and defeat.

After his 1551 ordination, Crowley followed Hugh Latimer, Seymour's pulpit spokesman, as a proponent of commonwealth reform. As an Erastian, Crowley envisioned a theocratic monarchy instead of the Genevan model for reform—he looked to Edward VI for the doctrinal fulfillment of Henry VIII's political Reformation. Crowley felt that the key to social reform lay in reorganization of the church, because a new elite of Protestant clergy and landlords had taken the place of the old Roman clergy in exploiting the commonwealth. His tracts appeal to king and Parliament to fulfill the broken promise that the dissolution of the monasteries would redress the misery of the impoverished commons. Because the potential of the Reformation had not yet been achieved, Crowley assaulted residual medieval abuses: clerical simony and misappropriation of tithes, as well as enclosure of land, rack-renting, and price-gouging by property owners. These objects of attack differed little from those denounced from the medieval pulpit and in such medieval classics as *Piers Plowman* and Chaucer's *Pardoner's Tale*,[1] topics that were still very much alive in the earlier part of Crowley's own century.

Crowley proposed a radical Christian solution to the problem of poverty. On the assumption that avarice is the fundamental cause of religious and social ills, he formulated a stewardship theory of property ownership whereby one should use no more than a sufficient and moderate amount of wealth—any surplus should be distributed as charity. In applying the Parable of the Steward (Luke 16:1-13) to contemporary England, Crowley concluded:

> Knowe that your office is to distribute & not to scrape together on heapes. God hath not sette you to surveye hys landes, but to playe the stuardes in his householde of this world, and to se that your pore felow servantes lacke not theye [their] necessaries.[2]

[1] See G. R. Owst, *Literature and Pulpit in Medieval England* (Oxford, 1933), p. 287.

[2] *An Informacion and Peticion agaynst the Oppressours of the Pore Commons* (1548), A7ᵛ.

Although all citizens are responsible for the welfare of the commonwealth, gentlemen and clergy have a special responsibility to ensure that the poor commons receive their fair share of wealth. Qualified by his desire to redistribute wealth, Crowley retained the medieval ideal of a hierarchal society strictly governed by obedience to the monarch.

Crowley's major project was his edition of *The Vision of Pierce Plowman*. In the history of editing, his 1550 publication of the first printed edition of *Piers Plowman* is important as an early effort to provide a critical edition of a classical English text. Its chief importance lies, however, in bringing into sharp focus—through the violent exaggerations and biting invective of a radical gospeller—the persuasive value of literature in the bitter controversies of the English Reformation. Crowley kidnapped this orthodox medieval demand for reform of monasticism and society, converting it, through his preface and marginal notes, into a powerful revolutionary attack against monasticism and the Roman Catholic hierarchy. Crowley's application of the fourteenth-century apocalypse transforms it into a prophecy of the advent of the Protestant millennium of the sixteenth century.[3]

Unlike the Elizabethan critics George Puttenham and Francis Meres, Crowley revered Langland not as a malcontent, but as a prophet and religious visionary. Concerned in particular with the recent suppression of monasticism, Crowley interpreted *Piers Plowman* as a prophecy of the English Reformation. Because of its anticlerical bias, this theological epic was the only Middle English model for satirical poetry acceptable to the reformers. Although the poem's obscurity conformed to the Tudor assumption

[3] Morton W. Bloomfield approaches *Piers Plowman* as an orthodox medieval apocalypse in *"Piers Plowman" as a Fourteenth-Century Apocalypse* (New Brunswick, N.J., 1961), pp. 98-126.

that satire ought to be rough and harsh, Puttenham disapproved of the poem as a model for imitation because the language was so "hard and obscure" that "litle pleasure [was] to be taken." His strictures linked Langland to Chaucer, another Reformation hero: "Our maker therfore at these dayes shall not follow *Piers plowman* nor *Gower* nor *Lydgate* nor yet *Chaucer*, for their language is now out of use with us. . . ."[4]

Crowley's reformist interpretation marks the culmination of the *Piers Plowman* apocrypha that had grown up during the previous two centuries. Originally an exemplary figure representing the simplicity of Christ and the Christian life, the devout medieval plowman had undergone by Crowley's time a metamorphosis into a harsh anticlerical spokesman. Sixteenth-century reformers mistakenly identified the *Piers Plowman* tradition with the Wyclifite movement, reinterpreting these medieval appeals for reform as Protestant propaganda.[5] Publication of *Piers Plowman* thus had to await the Edwardian repeals act. The reformers first eluded crown censorship under Cromwell by disguising the virulently anti-Roman Catholic *Plowman's Tale* as a gathering out of a legitimate Chaucer edition. The transformation of the medieval plowman began in *Pierce the Ploughmans Crede* (first printed in 1553), a late fourteenth-century imitation of *Piers Plowman*. By the sixteenth century, the plowman figure had become a shallow device for disguising both a prose attack on transubstantiation[6]

---

[4] *Essays*, ed. Smith, II, 65, 150.

[5] For a detailed account of the *Piers Plowman* tradition in the sixteenth century, see Helen C. White, *Social Criticism in Popular Religious Literature of the Sixteenth Century* (New York, 1944), pp. 1-40.

[6] *A Godly Dyalogue & Dysputacion betwene Pyers Plowman, and a Popysh Preest* (c. 1550).

and an updated Lollard prayer for reform.[7] Advocating religious reform through the millennial Christian king, *I Playne Piers Which Can Not Flatter* anticipates Crowley's apocalyptic rendering of *Piers Plowman*.[8] The medieval plowman is almost unrecognizable in a contemporary Edwardian complaint, having become a radical spokesman for the commons against the enclosure movement and the misappropriation of monastic lands by the nobility.[9] As Crowley interprets it, *Piers Plowman* prophesies the eradication of these abuses from the Protestant millennial kingdom.

In addition to the English Bible and the *Piers Plowman* apocrypha, Bale's *Image of Both Churches* is the main source of Crowley's millenarian application of *Piers Plowman* to contemporary history. According to Bale, the apostolic purity of the English church survived until the time of Bede and Alcuin. The blowing of the fifth trumpet then announced the arrival of Antichrist and the age of "innumerable locustes" during the reigns of Edward III and Richard II. Crowley's identification of this epoch with the time of Langland and Wyclif follows Bale in associating the Age of Locusts with the scholastic philosophers and the Roman hierarchy of the later Middle Ages (*True Copye*, A1ᵛ). Crowley shares Bale's belief that the present reign of Edward VI, after the dissolution of the monasteries but while Antichrist still rages on earth, is immediately prior to the advent of the Messiah and the end of the world. We

[7] *The Praier and Complaynte of the Ploweman unto Christe* (Antwerp, c. 1531).

[8] Although written during the reign of Henry VIII, this tract appeared in print at roughly the same time as Crowley's *Piers Plowman* editions (c. 1550).

[9] *Pyers Plowmans Exhortation, unto the lordes, knightes and burgoysses of the Parlyamenthouse* (c. 1550). Attributed to Crowley (below, p. 474).

know that Crowley pondered Bale's commentary as he prepared his editions of *Piers Plowman*, because on 29 November 1549 he published *The Voyce of the Laste Trumpet Blowen bi the Seventh Angel*, a versification of Bale's ideas. An extension of the prophecies in *Piers Plowman*, this poem singles out avarice as the fundamental cause of religious and social problems. The fact that the apocalyptic angel is still in the process of blowing the last trumpet marks the reign of Edward VI as the advent of the millennium.

Bale's initial attribution of *Piers Plowman* to John Wyclif, his prototype of the English reformer, supplied its claim to authority as a Protestant prophecy. As the reformers assimilated medieval anticlerical or Lollard works into their literary canon, Langland's theological epic exerted the strongest appeal. Despite Langland's use of the Vulgate Bible, they could accept him as a crypto-Protestant because of the heavily biblical texture of his poem. Its dense scriptural paraphrases and the reduced role of apocryphal materials make *Piers Plowman* a close medieval analogue to Reformation gospelling poetry. Unlike the *Legenda Aurea* and the external forms of visual art that the iconoclasts destroyed, Long Will's dream visions represent an uncommonly subjective, inward form of medieval piety. Langland and the Protestants share the habit of applying biblical archetypes to individual spiritual experience. Long Will's spiritual turmoil thus lent itself readily to the sometimes despairing search of the Tudor Protestant for certainty in a world full of competing images of faith and claims to salvation. Because of Long Will's habit of looking within and to the Bible for spiritual guidance, he and Piers Plowman were natural heroes for Reformation Englishmen.

In his preface Crowley claims to have conducted a thorough search to determine the authorship of *Piers Plowman*:

[325]

I did not onely gather togyther suche aunciente coppies as I could come by, but also consult[ed] such men as I knew to be more exercised in the studie of antiquities, then I my self have ben. And by some of them I have learned that the Autour was named Roberte langelande, a Shropshere man borne in Cleybirie, about viii. myles from Malverne hilles. (*2ʳ)

It is probable that John Bale was among the antiquaries Crowley consulted, since they are in ultimate agreement about the problem of authorship. A firm attribution for *Piers Plowman* would strengthen its authority as a valid historical document rather than a lying fable. Although Crowley's attribution to Langland remained unchallenged until recent times,[10] in his own time conservatives were by no means willing to concede that the poem was a prophecy of the Protestant Reformation. As late as 1534, Sir Adrian Fortescue interpreted the poem as an orthodox pietistic work in his notes on his holograph copy (Bodl. MS Digby 145, fols. 2ᵛ-130ʳ).

The Vision of Pierce Plowman was Crowley's most ambitious project, resulting in three separate quarto editions within one year (1550). Owen Rogers reprinted Crowley's text in 1561, marking the end of its sudden vogue; following this edition the poem remained out of print until the nineteenth century.[11] Aside from the three editions of *Piers Plowman*, Crowley published only one other quarto vol-

[10] John E. Wells disproved the Wyclif connection in 1916 (*A Manual of the Writings in Middle English: 1050-1400* [1916], p. 266). See George Kane, *"Piers Plowman": The Evidence for Authorship* (1965).

[11] Rogers appends "Pierce the Ploughmans Crede" to the careless copy of Crowley's second edition that he describes as "newlye imprynted after the authours olde copy." T. D. Whitaker's edition of the C text, *"Visio Uuillim de Petro Plouhman," Or The Vision of William concerning Peirs Plouhman* [*sic*] (1813), is the first modern edition.

ume (the *Psalter*). All of his other publications were plain
and inexpensive octavo editions aimed at a broad, popular
audience. The title page, borders, and typefaces of *Piers
Plowman* are the most elaborate of all his publications. Because Crowley lavished attention on his text, each edition
embodies corrections and a new typesetting. Although he
calls attention to only two separate editions, the title page
of one of these impressions (*STC* 19907) reads "Nowe the
Seconde Tyme Imprinted," whereas the title page of another (*STC* 19907a) reads "Nowe the Seconde Time Imprinted." Bishop Percy first observed that there were three
different printings, each containing "evident variations in
every page."[12] W. W. Skeat later supported Percy's ob-
servation by quotation of several illustrative variants.[13]
Complete collation of the three texts reveals new typesetting, correction of errors, and further emendation in each
successive edition.

Crowley edited and corrected his text carefully, using
an emended copy of the first edition as the basis for later
versions. The second and third editions agree closely, em-
bodying essentially the same revised text, and *STC* 19907
may actually be the third edition.[14] Crowley included a
preface and a small number of marginal notes in the first
edition. Retaining the preface, he added a précis and greatly
expanded his marginal glosses in the second and third edi-

[12] *Reliques*, II, 262.
[13] W. W. Skeat, ed., *The Vision of William Concerning Piers the Plowman* (Oxford, 1886; 2 vols.), II, lxxii-lxxvi. Unless otherwise noted, all
line references are to the version of the B text in this edition. Quotations
from Crowley's text follow the third edition (*STC* 19907a), which represents the editor's most complete and final thought on the poem.
[14] William R. Crawford, "Robert Crowley's Editions of *Piers Plowman*:
A Bibliographical and Textual Study" (Ph.D. diss., Yale University, 1958),
pp. 31-33 and passim. My collation of a page of each forme in each of
the three editions corroborates the results of Crawford's complete collation.

tions. In presenting *Piers Plowman* as the outstanding English satire and appeal for religious reform, Crowley gave it the appearance and apparatus of contemporary editions of the Greek and Latin classics; evidently he wanted the poem to be appealing and acceptable as a trustworthy ancient authority. The later editions differed further from the first through Crowley's addition of six leaves, a new title page, new headlines indicating the number of each passus in place of the running titles of the first edition, and a variety of new lines and readings.

Crowley's primary editorial effort went into an uncritical attempt to reproduce an authoritative text of the poem, using a lost manuscript of the B text as his copy text. Although Crowley's printed text is full of errors, Skeat points out that he was often unable to read his text correctly and that the frequent mistakes are Crowley's own. After collating Crowley's edition, Skeat accorded it manuscript status in his monumental parallel-text edition of *Piers Plowman*, arguing that the errors result from the editor's inaccurate rendering of his "extremely good" manuscript. Skeat's suggestion that he consulted at least four different manuscripts is borne out by collation of the three editions.

Crowley says in his preface that he searched out many "aunciente coppies" (✳2ʳ), and his quotation of a variant reading proves he had access to a C-text manuscript.[15] He employed at least one manuscript of each of the three texts of *Piers Plowman* to correct the copy of his first edition by introducing new lines and many variant readings in a random and scattered fashion. Crowley inserted into the later editions a six-line passage from the A text after line 215 of the prologue.[16] Some lines omitted from the first edition

---

[15] Skeat, *Piers Plowman*, II, lxxv, lxxvii (see ✳2ᵛ, C.9.351-52).

[16] Ibid., lxxvi (see A4ʳ, A. Prol. 90-95).

were restored by reference to other manuscripts (A3ᵛ, B. Prol. 170; F1ᵛ, B.5.73). His lost manuscript was closely related to MS W of the B text. The addition of several new readings into the later editions, including three entire lines that are absent from both Crowley's first edition and MS W, suggests that Crowley haphazardly corrected his first edition with a B-text manuscript closely resembling MSS Y, O, C2, C, B, Bm, and Cot.[17] Crowley's effort at correction may be seen in one instance by the restoration of alliteration which had been lost in the first edition; where the first edition reads "Tyl he had mony for hys service," the later editions return to the correct manuscript reading, "Til he had silver for his service" (C2ʳ, B.2.142).

Crowley's secondary goal as editor was to popularize *Piers Plowman* by providing a text that could be read easily by his contemporary reader. Thus he thoroughly modernized his text to accord with sixteenth-century standards of usage and orthography. Unlike Edmund Spenser, who sometimes revived certain archaic words for nationalistic and stylistic reasons, Crowley treated the archaisms of *Piers Plowman* as obstacles. In imitation of Chaucer, Spenser periodically introduced the archaic perfective *y*-prefix used in forming the Middle English past participle into *The Shepheardes Calender* and *The Faerie Queene*. Crowley, on the other hand, invariably deleted the *y*-prefix and introduced the Modern English past participle (see A1ᵛ, B. Prol. 41). Lacking Spenser's stylistic and ornamental interest in some older usages, Crowley altered his already difficult text to render it simpler for the modern reader. Sometimes he changed syntax to introduce a modern subject-verb-object order. Crowley sporadically simplified the Middle English verbs by eliminating inflections in the

---

[17] Crawford, pp. 58-59 (see B.3.161-62, B.4.9-10, B.18.292-93).

present and past tenses other than the third person singular—for example, in his altering the original "have ybounden" into "bind" (A3ᵛ, B. Prol. 178). He modernized Middle English pronouns, rendering "hij" as "I." The obsolete Middle English conjunction "ac," surviving in the sixteenth century only in the north, was invariably printed as "and."

Although he admitted that Langland's dialect was archaic and "the sence somewhat darcke" (✱2ᵛ), Crowley still expected his readers to understand the poem without a glossary or lexical notes. Owen Rogers, on the other hand, appended a brief glossary to his 1561 reprint of Crowley's text. Crowley's most significant alterations were of archaic diction, and although most of these changes were deliberate, some were naive misreadings of his text. For example, "poverty" was substituted for the more precise Middle English "poraille" ("the poor people"). The original "cracche us, or clowe us" was printed as "scratchynge us & clawyng us," and in the same line "clawes" is substituted for "cloches" (A3ʳ, B. Prol. 154). One of Crowley's many mistakes was his rendering the original "ac I swere now, so the ik that synne wil I lete" as "and I swere now sothelich that sinne wold I let" (F4ʳ, B.5.228).

In order to preserve the authority of *Piers Plowman*, it was essential for Crowley to print his text in as unaltered a state as possible. Thus he introduced only a very small number of substantive alterations where he found the original doctrinally unacceptable. He introduced an anti-Marian bias into the poem by substituting the name of Christ for that of Mary (K3ᵛ, B.7.196). In altering "for goddes body myȝte nouȝte be of bred, withouten clergye" (B.12.87) to "for bread of gods bodi. myght not be without cleargy" (Q1ʳ), Crowley omitted reference to transubstantiation. The Roman Catholic doctrine of purgatory was deleted by altering "and many a prisone fram purgatorie thorw his preyeres he delyvereth" (B.15.339) to "and mani prisoners bi his praier. he pulith from paine" (X2ᵛ). Crowley's most sweeping alteration was his complete omission of a thirteen-line passage in praise of the Gregorian rule and monastic ideal (N2ʳ, B.10.291-303).[18] This departure from his general policy of making only very few minor alterations to his text was prompted by the context of this praise of monasticism. The deleted passage immediately preceded what was for Crowley the central prophecy of *Piers Plowman*, the vision of the reforming monarch who will punish the religious orders. Crowley would have negated his marginal interpretation of this vision as a prophecy of the "suppression of Abbayes" (N2ʳ) had he retained the omitted passage; instead he transformed what was originally a call for monastic reform into a destructive attack on the very principle of monasticism.

Crowley's reverence for the fidelity of his text reveals the evangelical reformer's respect for the authority of primitive religious documents. Disregarding the temptation to rewrite *Piers Plowman* thoroughly from his Protestant bias, Crowley relies on the comments and interpretations in his preface, summary, and marginal notes to convert the work into Protestant propaganda. His preface first introduces *Piers Plowman* as a prophecy of the English Reformation:

> In [this] tyme it pleased God to open the eyes of many to se hys truth, geving them boldenes of herte, to open their mouthes and crye oute agaynste the worckes of darckenes, as dyd John Wicklefe, who also in those dayes translated the holye Bible into the Englishe tonge and this writer who in reportynge certayne visions and

---

[18] Skeat notes the first two examples of Crowley's falsification of his text (*Piers Plowman*, II, lxxvii).

dreames, that he fayned hym selfe to have dreamed: doth moste christianlie enstructe the weake, and sharplye rebuke the obstynate blynde. There is no maner of vice, that reygneth in anye estate of men, whyche thys wryter hath not godly, learnedlye, and wittilye rebuked. (✳2ʳ)

Marginal glosses provide the most effective device for reshaping *Piers Plowman*. Although Crowley justifies his annotation on the lexical ground that the language of the poem is archaic and "the sence somewhat darcke" (✳2ᵛ), his manifest purpose is to interpret it as reformist propaganda. The marginal glosses provide a running commentary on the poem. Not all of his notes have a doctrinal purpose, and because he finds it impossible to separate religious from social reform, many notes contain proverbial moral advice. He moralistically labels the habitués of Gluttony's tavern as "Commen drunkerds" (G1ᵛ, B.5.316-17). Sloth's rejection of Repentance is read as an "admonition of beware of dispair in repentaunce" (G3ᵛ, B.5.451-55). An attack on bribery provides an opportunity to warn that "Lawiars [lawyers] shold take no money" (K1ʳ, B.7.44-46). Identifying *Piers Plowman* with the welter of mid-Tudor tracts calling for social reform, the editor's sympathies clearly lie with the poor commons. Where Langland praises poverty as a way to moral virtue, Crowley comments approvingly "Lecherye and glotony raigne not much in povertye" (T3ᵛ, B.14.248-52) and speaks in "praise of povertie" (T4ʳ, B.14.283-85). Against a reference to Christ as the exemplar of humility, Crowley gnomically reminds the reader that "Christe was pore" (O3ᵛ, B.11.178-80). The commons are exploited by the wealthier estates: "Pore folke fede hunger" (I3ᵛ, B.6.296-98). He censures the wealthy, on the other hand, for their pride: "Rych men be compared to the Pecocke" (Q3ᵛ, B.12.240-43).

Crowley's apocalypse looks backward to the foundation of the primitive church. Protestant reliance on the scriptural traditions of the primitive "house unitie, holy churche in englysh," figured allegorically by the plowing of Piers, provides authority in matters of ecclesiastical discipline and polity. His notes explain that in supplying the blood for its "mortare" the Crucifixion provides "the foundation of the church" (2E1^r, B.19.320-25). This simple Christianity of the primitive church survived until the accumulation of sacerdotal abuses during the medieval Age of Locusts. Long Will's climactic vision of Antichrist's uprooting of the crops of truth (2E3^v-2G1^v, B.20) represents the degeneracy of the papacy and religious orders. Crowley describes pre-Reformation England as a time of dearth and flourishing of weeds. He glosses the friars as those "who receyved Antichriste fyrste" (2E4^r, B.20.57-59), explaining that England was first undermined and eventually conquered through the religious orders; current failures of both church and society are therefore due to the continued raging of the fiend. The editor does distinguish between the corruption of the monks and friars and the unwitting acquiescence of kings and holy men by noting of the latter, "How Antichriste doth seduce many good men" (2E4^v, B.20.63-68). Contemporary poverty, plagues, and misery arrive mysteriously as "the maner of goddes visitation" (2F1^r, B.20.98-100).

Crowley finds that lechery governs the relatively few survivors into the latter age, a time marked by the degeneracy in "the maner of men . . . when plages cease" (2F1^v, B.20.110-12). Clerical corruption is at the center of the problem, as when he notes that "Covetise & Simony make prelates" (2F1^v, B.20.125-27). When Antichrist's army of clergy attacks House Unity, he laments, "Woulde god there were no such priestes in englande" (2F3^r, B.20.221-

25). Eradication of the poverty and ignorance of many clergymen would provide a partial solution: "Curates oughte to have a competent lyvyng certayne" (2F3^r, B.20.232-36). Crowley blames civil and church authorities for condoning abuses like the holding of multiple benefices: "Nother patron nor bishop, regardeth his dutye" (2F4^v, B.20.324-27). Much of the problem results from more general moral failure, as when the editor comments that "Hypocrisi woundeth preachers" (2F4^r, B.20.300-301).

Crowley's persistent attack on contemporary clerical abuses may only be understood within the context of Antichrist's apocalyptic assault on the English church. Eradication of Roman Catholic influence will not eliminate Antichrist unless the clerical discipline and ecclesiastical polity of the English church are reformed. He censures clerical venality, exclaiming, "How covetise of the cleargy wyll destroye the church (Y1^r, B.15.502-506), and calling for "a medicyne for the Cleargie" (Y1^v, B.15.526-28). Insisting that "Prechers muste do as they preach" (U2^v, B.15.93-96), Crowley holds up the biblical Levites as a model and "admonicion to the cleargy" (Y1^v, B.15.515-17). Other abuses include "the fruites of Popishe penaunce" (C4^v, B.3.51-53), "the auctority of Popes" (K3^r, B.7.171-75), and the turning of "tithes to private use" (L2^v, B.9.67-70).

If Antichrist is roaming earth unchecked, the millennium must be at hand. Accordingly the only hope for redress lies in the advent of the reforming Christian king (2E1^v-2^r). Viewing the Edwardian reforms as preparation for the millennium, Crowley associates Edward VI with the longstanding tradition of the emperor of the last days, the just and pious Christian ruler who is to precede the Second Coming of Christ. Although Edward VI lacked the obvious trappings of the emperor of the last days, Crowley explains away the quotation "V[a]e terre, ubi puer Rex est" (Eccles. 10:16) as a reference to a "childish king" who is lazy, foolish, or incompetent, not to his age in years (above, Chapter 4 at n. 3).

Crowley identifies Edward VI as the millennial Davidic ruler through his gloss on the vision of "one christen kinge" who will govern his realm in reason and truth: "This is no prophecy, but a reasonable gathering" (D4^{r}, B.3.282-90). Explicitly linking Edward VI with the kingdom of the last days, Crowley says of the following lines, "Thys is no prophecye, but a truth gathered of the scriptures":

> And kind love shall come yet, and conscience togither
> And make of lawe a labourer, such love shall aryse
> And such a peace among the people, & a perfite truth,
> That Jewes shal wene in their wyt, & wax wonders glad
> That Moses & Messia, be come into this erth. . . .
> (D4^{v}, B.3.297-301)

The conversion of the Jews traditionally heralded the Second Coming.

Crowley's distinction between "prophecy" and "truth" alludes to the ancient tradition of pagan prophecy that survived into medieval and Renaissance astrological prognostication. Cast in the form of an almanac, the earliest English printed prognostication dates from the year 1498 and contains traditional predictions about the weather, periods of illness and plague, deaths of the great, and insurrection and turmoil. Coming out of medieval manuscript traditions linked to Merlin, Geoffrey of Monmouth, John of Bridlington, and other English "prophets," such foretellings incorporate occult symbolism, deliberate vagueness, and obscure self-fulfilling references to recent events. For example, a 1498 fragment at the Bodleian Library (Douce fragm. e. 11) voices a warning to those "that make insurreccyons ayenst the prynce, for they shall have the werse."

This threat alludes to a prediction that the same author had made the previous year, which had been "proven" by a 1497 rebellion in Cornwall: "as sayd the last yere in my pronostycaconns, wherby [the] Cornyshmen yf they had ben wyse myght have ben ware." During Crowley's time, the French astrologer Nostradamus was the most famous inheritor of the medieval tradition of prophecy and prognostication.

The gospellers identified this pagan tradition with the false church of Antichrist. Miles Coverdale, for example, translated *A Faythfull and True Pronostication upon the Yere .M.CCCCC.xlviii. and parpetually after to the worldes ende gathered out of the prophecies and scriptures of god*. . . . By means of a *double-entendre* that identifies Christ with the sun, this "true" prognostication parodies traditional weather predictions with an evangelical assurance that "the sonne sheweth playnly: that all soch as feare god, shall have a verye frutefull yeare. Psal. C.xxvii." (A4^r, A6^r). The predictions of John Partridge attest to the extreme conservatism of the pagan tradition of prognostication. Swift's lethal parody of Partridge's almanac, *Predictions for the Year 1708* by Isaac Bickerstaff, mocks prognostications identical in kind to those of the 1498 almanac.

Crowley's glosses reject pagan "prophecy" in order to protect the authority of *Piers Plowman* as "Christian" prognostication, asserting that Langland utters truths "gathered of the scriptures" in the manner of Coverdale's 1548 "prophecy." At the same time that he denies pagan conventions, however, he retains the characteristic self-fulfillment device from the old almanacs and horoscopes in order to apply the poem to contemporary conditions. Just as Lynne and Ochino exploited the Joachimist yearning to identify the exact moment at which prophecy turns into history,

Crowley fortuitously found a "proof" for his reinterpretation of *Piers Plowman*.

Glossing it with approval as "the suppression of Abbayes," the editor interprets the following passage as a prophecy of Henry VIII's dissolution of the monasteries:

> And there shal come a king, and confesse you religious
> And beat you as the bible telleth, for breking of your
> rule
> And amende moniales, monkes, and chanons
> And put hem to her penaunce. . . .
>
> (N2^r, B.10.317-20)

He underscores the importance of this prediction by commenting elsewhere on Reason's threats against lapsed clergy: "The Suppression of Abbayes. Good counsell" (F1^r, B.5.46-49). Crowley's smug gloss, "the Abbott of Abington," marks a prophecy that this abbot would receive "a knocke of a kynge, and incurable the wound" (N2^v, B.10.327). Indeed he had reason to be smug, because the abbey at Abington was one of the first to be suppressed after the abbot resisted the reforms of Thomas Cromwell. Concerned especially to stress this attack on the monks and mendicant friars, Crowley admonishes his reader, "Reade thys" (N2^r. B.10.306-307). During the Reformation, Bishop Cox also cited an ancient Latin prediction of the dissolution. John Bale found a prediction of the Reformation in the Merlin prophecies.[19]

Crowley's "proof" enables him to capture *Piers Plowman* and reshape it into Reformation propaganda. Langland's "true" prognostication of the suppression of the abbey at Abington permits Crowley to introduce his defense of royal authority and the program of religious and moral reform

---

[19] Thomas, *Religion and Decline*, p. 408.

associated with it by means of his glosses. He adopts the voice of a Tudor "prophet" when he explains that "pestilences come for sinne" (E4^v, B.5.13-14) and interprets contemporary religious turmoils as signs of the millennium. He warns his reader to "forgette not that the last daie wil surely come" (F4^v, B.5.280-83). The Christian monarch must be stern, and "due correction muste be had" (F1^r, B.5.33-35).

Crowley's effort failed with at least one contemporary reader. Andrew Bostock, an educated Roman Catholic, saw through the editorial distortions and entered a private protest in his marginalia to a copy of the third edition (Bodl. Douce L 205). Basing his argument on a more historically accurate reading, Bostock returns to the traditional interpretation of *Piers Plowman* as an orthodox appeal for reform within the established church. Bostock's refutation hinges upon Erasmian adiaphorism, which argues that many of Crowley's revolutionary issues are doctrinally indifferent.[20] The Bodleian copy, with Crowley's puzzling notes

---

[20] This volume is inscribed "Andrew Bostock/1613" (¶4^v). Another note reads "Andrew Bostock his booke of Loppington" (R1^v). The village of Loppington is in Shropshire, ten miles north of Shrewsbury. Andrew Bostock calls into question the premises of Crowley's revisionist interpretation by repudiating the previously quoted attribution of authorship to a disciple of John Wyclif: "Wyckliffe wa[s] a corruptor o[f] the truth and the Master of a sect of Rebe[ls] who being led b[y] Sr. John Oldcastle rose against the Soviraign, and t[he] Cheif of them executed as they w[ell] deserved, as our chronicles read and these were men that this Printer says h[ad] their eyes open, and so they had, [not] upon truth but rapine and plunder, an[d] their mouth op[en] not to cry ou[t] against the wo[rks] of darkness, but [. . .]vent heresie and sedition" (✱2^r). Bostock undercuts Crowley's central assertion that the "Abbayes shoulde be suppressed," arguing correctly that "this is false, for the Author speaks against abuses onely" (✱4^v). He qualifies Crowley's attack on "The fruites of Popishe penaunce" by noting, "Not the fruits but abuse of Penance (C4^v, B.3.52-58). In answering the editor's gloss, "Note howe he scorneth the auctority

and Bostock's handwritten replies, enables the modern reader to discover that such masterpieces as *Piers Plowman* can be creatures of history. In it are to be seen various conflicting ideas of the fourteenth century, some of which continued to play an important role in the intellectual life of later centuries. These enigmatic prophecies and dark visions attracted their first editor because he found in them, in all apparent sincerity, some clue to understanding the upheavals of the English Reformation. Although Andrew Bostock, a man of the seventeenth century, penetrated the mysteries and half-truths of these editions, some of Crowley's distortions would survive into recent times. Through Crowley's editions *Piers Plowman* may be read as an important text in the history of ideas, as much as it is the enigmatic masterpiece familiar to students of medieval literature.

A TUDOR PROPHET

Crowley's editions triggered a brief vogue for *Piers Plowman* and alliterative imitations of the medieval poem. Public demand warranted three separate editions of *Piers Plowman* within one year. Valuing the poem as a pure ancestor

---

of Popes," the sweeping implications of Bostock's reply call into question the whole of Crowley's interpretation: "No Catholick Doctor can be shewd to have writ or ever taught that the Pope hath power to pardon without any penance or obligation to live well. The Pope's Bull or pardons are for remitting of canonical penances, or temporal punishment, which remains to be suffered after the sin as far as it incurred eternal damnation is forgiven by the Sacrament of penance. And the pardons or Indulgences ever suppose a fit disposition in the persons to whom they are applied. And that must be a sincere resolution of forsaking evil and of doing good. And the Author must not be understood to scorn the Authority of the Cheif Pastor, as the Heretical margin wold suggest, but to reprove those who must, or presume upon such pardons whilst they live vitiously" (K3^r, B.7.170-86).

for modern verse, Crowley used the text as the model for his own prophetic poems. Although Crowley's rationale resembles Spenser's discipleship of Chaucer in writing *The Shepheardes Calender*, *Piers Plowman* offered far less scope for imitation. Crowley agreed with Puttenham to the extent of avoiding archaic diction in his imitations. He did, however, take from *Piers Plowman* the formula for all of his Edwardian poems: prophetic estates satire. He even attempted to imitate Langland's alliterative long line in *One and Thyrtie Epigrammes*. In these activities Crowley was not a narrow antiquarian. Thomas Churchyard based *Davy Dycars Dreame*, his 1552 appeal for commonwealth reform, on Langland's prophecy of the poor ditcher's death by starvation; he and William Waterman acknowledge the influence of Crowley's text on the Churchyard-Camel flyting. Although *Piers Plowman* went out of print in 1561, only a few years before Stow issued the last Renaissance edition of Skelton's *Works*, George Gascoigne's *The Steele Glas* (1576) kept the *Piers Plowman* tradition alive in the 1570s. This medieval tradition survived into the 1590s in the form of homiletic prose satires such as Thomas Nashe's *Pierce Penilesse his Supplication to the Divell* (1592).

Although he was a major participant in the intellectual revolution of the English Reformation, as a much-respected author Crowley was a throwback to earlier times. In style and conventions, his homiletic satires have much in common with the moralistic tradition that encompassed the twelfth-century *De Contemptu Mundi* of Bernard of Cluny as well as Skelton's poetry. Although Crowley exerted no stylistic influence on such giants as Sidney and Spenser, he and his colleagues exerted a profound technical influence on the development of the distinctively Protestant literary forms, genres, and modes of thought that are omnipresent in Elizabethan literature and the works of seventeenth-century authors, both Anglican and Puritan.

Even though Crowley received a humanistic education, only the Bible and medieval English literature noticeably influenced his poetry. Rarely referring to the classics, he rejected Horace, Persius, and Juvenal as satirical models. Sir Thomas Wyatt, on the other hand, anticipated the late Elizabethan flowering of Renaissance verse satire. In "A Spending Hand," "My Mothers Maydes," and "Mine Own John Poyntz," Wyatt supplements the dominant native influence of Chaucer with imported satirical techniques and conventions modeled on Horace and Luigi Alamanni. Although Persius and at times Juvenal are more important than Horace as influences on the 1590s satires of Marston, Hall, Donne, Guilpin, and Lodge, the latter were instrumental in the establishment of neoclassicism as the dominant mode of English verse satire. Instead of the more fully developed and realized individuals of Wyatt and his successors, Crowley used the type characters and abstract personifications of medieval allegory. Adopting the posture of Long Will (or the related voices of the preacher or Old Testament prophet), Crowley employed techniques that late medieval satire had derived from *Piers Plowman* and homiletic tradition. Classifying individuals either by type or social function, Crowley retained the essentially medieval hierarchy of estates.[21] His affinities were with Dunbar and Skelton, as well as his contemporary Luke Shepherd. Only in Crowley's religious thought do we sense participation in the opening of a new epoch, but he even regarded the

[21] John Peter analyzes the Renaissance transition from medieval "complaint" to neoclassical "satire" in *Complaint and Satire in Early English Literature* (Oxford, 1956), pp. 9-12, 106-22. K. W. Gransden's contrast between "homiletic" and "neoclassical" satire mirrors Peter's distinction in *Tudor Verse Satire* (1970), pp. 2-13.

English Reformation as a return to apostolic faith, not as something radically new.

The Voyce of the Laste Trumpet was a companion to the *Piers Plowman* editions. Crowley's octosyllabic verse is awkward and harsh, in keeping with the Tudor fashion for rough satirical style. Yet by adopting the *persona* of the archangel Gabriel, the last trumpeter of Revelation, he chooses an elegant apocalyptic conceit. In the manner of *Piers Plowman* and the *Psalter*, poet and prophet merge in Crowley's verse. The blowing of the last trumpet fuses Bale's theory, that the reign of Edward VI marks the advent of the millennium, with Crowley's social gospel. His epigraphs (Luke 3:4 and Isaiah 40:3-5) link this call for reform to biblical appeals for moral and spiritual renewal in preparation for the Second Coming. In blaming England's ills on avarice and social mobility, Crowley urges obedience, a return to Langland's fixed hierarchy of estates, and implementation of his own stewardship theory of property ownership. His successive lessons to twelve hierarchal estates ranging from beggars to magistrates adapt Langland's prophecies to England's time of crisis. In reference to the recent rebellions, Crowley urges the poor to accept their lot, because God alone can avenge their misery; scholars and priests must, however, resist their special sin of idleness. Gentlemen and clergy must ensure that the poor commons receive their fair share of wealth.

Appearing barely more than one month later, on 31 December 1549, *A New Yeres Gyfte, wherein is taught the knowledge of our selfe and the feare of God* is even more harsh and crabbed than *The Voyce*. Crowley's metrically irregular rhyme royal typifies decadent late medieval versification of the mid-century. Pieced together out of scriptural paraphrases, this précis of Christ's gospel teaching adopts the homiletic structure of a medieval sermon on the seven deadly sins, a pattern that Langland had vividly exploited in *Piers Plowman*. Despite his apparently gloomy doctrine of original sin, Crowley remains optimistic that a New Year's resolution for moral reformation may avert the apocalypse and merit "speciall grace" and salvation. In addition to avarice and lust, agelong objects of pulpit attacks, he concentrates on sloth, the special sin of property owners. In demanding reform from the wealthy, Crowley calls for controls on prices and rents, as well as for protection of the innocent poor. The apocalyptic alternative to reform within the coming year is stressed again and again through the anxious medieval *memento mori* and *de contemptu mundi* formulas.

Instead of passively reusing an old medieval verse form, in *One and Thyrtie Epigrammes* Crowley reinvigorates Langland's four-stress long line by adapting it to his Tudor audience. The title is misleading, for the collection actually contains thirty-three epigrams. Occasionally he employs alliteration, as in the line "Solomon the sage in Sapience doeth saye" (C1ᵛ). Crowley realizes that the alliterative tradition is very old-fashioned, for his preface to *Piers Plowman* acknowledges that Langland

> . . . wrote altogither in miter: but not after the maner of our timers that wryte now adayes (for his verses ende not alike) but the nature of hys miter is, to have three wordes at the leaste in every verse which begyn with some one letter. (∗2ʳ)

Crowley's epigrams are all the more impressive because alliterative verse, which had survived into the early sixteenth century in the works of Dunbar and Skelton, as well as in the northern masterpiece *The Scotish Feilde*, had atrophied by the mid-century. Although his juncture of the indigenous alliterative tradition with the imported tradition of rhymed couplets creates a much more jarring effect than the long, unrhymed verse paragraphs of *Piers Plowman*, Crowley's four-beat accentual rhythm has a lively and pleasing movement. Inheriting the strong caesura of Anglo-Saxon poetry, he prints each line as two half-lines.

This collection of satires on different institutions and estates resembles the vivid anecdotes and tales in medieval handbooks of pulpit *exempla* such as the *Gesta Romanorum* and Robert Mannyng of Brunne's *Handlyng Synne*. Included among these parables and fables illustrating human vices and failings are tales of the bribe-taking bailiff ("Of Baylife Arrantes"), the wealthy coal miner who "myght have bene a knight" ("Of the Colier of Croydon"), the recusant friar who had to travel to Louvain in order to wear his habit again ("Of Obstinate Papistes"), and two tales of a reforming king ("Of Double Beneficed men" and "Of the Exchecker"). Although the alphabetical arrangement of the collection borrows the structure of moralized Renaissance hornbooks, *Epigrammes* is not a children's *A. B. C.*; Crowley addresses his epigrams to a mixed audience including humble and educated readers.

Crowley defines the epigram as a species of short satire that aims "to blame and reprove / The faultes of al menne boeth hyghe and lowe" (A3^r). He attacks abuses of the time according to such types as Alehouses, Beggars, and Brothels. George Puttenham also defined the epigram as a close relative of satire, which is marked by the presence of "bitter taunts, and privy nips or witty scoffes, and other merry conceits."[22] The epigrams were well received, for Bishop John Parkhurst, the eminent Latin poet, linked Crowley with John Heywood as England's foremost epi-

---

[22] *Essays*, ed. Smith, II, 56.

grammatists.[23] The collection was reprinted during the reign of Edward VI and again under Queen Elizabeth.

Crowley adopts as his satiric *persona* the voice of the Old Testament prophet:

> If bokes may be bolde to blame and reprove,
> The faultes of al menne boeth hyghe and lowe:
> As the Prophetes dyd whom Gods Spirite did move
> Than blame not myne Autor for right well I knowe:
> Hys penne is not tempered vayne doctrines to sowe,
> But as Esaye hath bidden so muste he neades crye,
> And tell the Lordes people of their iniquitie.
>
> (A3ʳ)

The biblical narrator merges with Langland's Long Will, the truth-seeking wanderer who observes the moral anarchy of the world and tries to correct it by directly attacking vice. The kaleidoscopic scene of *Epigrammes* recreates Langland's "felde ful of folke." Once again Crowley contemplates the dissolution of the abbeys:

> As I walked alone and mused on thynges,
> That have in my tyme bene done by great kings,
> I bethought me of Abbayes that sometyme I sawe,
> Whiche are now suppressed all by a lawe.
>
> (A5ʳ)

Finding the same abuses that he glossed in *Piers Plowman*, Crowley laments the obstruction of the Henrician reforms.

---

[23] When Parkhurst held back publication of *Ludicra sive Epigrammata Iuvenilia* (1573), his friends argued that public esteem for the vernacular epigrams of Heywood and Crowley was a precedent for publication: "Illi autem orare, instare, urgere, & preces, blanditias, convitia, iurgia cumulare: & Heywodi, Crowleique; etiam patrio sermone scripta Epigrammata celebrari, & magno in pretio haberi, dicere" (A2ᵛ).

Only the millennial reign of Crowley's just king, evidently Edward VI, can bring reform (C3^{r-v} and D4^{v}-5^{r}).

Philargyrie of Greate Britayne (1551) is Crowley's masterpiece. By depicting the "great Gigant" Philargyrie as a fur-clad Protestant aristocrat who rakes gold coins into a sack with a Bible, the title-page woodcut (Figure 14) furnishes a negative variant of the royal emblem of the Sword and the Book. This image announces Crowley's central topic of the potential for misgovernment brought by the Reformation. In the well-ordered Protestant commonwealth, the ideal king would follow the Bible in overseeing the equitable distribution of wealth according to the Parable of the Steward. This work is Crowley's uniquely Protestant contribution to the debate on royal counsel that motivated four works that appeared in the remarkable year 1516: More's *Utopia*, Castiglione's *Il cortegiano*, Erasmus's *Institutio Principis Christiani*, and Skelton's *Magnyfycence* (not printed until 1528). Although he grounds the work in the specific occasion of the Reformation, Crowley transcends particular events of recent history in achieving a classic of mid-Tudor art. He does so by subsuming contemporary political problems into themes, conventions, and techniques derived from the tradition of moral tale and allegory that includes *Piers Plowman*, Tudor interludes, Chaucer's *Pardoner's Tale*, and many other works. In order to appreciate Crowley's satire on courtly misrule, one need not reduce his allegory to an attack on specific historical personages. The court and its habitués constitute an ancient *topos* that Crowley combines with a strident attack on Pride and Avarice that is as old as the Bible itself.

Philargyrie fuses two crucial questions: who is the ideal royal counselor and how does one recognize him? One might argue that this question underlies all Tudor political art. Indeed it had great urgency during the mid-Tudor period when four monarchs willfully changed advisors, court personnel, religious creeds, and political loyalties. The problem of royal counsel had special meaning during a period of minority government when few people knew with certainty whether Edward VI was a figurehead or a philosopher king of Solomonic wisdom. Crowley's allegory analyzes the English Reformation as a contest between personified virtues and vices for the spiritual welfare of Great Britain. Until the very end of the work the King is strangely absent, his proper role usurped by the tyrant Philargyrie.

Crowley's rhyme royal preface defines allegory as a satirical vehicle:

If Poetes maye prove and trye theyr owne wytte
In feyneyng of Fables greate Vices to blame:
And if they be blamelesse although they do hytt
The Treuth in theyre Treatyse under a straynge name
Then maye I by ryght (me thyncke) do the same
Wherefore though I touth [touch?] the take it in good
    parte,
For I wyll the noue [no?] Ill as God knoweth myne
    herte.

                        (ll. 1-7)

This disclaimer derives from his analysis of the allegory of *Piers Plowman* as the nutshell which must be broken "for the kernelles sake" (✱2ᵛ). He avoids Langland's obscurity, however, in clearly applying his tale to Reformation England. The epigraph from Mark 4:11 ("Unto suche as be yet wythoute All thyngis shalbe spoken in Parables") identifies Crowley's fable as "Christian" fiction and the comprehending reader as the elect Christian. In addition to their agelong association with Christ's ministry, William Baldwin also identifies the didactic operation of parables with fables (*Treatise*, A6ʳ).

Despite the formal obscurity of the allegory, Crowley's style is extremely simple and unadorned. Opening the poem with a simple minstrels' formula for beginning a romance, he calls attention to his deliberate choice of a plain style and conversational diction:

> Geve eare awhyle
> And marke my style
> You that hath wyt in store
> For wyth wordes bare
> I wyll declare
> Thyngs done long tyme before.
>
> (ll. 29-34)

Although he imitates alliteration (see ll. 727, 730, 742, 856, and 931-32), he introduces the medieval forms of rhyme royal and tailed rhyme in place of Langland's four-stress long line. Crowley wrote the body of the poem in the latter measure, a six-line stanzaic variation of ballad meter that alternates iambic dimeter couplets with one trimeter line and rhymes *aabccb*. This popular minstrel form is marked by insistent rhyme and an emphatic beat; similar forms of tailed rhyme may be found in *Sir Launfal* and other metrical romances. The extremely simple rhyme scheme and abundance of tag lines make it a very memorable and popular form.

Crowley adapts the format and techniques of the Tudor moral interlude. The text might lend itself to performance, except for the length of particular speeches, as well as the presence of narrative links and subheads that identify the work as a tale. The structure of his narrative has undergone rudimentary dramatization; time and again various characters orate, preach, supplicate, engage in dialogue, and pray. A narrative link at the end of Philargyrie's first oration to the "people of Britaine" illustrates this pattern:

> Dixi, quoth he
> And bowed his knee
> Unto his audience
> Thankyng them all
> Boeth greate and smale
> For theyr quiete scilence
>
> Then wyth one voyce
> All dyd rejoyce
> And clapt theyr handes apase
> And after that
> They fell all flatte
> Prostrate before his face.
>
> (ll. 263-74)

The communal audience that represents the British people repeatedly listens to orations and sermons. The populace takes on some of the attributes of the Mankind figure of morality tradition. In one of the more explosive scenes, Hypocrisy's sermon dramatizes the doctrine of purgatory and the sale of indulgences, practices that had obsessed the reformers ever since Martin Luther first tacked up his ninety-five theses on the door of Schlosskirche, Wittenberg.

The allegory centers on Philargyrie ("love of silver"), a Gargantuan, gold-eating giant who devours Great Britain until the just King, urged on by Truth, expels him from the kingdom. The giant might occupy the vestigial Mankind role, except that he never wavers, possesses no virtue, and is urged on by two Vices. In a curious doubling, the single corresponding Virtue, Truth, attends the missing King, who never acts until the conclusion. If one treats them as a composite figure, Philargyrie and the King embody the negative and positive capacities of the ruler in the manner of a true Mankind figure like the flawed tyrant of Skelton's *Magnyfycence*. The giant personifies avarice, for Crowley the underlying cause of the failure of reforms. As a conventional dramatic figure, he is the descendant of such medieval personifications as Avarice in the *Castle of Perseverance*. He anticipates characters like Sir John Falstaff and Sir Epicure Mammon. Philargyrie matches Chaucer's Pardoner, his most notable literary precursor, in both oratorical expertise and capacity for self-deception. The giant dramatizes Tyndale's *Parable of the Wicked Mammon*, which amplifies a famous Luther sermon. Luther and Tyndale also furnish the theological background for Milton's golddigging Mammon, who excels at the conventional sophistry attached to Protestant personifications of wealth (*PL*, I.678-90, II.229-83).

Hypocrisy and Philaute ("self-love"), the two Vices, serve in sequence as Philargyrie's chief minister. Through the transfer of power between characters who respectively preach Catholic and Protestant doctrines, Crowley constructs a metaphor that refers on one level to Henry VIII's ecclesiastical policy. In the manner of Thomas Cromwell, the Protestant Philaute supports the dissolution of the monasteries and religious houses. In a second instance of the doubling pattern from the moral interlude, however, Philaute is indistinguishable from the Catholic Vice Hypocrisy. Although Philargyrie receives counsel from each minister in turn, there is no essential difference between their policies. The reader's difficulty in keeping the two characters separate recapitulates the epistemological problem of Reformation faith that Bale formulated in the *Image of Both Churches*. Philaute's acquisition of vast wealth and property provides the key to Crowley's contention that the new Protestant elite has simply replaced the Roman clergy in oppressing the poor commons.

As in the moralities and interludes, inner character is revealed through both names and costumes (or disguises). A likely source for the name Philargyrie is Skelton's *Nigramansir* or William Turner's contemporary dialogue-trial of Mistress Missa. The lost Skelton interlude took its title from a minor character, the necromancer, and featured an allegorical trial of "Philargyria, or Avarice" and Simony before a devil who serves as judge.[24] In Turner's allegory, Sir Philip Philargyry defends the mass before an English court of law. Protestant authors used the name Hypocrisy as a familiar epithet for Catholic characters throughout the sixteenth century, as, for example, in the stage personifications of Hypocrisy as a Roman Catholic Vice, found in Bale's *The Three Laws* and Wever's *Lusty Juventus*. Comparison with the title-page woodcut identifies both Philargyrie and Hypocrisy as variants of the Papal Antichrist familiar from Reformation iconography.

Several possible precedents exist for Philaute. In *Archipropheta* Grimald used the name Philautus to link the Pharisees to medieval forms of devotion. It is improbable that Crowley drew the figure directly from the *Nichomachean Ethics* (IX. 8. 4), where the negative manifestation of φίλαυτος ("loving oneself") connotes the acquisition of excessive wealth, fame, or physical pleasure. Erasmus personifies Philautia as an attendant of Folly in *Moriae Encomium*. The vice is criticized frequently in Erasmus's colloquies, *Il cortegiano*, and Baldwin's *Treatise* (O2ᵛ). Of all these possible sources, however, Tyndale's attack on "philautia," or the fifteenth-century Aristotle of the scholastic commentaries, is the most likely:

[24] Warton, *History of English Poetry*, II, 360-63.

[351]

They will saye yet moare shamefully, that no man can understonde the scriptures without philautia, that is to saye philosophy. A man must fyrst be well sene in Aristoteles yer [ere] he can understonde the scripture saye they. . . . (*Obedience*, B8ᵛ)

In a Protestant metamorphosis of medieval Pride, Tyndale and Crowley link "self-love" to scholastic abuse of the Bible and Christian learning. Crowley also looked to the medieval miracle plays, taking, for example, the figure of Bishop Caiaphas ("Who rode with spear and shyld / Haveynge his corse / Armed with force") directly from passion plays in the mystery cycles. In presenting Caiaphas as the Roman Catholic governor of the capital city of Nodnoll (an anagram for London), Crowley transforms the Hebrew stage villain into another variant of the papal Antichrist. One can identify any number of historical persons with Caiaphas, but Edmund Bonner must have come to the minds of many readers. Bale identifies Bonner as "Cayphas" of London in the first part of Anne Askew's *Examinations* (C6ᵛ-D1ᵛ).

This proliferation of Antichrist figures and the unregenerate behavior of Protestant Philaute suggest that the English monarchy has achieved no substantial advance since the beginning of Henry VIII's political Reformation. Traditions of anticlerical and courtly satire coalesce in the doubling of Hypocrisy and Philaute. Crowley's metaphor articulates the following sentiment: where Avarice (Folly) reigns, Hypocrisy and Self-Love govern. Crowley follows *Piers Plowman* as the narrative model for his allegory when Truth brings corruption to the attention of the unknowing King. The history of the gold-eating giant runs parallel to that of Lady Meed, Langland's personification of avarice and bribery in passus 2-4. In the medieval epic Lady Meed corrupts England until the King, urged on by Reason, expels her from Westminster, the center of government. So also Philargyrie devours Great Britain until Crowley's just King, urged on by Truth, expels him from the kingdom. *Philargyrie* concludes with the advent of the millennial kingdom of truth and peace, which recalls Conscience's prophecy of an ideal kingdom at the end of the Lady Meed episode. In his marginalia to *Piers Plowman*, Crowley seizes upon this "Christian" prognostication in order to argue for contemporary reform: "This is no prophecye, but a truth gathered of the scriptures" (D4^v, B.3.297-301).

Crowley's conviction that the monarchy has never fulfilled its obligation to share the wealth of the monasteries with the entire commonwealth accounts for the intermixture of attacks on the monasteries with contemporary Edwardian objects of attack in the iconoclastic episode entitled: "Howe Philargyrie committeth the Governaunce of all hys Subjectes to Hypocrisie" (ll. 461-676). As strict historical allegory, the passage refers to the period prior to the break with Rome; it elaborates Crowley's interpretation of passus 5 of *Piers Plowman* as a prophecy of the dissolution of the abbeys. Philargyrie's devouring of "all the treasure that Hypocrisie had layed up in store" utilizes gold as a complex metaphor for the traditional deadly sins of avarice, pride, gluttony, envy, sloth, and anger. Philargyrie's sins even include lust if one conceives of gold metaphorically as an erotic object in the manner of Mammon's speech (*FQ*, II.vii.15-17) and Volpone's opening soliloquy. In addition to the minor abbey at Willesdon and the shrine at Winchcombe, Crowley's iconoclastic outburst attacks what were the wealthiest shrines in England except for those of Edward the Confessor at Westminster Abbey

[353]

(a special royal preserve) and Thomas Becket at Canterbury.

The dissolved shrines of the relic of the Virgin's milk at Our Lady of Walsingham, the relic of Christ's blood at Hayles, and the tomb of St. Audrey (Etheldreda) at Ely Cathedral exemplify the external forms of adoration and devotion that the iconoclasts demolished under Edward VI. Walsingham in particular had been known for its hoard of gold, precious jewels, and silver. In *Piers Plowman* Crowley calls attention to monastic abuses by citing "Hermets" in the margin. The text reads: "Hermets on a heape wyth hoked staves / Wenten to Walsingham, & her [their] wenches after" (A1ᵛ, B.Prol.53-54). Langland's Avarice promises to go on a pilgrimage "to Walsingham, and my wife also / And byd the rode of bromholme, bring me out of dette" (F4ʳ, B.5.230-31). London typography may account for Crowley's concern with the lesser shrine of St. Audrey, where miraculous cures were attributed to cloths placed on the saint's coffin (hence the "tawdry" laces on sale at the annual saint's fair). Crowley's bookshop at Ely Rents was adjacent to the church of St. Etheldreda, the chapel of the Bishop of Ely's town house, which the Protestants seized during the Reformation. The association of Hypocrisy's treasury with St. Paul's (ll. 671-76) recalls the 1548 destruction of the cloister, chapel, charnel house, church art, and monumental tombs at Edmund Bonner's cathedral (*Annales*, 3D3ᵛ). Crowley's identification of Hypocrisy's fortified city Nodnoll with Babylon ("It was all one / Wyth Babylon"), the birthplace of Antichrist and demonic counterpart to Jerusalem, had already applied Bale's millennial prophecies to contemporary London.

Truth, the sole Protestant Virtue, resolves the conflict by persuading the King to rescue his people. As he does in his other writings, Crowley looks to the ideal Christian ruler (in particular Edward VI) for the complete reform of religious and social abuses. When Truth reveals misrule to the godly ruler, he immediately springs into action:

> Wyth that the Kynge
> For feare gan sprynge
> Unto the Bible boke
> And by and by
> Ryght reverently
> That swerde in hande he toke.
>
> (ll. 1379-84)

The solution to the Reformation problem of royal counsel insists that the King as God's agent can receive counsel only from Truth, who personifies the divine revelation of the Bible. The King must recognize for himself that the Bible is the model for good government. The restoration of order and measure through the King's pious banishment of Philargyrie follows the interlude pattern of the royal drama *Magnyfycence*. Identification of divine revelation with ideal kingship argues for the royal supremacy; the realm prospers when the King governs as a providential agent and banishes Philargyrie. In going into exile, Philargyrie functions as a complex allegorical figure that incorporates Avarice, Hypocrisy, Self-Love, Abuse of Learning, Antichrist, the Pope, Images and Relics, and the Mass. The allegorical action turns full circle from Philargyrie's initial perversion of the scriptures when the King arms himself with the emblematic weapons of Reformation warfare: the Sword and the Book. Although the satire is grounded in the specific occasion of Edward VI's reign, Crowley so universalizes the action that readers could apply it with equal validity to every monarch from Henry VIII to James II.[25]

[25] In *Tudor Puritanism: A Chapter in the History of Idealism* (Chicago,

Crowley's final Edwardian apocalypse, *Pleasure and Payne,
Heaven and Hell* (1551), is a sequel to *The Voyce of the
Laste Trumpet*. Writing in the medieval octosyllabics of
The Voyce, a staple for popular narrative verse, Crowley
adopts the posture of the brother of "the trumpet" (D5ʳ)
who narrated the previous work. His scene has shifted
from millennial prophecy to a vision of the Last Judgment. Avarice remains the root cause of England's troubles: "gods Ire . . . wyl fal upon this realme very shortly,
if oppression and gredye covetise cease not . . ." (A2ᵛ). As
an amplification of his epigraph, which describes Christ's
separation of the blessed and the damned on Judgment Day
(Matthew 25:34, 41), this poem is Crowley's most disillusioned work. When he edited *Piers Plowman* and wrote
The Voyce, he confidently envisioned Edward VI's reign as
the time of peace and justice preceding the millennium.
Philargyrie in turn articulated the ideal of commonwealth
reform. In *Pleasure and Payne*, however, Crowley identifies Christ's sufferings with the misery of the poor and
offers little hope that the landlords will reform. Abandon-
ing all hope for change from above, he now uses millenarian prophecy to frighten his audience and warn of the
Second Coming.

1939), M. M. Knappen suggests that *Philargyrie* refers in general to the
English Reformation (pp. 414-15). Ralph Maud interprets the text as an
analysis of the Edwardian Reformation in "Robert Crowley, Puritan Satirist," *Costerus*, 7 (1973), 81-92. This uncritical argument identifies Crowley as a "printer" and a "Puritan," even though the Puritans coalesced into
a faction only after the Elizabethan Compromise (see Knappen, *Puritanism*,
pp. 163-216, 488, passim). Maud's contention that *Philargyrie* jointly attacks Seymour and Dudley ignores Seymour's contemporary reputation as
a social reformer, as well as Crowley's open partisanship for the former
and animus toward the latter (above, pp. 181-83). Becon's *Confortable
Epistle* identifies Dudley as a much more probable object of topical attack
than Seymour (A3ʳ).

Crowley fell silent after *Pleasure and Payne*, perhaps as a consequence of his 1551 ordination by Nicholas Ridley. He fled into exile after Edward VI's death, at the reversal by Mary of reforms. Unlike Bale, Foxe, Becon, and other fellow exiles, Crowley maintained complete silence during his residence at Frankfurt. Within one year of Elizabeth's accession, however, he welcomed the new queen as the ideal Christian ruler in terms almost identical to those that he had once applied to her brother. His continuation of Lanquet's *Epitome of Cronicles* comprised the first published analysis of the failure of Reformation under Edward and Mary. Consideration of this text leads, however, to the conclusion of this study. Such discussion must await examination of a final Edwardian author, the learned satirist William Baldwin.

CHAPTER 8
William Baldwin and the Satirist's Art

William Baldwin, a man of much learning and wisdom as it appears
from his writings, who was skilled in many things and shined forth
in the same manner as Cato himself.

John Bale, *Catalogus*, Volume II.

ATHENS AND JERUSALEM

Judged on the strength of his satire, *Beware the Cat*, and
other writings, William Baldwin is the preeminent imaginative author of the English Reformation. Yet his life is
much more shadowy than those of such figures as Crowley
or Bale. Before John Bale began his Marian exile, he appears not to have heard of Baldwin, for he fails to mention
him in any pre-exile books or manuscripts. Other than the
lost comedies that he wrote for court performance, *A Treatise of Morall Phylosophie* is the only Baldwin work cited
in *Catalogus*.[1] Anthony à Wood's claim that he supplicated

---

[1] Bale lists the four parts of the text as separate titles (II, 108). Baldwin
dedicated this work to Edward Beauchamp, Earl of Hertford and son of
Edward Seymour. Use of the latter's title of protector shows that Whitchurch dated publication on 20 January 1547/8. Paul M. Gaudet edits the
work in "William Baldwin's *A Treatise of Moral Philosophy* (1564): A
Variorum Edition with Introduction" (Ph.D. diss., Princeton University,
1972). The 1564 edition, the last one overseen by Baldwin, had undergone

for the M.A. degree from Oxford University carries no authority.[2] Baldwin's publications furnish the most concrete details about his own life. According to its colophon, *The Canticles or Balades of Salomon* was "Imprinted at London by William Baldwin, servaunt with Edwarde Whitchurche." Because he never set up shop independently of his master, his imprints imply that he collaborated with Whitchurch as a publisher. A scholar like Baldwin would have edited books and read proof at the Whitchurch printing house. The prologues of *Beware the Cat* and *The Mirror for Magistrates* link him to George Ferrers and Thomas Chaloner, both of whom participated in the Christmas revels of 1552-53. As editor of the *Mirror*, Baldwin identifies himself as a Welshman as well as "a Minister and a Preacher" in the 1587 prologue to Churchyard's *Shore's Wife*.

The brevity of the above-quoted tribute in Bale's *Catalogus* distorts Baldwin's high stature as a Reformation artist and editor. Introducing innovations that point toward major developments in Elizabethan literature, his publications were among the most successful and influential books circulating between 1550 and 1560. Baldwin's authorship of the first printed sonnet in English places him well in advance of public taste. This dedicatory poem for Christopher Langton's *Treatise of Phisick* (10 April 1547) looks forward to *Songs and Sonnets* and the Elizabethan vogue for printed sonnet cycles. Baldwin apparently edited or corrected the Langton text for Whitchurch. Inclusion of "The thinges that cause a quiet lyfe, written by Marcial" in Baldwin's *Treatise* (Q2^r) led to the second printing of a

---

expansion to ten books and 151 verse tags. Quotations follow the second edition, hereafter cited as *Treatise*.

[2] *Athen. Oxon.* (1691), col. 113.

Surrey poem;[3] Baldwin must therefore have had direct or indirect access to one of the manuscript miscellanies of courtly verse.

Baldwin is the only imaginative author of the English Reformation to escape the 1580s censure of earlier Tudor literature and to provide a consciously acknowledged influence on Elizabethan literature. Appearing in seven editions under Baldwin's general editorship, *The Mirror for Magistrates* is the only mid-Tudor work that Sidney admits into the select company of *The Shepheardes Calender* and *Gorboduc*. As such, the *Mirror* became the major conduit that channeled medieval notions of *de casibus* tragedy into the Elizabethan age. The twenty-four Renaissance editions of the *Treatise* (Palfreyman's pirated text diverges from the five editions supervised by Baldwin) show that this extremely popular text filled a genuine need for a popular encyclopedia of classical wisdom. Baldwin's translation of *Wonderfull Newes of the Death of Paule the .III.* marks one of the earliest shifts away from native English estates satire toward the Italianate malcontent satire that would become fashionable under Elizabeth. In breaking away from the medieval tradition of exemplary tales, *Beware the Cat* is arguably the first English novel and a very early example of the kind of experimentation with modes of narration and point of view that characterizes modern fiction.

The entry in Bale's *Catalogus* does attest to Baldwin's contemporary reputation as a moral philosopher. Concern for prudential wisdom unifies all of his publications, which fed the Tudor hunger for gnomic sayings, proverbs, aphorisms, and parables. The Langton sonnet reflects this preoccupation, for Baldwin's choice of medicine as the subject for this occasional poem and his sententious conclusion

---

[3] *Poems*, No. 40.

"Consule valetudini" ("Take care of your health") substitute didactic instruction for traditional sonnet themes of
erotic love:

> Great knowlege wherof, this boke wil him show.
> Whiche smal though it seme contayneth as much
> Of arte to be knowen of them that are wyse. . . .
>
> (A1ᵛ)

According to the *Treatise*, "phisicke" or medicine joins logic
and moral philosophy as one of three branches of natural
philosophy (A3ʳ⁻ᵛ).

As the major public author of the time to fuse humanistic learning with Christian truth, Baldwin avoids the gospelling manner of Bale and Crowley—he continues instead
in the tradition of Protestantized Erasmianism established
by Udall, Taverner, Cheke, and Ascham. Baldwin's harmonization of classical and Christian wisdom thus contradicts Bale's declaration of the incompatibility of the Bible
and classical learning (*Image*, p. 515). In the prologue to
his *Treatise*, Baldwin defends secular learning against such
Protestant radicals as John Hall and Thomas Becon: "For
although . . . Philosophie is not to be compared with the
most holy scryptures, yet it is not utterly to bee despysed"
(¶5ʳ). He follows the Augustinian principle that philosophy serves as the "handemayden" to the Bible rather than
the "Scriptures Interpretour" wherever the pagan philosophers agree with Christian revelation (*De Doctrina Christiana*, 2. 40. 60). The Christian should follow Augustinian
practice by "takyng the good, & leavinge the bad" (¶5ᵛ,
6ᵛ). Socrates is especially important as a pre-Christian authority because unaided reason led him, in the manner of
More's Utopians, to belief in the immortality of the soul
and monotheism (A4ʳ, E5ʳ; see C1ᵛ).

Bale's classification of Baldwin as an English Cato endorses him as a learned moralist, perhaps by allusion to the reputations of the elder and younger Cato as defenders of Roman virtue. By Dante's time, Cato the Younger personified the harmonization of pagan and Christian ethics (*Purgatorio*, II. 119-23). Bale's epithet places Baldwin in the same league as Walter Map, the reputed author of *Apocalypsis Goliae*, who "compared himself to a third Cato" (*Rhithmi vetustissimi*, A3ʳ). Bale doubtless refers to the *Catonis disticha* attributed to Dionysius Cato, the pseudepigraphous collection that acquired extensive moral authority during the Middle Ages and Renaissance; Baldwin's *Treatise* is a Renaissance reformulation of this encyclopedia of prudential wisdom. The collection of distichs in Latin hexameters supplied Baldwin's model for appending to the third book of the *Treatise* a compendium of sixty-two epigrammatic tags entitled "Pyththie [*sic*] meters of divers matters." After use as a remarkably influential medieval schoolbook, the *Disticha* began to appear in print with Caxton's Latin-English edition. Its assimilation into the humanistic curriculum through Erasmus's edition furnished Baldwin's general precedent for structuring his text as an encyclopedia made out of sententious precepts attributed to classical authorities. After Richard Taverner edited the Latin text for use in grammar schools,[4] Robert Burrant issued an English translation.[5]

In bringing together selections from many otherwise unavailable authors, Baldwin's *Treatise* served to introduce ancient learning to a reading public with an avid commitment to self-education. Baldwin specifically refers to *Toxophilus*, Ascham's Christian-humanistic synthesis. Eras-

---

[4] *Catonis disticha moralia ex castigatione D. Erasmi Roterodami cum annotationibus & scholiis R. Taverneri* (1540).

[5] *Preceptes of Cato the Sage, with Annotacions of D. Erasmus of Roterodame* (1545 [no copy extant?]; 1553).

mus's collections of maxims and proverbs taken from classical authors, the *Adagia* (1500) and *Apophthegmata* (1514), also helped to satisfy the Tudor demand for aphoristic literature. It is no wonder that these works went into edition after edition. They function as general models for the didactic form and structure of the *Treatise* rather than as specific textual sources.[6] Baldwin's titles for books three and four confer an unmistakable Erasmian coloring upon the text: "The thyrde boke, of Proverbes and adages" and "The laste boke, of Proverbes and Semblables." Nevertheless, when he mentions *Apophthegmata*, he cites it as a literary model rather than as a source (F6[r]). Baldwin does refer to Diogenes Laertius's *De vita et moribus Philosophorum* as the chief source both for the framework and content of book one as a set of lives and sayings of the philosophers.

Baldwin's *Treatise* is an outstanding example of the coexistence of medieval and humanistic ideas throughout the English Renaissance. Formal and structural imitations of Erasmian texts are devices for concealing the intellectual conservatism of his text; he remains pointedly silent about a major source for the texts of specific aphorisms: Caxton's edition of the translation of the medieval *Dicts or Sayings of the Philosophers* (1477) by Anthony Woodville, Earl Rivers.[7] Ultimately derived from an eleventh-century Arabic compilation, this work had become a medieval favorite by the time Woodville translated a French version. Although the general form and doctrine of the *Treatise* accord

---

[6] Wilbrahim F. Trench fails to support his generalization that Baldwin drew the first and third books from *Apophthegmata* and the second book from *Adagia* in "William Baldwin," *Modern Quarterly of Language and Literature*, 1 (1899), 260.

[7] Curt F. Bühler, "A Survival from the Middle Ages: William Baldwin's Use of the *Dictes and Sayings*," *Speculum*, 23 (1948), 76-80.

with classical modes of thought, one cannot rely on Baldwin's attributions to such historical and mythical philosophers as Socrates, Plato, Aristotle, Pythagoras, and Hermes Trismegistus.[8]

Baldwin's choice of moral philosophy as his subject is not unusual—Tudor Englishmen were preoccupied with ethics. His stated purpose of fashioning a guide "to lyve together well and lovyngly" explains Baldwin's motto "Love and Lyve." A gloss for a precept on friendship ("It is the propertie of frendes to lyve and love together") attributes this tag phrase to Aristotle (¶6ᵛ-7ʳ, K3ʳ). Baldwin shares the belief that moral philosophy is the rational complement to revealed truth with St. Thomas Aquinas and the scholastic philosophers, as well as such Renaissance contemporaries as Erasmus, Montaigne, Spenser, and Donne. Baldwin's intention of balancing "lawfull praise" of philosophy with "due service" to the scriptures mirrors the Erasmian program (✳3ᵛ). His epigraph "Ne quid nimis" comes directly from *Adagia* (¶7ᵛ).

It is a mistake, however, to reduce Baldwin's thought to an expression of Erasmian pietism; one must recognize the Protestant character of Reformation humanism. Without any qualification, P. M. Gaudet applies to the *Treatise* McConica's argument concerning the continuity of Erasmian humanism ("Variorum Edition," p. 38). He fails, for example, to acknowledge that the ultimate, homiletic purpose of the *Treatise* mirrors Cranmer's redefinition of *caritas* and good works as posterior "fruits of faith." Nevertheless, Baldwin states unequivocally "that oure love and charitye used towardes oure bretherne, maye testify oure fayth and love towardes GOD" (¶7ʳ). His works

[8] D. T. Starnes, "Sir Thomas Elyot and the 'Sayings of the Philosophers,'" *Texas University Studies in English*, 13 (1933), 5-35.

reflect the Reformation tendency to transform Erasmus into a Protestant authority, which is shared by Coverdale's edition of the second volume of the *Paraphrases*. Whitchurch printed that text while Baldwin worked at his printing house.

In the manner of the Lucianic satires of Thomas More and Erasmus, Baldwin identifies truth with fiction. This juncture is akin to the Reformation defense of fiction articulated by Crowley and Wever, and it may account for the apparent ease with which Baldwin, a serious moralist, gives the *Treatise* a "fictional" garment as a collection that comes out of the tradition of Erasmian humanism. During the Renaissance, license to invent fictions is associated with dialogue, comic drama, Lucianic satire, allegory, and beast fable. It was the early Christian identification of truth with canonical scriptures and fiction with lying fables that led to the disguising of apocryphal tales and pseudepigraphous works as documented Christian "history" rather than freely invented fiction.[9] It might be argued that so long as one relates spiritual "truth," no fiction can lie. Baldwin anticipates Sidney's distinction between the three kinds of "poetry": divine, philosophical, and "right" fiction. In organizing the *Treatise* by means of progression from simple precept to complicated and indirect parables, Baldwin chooses Aesop as the model author of philosophical fiction (A6[r]). Crowley similarly moves from the prescriptive truths of *The Voyce of the Laste Trumpet* and *Pleasure and Payne* to the anecdotal satires of *One and Thyrtie Epigrammes*. The latter fables are fictions of a lower order than the complex parable of *Philargyrie*.

At its highest level, moral philosophy teaches by means of intricate and ambiguous fiction. The proverbs, parables,

[9] William Nelson, *Fact or Fiction: The Dilemma of the Renaissance Storyteller* (Cambridge, Mass., 1973), pp. 22, 31, 48.

and similitudes that Baldwin collects in books three and four are little "fictions" that satisfy the three intrinsic purposes of instruction, delight, and moving to good action that Sidney identified with "right" poetry. Baldwin includes epigrams by himself and other hands in book three because they will encourage "suche as delyte in Englyshe meter" to enjoy and remember his maxims (M8ʳ). Literary pleasure is the principle by which readers should evaluate his collection, for he recommends that "suche as therein delyte, to set forth the reste, and not to loke for all thynges here, in whyche nothinge lesse than perfection is pretended" (Q3ʳ). Baldwin's theory of fiction anticipates Sidney's dismissal of the philosophical precept as an inferior form because of its inability to move one to action by means of aesthetic pleasure. The sayings gathered in the first two books of the *Treatise* cannot provide the complete picture of human life furnished by proverbs and parables:

> . . . although preceptes and counsayles bee the most playne and easye, yet lacke they the grace of delyte, whyche in theyr Proverbes they have supplyed: and that so finely and so wyttely, that they both delyte and perswade excedynglye, mixed with suche piththynes [*sic*] in wordes and sentence, as maye minister occasyon to muse and studye, or cause to fixe the better in memory. . . . (M7ᵛ)

Solomon's "divyne and holy counsayles" furnish the best precedent for Baldwin's *Treatise*, even though they pertain rather to "divine than morall" wisdom (A5ʳ). Baldwin's *Canticles or Balades of Salomon* (1549), on the other hand, constitutes a collection of divine wisdom analogous to moral philosophy. Because of the Hebrew king's reputation as author of Proverbs, Ecclesiastes, and the Song of Songs, Baldwin found in him the precedent for his own authorship. Solomon was the model for Baldwin as a Reformation philosopher and singer of songs. Separately printed octavo editions of *The Books of Solomon*, which included Proverbs, the Song of Songs, Ecclesiastes, Sapientia, and Ecclesiasticus, fostered the myth of the wise and godly ruler.

The *Canticles or Balades* appeared on 1 June 1549 soon after the prayer book and the Psalms of Sternhold and Crowley. At roughly the same time that he prepared his own version, Baldwin may have read proof for Whitchurch's 29 December 1549 edition of the Great Bible, which includes the following title: "The Ballet of Balettes of Salomon: called in Latin, Canticum Canticorum." He conceives of his collection as a sequence of ballads or love songs, thus insisting on the nature of the text as verse. He explains that he chose versification as the best means of clarifying Solomon's meaning: "And because the rediest way was to make a paraphrase, I have attempted it: & that in meter, because they bee balades" (A1ᵛ). Publication of *A Boke of Ballettes* (c. 1549) provided a secular precedent. The application of the term "ballad" to a Bible translation would at the same time offend Catholics who disapproved of the popularization of the scriptures[10] and placate the gospellers who advocated the sacred parody of secular song. The complex format for each chapter of *Canticles or Balades* combines the prose text from the Great Bible with a commentary, a division of each chapter into individual lyrics in Baldwin's own prose translation, and an amplified verse paraphrase set off from the black-letter text in italic type. He assimilates his own commentary into the verse paraphrase.

Baldwin knew that he had chosen a controversial text. After the Psalms, the Song of Songs is the collection of

---

[10] See Campbell, *Divine Poetry*, p. 57.

biblical poetry that had greatest impact on Reformation spirituality;[11] only the Psalms exceeds it in the number of commentaries that it evoked. It is no accident that *Canticles or Balades* is the first poetic version of the text to appear in English, for the literalistic gospellers would have had great difficulty in accommodating the sensual language of the work to their principle of the plain simplicity of biblical truth. Despite its popularity with commentators, few poets found that it served so well as the Psalms as a mirror for the inner state of their souls. Protestant interpretation of the songs as allegories and parables obviously appealed to the man who had praised parables in the *Treatise* because of their allusiveness, complexity, and utility as vehicles for truth.

In his dedication to Edward VI, Baldwin's attack against the "baudy balades of lecherous love that commonly are indited and song of idle courtyers in princes and noble mens houses" (A3ᵛ) explicitly raises the problem of interpretation. The primary reason for the proliferation of commentaries, including that by Baldwin himself, is the overwhelming concern with erotic love in the literal text. Despite his praise of Sternhold, Baldwin's affinities as a poet lie with Marot and Sidney rather than with Crowley or Sternhold. He had no English precedent for designing the collection as a private anthology of diverse metrical forms rather than as a congregational songbook. In contrast to the mechanically iambic fourteeners of the gospellers, Baldwin experiments in such varied forms as heroic couplets, poulter's measure, hexameters, trimeter lines, fourteeners, ballads, iambics, and anapestics.

The presence of *Canticum Canticorum* among the canonical scriptures required some effort to harmonize its ap-

---

[11] Lewalski, *Protestant Poetics*, pp. 59, 67.

parent profanity with divine truth. During the Middle Ages it served as a magnet for allegorical interpretation. In addition to their rejection of fourfold exegesis, the Protestants refused to accept Solomon as a historical figure in the poem or the presence of themes of erotic love.[12] Calvin in particular became embroiled with Sebastian Castellio in a controversy over the text. Ruling out the validity of spiritual interpretation, Castellio condemned the Song of Songs as an obscene and carnal colloquy between Solomon and the Shulamite. Although he rejected the book of Revelation, Erasmus accepted Canticles as part of the historical canon. Calvin defended the traditional canon on the ground that Canticles was an epithalamium not unlike Psalm 45.[13]

Baldwin came down on Calvin's side, and his preface enters the volume in the debate:

> No doubt but it is an hie and misticall matter, and more darkely hyd than other partes of the scripture, by meanes of the wanton wordes: which also cause many to deny it to be Gods wurde. Whose errour to redresse is the chief cause why I have medled with the matter.

He follows his own hermeneutic advice: "Doubteful thinges oughte to bee interpreted to the beste" (*Treatise*, M6ᵛ). The Reformation controversy explains his rejection of scholastic commentaries, which discovered elaborate allegories concerning spiritual love. Baldwin favors the earlier exegeses of Origen and Anselm, and follows them in finding a coherent statement concerning the historical development of the church. According to his preface, Anselm

---

[12] George L. Scheper, "Reformation Attitudes toward Allegory and the Song of Songs," *PMLA*, 89 (1974), 553-56 et seq.

[13] Roland H. Bainton, "The Bible in the Reformation," in *Cambridge History of the Bible: The West from the Reformation to the Present Day*, ed. Greenslade, pp. 8-9.

"taketh it . . . [as] a prophecie, describyng the estate of the churche, and with what affeccion she desyred Christ in all tymes, bothe under the lawe of nature, of Moyses, and of the gospell" (A1ᵛ). Thus the historical and millennial prophecies of Canticles correspond to those in Revelation.

Assimilating Bale's reading of the Revelation of St. John as a prophecy of the English Reformation, Baldwin's commentary interprets the Hebrew nuptial song as a prophecy of contemporary religious turmoil. *Canticles or Balades* is unique in its interpretation of the text as a Reformation allegory, yet, despite its topicality, Baldwin's commentary tends to be abstract and contains little religious polemic. Interpretation of Solomon's building of the temple as a figure for the spiritual church ("the primative churche of . . . [Christ's] Apostles") was a familiar *topos* for religious reform. The union between Solomon and his spouse stands for the communion between Christ and the faithful, who are represented individually by the bride's attendants. So also the bride's loins engender faithful Christians, and her navel is the Bible that nurtures them. The wavering of the attendants marks the onset of the "troubles and persecusion" that succeed the apostolic age; the latter difficulties lead directly into the ensuing period of church history, which brings the degeneration of the unified congregation into two churches.

Baldwin's account of conflict between "true fayth" and "false hypocrisie" follows Bale's apocalyptic vision of history. He focuses on what reformers from Tyndale to Spenser perceived as the real difficulty that individual Christians face in distinguishing true doctrine from false spirituality. Sharing Duessa's ability to disguise herself, "the churche malignant" conceals itself by means of false doctrine. Thus the little foxes that enter the garden and waste the vineyards are the false clerics who "fayne themselves to be the spouses healpers." Those who persist in working the "fields and vineyards" despite persecution are the Wyclifites and Lollards, who defended true faith during the Age of Locusts. Baldwin sees the Reformation as a return to gospel preaching by the "true and constaunt preachers." The entire collection of songs from "Christe to his Spouse" therefore holds out the promise of salvation by means of the "good gyftes" of imputed grace and justification by faith.[14]

THE ROMAN BABYLON

William Baldwin brings to life the full animus that Reformation Englishmen felt toward the Vatican in his translation (c. 1552) of *Wonderfull Newes of the Death of Paule the .III.* (ascribed to Publius Aesquillus). The designation "Englyshed by W. B. Londoner" must refer to Baldwin because of the presence of his motto "Love and lyve" at the end of the preface.[15] Although it is the second pasquinade to appear in English, the text is extremely important as the earliest sign of a shift toward the imported standards of Italianate and neoclassical satire that would take hold in England by the end of the century. Despite the apparent incongruity of their respective scriptural themes and erotic imagery, *Wonderfull Newes* complements *Canticles or Balades*. The phantasmagorical images of perverse sexuality in the antipapal satire, which include narcissism, incest, and sodomy, invert the major themes of the preceding publication. Just as Baldwin insisted that the carnal imagery of

[14] *Canticles*, a2^r, a4^r-b1^r, b2^v-3^r, c3^r, d2^r, d3^r, e2^r, e3^{r-v}, i2^v, k3^v, and passim.

[15] William A. Ringler, Jr., attributes the translation on the basis of the motto. George B. Parks conjectures translation by William Barker in "William Barker, Tudor Translator," *PBSA*, 51 (1957), 134-35.

the Song of Songs provides a dark metaphor for divine wisdom and love as it is embodied in the true, reformed church, so he intended the grotesque sexual images of *Wonderfull Newes* to approximate the false wisdom and spiritual fornication of the Roman church. The common origin in Revelation imagery of *Wonderfull Newes* and Baldwin's commentary on *Canticles* helps to account for the convoluted parallels between the works. Spenser makes a similar inversion in the comparison between Una and Duessa.

Baldwin's possession of a copy of *Epistola de Morte Pauli Tertii Pontifex Maximus* documents the influence of Continental reformers on their English counterparts. The work appeared with a false colophon stating that it was composed at Rome on 11 November 1549, only one day after the death of Paul III, and published in Piacenza in December of the same year. The piece is disguised, therefore, as a satirical newsletter. These spurious circumstances identify Pier Luigi Farnese, the late son of Paul III who ruled from Piacenza as Duke of Parma and Modena, as a major object of attack. In actual fact Joannes Oporinus published the Latin text in Basel. The anonymity of the title entries for the octavo text in Oporinus's *Librorum Index* (Basel, 1567) shows that the Swiss printer realized that the name Publius Aesquillus was a pseudonym (c6^r, c7^r). One of ten printers who were active in Basel in 1549, Oporinus published books produced by his own presses in addition to those printed for him at Bern and Strasbourg.[16] According to Oporinus's *Index*, *Epistola* joined a book list that included many editions of Greek and Latin classics, the Greek New Testament, patristic texts, and works by Continental

---

[16] Josef Benzing, *Die Buchdrucker Des 16. und 17. Jahrhunderts im Deutschen Sprachgebiet* (Wiesbaden, 1963), pp. 33-38.

humanists and reformers. He imprinted very few medieval texts, such as his minor sixteenmo edition of "Aeneae Sylvii de Euryali & Lucretiae amore libell" (a2ᵛ), and no works by Catholic partisans. Matthias Flacius Illyricus conceded authorship of *Epistola* in the preface of his own translation into German.[17] With eight of his antipapal polemics to his credit, Oporinus was Flacius's Basel publisher. His long list of classical and biblical editions, which included an annotated Greek edition of Aristotle's works (Basel, 1550), identifies this contentious professor of Hebrew as one of the most eminent Lutheran humanists. His edition of *Historia ecclesiastica* (Magdeburg, 1560-74), a thirteen-volume account of European history as an apocalyptic battle between the true and false church, shows the influence of Bale's *Image* and *Acta Romanorum Pontificum*.[18] Archbishop Matthew Parker, who had acquired Bale's library after his death, thanked Flacius in a letter dated 18 July 1562 for sending parts of the "Magdeburg Centuries" to him by private courier. At Flacius's request, Parker sent several medieval manuscript

[17] *Ein Sendbrieff, P. Aesquillij von dem tode Pauli des dritten Babsts dieses namens* (n.p., c. 1550). "Mit zwein Vorreden" signed "Matth. Fla. Illyr." (A2ʳ). Baldwin worked from the original Latin edition. Friedrich Hubert does not document his attribution to Pietro Pauli Vergerio in *Vergerios publizistische Thätigkeit nebst einer bibliographischen Übersicht* (Breslau, 1893), p. 51. Authorship is assigned to Flacius by Emil Weller in *Die falschen und fingirten Druckorte Repertorium* (Leipzig, 1864), p. 244, and Marino Parenti in *Dizionario dei Luoghi di Stampa Falsi Inventati o Supposti* (Florence, 1951), p. 254. The name Publius Aesquillus had become common coin in pasquinades by the time Jacob Bobhard, a German Protestant, employed it as a pseudonym assigned to a member of the Society of Jesus in *Eygentliche, gründliche und warhafte Beschreybung Dess heyligen Römischen und Catholischen Hafenkass* (n.p., 1617). See Emil Weller, *Lexicon Pseudonymorum* (Regensburg, 1886), p. 7.

[18] Published in Basel by Oporinus in July 1558, four months before Mary Tudor's death, this pessimistic account went into *Catalogus*.

commentaries from Bale's collection to Zurich on a one-year loan.[19] Baldwin acquired the *Epistola* by a similar exchange of books between Basel and London or by the usual process of book importation. Bale and William Turner had established contacts in Basel during their Henrician exile, and Bale, Foxe, and Laurence Humphrey would flee to Basel during Mary's reign.

Flacius shared Bale's fondness for anonymity and facetious pseudonyms as satirical devices. Because of the general Protestant anxiety over the Council of Trent, Flacius attacked Paul III in other satirical works. The Croatian Lutheran issued his spurious *Bulla des Antichrists, dadurch er das volck Gottes widderumb inn den eisern ofen der Egiptischen gefengknis denckt zuziehen . . . Verendscht* (Magdeburg, 1550) under the name of the pope who convened the council that met intermittently between 1545 and 1563. In calling the reader's attention to "Gomorrischer unzucht" ("the sexual offense of Gomorrah") in his preface to *Ein Sendbrieff* (A3ʳ), Flacius mirrors Bale's attacks on clerical immorality in *Actes of Englysh Votaryes* and other works.

Reformation England was insatiably curious about the Vatican and contemporary Italy. This shift away from the humanistic concern for classical Rome and Latin learning developed inevitably from the religious controversy and English fears of encirclement by hostile powers which came about as a result of the Council of Trent.[20] *Wonderfull Newes* followed in the wake of William Thomas's *Historie of Italie* (1549) as the second English description of modern Italy. Thomas mingles enthusiasm for Italian cultural superiority with antipathy toward papal Rome, which would

[19] Hastings Robinson, ed., *The Zurich Letters: 1558-1602* (Cambridge, 1842-45; Parker Soc., 2 vols.), II, 77-82.

[20] See J. R. Hale, *England and the Italian Renaissance: The Growth of Interest in Its History and Art* (1954), pp. 12-14 et seq.

remain the conventional attitude of English Protestants as late as Milton's Grand Tour.[21] By contrasting Italian political disunity with the Tudor commonwealth ideal, Thomas's description of Italy luridly confirms Protestant stereotypes. He juxtaposes eyewitness descriptions of the pomp of Paul III and a high mass at St. Peter's basilica with leering hearsay about clerical patronage of Roman brothels along a street called "Julia": "Briefelie by reporte, Rome is not without .40000. harlottes mainteigned for the most parte by the clergy and theyr folowers" (K1^r-4^v). He also regales the reader with details about the sexual propensities of the Farnese family, such as the rumor that in his dotage Paul III "is nourished with the sucke of a womans breasts: and . . . two younge girles . . . lie by hym in his bedde a nights (S4^v)." Moreover, Pier Luigi is said to have been slain by the nobility of Piacenza because of his misrule and "abhominacion in all kinde of vices, and specially in the unnaturall" (3I1^v). When Thomas was hanged, drawn, and quartered for taking part in Wyatt's Rebellion under Queen Mary, the hangman burned copies of his banned *Historie*.

Wonderfull Newes is an unusual example of a full-length attack on an individual pontiff, for most antipapal satires attack the pope as a generic figure or a line of popes as exemplary types. The portrait of the luxurious, worldly majesty of Paul III as a great Renaissance prince epitomizes the Protestant obsession with papal usurpation of temporal, political authority. The historical core is accurate. Alessandro Farnese (b. 1468) rose to favor under the patronage of Rodrigo Borgia after his sister Giulia had a scandalous affair with the cardinal. Appointed to the car-

---

[21] George B. Parks discusses the ambiguity of Tudor attitudes toward Italy in "The Decline and Fall of the English Renaissance Admiration of Italy," *HLQ*, 31 (1968), 341-57.

dinalate in 1493 soon after his patron was crowned as Pope Alexander VI (1492-1503), Farnese became Legate of Ancona in 1502. Julius II legitimized his natural offspring Pier Luigi, Paolo, and Costanza. As the senior cardinal and Dean of the College of Cardinals, Farnese was elected pope in 1534 as a transitional figure who was not expected to reign long. In actual fact, fifteen years remained to his life. He detached territory from the papal states to create the hereditary Duchy of Parma and Modena for Pier Luigi and made his grandsons, Guido Sforza and Alessandro Farnese, cardinals.

The satire suppresses reference to the great learning of Paul III and the extraordinary influence that he had on Renaissance religion and culture. He commissioned Michelangelo to paint the Sistine Chapel, with the Herculean Christ and unprecedented nude figures in his "Last Judgment." Embarking on a much-needed program of church reform that has come to be known as the Counter Reformation, his calling of the Council of Trent is the most important religious event of the time other than the Reformation itself. In any case, Paul's excommunication of Henry VIII would have won him the hatred of the English people. His elevation of the Catholic reformers Giampetro Carafa (the future Paul IV), Jacapo Sadoleto, Gasparo Contarini, and Reginald Pole to the sacred college counterbalanced his nepotistic appointments. He revived the papal Inquisition in 1542 after recognizing the austere order of the Society of Jesus under the leadership of Ignatius Loyola. Bernardino Ochino was a candidate for the cardinalate after Erasmus declined Paul's offer of the red hat.[22]

Wonderfull Newes amplifies Thomas's skeletal account of

[22] For a sympathetic account of Paul III, see Ludwig Pastor, *The History of the Popes*, trans. R. F. Kerr et al. (1891-1953; 40 vols.), XI, 18-23, 357-58; XII, 1-5, and passim.

Vatican depravity by recounting scabrous allegations about the Farneses that have no basis in historical record. According to Baldwin's translation, Alessandro Farnese poisoned his nephew and mother in order to gain his inheritance. After forcing his sister Giulia to yield herself to Rodrigo Borgia, he went on to poison her when she fell in love with another man. Pier Luigi was conceived after his father seduced a woman during his legation to Ancona; the pope is also said to have seduced a niece and committed incest with his daughter Costanza. The most gruesome accusations are made against Pier Luigi, who is alleged to have committed sexual assault on Cosimo Gheri, Bishop of Fano, and to have poisoned his victim afterward. The last legend may be traced to a piece of Cromwellian propaganda written by Sir Richard Morison: *An Exhortation to Styrre all Englyshe Men to the Defence of theyr Countreye* (1539). Morison, in turn, picked up Roman rumors about Pier Luigi's "ungovernable passion" that had gone into lost Latin books that were sold in Protestant Nuremberg in 1538.[23]

Even for an age that would come to associate Italy with sensational tales of intrigue and depravity, Baldwin's translation depicts an extraordinarily sinister pattern of papal corruption. Its lurid vision of poisoning, licentiousness, betrayal, and nepotism soon became the average Elizabethan's image of Italy. The account of Paul III in Bale's *Acta Romanorum* comes from *Wonderfull Newes* or directly from *Epistola*; Bale embroiders Flacius's fiction with details from Thomas's *Historie*.[24] In *The Scholemaster*, As-

---

[23] On the Morison text, see George B. Parks, "The Pier Luigi Farnese Scandal: An English Report," *Renaissance News*, 15 (1962), 193-200.

[24] *Acta*, I3^r-8^r. Where Thomas describes Paul III as an astronomer, Bale makes him an astrologer and conjurer. Bale increases the number of Ro-

cham records his horror of Italy in the course of warning young Englishmen against the corrupting influence of Italianate books and manners. In reporting that the pope assigns "both meede and merite to the maintenance of stewes and brothelhouses at home in Rome" (K1ᵛ), Ascham follows his contemporaries in singling out sexual license as the most obvious sign of spiritual decay.

The Italianate settings of Jacobean plays inherit a polemical Protestant edge. Thus Shakespeare and his successors recreate the Reformation image of Italy in such plays as *Othello*, *Volpone*, and *The Duchess of Malfi*, which convey a steamy atmosphere of sexual corruption, jealousy, and revenge. In the revenge tragedies of Webster, Tourneur, and other dramatists, poisoning by means of such ingenious vehicles as leaves of a book, the painted lips of a picture, the pommel of a saddle, an anointed helmet, and even the covers of a Bible furnishes a staple device for intrigues set in Italy. The hypocritical pope or cardinal becomes a stock villain, as, for example, in Marlowe's set-piece scene where Mephistophilis leads Faustus into the Vatican through his own private entrance.

As a pasquinade, the Italianate form of *Wonderfull Newes* provides a precise analogue to the English *topos* of the papal fall. The work imitates the satirical form of a letter sent by Pasquillo to Marforio reporting on the papal descent into hell. The extended monologues or dialogues in pasquinades originated in the Roman custom of fixing scurrilous verses attacking the powerful on the ancient statue of Pasquillo (or Pasquino), which was set up in the Piazza Navona in 1501. Discovery of a second statue in the Campus Martius ("a foro Martius") gave rise to the name Marforio for Pasquillo's interlocutor or correspondent.

---

man prostitutes to 45,000 and has them pay monthly tribute to the pope. Also see *Catalogus*, I, 639, 663-64.

These quasi-journalistic pieces had become identified with antipapal attacks by the time Aretino lampooned the conclave that sat after the death of Leo X in 1521. Thomas Elyot introduced Pasquillo into England in *Pasquil the Playne* (1532); however, he Anglicized the sardonic Italian narrator by assimilating him into the native tradition of the plain-speaking satirist.

During the Reformation, Protestants adopted the indigenous Roman formula for the pasquinade. *Pasquillus ecstaticus* (written c. 1539) by Coelius Secundus Curio appeared, for example, in *Pasquillorum Tomi duo*.[25] Seymour recognized the pasquinade as an antipapal form of satire when he cited to Gardiner the pope's inability to suppress "Pasquill's rhymes and verses" as a precedent for the circulation of unauthorized works in England. *Pasquillus ecstaticus* eventually reached the English reading public through *Pasquine in a Traunce* (c. 1566), translated by W. P[histon?]. Pasquillo reappeared in the 1580s in the Martin Marprelate pamphlets, and Nicholas Breton's *Pasquil's Mad-cap* (1600) completed the transformation of Elyot's Plain Pasquil into the sarcastic narrator of Elizabethan malcontent satire.[26]

In *Pasquillus ecstaticus* Curio conflates the Dantesque device of sequential visions of hell, purgatory, and heaven with anti-Farnese propaganda. During his "ecstasy," Pasquillus has an apocalyptic vision that contrasts the true Christian heaven with the false papal heaven that fell when Luther and Zwingli undermined it. The imagery of the beast, scarlet whore, blood of the saints, and golden cup comes directly from Revelation (B2ᵛ; cited from W. P.'s

---

[25] Basel?, 1544; II, K8ʳ-R3ʳ. The false imprint "Eleutheropolis" ("Jerusalem") is a satirical analogue of the "Marburg," "Winchester," "Rome," and "Piacenza" imprints used in other Reformation texts.

[26] See Alvin Kernan, *The Cankered Muse: Satire of the English Renaissance* (New Haven, 1959), pp. 51-53.

translation). Pasquillus's hell vision adopts the conventional self-fulfillment formula of medieval and Renaissance prophecy. Arriving at the entrance to hell, for example, he finds the papal arms over the gate as well as a place prepared to put up the coat of arms of Paul III when he arrives to join his line of predecessors: the infamous Pope Joan, Boniface VIII, Gregory VII, Alexander VI, Julius II, and Leo X (compare *Inferno*, XIX. 52-57). Curio reflects contemporary vilification of the Farneses by reserving the place of special honor for the pope and his son: "And yet was there one much fayrer, that was preparing for *Peter Lewes*, some [*sic*] to Pope *Paule* the third, and one for his father also" (2C1ʳ). The second part of the satire styles Pasquillus as a conciliar delegate: "Questions . . . to be disputed in the Councell nowe holden at Trent" (2D2ʳ-2E4ᵛ). Pasquillus learns that loyal Catholics hate the renegade pope because he became "a Rebell to this [papal] heaven" and proves Rome to be the seat of Antichrist (G3ʳ, 2B3ʳ).

Ochino imitated Curio's pasquinade to the extent of setting the papal dialogues of his *Tragoedie* in hell. The anonymous hell vision in *The Wyll of the Devyll* (c. 1548) inverts this formula by having the devil draw up a final testament bequeathing his belongings to sinners and clerics prior to burial beneath the high altar at St. Peter's basilica, the traditional resting place of St. Peter. Later English examples of this satirical sub-genre of the Protestant hell vision, with its conventional attack on the consistory of cardinals, may be found in Donne's *Ignatius His Conclave* (1611) and Milton's description of the "close recess and secret conclave" of the devils in Pandaemonium (*PL*, I. 795; II.1-505).[27]

[27] R. W. Smith suggests that St. Peter's basilica is the architectural

In *Wonderfull Newes*, Pasquillo speaks in English for the first time *in propria persona*. Baldwin parts from his source in acknowledging its fictionality, for his preface states openly that the name Publius Aesquillus is a pseudonym for "some wittie man" who "fayneth a poesie in manner of a vision." For Baldwin, the work functions as allegory that veils the truth "under the shadow of dreames and visions." W. P., by contrast, insists that *Pasquine in a Traunce* is not fable but real truth (A4^r). The element of obscenity and slander that characterizes the pasquinade might seem incompatible with the satirist's claim to attack vice, except that the Protestants accepted violent hyperbole as a permissible corrective device. Personal vilification and obscenity would become conventions of satire by the time of Ben Jonson and John Marston.[28]

Baldwin's preface defends the validity of fiction. Although the author may record details that are not matters of historical fact, Baldwin contends that "he fayneth properly, but lyeth not" (A1^v-2^r). The text therefore serves as an amplified parable that supports Baldwin's definition of the proverb as a satirical form that teaches "grave and wayghtye matters" by means of an apparently unreasonable fable: "lyke a playster both corrosyve and incarnative, tauntynge vyces, and shewyng the remedyes: beyng therwithall so briefe, that without trouble they maye bee contayned" (*Treatise*, A6^r, M7^v). The work's proverbial wisdom enables Baldwin to justify it on traditional didactic grounds as a work necessary for "al christen men, especially princes" to comprehend the truth about papal usurpation of temporal power (A2^v). The reader should ap-

---

model for Pandaemonium in "The Source of Milton's Pandemonium," *MP*, 29 (1931), 187-98.

[28] Peter, *Complaint and Satire*, pp. 118-20.

proach such "Christian" fiction in a devotional manner appropriate to prayer:

> . . . to thentent that all Englishe men myghte thanke God the more for his aboundant mercy, in delivering them through knowledge of his truth from the tiranny of so corrupt and stinking an heade, and the better love and obeye our soveraygne lord and kyng, theyr head by God appoynted. . . . (A2^v)

The satire is a very free biblical adaptation. Baldwin's description of the work as an expansion of Revelation therefore implies the compatibility of fiction and divine truth. His added epigraph from Revelation 18:4, which summons the elect Christian to flee the City of Destruction, equates papal Rome with fallen Babylon. The title *Wonderfull Newes* relates the work to the "good news" of the gospel. Any "epistle" sent out of Rome would necessarily remind the Reformation reader of the apostolic letters that St. Paul sent out of imperial Rome under great duress to congregations of the faithful. Such contemporary editions as the 1550 Great Bible published by Whitchurch stress the epistolary nature of Pauline texts through such colophons as "The Epistle unto the Galathians was sent frome Rome," "Sent from Rome unto the Ephesians by Tichicus," and "The second Epistle unto Timothe, was written from Rome, when Paul was presented the second tyme unto the Emperour Nero." Bale and others wittily exploited the same formula through their satirical "Rome" colophons.

The topicality of the preface and epigraph, as well as Baldwin's tendency toward more colloquial language, make the text read more like a British broadside than the letter of an "Italian humanist." He follows his original very closely; thus the few variations result from substitution of

racy diction that exaggerates the scurrility of the more re-
strained, humanistic Latin of the original. Where *Epistola*
speaks of "fabulas," Baldwin uses the idiom "tales of
Robin hode." In place of Flacius's more elegant periphrase
"pusio" (lit. "little boy"), Baldwin introduces "pintell," a
more vulgar archaism for "penis." "Nates" is a more dec-
orous word than "arses." The shift from "lenonum & parri-
cidarium" (lit. "pimps and parricides") to "Baudes and
manquessers [whores]" emphasizes the sexual transgres-
sions of the Farnese family.[29]

By defining the work as a "tragedie," Baldwin places the
fall of Paul III within the tradition of *de casibus* tragedy.
The fictional report of Paul III's arrival in hell and the
pageant of abominations celebrating the occupation of his
final resting place function as a sequel to the prophetic
dream that Pasquillus recorded in *Pasquillus ecstaticus* a
decade earlier. The same Genius who had carried Pasquillus to heaven in Curio's pasquinade leads Publius Aesquillus to the underworld. Flacius's collapsing together of
Renaissance notions of Genius as both the beneficial guardian spirit of the individual soul and the universal god of
generation inverts his major theme of the "sterility" of the
Roman church. Spenser similarly combines the two concepts in the "Old *Genius*" of *The Faerie Queene* (III.vi.31).[30]
The Protestant Genius embodies spiritual "procreativity."
The pillars of hard red salt that jut up from the great field
of Plutonium, and Aesquillus's recollection of Lot's wife
when Genius warns him against turning back during their
eventual departure, conflate papal Rome with biblical Sodom
and its associated crimes against the Lord (B4[r], C2[r]; see
Genesis 19:26).

[29] *Epistola*, a6[r], a5[r-v], a7[v]; *Wonderfull Newes*, B1[r], A7[v], A8[r], B3[r].

[30] See C. S. Lewis's note "Genius and Genius" in *Allegory of Love*, pp.
361-63.

The centerpiece scene enacts the homage that Pier Luigi ("Peter Aloysius") pays to his father. The Bacchic animal imagery attached to the son and his retinue reflects the Renaissance assumption that homosexuality is a sin that denies the higher faculties of reason and will that distinguish man from beast:

> And he beyng wrapped in a Goates skinne, ryd upon a Goate, that was so byg, that he semed to be greater then a bul. At his brest in stede of a golden Bull, hong a great Priapus. And this Priapus . . . whiche I greatly wondred at, had a naked Pintell hanging in the middle parte of his body. About Peter Aloysius were Catamites innumberable, havyng all the partes of theyr body finely clothed, save only theyr arses, which beyng naked lyke Apes, they shewed forthe. The rest that were with hym, rode upon the very great she goates. And in theyr banners (whether it were to fraye byrdes or no I know not) they had images of Priapus. (A7ᵛ-8ʳ)

Paul III had received the epithet "Goatishe olde manne" ("senex hircosus") for the seduction of his niece. The tableau on the first triumphal arch leading into the City of Pluto celebrates the central allegation of anti-Farnese propaganda in obscene detail: "In the upper parte of this Arche, Peter Aloysius wroughte by force unnaturallye with the Byshoppe Fanensis, whereof that good yong man dyed. And there his father Paule smylyng, dyd absolve hym" (B3ᵛ; *Epistola*, a7ʳ).

Only an English reformer could compound Flacius's grotesque phallic conceit with a pun on "bull." The Latin "taurus," of course, is not related to "bulla," a term denoting a round lead seal, attached to charters, that refers by extension to papal edicts (*Epistola*, a5ʳ). Contemporary iconography linked goats and monkeys to both uncontrollable lechery and cuckoldry. Thus Othello spits out the epithet "goats and monkeys" at Desdemona after Iago has poisoned his mind (IV.i.263). Malbecco ("wicked he-goat") rushes "like a Gote emongst the Gotes" when he discovers his wife Hellenore ("Helen-whore") among the proverbially lustful and goatlike satyrs prior to his final metamorphosis into Gealosie (*FQ*, III.x.44-47).

The embroidered animal imagery of scorpions, frogs, and vipers that adorns the gray costume of Paul III, the man-size locusts with human faces that gallop into battle like horses, and the battle between the sheep and wolves come directly out of Revelation 9:3-10 and 16:13. Except for retention of the miter, Paul's drab dress inverts the ornateness of papal regalia. The seven-headed beast ridden by the Whore of Babylon was recognized universally during the Reformation as a Protestant image for the Church of Rome (Figure 4). The most deliberately offensive imagery appears in the phantasmagorical conclusion that merges Paul III with the Scarlet Whore:

> Into the which cup, she shead fyrst the filth of her menstrue, and after her all the devils put in theyr engendryng seede. Than came the kinges of the yearth crepyng unto her, to whome after they had kyssed her blessed feete, she fetched her lovesome [lovely] cup. Of whiche they drunke, and whan they had doen, all the kynges medled with her, with abhominable advoutry. But whan this act was finished, came Pluto his ministers, and whan they had caughte that whore Babilon, that is, the chiefe Byshop, (an horrible thing to be heard) they drewe her into the butcherye and there played the butchers with her, and than brought her to the table, and sette her before the kinges to be eaten. Which fed straight upon the fleshe of the Romyshe whore, and in a while after

provoked to vomite, they spewed up theyr Gobbettes of fleshe, smellyng of that moste filthy wine. Of whiche Gobbets (a wonderfull matter) put together, I sawe the Byshop newe made agayne. (C1ᵛ)

This passage personifies the intense hatred that Protestants felt toward the Roman mass and doctrine of transubstantiation, which interpreted the eucharist as a continuing sacrifice of Christ's body. Nevertheless, it represents little more than a literalistic application of St. John of Patmos's description of the great whore, who held "in her hand a golden cup full of abominations and the impurities of her fornication. . . . all nations have drunk the wine of her impure passion and the kings of the earth have committed fornication with her" (see Revelation 17:1-18:3).

Alimentary imagery became a convention of Protestant polemical tradition. The cartographical allegory of J. B. Trento's *Mappemonde Nouvelle Papistique* (Geneva, 1566) depicts priests as "Bouchers du Pape" and the eucharist as "Boucherie" ("Butcher shop"). Communicants at the banquet table drink blood from a goblet and eat "chair" ("meat"). On the back of her many-headed beast, Duessa goes into battle at Orgoglio's castle with the golden cup that "still she bore, replete with magick artes" (*FQ*, I.viii.6, 12-15). Milton adds a scatological nuance to such satire in suggesting that Adam and Eve enjoyed true communion with the gods prior to the Fall:

> So down they sat,
> And to their viands fell, nor seemingly
> The angel, nor in mist, the common gloss
> Of theologians, but with keen despatch
> Of real hunger, and concoctive heat
> To transubstantiate. . . .
>
> (*PL*, V.433-38)

The binding of the whore and her entire retinue in the bottomless pit (C2^r; see Revelation 20:1-3) brings the vision to a rapid conclusion as Genius guides Publius Aesquillus up "a certayne narrow pathe" (Matthew 7:13-14). Like a latter-day Dante led upward by Virgil, Publius Aesquillus ascends out of this Reformation Inferno. The "comedic" ending illustrates the mysterious pattern that the reformers found in God's providential design (above, Chapter 6 at n. 13).

ENGLAND TRANSFORMED

A Marvelous Hystory Intitulede, Beware the Cat (written 1553; printed 1570) intermingles, as devices of satire, the imagery of butchering and eating men with elements of the medieval beast fable. Baldwin's preface to *Wonderfull Newes*, which attacks Roman Catholicism as a "cannibalistic" faith, had already contrasted works offered "under the persons of specheles beastes" with "fayned histories" and dream visions as one of three kinds of fiction (A1^v). *Beware the Cat* as a whole is not cast into fabular form; instead it contains many smaller beast tales within its overall structure as the earliest freely invented English work of long narrative fiction that may be characterized as a novel.[31] Prior to Elizabeth's reign, romances and a few Tudor jest books were the only other examples of native prose fiction. *Beware the Cat* contains the outrageous mixture of genres that distinguishes satire. Under the guise of parody, it combines the conventional devices and forms of proverb, history, tale, oration, dream vision, beast fable, skeltonics, medical exposition, and hymn.

[31] William A. Ringler, Jr., *"Beware the Cat* and the Beginnings of English Fiction," *Novel*, 12 (1979), 113-26. Quotations follow the typescript of Ringler's forthcoming annotated edition.

Baldwin constructs a hypothetical world of cats as a foil to Reformation England of his own time. Sharp juxtapositions of the frankly fictional with the fictionally real worlds shock the audience into criticism of both; these jolts should lead the reader into critical awareness of the modes of description and narration operative in fiction. Literally and metaphorically, the book is a macaronic composition that moves not only between English and Latin, but also between the speech of beasts and that of men. The central character, Gregory Streamer, is reputed to know Arabic, Chaldean, and Greek. No one could read Egyptian hieroglyphics in the sixteenth century, but Streamer is said to have that ability. In debating the ancient question of whether speech and reason are the special preserve of mankind, *Beware the Cat* calls into question the nature and rationality of man. Baldwin relies on the deceptively simple parodic pattern of turning the world upside down, the best contemporary examples of which are *Moriae Encomium*, *Gargantua and Pantagruel*, *Utopia*, Skelton's satires, and Shepherd's dramatic monologues. In bewildering succession, Baldwin compares radically different times, places, and levels of the chain of being (the society of cats as opposed to that of man).

Baldwin's title comes from the made-up proverb that he inserts into both his dedication ("learn to Beware the Cat") and moralized conclusion. The special meaning that he attaches to the phrase treats the cat as a figure for Protestant conscience, in the form of house pets who see all that goes on behind their owners' doors, or the devil's cat, whose all-encompassing vision may earn one damnation. The providential and diabolical associations of cats are preserved in such proverbs as "a cat hath nine lives" and "a witch may take on her a cat's body nine times" (p. 13). Baldwin equates proverbs and fables as vehicles for "allud-

yng & bryngyng unreasonable thinges, to teach & instruct men, in grave and wayghtye matters" (*Treatise*, A6ʳ).
In the manner of a proverb, *Beware the Cat* instructs by
means of "corrosive" satirical fiction (*Treatise*, M7ᵛ).
Proverbs and adages differ from precepts in their use of
paradox as a means of instruction.

Baldwin is the first writer of fiction in English to construct an elaborate mock apparatus for his book as a comical or satirical device. In addition to his naive *persona* as
a character within the narrative, he plays the roles of "publisher," "editor," and "commentator" in the satire. He may
have had in mind More's burlesque of the humanistic devices of prefatory epistles, dedicatory poems, maps, alphabets, and dedications in *Utopia*. The seriocomic marginal
glosses that he adds by way of commentary undercut
Streamer's narrative in a manner similar to the obtuse annotations that Pope added to *The Dunciad*. If Spenser himself supplied any of E. K.'s notes on *The Shepheardes Calender* as an ironic commentary on the eclogues that he
presents with great seriousness, they furnish another Tudor
example of this kind of learned hoax. Despite *persona* Baldwin's approval of Streamer's narrative, Baldwin the "editor" uses marginalia to rebut the speaker's absurd assertions. Latin notes often contradict English narrative.

Baldwin imitates Chaucer's pose of timid innocence in
creating his *persona* as a "reporter" who merely retells one
of the pleasant "stories" told by a Master Streamer the
previous Christmas; Publius Aesquillus had similarly served
as a "reporter" of current events in Rome. Streamer's reference to *The House of Fame* shows that Chaucer is on the
author's mind. Grounding the text in the reality of Reformation England, the dedication asserts the representa-
tional accuracy of the fiction:

. . . I so nearly used both the order and words of him
that spake them . . . that I doubt not but that he [Fer-
rers] and Master Willot shall in the reading think they
hear Master Streamer speak, and he himself in the like
action shall doubt whether he speaketh or readeth.

The only role that Baldwin acknowledges in constructing
the work is the "editorial" task of dividing Streamer's "oration" into "book-like" parts introduced by an "argument"
and concluded with a moralized "instruction" or "exhortation." Baldwin's inside knowledge of Reformation book
publication thus becomes a constituent element of the satire. He advances the joke by announcing the imminent
"printing" of the satire as a companion to Streamer's forthcoming translation from Arabic of the *Cure of the Great
Plague* (a nonexistent book). His request that John Young,
the courtier to whom he dedicates the edition, convey his
manuscript copy-text to Streamer for last-minute correction advertises his concern for scrupulous textual accuracy:
"I beseech you . . . that he peruse it before the printing
and amend it if at any point I have mistaken him." The
obtuse attack on Baldwin for slandering Streamer (an author of "many witti things . . . for his countrys sake") in
A Short Answere to Beware the Cat (1570) attests to the
success of the fabrication.

Baldwin's strategy resembles that of the *Decameron* and
Canterbury Tales by setting smaller stories within an en-
compassing narrative framework. He carries the reader
one step back from the witty devices of publication by
describing the circumstances under which Streamer "or-
ated" his tales the previous Christmas. In so doing, Baldwin's "Argument" introduces the tale-within-the-tale format that governs the entire work. The outer episode is set
within the realistic historical context of the 1552-53
Christmas revels at court:

It chanced that at Christmas last I was at Court with Master Ferrers, then master of the King's Majesty's pastimes, about setting forth of certain interludes, which for the King's recreation we had devised and were in learning. (p. 3)

In addition to Baldwin and Ferrers, the auditors sleeping at Ferrers's lodgings include the apparently fictional characters Streamer and Willot, who are described respectively as Ferrers's astronomer and divine. The Revels Accounts list a "divine" and an "astronomer" in Ferrers's retinue as Lord of Misrule. The nightly conversations of these revels collaborators touch upon "sundry things for the furtherance of such offices wherein each man as then served." Baldwin's "verisimilitude" extends to his recollection of the night of 28 December as the exact time when he and Streamer debated the question of whether birds and beasts possess reason. The occasion for their argument was the report that Baldwin had heard that the King's Players were rehearsing "a play of Aesop's Crow" in which most of the characters played the parts of birds. Although he approves of the beast fable as an author, *persona* Baldwin protests its appropriation to the stage because of the lack of suitable "comical" [dramatic] precedent:

. . . the device whereof I discommended, saying it was not comical to make either speechless things to speak or brutish things to common [commune] reasonably; and although in a tale it were sufferable to imagine and tell of something by them spoken or reasonably done (which kind Aesop laudably used), yet it was uncomely, said I, and without example of any author, to bring them in lively personages to speak, do, reason, and allege authorities out of authors. Master Streamer, my lord's Divine, being more divine in this point than I was ware of, held the contrary part, affirming that beasts and fowls had reason, and that as much as men, yea, and in some points more. (p. 3)

Despite its apparent simple-mindedness, Baldwin's argument from authority announces the work's central concern with Reformation epistemology. The discussion turns on the question of logical proof, and it should come as no surprise to find the editor of the *Treatise* arguing that proof consists of the "authority of the most grave and learned philosophers." Describing such proof as "hearsay," Streamer argues from personal experience: "what I myself have proved." In contrast to Ferrers's laughter, *persona* Baldwin's naive response to Streamer's assertion that he himself has heard animals "both speak and reason as well as I hear and understand you" is to take it under serious consideration on the authority of *The Booke of Secretes of Albertus Magnus, the Vertues of Herbes, Stones and Certayne Beastes* (1549). Baldwin the author ridicules Streamer by citing this collection of fantastic marvels, which Tudor readers laughed at as entertaining fiction, as the source for the comic formula of the potion that enabled him to hear animals speak.

The pun on Streamer's "divine" understanding as Ferrers's "Divine" labels his narrative as a burlesque of scholastic "proof" based on nonscriptural traditions. In his plain simplicity, however, *persona* Baldwin "thought there might be somewhat more than I did know" and questions Streamer by means of the traditional categories of what, where, and when. Streamer insists on haranguing his listeners in the manner of Raphael Hythlodaeus, another recently returned traveler from a remote land that also turns out to be "no place." In agreeing to listen in silence to Streamer's "story of one piece of mine own experimenting [experiencing]," Baldwin gives up active participation as an interlocutor.

[392]

Streamer's involuted tale thus functions as an elaborate "proof" in a vestigial debate with Baldwin.

The question under discussion is a traditional one that the *Treatise* analyzes without irony. In that work, Baldwin defines reason as the intrinsic distinction between men and beasts:

> . . . knowlege of preceptes of al honest maners, which reson acknowledgeth to belong and appertayne to mannes nature (as the thyng in which we diffre from other beastes) and also is necessary for the comly governance of mannes lyfe. . . . (A3ᵛ)

Such "preceptes and counsayles" are the foundation of man's distinctively ethical consciousness "in whiche whoso is ignorante, is worse than a brute beast" (I1ʳ). According to Baldwin, Pythagoras was superior to other philosophers because he affirmed the immortality of the soul, which is linked in essence to reason: "Whan a resonable soule forsaketh hys divyne nature, and becommeth beaste lyke, it dyeth: For although the substaunce of the soule be incorruptible, yet lackyng the use of reason, it is reputed dead: for it loseth the intellectyve lyfe" (I5ᵛ). Streamer's argument, on the other hand, leaves him open to the same accusation that Sidney leveled against those who say that fables lie:

> Which as a wicked man durst scarce say, so think I none so simple would say the *Esope* lyed in the tales of his beasts: for who thinks that *Esope* writ it for actually true were well worthy to have his name cronicled among the beastes hee writeth of.[32]

[32] *Essays*, ed. Smith, I, 185.

The underlying question of *Beware the Cat* is what kind of creature man, as a species, really is. The initial assumption that man is rational gives way to the question of whether man may be defined in essence as rational. A gloss points to the truth that although reason differentiates between men and beasts, rationality does not inhere in all men: "There be churls among cats as well as among christian folke" (p. 45). This problem alludes to the well-known definition found in Latin logic texts: "Homo est animal rationale" ("Man is a rational animal"). The assumption of Baldwin and Sidney that man must make a conscious effort to fulfill his potential for rationality parallels Swift's revision of the ancient axiom in his letter to Pope: "Homo est animal capax rationis" ("Man is an animal capable of reason").[33] Streamer's absurdity makes him a negative example of the human capacity for rationality and moral regeneration. Like Paul III and Pier Luigi in their goatishness, Streamer willingly denies his rationality.

Streamer's "oration," as Baldwin "reports" it, represents a further step back from the outer framework. The enveloping of many different tales within Streamer's narrative constructs an onionlike structure of many different stories that furnish varied refractions of the beast fable. This inner narrative, which includes Streamer's account of personal experiences with rational animals, mirrors the division of *Utopia* into a series of secondhand examples. It even resembles the travelogue of Raphael Hythlodaeus in carrying the reader back in time to isolated Staffordshire as well as to even more remote and distant Ireland, before the metaphoric journey into the world of cats. Streamer

---

[33] R. S. Crane cites examples from traditional logic texts in "The Houyhnhnms, the Yahoos, and the History of Ideas," *The Idea of the Humanities and Other Essays Critical and Historical* (Chicago, 1967; 2 vols.), II, 274-77.

met the four companions who told him tales about the cats at the Aldersgate residence of John Day. He then occupied "a chamber hard by the Printing House" in order to correct his "Greek alphabets" that were then in press; Day printed no such edition under Edward VI. Baldwin may ascribe this third fabricated authority to Streamer in imitation of the Utopian alphabet that Hythlodaeus brought back from his travels.

Even Streamer's narrative has an outer framework into which he fits his inner tales. The meeting at Day's lodging reflects the grouping of collaborators in the Christmas revels to whom Streamer recounts the Aldersgate gathering. The other speakers include a Staffordshire man, another named Thomas who had been to Ireland, a skeptic who questions Thomas's tale, and a scholar. Baldwin's gloss states of the latter: "Some think this was Master Sherry." In 1550 Day printed *A Treatise of Schemes & Tropes* and one other book by Richard Sherry, one-time headmaster of Magdalen College School. Their discussion of whether cats have speech and reason was occasioned by the sleepless night that Streamer spent because of the noisy cats gathering among the quarters of executed men that were displayed on poles outside the window of his Aldersgate chamber:

> And I marvel where men have learned it or for what cause they do it, except it be to feed and please the devils. For sure I believe that some spirits, Misanthropi or Molochitus [Moloch], who lived by the savour of man's blood, did, after their sacrifices failed (in which men were slain and offered unto them), put into butcherly heathen tyrants' heads to mangle and boil Christian transgressors and to set up their quarters for them to feed upon. And therefore I would counsel all men to bury or burn all executed bodies, and refrain from mak-

> ing such abhominable sacrifices as I have often seen—
> with ravens or rather devils feeding upon them, in this
> foresaid leads [roof]—in the which every night many
> cats assembled, and made such a noise that I could not
> sleep for them. (p. 6)

Tudor custom dictated that the remains of quartered traitors be displayed at the gates of the city as a warning to
malefactors, with the heads on stakes at the London Bridge
entrance.

The obvious and grisly application of the proverb "Beware the Cat" escapes both Streamer and *persona* Baldwin.
Cats as well as devils can scavenge outside the chamber
window. Baldwin's gloss ("Evil spirits live by the savor of
man's blood") and his repeated references throughout the
narrative to cats eating men mock transubstantiation and
the Roman mass in a manner analogous to the allegorical
butchery at the end of *Wonderfull Newes*. The roasting and
eating of a cat by Thomas and his friends, as well as
Streamer's recipe for the lozenge that enables him to understand cat speech, invert Protestant alimentary satire in
a blasphemous parody of the eucharist:

> And then I took a piece of the cat's liver and a piece of
> the kidney, a piece of the milt and the whole heart, the
> fox's heart and the lights [lungs], the hare's brain, the
> kite's maw, and the urchin's kidneys. All these I beat in
> a mortar together until it were small, and then made a
> cake of it, and baked it upon a hot stone till it was dry
> like bread. And while this was a-baking . . . took I the
> galls of all these beasts, and the kite's toe, and served
> them likewise, keeping the liquor that dropped from
> them. At twelve of the clock, what time the sun began
> his planetical dominion, I went to dinner. But meat I
> ate none, save the boiled urchin; my bread was the cake

mentioned before; my drink was the distillation of the urchin's broth, which was exceeding strong and pleasant both in taste and savor. (pp. 25-26)

Ringler argues that the "fundamental fictional construct of *Beware the Cat* . . . [is] that belief in the physical efficacy of the mass is as absurd as belief in animals having the power of speech" (note to pp. 15-17). Baldwin supports such an interpretation by annotating Streamer's recipe with an ironic gloss that he attributes to Hermes Trismegistus: "Omne totum totaliter malum" ("All everything is entirely evil").

The impenetrable regress of narrators and narratives in Streamer's account provides a metaphor for the Catholic oral traditions that came under attack during the Reformation. The inner debate at Day's lodgings takes on a reflexive quality because at that time Streamer argued Baldwin's position and denied cat rationality: "And some affirming, as I do now (but I was against it then), that they [cats] had understanding. . . ." Baldwin the editor adds a double-edged gloss: "A wise man may in some things change his opinion" (p. 7). Both of the tales that Streamer listened to as proofs that cats can speak carry the reader back to the earliest layer of the narrative, which can be dated c. 1510. Baldwin's scrupulous concern for chronology is another device for creating satirical verisimilitude.

Set in Staffordshire and Ireland, these parallel tales derive from oral traditions going back to talking cats. An account derived from a long-dead Staffordshire man commemorates a cat that told him, " 'Commend me unto Titton Tatton and to Puss thy Catton, and tell her that Grimalkin is dead.' " At this point in the narrative, the reader receives the tale through six layers of narration. On overhearing the man recount this marvelous happening to his wife that night, their house cat said, " 'And is Grimalkin dead? Then farewell dame,' . . . and was never seen after" (p. 7). The Irish "churl's tale" told by Thomas confirms its English counterpart. The insatiability of the cat that devours a stolen cow quartered by the Irish churl gives a new refraction to Baldwin's burlesque of the mass. When the voracious beast threatens to move on to the man, the churl slays him with his dart. The Irish episode outdoes the cat gathering outside Streamer's Aldersgate window, to which it is linked by the imagery of butchery, when a vengeful pack of the slain cat's followers devour the churl's boy. On overhearing the churl retell the day's adventure at home that night, his wife's pet kitten strangles her master with her teeth in revenge for the death of Grimalkin, ruler of cat society.

The regress of narrators throughout *Beware the Cat* as a whole functions as a device of satire. Baldwin's written texts, which Streamer labels as "hearsay," are more tangible than the bewildering oral tradition that the divine offers by way of firsthand experience and "proof." The dubiousness of Streamer's sources validates Baldwin's textual authorities, be they pagan philosophy or scriptural texts. Even though Baldwin attacks religious abuses, the worldliness of his satire affirms rational discourse as a valid mode of inquiry. Such argument operates independently of the self-validating affirmations of the gospellers at the same time that it upholds them. To the knowing reader, the indirect defense of human rationality in *Beware the Cat* may be as effective and certainly more entertaining than the explicit argument of Baldwin's *Treatise*.

The Aldersgate auditors draw varied lessons from the tales. The skeptic remains unconvinced by the "proofs." An analogical argument drawn by Thomas to defend the special status of Grimalkin introduces the first overtly antipapal satire:

> . . . as the Pope hath had ere this over all Christendom, in whose cause all his clergy would not only scratch and bite, but kill and burn to powder (though they knew not why) whomsoever they thought to think but once against him—which Pope, all things considered, devoureth more at every meal than Grimalkin did at her last supper. (pp. 11-12)

Baldwin's gloss notes a significant application of his proverb "Beware the Cat": "The Pope's clergy are crueller than cats." At one point in the debate, the learned scholar attacks Streamer as either a witch (who may assume the shape of a cat) or a papist:

> . . . but where you spake of intrusion of a woman's body into a cat's, you either play Nichodem, or the stubborn Popish conjurer: whereof one would creep into his mother's belly again, the other would bring Christ out of Heaven to thrust him into a piece of bread. . . . (p. 14)

A marginal gloss clarifies this identification: "Transubstantiationers destroy Christ's manhood." The scholar closes the debate with an argument that stands very close to the position of Baldwin as translator of *Wonderfull Newes*:

> . . . like as we silly fools long time, for his sly and crafty juggling, reverenced the Pope, thinking him to have been but a man (though much holier than we ourselves were), whereas indeed he was a very incarnated devil, like as this Grimalkin was an incarnate witch. (p. 18)

As the gathering dissolves, Streamer stands identified as the embodiment of the man-made traditions of the medieval church by having accepted the two tales as "proof of natural knowledge."

After the bewildering array of narrators and tales in part one, the remainder of *Beware the Cat* follows a relatively straightforward course; Streamer's solitary Aldersgate chamber is the setting for the rest of the story. Because his new belief in cat rationality convinces him that the animals gather in organized assembly outside his window, part two is given over to preparation of the magical lozenge and Streamer's initial entry into the world of cats. The learned reader would laugh at Baldwin's invention of the meaningless gibberish that the cleric attributes to *The Booke of Secretes*, his only acknowledged written source (pp. 23-24, 27, and notes). The mock-heroic, astronomical details are all wrong, and he succeeds in hearing cats speak despite repeated violations of the recipe for his "prescienciall pills." The mixture of noises and voices, human and divine, that Streamer hears after taking his philter parodies *The House of Fame*. Streamer's moral confusion and the feigned naïveté of *persona* Baldwin merge in imitation of the point when obtuse Chaucer soars heavenward borne by the Eagle who chides: "Awak! / And be not agast so, for shame!" (ll. 556-57). Baldwin would have accepted Chaucer as a Protestant authority on the strength of William Thynne's edition. Although it is printed as prose, the din that Streamer hears in ecstasy imitates the word torrents, alliteration, and rhyme-spinning of skeltonics. Baldwin's gloss states simply: "Here the poetical fury came upon him" (p. 30).

The rising of the moon in part three marks the point of deepest human penetration into the world of cats. Even in pre-Copernican England, Streamer's geocentric inversions of Ptolemaic theories mock the astronomical description that he offers by way of "natural philosophy" as effectively as the absurd ramblings of the mad astronomer in chapter 42 of Samuel Johnson's *Rasselas*. He plans to set forth his revisionist theories "by reason and experience proved" in yet another "authoritative" text, his "book of heaven and hell" (pp. 33-34). When the cats begin to howl beneath the newly risen moon, Streamer's ecstasy enables him to deny rational humanity and assume the by now conventional role of feline eavesdropper.

The four tales that Streamer hears Mouse-slayer tell are grounded in the reality of Reformation England. The basic device is that house cats go everywhere and see their masters with their disguises stripped away, in actuality or in metaphor. In clinging to illegal religious beliefs and in their endemic adultery, Englishmen are less faithful to their laws than the pets that they keep. Feline jurisprudence, which rests upon the mandatory law of promiscuity, parodies that of English society in its codification of laws and precedents. The rational laws and norms of feline society give prominence to the contrasting failures and irrationality of Reformation England.

The comic fiction of Mouse-slayer's picaresque wanderings furnishes the narrative core of Baldwin's satire. The first tale recounts the life of Mouse-slayer and her mate Bird-hunt in the house of a recusant couple "in the time when preachers had leave to speak against the Mass, but it was not forbidden till half a year after" (i.e., December 1548). The episode parallels the stage *topos* of Youth and Age, for in the village of Stratford the aged cling to old beliefs despite protests by their children. After the old woman's sight fails on the verge of her conversion, it can return only through the agency of the forbidden mass. The restitution of her vision during the elevation of the host, at the priest's words "Wipe thine eyes thou sinful woman

[401]

and look upon thy Maker," constitutes a "miracle" of the kind familiar from medieval saints' lives. This dramatization of the supernatural power of the host mocks stories of the Corpus Christi and related saints' lives contained in *The Golden Legend* and similar collections. In addition to the satirical glosses, the credulous suggestion that the same remedy be used to cure the blindness of newborn kittens constitutes a *reductio ad absurdum* in an ostensibly straightforward narrative (pp. 35-38).

Mouse-slayer's second mistress was a bawd and receiver of stolen goods. The trading in false appearances of the second old woman embodies the work's central theme of transformation, which Baldwin equates metaphorically with transubstantiation; it also embodies the epistemological problem of the English Reformation as a whole. Once again it is the older generation that is more corrupt than the younger. Only her cat sees the forbidden image of the Virgin and the candles that the woman keeps hidden away in her coffer. Two glosses link the image to her profession. The first note ("A Catholic quean") suggests a pun on the sixteenth-century idiom for prostitute ("quean"), whereas the second states the accusation without irony: "Our Lady is hired to play the bawd." Another gloss mocks the rosary: "The image laughed to see the cat play with her dame's beads." When she pandered for a lustful young gentleman by procuring the chaste wife of a London merchant, the old woman even transformed the appearance of Mouse-slayer into a false image of pity. After feeding her pet mustard and pepper in order to make her weep, the old woman presented Mouse-slayer to the faithful wife as a moral "exemplum." According to the bawd's lying tale, her own daughter had lost her human form because her chaste spurning of a young suitor had caused him to pine away and die of lovesickness. The pitiful suffering of the cat-daughter parodies the efficacy of religious images by converting the young wife. Despite her mistress's success, Mouse-slayer takes revenge in a comic variation of the motif of cats eating men: "And I, to amend the matter, making as though I leaped at the mouse, all to-bescrat her thighes and her belly, so that I dare say she was not whole again in two months after."

Mouse-slayer's tale about the practical joke played against her when a man affixed walnut shells filled with soft pitch to her feet eventually redounds against an unregenerate priest, who furnishes another object for anticlerical satire. Fully believing that only the devil could make such a din in the garret, the priest attempts to exorcise the spirit by means of the forbidden instruments of holy water, holy candle, a chalice, and unconsecrated wafer. In her eagerness to witness yet another illegal mass "as many nights before in other places I had," Mouse-slayer knocks over the terrified priest who lands with scatological indelicacy amid a naked boy and another priest down whose breeches the holy candle has fallen.

The satirical themes of the stripping away of disguises and the idea of cats eating men merge in the final tale. In the conventional manner of the cuckold's tale, the unexpected return of the husband surprises his unfaithful wife with her lover, who has time only to grab his clothing and leap behind an arras. The excruciating revenge that Mouse-slayer metes out inverts the initial imagery of human execution and feline scavenging in a comic explosion:

> But I, minding another thing, and seeing that scratching could not move him, suddenly leaped up and caught him by the genitals with my teeth, and bote [bit] so hard that, when he had restrained more than I thought any man could, at last cried out, and caught me by the

neck thinking to strangle me. My master, not smelling but hearing such a rat as was not wont to be about such walls, came to the cloth and lift it up, and there found this bare-arst gentleman strangling me who had his stones in my mouth. And when I saw my master I let go my hold, and the gentleman his. (p. 49)

This mixture of wisdom and bawdry characterizes the satirical humor of Baldwin and other Reformation "wits." Like Bale and Flacius, he mixes sacred and profane in order to fashion a metaphor for religious error.

Only in his conclusion does Baldwin return to the kind of estates satire favored in *Piers Plowman* and Crowley's prophecies. Here he allows the harsh invective of the Juvenalian satirist to break through the whimsical tenor of the work. Streamer reports the moral drawn by the cats, who accept Mouse-slayer's tales as a cross-section of human society:

Wherof in the first two years . . . she had five masters: a priest, a baker, a lawyer, a broker, and a butcher; all whose privy deceits which she had seen she declared the first night. In the next two years she had seven masters: a bishop, a knight, a pothecary, a goldsmith, an usurer, an alchemist, and· a lord; whose cruelty, study, craft, cunning, niggishness, folly, waste, and oppression she declared the second night. . . . As for what was done and said yesternight, . . . which is nothing in comparison of any of the other two years before, I need not tell you for you were present and heard it yourself. (pp. 50-51)

Like Raphael Hythlodaeus and his descendant Lemuel Gulliver, Streamer obtains no insight into his own pride. Although the breaking of his fast entails the loss of his marvelous linguistic abilities and return to real life, like those other voyagers he condemns himself to an absurd quest to recover his golden world. The last words that he heard the cats utter announced reassembly on the feast day of St. Catherine ("the saint of cats"?) at "Catnes" (Caithness) in northern Scotland, a locale as wild as Ireland. Despite his every intention, Streamer has yet to reach his destination: "In the meanwhile, I will pray you to help to get me some money to convey me on my journey to Caithness, for I have been going thither these five years and never was able to perform my journey" (p. 52).

With the conventional ambiguity of the satirist, Baldwin retreats from the total pessimism of the feline judgment of human society in the final editorial intrusion of his "Exhortation." Although he preserves the obtuse naïveté that characterized the "reporter" at the beginning of this prolonged winter's tale, the seriocomic moral drawn from his proverb "Beware the Cat" does not belie the macabre setting for the events outside John Day's Aldersgate window:

> I would counsel all men to take heed of wickedness, and eschew secret sins and privy mischievous counsels, lest, to their shame, all the world at length do know thereof. But if any man, for doubt hereof, do put away his cat, then shall his so doing testify his secret naughty living, which he is more ashamed his cat should see than God and his angels, which see, mark, and behold all men's closest doings.

No less than the sober gospellers, he treats serious questions of faith and salvation (or damnation, as the case may be).

Only in conclusion does Baldwin make explicit the underlying importance of analogy in the tale. According to the Tudor doctrine of correspondences between the planes of nature and grace, man is like a beast but he may be like an angel. God did create man in his own image and gave him power to rule over and communicate with the beasts (Genesis 1:26-31). But Streamer, like Adam, exemplifies the folly of looking downward rather than upward on the scale of being. The all-seeing vision of the cat may serve as a figure for both the providence of God and the vigilance of the devil. The paean to universal harmony, in the halting heroic couplets of the concluding "Hymn," complements the scriptural truth of the gospelling ballads at the same time that it offers a mock eulogy to the scholar who fathomed the "course of things above and here below." At the Creation God did give "wit to whales, to apes, to owls" and "spirit to men in soul and body clean, / To mark and know what other creatures mean." He may yet grant "grace to Gregory, no Pope . . . / But silly priest, which like a streamer waves."

CHAPTER 9

Continuities: Foxe, Spenser, and Milton

MARTYRS AND MAGISTRATES

A distinctively Protestant literary tradition took root in
England under Edward VI. Although Edward's reign was
cut short, the literary practices of the reformers retained
their influence. Despite the perturbations of succeeding
generations, Protestant genres, themes, and conventions
enriched the writings of a diverse array of authors coming
out of the increasingly fragmented spectrum of reformist
orthodoxy and sectarianism. This diversity notwithstand-
ing, one may trace the development of a unified Protestant
literary tradition through the complexities of later centuries. Although his ideas were not original, John Bale first
articulated the apocalyptic vision of Reformation literature
in his tendentious plays and the seminal argument of *The
Image of Both Churches*. The prophetic tradition descending
from Bale and his contemporaries furnishes a common thread
running through the landmark texts of later years—*Actes
and Monuments*, *The Faerie Queene*, *Paradise Lost*, and *Paradise Regained*—as well as a host of less-known works written in England and America. It would take many volumes
the size of the present one fully to document the complexities of the Protestant tradition. This concluding chapter

aims to provide an overarching view of the literary legacy of the mid-Tudor Reformation.

By the end of Edward VI's reign, Reformation literature had assumed a tragic tenor that would not soon abate. Edward's last days were filled with foreboding—it seemed that the wheel of Fortune stood ready to move once more, leaving unresolved agelong problems of faith and wealth as it toppled the young king in the inevitable downward turn of the *de casibus* cycle. Although the settlement in religion rested upon the king's person, he himself escaped the increasingly critical scrutiny that the reforms received from different Protestant groupings. These factions still maintained a united political front in support of the ideal Christian ruler who provided the sole means of reform. Nevertheless, gospellers like Thomas Becon and Thomas Lever began to attack the Protestant aristocracy and clergy for perpetuating Catholic abuses. To the dispassionate observer, it must have seemed that the English Reformation had settled nothing. *Beware the Cat* concludes with a universal vision of a society that hypocritically tailors its behavior in outward conformity to the new custom. *Philargyrie of Greate Britayne* and *Pleasure and Payne* articulate Robert Crowley's attack on courtiers whose greed undermines the potential for commonwealth reform offered by the dissolution of the monasteries and chantries. After incessant warnings of divine retribution against a sinful people, moralists found no difficulty in perceiving the hand of a wrathful God when the "sweating sicknesse" swept London in 1551 and the king fell ill of consumption in 1553 (*Annales*, 3E2^r, 3E4^r).

The king blamed himself for moral decay in the land, unlike the gospellers, who attacked the communal sin of the English people. His acceptance of responsibility accords with the prevailing temper of a histrionic court that took seriously the themes of mutability and *de contemptu mundi*. Manuscript Harley 2194 shows Edward dramatizing his own consciousness according to the conventions of *de casibus* tragedy. Although the document agrees outwardly with the chronicles that interpret court revels as part of a Dudley plot against Seymour, it differs in describing a youth who blames himself privately for failing to save his uncle because it is "not agreeable to Ma[jes]tie openly to declare himself." Upon mention of his uncle, he is reported to have cried:

> Ah. how infortunate have I beene to those of my bloud, my mother I slew at my birth, and since have made away two of her brothers, and happily to make away for others against my selfe, was it ever knowne before that a Kings Unckle, A Lord Protectour one whose fortunes had much advanced th[e] Honour of the Realme, did lose his head for a felony; ffor a felony neither cleere in Law, and in fact weakely proved. Alas so how falsely have I beene abused? How weakely carried? How little was I master of myne owne Judgement? (fol. 20^{r-v})

Protestant piety fuses with Boccaccian tragedy in the death accounts of magistrates and martyrs that began to pour out at the end of Edward's reign. During the last stages of the king's illness, a final piece of royalist propaganda appeared on 19 June 1553 at the orders of John Russell, Earl of Bedford.[1] Another broadside purported to be a verbatim record of a prayer that the king said on 6 July, three hours before his death, "to hym self, his eyes beynge closed, and thynkyng none had heard him." This sensational dramatization of the king's death acknowledges its own fictionality, for Dr. Owen, who is cited as a witness, states, "We hearde you speake to your selfe, but what ye sayde, we knowe

---

[1] *A Prayer Sayd in the Kinges Chappel in the Tyme of Hys Graces Sicknes, for the Restauracion of His Helth.*

not." Shaped according to *ars moriendi* conventions, Edward's last words bring him into the company of Anne Askew and Edward Seymour as a Protestant saint and martyr. This idealized portrait conflicts with the king's Calvinistic perception of himself as a sinning reprobate, according to MS Harley 2194.

From the early paeans to a precociously learned boy until the saintly composure of his end, the public appearances of the king had been consistently stage-managed as Reformation propaganda. The broadside prayer shows him resigning himself to death, by adopting the prescribed stance of contempt for a sinful world. Utterance of the last words of Christ on the cross (Luke 23:46) idealizes the king as a Christlike redemptive agent, who suffers as a surrogate victim for his people's sin:

> Lorde God deliver me oute of this miserable & wretched lyfe, & take me among thy chosen: howebeit not my wyll, but thy wyll be done. Lorde I commit my spirit to thee. Oh lorde thou knowest howe happy it weare for me to be with thee: yet for thy chosens sake send me life and helth, that I may truely serve thee. Oh my Lorde God blesse thy people, and save thy enheritaunce. Oh Lorde God, save thy chosen people of Englande. Oh my Lorde God defende this Realme from papistrye, and mayntayne thy true religion, that I and my people may prayse thy holy name.

His last reported words were: "I am faynte, Lorde have mercy upon me, and take my sprite." Crowley states that the item was printed "at the same tyme" as the 10 July proclamation of Edward's death, which also declared the accession of Lady Jane Grey as queen (*Epitome*, 4E4r). Despite the ephemerality of the original broadside, its regular reprinting in chronicles by Bale, Foxe, Holinshed, and others shows that it was accepted as the authoritative account of the king's death.

William Baldwin's *Funeralles of King Edward the Sixt* is the only published record of Edward's death to diverge from the broadside prayer. Although it did not appear until 1560, it was "penned before his corse was buryed." The downfall of Queen Jane had blocked publication—according to the Elizabethan preface, Baldwin had "endevoured since by many meanes to have had . . . [the book] printed: but such was the time, that it could not be brought to passe" (A1ᵛ). As Baldwin's most homiletic composition, this funeral elegy links him to Crowley and the gospellers. The winter opening imitates the *Canterbury Tales*. The reversal of the conventional springtime opening of the *General Prologue* thus serves as a figure for the destruction of England's hopes:

> When bytter Wynter forced had the Sun
> Fro the horned Goat to Pisces ward to run,
> And lively sap, that greneth gardins soote,
> To flye the stocke to save her nurse, the roote. . . .
>
> (A2ʳ)

Such incipits function in Renaissance poetry as expressions of the transience and mortality of worldly existence.[2]

Baldwin's attack on the times presents avarice as the universal failure of all estates. His combination of personification allegory in the *Piers Plowman* tradition and dialogue between God and man reminiscent of Ochino's *Tragoedie* idealizes Edward as an innocent surrogate for his people's sin. Edward's tragedy suggests nascent possibilities for the tradition of the Fortunate Fall that Milton would develop

[2] Alan T. Bradford, "Mirrors of Mutability: Winter Landscapes in Tudor Poetry," *ELR*, 4 (1974), 3-39.

fully in *Paradise Lost*—the king must die in order to purge the kingdom and warn England to amend. Only royal martyrdom can preserve the covenant between God and his chosen people.

The accession of Mary Tudor heralded complete defeat for the Protestant reformers. Leaving John Hooper and John Rogers behind, Bale, Turner, and Coverdale went into a second exile. Crowley, Whitchurch, Becon, Foxe, Ponet, and approximately eight hundred other exiles joined them on the Continent during the early years of the reign; the Duchess of Suffolk was the highest ranking emigré.[3] Foreign theologians fled the country. Although Grafton printed the proclamation that declared her queen, Mary deprived him of the office of royal printer for having published an identical edict on behalf of Lady Jane Grey. After imprisonment in the Tower of London on 16 October 1554 for the printing of "noythy [naughty] bokes,"[4] John Day went underground in England or on the Continent. If two leaves of a printer's ledger that were recovered from the spine of an Elizabethan edition by Day are from his own account books, he was actively selling New Testaments, copies of Hall's chronicle, and other Protestant books prior to his imprisonment (MS Egerton 2974, fols. 67^r-68^v). William Cecil and Thomas Smith withdrew from court into the discreet silence of rural retirement. Led by John Rogers, those who could not conform began to go to the stake in February 1555. At least 274 Protestants were burned under Mary. Most of the condemned were artisans and their wives, but they also included the prime movers of

[3] For a valuable census that should be checked against its sources, see Christina H. Garrett, *The Marian Exiles: A Study in the Origins of Elizabethan Puritanism* (Cambridge, 1938).

[4] Henry Machyn, *Diary*, ed. J. G. Nichols (1848; Camden Soc., o.s. 42) p. 72.

the English Reformation who chose to remain in England as witnesses to their faith: Thomas Cranmer, Hugh Latimer, Nicholas Ridley, and John Hooper. Alone among prominent Edwardian writers and publishers, William Baldwin remained visibly active in London. He collaborated with John Wayland, Whitchurch's successor at the sign of the Sun, and wrote a lost moral interlude entitled *Love and Live, or The Way to Life* for production before the queen and at the Inns of the Court (c. 1556-57).[5]

Literary creativity dried up as the London book trade reverted to the noncontroversial publication that had characterized Henry VIII's reign. *The Saying of John Late Duke of Northumberlande Uppon the Scaffolde*, appearing immediately after Dudley's execution on 22 August 1553, was the government's only effective counterattack against the Protestants. Although he remained a traitor to both sides, Dudley's startling apostasy and denunciation of "these seditiouse preachers, and teachers of newe doctryne" (A3r-v) gave Mary her greatest propaganda coup. John Heywood and Miles Hogarde produced manuscripts written under Edward, and William Forrest complimented the queen through his conceit on the Blessed Virgin in *A Newe Ballade of the Marigolde* (c. 1553). Dream visions and personification allegories replaced gospelling paraphrases. *An Epitaph Upon the Deth of Kyng Edward* exploited the late king's residual popularity by treating him as a ballad *exemplum* for obedience and loyalty to his sister.

Few new writings appeared. In stark contrast to the abundant dramatic records for Edward's reign, *Respublica* stands alone as an analysis of the English Reformation. Two "new" books are both retrospective collections: William Rastell's edition of Thomas More's *Workes Wrytten in*

[5] Feuillerat, pp. 215-17.

the Englysh Tonge (1557) and Tottel's *Miscellany*. Popular literature included reprints of noncontroversial medieval classics; however, publishers avoided the Protestant favorites, Chaucer and Langland. John Cawood, the Queen's Printer, produced Dares Phrygius's *Storye of the Destruction of Troye* (1553; *STC* 6274.5). *Le Morte d'Arthur* reappeared, and John Bourchier's translation of *Arthur of Lytell Britayne* was published. Forgotten works came back into print. Berthelet reissued Caxton's 1483 version of Gower's *Confessio Amantis* (1554). The startling vogue for Hawes's *Pastime of Pleasure* (1554-55; 3 eds.) epitomizes the backward-looking taste of Mary's reign.

As Lord Chancellor, Stephen Gardiner suppressed the only original composition worthy of note written under Mary. John Wayland commissioned William Baldwin to prepare *A Memorial of Suche Princes, as Since the Tyme of King Richard the Seconde, Have Been Unfortunate in the Realme of England* (c. 1554) as a sequel to his edition of Boccaccio's *The Fall of Princes* (c. 1554). Most conjectures about the suppression rely on extrapolation from the nineteen tragedies that appeared in *The Mirror for Magistrates* (1559), as well as the delayed publication of George Ferrers's tragedies of Humphrey, Duke of Gloucester, and his wife Elianor Cobham in the 1578 edition of the *Mirror*. Circumstantial correspondence to the discord between the Seymour brothers, and their wives Catherine Parr and Anne Stanhope, leads E. I. Feasey and L. B. Campbell to interpret Duke Humphrey's lamentation as a thinly concealed account of Edward Seymour's fall. Unlike Feasey, who reads "Elianor Cobham" as an account of Anne Stanhope,[6] Campbell constructs an ingenious topical argument

---

[6] "The Licensing of the *Mirror for Magistrates*," *Library*, 4th ser., 3 (1923), 178-88, and "William Baldwin," *MLR*, 20 (1925), 413-14.

to prove that it refers to Princess Elizabeth and the magus John Dee.[7] They both read the *Mirror* as pro-Seymour propaganda.

Nevertheless the mirror pattern that Baldwin defines in his dedication is generalized rather than particular:

> For here as in a loking glas, you shall see (if any vice be in you) howe the like hath bene punished in other heretofore, whereby admonished, I trust it will be a good occasion to move you to the soner amendment. This is the chiefest ende, whye it is set furth, which God graunt it may attayne. (ll. 57-61)

Individual tragedies are universal examples of the fickleness of Fortune and the fall of the illustrious from high estate. The continuing favor at court of the four original collaborators, Baldwin, Chaloner, Ferrers, and Phaer, argues against the Feasey-Campbell reading. In imitation of Boccaccio's role as commentator and interlocutor, Baldwin reports and comments upon dramatic speeches delivered by the souls of dead politicians. Baldwin suggests a generalized concern with Reformation England in his original plan "to have continued it to Quene Maries time." The twenty-one tragedies in the first part, ranging from the time of Richard II to that of Edward IV, stress the broad issue of minority rule. Duke Humphrey's fall thus raises the political problem of any protectorship, rather than individual topical history. Repetition of the proverb "that pryde wil have a fall" at the beginning and end of "Elianor Cobham" runs counter to a particularized reading of the tale (ll. 7, 329). Even these political readings apply to the

---

[7] "Humphrey Duke of Gloucester and Elianor Cobham His Wife in the *Mirror for Magistrates*," *Huntington Library Bulletin*, no. 5 (1934), 119-55. See "The Suppressed Edition of *A Mirror for Magistrates*," *HLB*, no. 6 (1934), 1-16.

two tragedies by Ferrers that were dropped from the first Elizabethan edition, rather than to the *Mirror* as a whole.

The use of specific Protestant sources in a work that could be applied to the previous reign would have distressed Marian authorities. Although the collaborators cite a variety of sources, for the most part they follow Hall's chronicle. This Protestant interpretation of Tudor history was banned on 13 June 1555 (*Proclamations*, II, no. 422). Allusion to *Piers Plowman* (A3ʳ-4ʳ, B. 146-206) in Seager's "Richard Plantagenet, Duke of Gloucester" (ll. 92-98) could have incurred official disapproval because of Langland's credentials as a Protestant prophet. Ferrers refers to the most highly charged precedent from Edward VI's reign in the tragedy of Edmund, Duke of Somerset, who was slain under Henry VI:

> True is the text which we in scripture read,
> *Ve terrae illi cuius rex est puer.*
> Woe to the land whereof a chylde is head,
> Whether chylde or childyshe the case is one sure. . . .
>
> And no lesse true is this text agayne,
> *Beata terra cuius rex est nobilis.*
> Blest is the land where a stout kyng doth rayne, . . .
> Where the prynce prest hath alway sword in hand. . . .
>   (ll. 78-81, 85-87, 90)

The application of these verses to Edward's minority would have escaped no knowledgeable reader. Ferrers's reference to a "childyshe" king alludes to Crowley's gloss on the Vulgate text (above, Chapter 4 at n. 3).

Boccaccio's *Fall of Princes* manifestly influenced a different series of *de casibus* tragedies that mirror Reformation history: the metrical visions of George Cavendish. According to the envoy, he wrote them for publication under

Mary but withheld them at the queen's death. The prose life of Cardinal Wolsey that he wrote at the same time in the same manuscript (MS Egerton 2402) also imitates Boccaccio in the unfolding of Wolsey's life according to the pyramidal pattern of the fortunate rise and tragic fall of the hero.[8] Although he did not know the *Mirror for Magistrates*, Cavendish wrote verse that is the closest analogue to Baldwin's collection. The most obvious contrast to the *Mirror* is the open concern of his dream visions with contemporary politics. As in writing the life of his patron, Cardinal Wolsey, Cavendish sets himself the task of correcting Protestant distortion of recent history.

By detaching Mary's father and brother from the Protestant cause, Cavendish artfully rewrites the history of the past twenty years; he sees dynastic politics rather than religious ideology at the center of the turmoil. Cavendish seizes upon the human failing of uncontrollable lust rather than religious error as the cause of the tragedy of Henry VIII. In the process, he idealizes Catherine of Aragon as a "pacient Greseld" in compliment to the reigning Hapsburg queen. His eulogy on Edward VI praises the late king's wisdom and learning without reference to religion. Although the complicated confession of Edward Seymour acknowledges personal sin and guilt, diversion of responsibility to the jealousy of Anne Stanhope and the plotting of Dudley (the "whyly *Beare*") exculpates Seymour for his role in the tragic fall of his own brother. Dudley and Latimer are, for Cavendish, the only Protestant villains. Dudley's open confession to crimes ranging from "covetous pryde and hyghe presumpcion" to murder and treason dramatizes his traditional reputation as a master intriguer.

[8] *Life of Cardinal Wolsey and Metrical Visions*, ed. S. W. Singer (1825; 2 vols.); see Richard S. Sylvester, "Cavendish's *Life of Wolsey*: The Artistry of a Tudor Biographer," *SP*, 57 (1960), 44-71.

Lady Jane Grey comes forward as the innocent instrument of Dudley and his fellow traitors. The portrait of Latimer, the recently executed leader of the gospellers, contradicts the later Protestant tradition that is rooted in Foxe's version of the Reformation; his tragedy reflects the intense hostility that even a moderate Catholic felt toward the leader of the Protestant intelligentsia. Thomas Seymour's apostrophe against Latimer for fabricating the evidence that brought about his downfall treats Latimer as a generic example of the Protestant distortion of priestly vocation:

> O Precher! what moved the, me to defame?
> Was it thyn office, or was it thy profession,
> To applie Goddis scripture to the slaunder of my name?
> Are not ye therfore brought to confusion?
> You may se, howe God wyll in conclusion
> All suche punyshe that slander invents;
> Therfore preache no slaunder of innocents.

It was the Protestant preachers, however, who led the counterattack from Continental exile; their smuggled tracts and pamphlets flooded England. Even during this period of intense distress, they took time to shape their works into rudimentary fictions and dialogues. John Bale reverted to his Henrician practice by issuing works bearing a sardonic "Rome" colophon or the mystifying "Rouen" imprint of Michael Wood. Mistress Missa returned from Rome in *The Resurreccion of the Masse* in order to hector the "Gospelers" over their failure. Becon's *Confortable Epistle* bore the same false imprint as the ironic *Resurreccion*: "Strasburgh in Elsas, at the signe of the golden Bibel." In actuality these works were printed at Geneva, Wesel, or in London itself at the underground press of Hugh Singleton.

Appearing soon after Edward VI's death, Bale's *Voca-*

cyon (Wesel, December 1553) gives a unique glimpse of the consciousness of a Tudor reformer. Written during flight from Ireland, it dramatizes Bale's life as a radical bishop and its immediate aftermath in terms of his familiar roles of missionary and exile. Bale faced genuine danger before he fled Ossory, for one of his Irish servants was murdered for cutting hay on a feast day. He found little safety during encounters with pirates and Cornish Catholics, who threatened to send him to London for interrogation by the Privy Council. Regardless of whether one finds Bale in the Low Countries, Hampshire, or Ireland, he plays variations of the same role in the eternal apocalyptic drama. With the "Irishe Papist" attacking "The English Christian," the title-page woodcut depicts Bale's Irish ministry as yet another encounter between the true and false churches. In going into his second exile, Bale equates his journey to Germany with St. Paul's last voyage—just as Paul moved from Jerusalem to Rome, Bale's exile carries him out of his spiritual homeland into the land of his enemies. Bale's spiritual direction symbolizes both his Pauline role as missionary to the Gentiles and the danger of imminent martyrdom. The satirical colophon ("Imprinted in Rome, before the castell of S. Angell, at the signe of S. Peter") presents him as one who figuratively preaches against error at the seat of papal power. Bale styles himself and other Protestant saints as true apostolic successors: "From the schole of Christe hymselfe have we receyved the documentes of oure fayth. From Jerusalem & not from Rome, whom both Peter & also Christe hath called Babylon . . ." (B4ʳ).

A fugitive press published the most powerful contemporary Protestant attack on the Marian regime: the "last words" of Lady Jane Grey. This 1554 chapbook carried the title *An Epistle of the Ladye Jane to a Learned Man.*

With as great a reputation for youthful learning and piety as King Edward himself, the one-week queen adopts the plain style and manner of the gospellers in her scriptural paraphrases. Like Anne Askew and Edward Seymour, she assumes the characteristic voice of the Protestant preacher. An earlier copy of the 1550 letter among Cecil's papers names the scholar who had "late falne from the truth of Gods most holy word" as John Harding (MS Lansdowne 2, fols. 87ʳ-89ᵛ). Foxe's later transcript makes the same identification (MS Harley 416, fols. 25ʳ-28ʳ). Circulation of manuscript copies both before and after publication of the text attests to the notoriety of Lady Jane's evangelical reply in Protestant circles.

Harding goes unnamed in the Wood edition in order to apply Lady Jane's homily against one man's apostasy to the beleaguered spiritual condition of all Protestants in England. The concluding couplet added by the editor, perhaps John Day, counsels faithful Englishmen: "Be constant, be constant, feare not for payne: / Christ hath redemed the, and heaven is thy gayne" (B2ʳ). The title page reassures the reader: "Read it, to thy consolacion." The Balean dichotomies of Lady Jane would have had special appeal to readers of the *Image of Both Churches*:

> That thou, which some tyme wast the lively member of Christ: but now the defourmed impe of the divel, some time the beutiful temple of God: but now the stincking & filthy kenell of Sathan, some tyme the unspotted spouse of Christe, but nowe the unshamefast paramour of Antichrist, sometyme my faithful brother: but now a straunger and Apostata: yea some tyme a stout christen souldier: but now a cowardly runawaye. (A2ʳ)

Well before the fires began to burn at Smithfield, three additions early in Mary's reign converted Lady Jane's *Epistle* into the first printed martyrology of the reign. The transcript of Lady Jane's interrogation by John Feckenham in the Tower of London four days before her execution adopts the dialogue structure of Anne Askew's *Examinations*. A second epistle ("written by the Lady Jane the night before she suffered, in the ende of the New testament in Greke, which she sent to her sister, Lady Katerine") belongs to the same literary tradition of the good death as the cento that Seymour inscribed into the pocket calendar that the same sister received (Figure 16). Unlike Seymour, however, who addressed his meditation to his own soul, Lady Jane exhorts her sister to remain steadfast. The editor readily converts her private letter into a public testimonial of faith.

The martyrdom imagery in this evangelical defense of the Bible anticipates Lady Jane's imminent beheading. In contrast to the gilded shrines and jewelled reliquaries of medieval church tradition, her only suitable monument is the gospel account of Christ's ministry: "which although it be not outwardly trimmed with gold, yet inwardli it is more worth then precious stones." Her words bear comparison with Caxton's praise of *The Golden Legend* as the best of all books "as golde passeth in valewe alle other metalles" (2K5ʳ). Lady Jane's spiritual legacy wittily furnishes her sister (and by extension any faithful Protestant) with the means of salvation: "It is his testament and last will, which he bequethed unto us wretches, whiche shall leade you to the path of eternall joye." Repeated citations identify the gospels as the only text necessary to "teache you to live and learne you to dye" (B6ʳ). Although both the letter and her last words could be a fiction, there is no reason to doubt the authenticity of the message to her sister and "The Lady Janes wordes upon the Scaffold." Marian authorities were notoriously remiss in allowing prisoners to send their writings out for publication. Lady Jane dramatizes her death according to *ars moriendi* conventions as a testimonial to her faith; these words as an apostolic witness mark her entry into the growing company of Protestant martyrs including Anne Askew, Edward Seymour, and Edward VI. Prior to the familiar words "Lorde save my soule, whyche now I commend into thy handes," her paraphrases compare her to the Woman Clothed With the Sun. Elizabethan readers would recognize this figure as a Reformation commonplace: "a true Christian woman" (B8^r). Spenser would later fashion Una according to this pattern of the One Woman of Faith.

The English exiles found refuge in the strongly Protestant cities of Germany and Switzerland. Bale surfaced first at Strasbourg and then at Frankfurt, where he rejoined his friend Foxe. Crowley issued no works during his Frankfurt exile, but William Seres's publication of his *Epitome* within five months of Elizabeth's accession shows that Crowley worked on his analysis of reformation and reaction during his exile. Bale and Foxe soon gravitated to Basel, where both men wrote for the press of Joannes Oporinus and Foxe found employment as a corrector. In *Librorum Index*, Oporinus granted Foxe, Bale, and their exiled colleagues Becon and Laurence Humphrey the same status that he gave to Continental humanists and reformers of the first stature. Foxe, Bale, and Humphrey lived in Basel at Oporinus's household, while other emigrés lived in a dwelling owned by Froschauer.[9]

The Englishmen continually returned to Revelation to explain current historical events. Oporinus published *Christus Triumphans* (Basel, 1556), the imitation of *Pammachius* that Foxe termed an "apocalyptic comedy," which

---

[9] Jennifer Loach, "Pamphlets and Politics, 1553-8," *Bulletin of the Institute of Historical Research*, 48 (1975), 35; see Firth, p. 88.

he sold along with the similar satire in Flacius's *Epistola*. The papal figure that Foxe named Pseudodamnus and the prostitute Pornapolis ("harlot-city") dramatize contemporary Rome as the current residence of Antichrist and the Whore of Babylon. Foxe had already issued the first installment of the Latin history that he completed in manuscript as tutor to Thomas Howard prior to Edward VI's death. Ribelius printed the octavo text in Strasbourg as *Commentarii Rerum in Ecclesia Gestarum* (1554). This account of apocalyptic conflict from the time of Wyclif and the Lollards through that of Hus and Savonarola analyzes the Age of Locusts that so obsessed Bale and Crowley.

Foxe brought his Latin chronicle through his own age in *Rerum in Ecclesia Gestarum Commentarii. Pars Prima* (Basel, 1559). (Henricus Pantaleon completed the text with *Martyrum historia. Pars secunda* [Basel, 1563].) Incorporating the text of *Commentarii Gestarum*, Foxe formulated this martyrology by fusing accounts of the Marian burnings with the apocalyptic interpretation of history that he derived from his friend Bale. He includes Anne Askew, Edward Seymour, and Lady Jane Grey as prototypes for the Marian martyrs. Contrary to William Haller's suggestion that Foxe relied on reports from John Aylmer for his account of Lady Jane,[10] he worked from her published *Epistle*. His Latin text quotes Anne Askew's *Examinations* without Bale's commentary, along with Seymour's execution speech. An elegiac distich on Seymour idealizes him as the father of reform:

> Innumeras uno laudes ut carmine dicam:
> Anglia tota ruit caede, Semere, tua.[11]

[10] *Foxe's Book of Martyrs*, p. 72.

[11] "In order that I may utter innumerable praises in one song: / All England is ruined by your death, Seymour" (II, E2ᵛ).

Citation of Coelius Secundus Curio as "Orator et Historicus" identifies the author of *Pasquillus ecstaticus* as a member of the Foxe-Bale circle. Curio contributed a dedication poem to the first volume of Bale's *Catalogus* (α6ʳ).

Bale continued his lifelong labor at his Swiss sanctuary. Between 1548 and 1557, his account of British authors ballooned from the 255 quarto leaves of *Summarium* to the encyclopedic folio that contains three times as many leaves. He increased to nine hundred the number of writers, whom he still organized into *centuriae*. Additions included such older authors as Caedmon, Walter Map, Robert Langland ("Robertus Langelande"), John Gower, and Stephen Hawes, as well as eminent Edwardians who had succumbed to the Marian burnings: John Rogers, Nicholas Ridley, John Bradford, and John Philpot. Along with Latimer, Hooper, and Cranmer, who had appeared in *Summarium*, he groups these reformers in a rough-and-ready martyrology. At Oporinus's house he and Foxe worked side by side on *Catalogus* and *Gestarum Commentarii* as complementary accounts of English history and literature. The historical appendices that Bale intersperses throughout the volume supply the apocalyptic context within which all these authors are said to work. The title page identifies the volume as an application of *The Image of Both Churches*, for it advertises a record of ". . . the deeds of the elect ministers of the church that are described in the Apocalypse of St. John, in the stars, angels, horses, trumpets, thunders, heads, crowns, mountains, phials, and plagues. . . ."[12]

Completion of the second part of *Catalogus* in February 1559 concluded the literary history that Bale had "collected with no small labor" ("non parvo labore collegit") from

[12] ". . . quam electorum Ecclesiae ministrorum facta, mysteriis in S. Ioannis Apocalypsi descriptis, in stellis, angelis, equis, tubis, tonitruis, capitibus, coronis, montibus, phialis ac plagis. . . ."

John Leland and other authorities. Five additional *centuriae* supplement the entries for English and Scottish authors in the first volume and add an entirely new section on the literature of Ireland, the Hebrides, and the Orkneys. The short notices for the following writers in Centuria XII complete the comprehensive account of Reformation authors that he had begun in *Summarium*: Richard Sherry, William Baldwin, Thomas Chaloner, George Ferrers, Luke Shepherd, John Dudley, William Thomas, John Heywood, and Miles Hogarde (Latinized to "Milo Porcarius," with a pun). Bale's grouping identifies Baldwin, Chaloner, and Ferrers as a literary circle (II, 108). Bale had announced his intention of adding many of these Edwardian authors in the outline for the planned second part of *Summarium*, which he published in 1549 as an appendix to his edition of Leland's *Laborious Journey*. *Catalogus* represents the fulfillment of this earlier plan, which he had advanced with the manuscript *Index* that he apparently began after his return from Wesel.

AN ELIZABETHAN RENASCENCE

The Protestant faithful focused their millennial expectations on Queen Elizabeth, whose accession seemed to offer a return to the halcyon climate of Edward VI's reign. John Bale spoke for the exiles when, as an "Englishman of Suffolk," he eulogized the new queen in *Scriptorum Illustrium maioris Brytanniae Catalogus*. His panegyrical dedication furnishes an exact parallel to his earlier praise of King Edward in *Summarium*. Although the second volume of Bale's *Catalogus* had gone to press prior to the arrival in Basel of news of Mary's death on 17 November 1558, a unique copy of the first volume contains four new leaves that Oporinus inserted after the original 1557 preface.[13] This insertion adds Bale's new dedication to Elizabeth: "AD POTENTISSIMAM AC SERENISSIMAM PRINCIPEM." Government by Antichrist had run full circle, for Bale's hyperbolic antitheses, in a manner identical to his previous greeting to her brother, welcome Elizabeth as the millennial ruler prophesied in Revelation. Her accession as the ideal prince ("bonus princeps") marks the return to true religion, justice, and virtue after the "yoke of the wicked tyrant" ("mali tyranni iugum"). Unlike John Knox, whose attack on female government was issued so inopportunely as to appear to attack Mary's successor,[14] Bale has no difficulty in eulogizing rule by a woman. It should be no paradox that government by this new woman has been instituted by Christ in contrast to prior enslavement by "woman, Pope, and Satan" ("femina, Papa, Satana"). The Protestant precedents for Elizabeth as the Woman of Faith are Anne Askew and Lady Jane Grey.

The millenarian iconography of Edward VI's reign was readily adapted to the glorification of his favorite sister. Bale's eulogy anticipates the labyrinthine praise of Elizabeth as the just virgin, Astraea. Added dedicatory poems continue Bale's dichotomies. According to Laurence Humphrey, woman may be a "cross" ("crux") but the "good woman" ("bona femina") may also be a governor. Just as Edward became the Young Josiah, the respective biblical archetypes for Mary and Elizabeth are Jezebel and Deborah ("Nam Iesabel quondam tortrix, sed Debbora vindex"). Elizabeth's coronation festivities had already eulogized her as the woman judge. The queen becomes for

[13] B.L. G 6026. The added leaves are foliated α2-4, [α5] and dated 4 March 1559.

[14] *First Blast of the Trumpet against the Monstruous Regiment of Women* (Geneva, 1558).

Oporinus an English Phoenix after the tyranny of the "Wolf in the fold" ("Lupus in terris"). Oporinus's tribute to Bale, "Gratulatio et Votum" ("Thanksgiving and Prayer"), styles the special dedication copy as a homecoming volume, very much in the manner that Bale had designed *Summarium* in 1548. The verse dialogue between himself and Bale, which Jacobus Hertelius contributed, dramatizes the close of Bale's second exile. After hearing of Bale's imminent return to serve the Protestant queen, Hertelius states: "May God guide your leaving and return you safe to your own." Bale's parting salutations ("Peace to you, peace to us" and "Farewell friend") envelop Hertelius's consolatory words on the loss of a friend:

> B. Pax tibi, pax nobis. H. Abitum DEUS ipse gubernet,
> Teque tuis saluum reddat. B. Amice vale.

Elizabeth rewarded those who had remained loyal to her during the dangerous days of her sister's reign by bestowing royal favor on such men as Matthew Parker, William Cecil, Nicholas Bacon, and John Harington. In contrast to his previous failure to obtain crown patronage from Seymour, Bale was appointed a prebendary at Canterbury Cathedral by Parker, whom Elizabeth had chosen, as the protégé of her mother, Anne Boleyn, to replace Cardinal Pole as the primate of the Church of England. Bale wrote nothing new after *Catalogus*, but he did issue his 1554 manuscript of *A Declaration of Edmonde Bonners Articles* (1561). Because of the Marian heresy prosecutions, Bale was the most important radical of the first reformist generation to live on into the new reign. He died in 1563 at the age of sixty-eight. *The Pageant of Popes* (1574), John Studley's adapted translation of Bale's *Acta Romanorum Pontificum*, appeared posthumously. Known otherwise as a translator of Senecan tragedy, Studley acknowledges the *de casibus* structure of Bale's Reformation apocalypse when he stresses the "tragicall partes, played by . . . [the popes]: both pleasant and profitable to this age."

Bale correctly predicted that a rebirth of literature and learning would occur under Elizabeth, for the concluding prayer to the amended copy of *Catalogus* states: "through you literature may be reborn and all writers had in honor" (". . . ut per te . . . bonae literae renascantur, scriptoresque omnes in honore habeantur . . ."). This first Elizabethan renascence is a throwback to the Reformation flowering that Roger Ascham spoke of as a golden age: "If kyng *Edward* had lived a litle longer, his onely example had breed soch a rase of worthie learned jentlemen, as this Realme never yet did affourde" (*Scholemaster*, G4ᵛ). The literature and culture of the two decades prior to publication of the "new poetry" of Spenser's *Shepheardes Calender* (1579) were strongly influenced by Reformation conventions, ideas, texts, and forms.

Reformation literature and thought supply the immediate background for the literary flowering at the time of Sidney, Spenser, Marlowe, and Shakespeare. Many mid-century texts came back into print during the early decades of Elizabeth's rule. Bale himself contributed *Actes of Englysh Votaryes* (1560), *The Image of Both Churches* (c. 1570), and his tragedy *God's Promises* (1577). This Protestant drama was only one of many Edwardian plays to be republished or, more usually, to appear in print for the first time: *Impatient Poverty* (1560), *Nice Wanton* (1560), *Lusty Juventus* (c. 1565), *Mary Magdalene* (1566), *Ralph Roister Doister* (c. 1566), *Jacob and Esau* (1568), and *Gammer Gurton's Needle* (1575). With its title-page woodcut, Lynne's *Beginning and Ending of All Popery* (1588) reappeared as an argument against the Jesuits. Like many other authors,

William Baldwin brought out old manuscript works such as *The Funeralles of King Edward the Sixt* (1560) and *Beware the Cat* (1570). In revision after revision, *The Mirror for Magistrates* and Baldwin's *Treatise of Moral Philosophy* went on to become two of the most popular texts of the time. Michael Lobley gathered together the 1552 flyting under the title *The Contention bettwyxte Churchyeard and Camell, upon David Dycers Dreame. Newlye Imprinted* (1560). Although Thomas Wilson's *Art of Rhetoric* and *Rule of Reason* had not appeared under Mary because of the author's Protestant zeal, they went on to achieve great fame through many Elizabethan editions.

The Elizabethan settlement rested upon Edwardian texts. The vernacular Bible was printed for the first time since Edward's death, and the Thirty-nine Articles revived the Forty-two Articles. Even though Bale's *Image of Both Churches* ceased to appear, his commentary lived on in the abridged form found in the annotations of the Geneva Bible (1560); government action forced the Puritans to moderate the Balean invective in later editions. The Bishops' Bible that Matthew Parker issued in 1568 to counter the Puritan text differed only slightly from the Great Bible. Like most educated Elizabethans, including Spenser and Shakespeare, Parker acknowledged the superior scholarship of the Geneva Bible through private use of the unauthorized version. The Elizabethan *Book of Common Prayer* was a modification of the 1552 prayer book; as a concession to the Puritans, the ballad versions of Sternhold and Hopkins regularly appeared after the prose psalter in the prayer book. Cranmer's sermon collection survived as the first part of the expanded Elizabethan *Book of Homilies*.

The book trade reverted to Edwardian norms. Although Whitchurch and Grafton never regained their mid-century stature, John Day went on under the patronage of Archbishop Parker and William Cecil, first Lord Burghley, to become the most successful and innovative printer of the century (MS Lansdowne 15, fol. 99ʳ; MS Lansdowne 17, fol. 126ʳ). His edition of *The Whole Book of Psalms* (1562) achieved remarkable acceptance as popular poetry. Day received monopolies on the collected sermons of Hugh Latimer and the ever-popular writings of Thomas Becon. Thus he issued the three folio volumes of Becon's *Worckes*, "whiche he hath hytherto made and published, with diverse other newe Bookes added," in addition to individual editions of mid-century writings. Two new Becon publications, *The Pomander of Prayer* (1558) and *The Sycke Mannes Salve* (c. 1560) appeared in thirty-five editions prior to 1640. Day published John Foxe's folio edition of *The Whole Workes of W. Tyndall, John Frith, and Doct. Barnes* (1573). Foxe also edited the gospels with an Anglo-Saxon text for the archbishop in 1571; Day printed the volume under the primate's patronage with the Anglo-Saxon font that he had previously cut for Parker.

In his continuation of Lanquet's *Epitome of Cronicles*, Robert Crowley issued the first analysis of the English Reformation and Counter Reformation. His example was followed in rapid succession by Cooper, Grafton, Foxe, Stow, and Holinshed. Crowley revives the factionalism of Edward's reign. On the basis of both firsthand experience prior to exile and the published version of Dudley's scaffold speech, Crowley contrasts Seymour and his successor as saint and villain. Shaped according to the formulas of *de casibus* tragedy, his is the most idealized version of Seymour's life and death. According to Crowley's account of the execution, Seymour "behaved hymselfe so soberly and humbly, that none [was] so harde herted about hym, that dyd not shedde teares" (4E3ᵛ). After blaming Dudley's deposition of Seymour as the cause of Edward's death and

of the failure of the reforms, Crowley's millenarian enthusiasm flares up once again when he interprets the Marian
persecutions as a sign of the Second Coming. As the first
martyrology for Mary's reign, Crowley's account anticipates Foxe's *Actes and Monuments*. Transferring his faith
in the Christian monarch of the Last Days from Edward
VI to Elizabeth, he concludes with the hope that the new
queen will usher in the millennium (4E2^v-3^v, 4G5^v-6^r).

Although Crowley never went back to his earlier career
as a publisher, the reprinting of *The Vision of Pierce Plowman* (1561) and *One and Thyrtie Epigrammes* (1573) does
attest to the continued popularity of his Edwardian works.
After his return from exile, he rose very high in the Elizabethan church establishment. Bishop John Scory, who had
examined him prior to his 1551 ordination, appointed
Crowley Archdeacon of Hereford Cathedral in 1559 and
a Hereford prebendary in 1560. He returned to London
on his appointment as a prebendary at St. Paul's Cathedral,
accepting also several related offices.[15] Like all millenari-
ans, however, Crowley became disillusioned once again.
His pamphlets fired the Elizabethan controversy over vestments, at the height of which the term "Puritan" first came
into use during the winter of 1567-68.[16] His fundamental
principle of restoring religious purity through a return to
gospel practices had not varied during the previous two
decades. Nevertheless, under the influence of Calvinistic
ideas that they had encountered in exile, Crowley and other
early Puritans were led by their individualistic interpretations of the Bible to question the royal supremacy that had
been axiomatic under Edward VI. The united Protestant
front of Edward's reign was shattered after the Elizabethan

[15] George Hennessy, *Novum Repertorium Ecclesiasticum Parochiale Lon-
dinense* (1898), pp. 38, 172, 375-76.
[16] Knappen, *Tudor Puritanism*, pp. 198, 488.

Compromise, and many old gospellers joined the Puritan movement.

It was at the height of the Elizabethan controversy over vestments that Crowley chose to publish his earliest apocalyptic poem. In all likelihood Crowley suppressed *The Opening of the Wordes of the Prophet Joell* (1567), which he had written in 1546 during the waning days of Henry VIII, because of his hope that Edward VI would fulfill the Henrician reforms. Evidently Crowley thought this catalogue of abuses to be as valid under Elizabeth as it had been decades earlier, for he scarcely revised the poem's portrayal of the cyclic pattern of reform and backsliding. Although the thumping meter of Crowley's tailed rhyme is inclined toward a singsong effect, it builds up a powerful momentum during the 2,802-line course of the narrative. He finds in the recently promulgated Elizabethan Compromise new signs of doom. The somber mood and threatening imagery of earthquake, famine, plague, and warfare come from the "little apocalypse" of Mark 13:

> Darke is the sunne,
> Bloud is the moone,
> From heaven are fallen the stars:
> Earthquakes are seene,
> Pestilence, famine,
> Rumors tel noght but wars.

> (A2ʳ)

Crowley achieved his greatest fame late in life not as a poet, but as a Puritan clergyman, an energetic pamphleteer, and an arbiter of public morality. Although he lost his benefices in 1566-67 because of his agitation, he never joined the separatist Puritans. Despite the displeasure of the bishops and queen, he retained the favor of the City of London authorities before whom he preached the election day sermon at Guildhall on 19 September 1574. He was restored to some of his earlier benefices in the late 1570s.[17] After regaining his position as a St. Paul's prebendary, he acted in 1582 as a censor on behalf of the Bishop of London when he authorized a manuscript for publication, stating: "I have diligently perused all these meditations, and everie parte therof: and have founde nothynge therin, that maye not be published to the edification of all Christians. By me Robert Crowley" (B.L. MS Add. 38170, fol. 16r).

The measure of Crowley's Elizabethan popularity is suggested by the dedications that he received and the prefaces that he contributed to other men's books. By 1575 his recommendation to the reading public was sufficiently valuable for him to be asked to write a preface for Richard Rice's *An Invective againste Vices*, which attacks dicing, dancing, and other forms of secular entertainment. In 1578, he (along with Foxe and other Puritans) endorsed *Whartons Dreame*, a millennial complaint against usury. Anthony Gilby dedicated *A Pleasaunt Dialogue, Betweene a Souldior of Barwicke, and an English Chaplaine* (1581) to Crowley and six other men as his "Reverent Fathers and Brethren in Christ." Of these six, Miles Coverdale, William Turner, and Thomas Lever had joined Crowley and Gilby as active Reformation publicists. Thomas Lovell dedicated his *Dialogue between Custom and Veritie* (1581) to Crowley and Thomas Brasbridge as "godly and faithful Ministers of Christe and Prechers of the Gospel." Crowley and Brasbridge had a considerable following in the reading public of the City of London, for both were "wel knowen to be careful furtherers of all godlynes" (A2r, B2r). Crowley's edition of Francis Seager's *The Schoole of Vertue* (1582) appeared during the thick of the moralistic attack on poetry

---

[17] Hennessy, *Repertorium*, p. 172.

and the stage, which occasioned Sidney's reply to works like Stephen Gosson's *Schoole of Abuse* (1579). Despite Sidney's insistence on neoclassical standards of style and decorum, Crowley affirmed Sidney's confidence in "right poetry" as the most powerful vehicle for moral education in the preface: "The Preachers counsell to Parents & Tutors" (A1ᵛ). Crowley added his own "Praiers and Graces" in meter. When he died in 1588 near the age of seventy, he was buried beneath the same stone at his old church, St. Giles Cripplegate, where his friend John Foxe had been interred the previous year (Stow, *Survay*, Q8ᵛ).

John Foxe's *Actes and Monuments* (1563) was the landmark Elizabethan work to appear prior to the literary flowering of the 1580s and 1590s. John Day expanded the folio edition of his most important publication to two volumes in 1570. "The Book of Martyrs" completed the martyrology that Foxe had advanced in *Commentarii Gestarum* and *Gestarum Commentarii*. Foxe returned to England after publication by Oporinus and Brylinger of the first part of the latter work. It too served as a homecoming volume, for Foxe followed Bale in adapting the text to the changed political circumstances back in England. He addressed his dedicatory epistle of 1 September 1559 to Thomas Howard, the fourth Duke of Norfolk. The reference to Howard as his "Maecenas" suggests the possibility that the Duke underwrote Foxe's expenses in exile. By giving Foxe a place in his household, Howard continued the patronage shown by his aunt, the Duchess of Richmond. His friendly correspondence with his mentor contained such salutations as "To my right loving schoolemaster John ffoxe," "Tuus Alumnus / Thomas Norfolke," and "Tuus scholasticus amantissimus / Tho. Norffol." Now in England, Foxe engaged in active correspondence with Queen Elizabeth,

Howard, Oporinus, Matthias Flacius, Laurence Humphrey, Thomas Lever, and John Parkhurst.[18]

Foxe retained the millenarian enthusiasm of Edward's reign; unlike the extremist Puritans, he never questioned Elizabeth's reforming zeal. Placement of chained copies of *Actes and Monuments* in cathedrals in 1571 gave it the location that Erasmus's *Paraphrases* had occupied alongside the English Bible under Edward VI. He collaborated with John Day in designing the volume as a formal compliment to the queen and a defense of the royal supremacy. Queen Elizabeth supplants Howard in receiving Foxe's dedication to the folio volume.

It has been suggested that the capital C of the initial word "Constantine" in the dedication portrays three counselors or figures representing the three estates standing at the side of the enthroned queen, who bears the sword of justice and orb of government.[19] Nevertheless, the woodcut occupies the traditional location of the dedication portrait and incorporates imagery from similar scenes in books dedicated to Henry VIII or Edward VI. It mirrors the initial E from the 1551 folio Bible (Figure 15) that Day reused at the beginning of Foxe's history of Edward's reign (*A & M* [1563]). Only one of the men wears the symbols of the councilor's office, and none wears the costume of a peer or bishop. As a dedication scene, the portrait would depict Foxe, Day, and probably Cecil. It was through Cecil's favor that Foxe was appointed a Salisbury prebendary upon completion of the book. As the queen's chief secretary Cecil returned to his function as the agent of crown patronage, which he had performed for Seymour and Dudley. The presence at the feet of the queen of a figure

[18] MS Harley 417, fols. 97ʳ-112ᵛ passim, 113ʳ, 115ᵛ, 118ʳ, 121ʳ⁻ᵛ.
[19] Yates, p. 43; Haller, *Elect Nation*, p. 119.

of the pope, who wears the tiara and carries the broken keys of St. Peter, conflates the allegorical imagery of the painting of Edward VI and the Pope (Figure 12) and Edwardian dedication portraits (Figures 5-6, 15). Day's woodcuts integrate many variations of this Reformation tableau into Foxe's text (above, pp. 193-96).

The overall pattern of *Actes and Monuments* descends from Bale's chronology.[20] Foxe's dedicatory comparison between the queen and emperor Constantine, with himself likened to Eusebius, transfers to Elizabeth's reign Bale's apocalyptic interpretation of Christian history. In his Revelation commentary, Bale had praised Constantine as the last of the true Christian emperors prior to the advent of Antichrist; he styled himself as a modern Eusebius when he applied precedents of the second-century persecution of Blandina under Emperor Antoninus Verus to the Anne Askew affair. In compiling his Protestant martyrologies, Foxe conceives himself to be the successor to Bale as the editor of the life of Oldcastle and Askew's *Examinations*.

Day announces this kinship between Bale and Foxe with the millennial woodcut on the title page. The dualistic illustration contrasts the persecution of the true Protestant church with the false religion of the Roman Catholic church. In the 1570 edition Day added a legend beneath the woodcut that alludes explicitly to the Bale connection: "The Image of the persecuted Church. The Image of the persecutyng Church" (Figure 18; compare Figure 4). Adoration of Christ the Judge by the ranked hierarchies of trumpeting martyrs, kings, and angels is supported by a panel depicting true gospel worship. In this inset the religion of the Book is practiced by a minister who preaches the Word to a congregation of Bible-reading Christians beneath the

[20] See Haller, *Elect Nation*, pp. 136-39, and Firth, pp. 70, 90, 106.

Tetragrammaton. On the right-hand side a priest in vestments speaks to a congregation that tells its rosary beads opposite a Corpus Christi procession followed by a throng of vain worldlings. The Latin address "Ad doctum Lectorum" contrasts Foxe's collection of Protestant saints' lives with the *Legenda Aurea*, from which the priest might read. In another panel the host is elevated to Antichrist as he falls toward hell surrounded by his attendant devils. As an image of Elizabethan piety, this frontispiece repeats themes from the frontispiece woodcuts in Caxton's *Golden Legend* and the earliest English Bibles (Figures 1-3). The fine woodcut that Day placed in the 1570 edition as an introduction to Edward VI's reign (Figure 19) is an iconographic variant of his title page.

Foxe imitates Bale in his scrupulous handling of source materials (*A & M* [1563], p. 98). Refuting accusations that he falsified his texts, Dickens notes that "it cannot sanely be maintained that Foxe fabricated this mass of detailed and circumstantial information . . . when so many of the people and the events remained well within living memory."[21] He invariably distinguishes between the hyperbole of his polemical commentary and verbatim quotation from manuscript and printed records. Collation of extant letters and documents by an extraordinary number of different hands in the eleven massive volumes of Foxe papers (MSS Harley 416-426) shows that where a source survives, *Actes and Monuments* contains an accurate transcript. Fragments of first drafts of Gardiner's letters to Seymour, for example, go directly into the printed text (MS Harley 417, fols. 84^r-89^v; pp. 740-42). Foxe corrected the Lady Jane Grey papers by reference to *An Epistle of the Ladye Jane to a Learned Man*. His possession of man-

---

[21] *English Reformation*, pp. 46 and n. 3.

uscript versions of both Lady Jane's letters and her interrogation by John Feckenham attests to his concern for her
as a prototype of the Marian martyr (MS Harley 416, fols.
25ʳ-28ᵛ, and MS Harley 425, fols. 83ʳ-84ʳ; pp. 917-20).

The writings of Protestant martyrs are the "monuments"
referred to in Foxe's title (also see *A & M* [1563], p.
98). His concept of texts as witnesses to faith plays upon
the different senses of "monument" as sepulcher, written
document, and funerary memorial. In addition to recounting the sufferings of the faithful, he edits extensive tran-
scripts of supporting documents. Wherever possible he
follows Bale by allowing martyrs to tell their own stories
in their own words. Foxe stresses vivid narrative because
exciting sacred stories can replace the "prophane" and
"heroicall" tales that kings and nobles usually delight in.
His Latin and English prefaces explicitly contrast his method
of compilation with the medieval "monuments" of "reliques," saints' lives, shrines, and images (see above, pp.
70-72, 421). Unlike the Catholic saints, Protestant martyrs are no different from ordinary laymen and possess no
miraculous, intercessory power as a special endowment from
God. As exemplary types, they illustrate how true faith
enables anyone to be a witness to Christ as an elect saint.

The title page of *Actes and Monuments* announces Foxe's
intention of describing "the great persecutions & horrible
troubles, that have been wrought and practiced by the
Romishe Prelates." The unforgettable accounts of the deaths
of Latimer, Ridley, Cranmer, and Hooper had to be the
centerpiece of such a collection. Within Foxe's overall pattern, the English Reformation under Edward VI functions
as a tranquil golden age prior to the final onslaught of
Antichrist during "these latter and perillous dayes"; Foxe
looks back with nostalgia to those "mild and halcyon days"
as a "breathing-time" and "haven of fairer and calmer

weather" (V, 697, 704). As the new Josiah, Edward is the only example of an "evangelical" monarch prior to Elizabeth herself. According to Foxe, his reign is the only period of godly rule between the beginning of the Age of Locusts and the present moment.

By positioning the story of Anne Askew's execution as an introduction to the English Reformation, Foxe presents Edward's reign as a brief interlude prior to the arrival in England of the Spanish Inquisition under Mary Tudor. The centrality of Askew's suffering is suggested by a holograph note in which Foxe describes with horror how Wriothesley and Sir John Baker "put of[f] their gownes, and racked her them selves" when Sir Anthony Knevet, Lieutenant of the Tower, "would not rack so vyhemently as they required" (MS Harley 419, fol. 2ʳ). In drawing his verbatim transcript of the *Examinations* directly from Bale's edition, Foxe brings to a close the long odyssey of the manuscript that had been smuggled out of Newgate prison in 1546. He alters his original only in omitting Bale's commentary and interpolating Anne Askew's confession from Edmund Bonner's diocesan records.

John Day collaborated with Foxe in the integration of woodcuts into the narrative text, and Foxe tailored his text to fit the historiated woodcut initials C and E. In order to illustrate the "trouble and persecution of Anne Askewe," Day used the wood block that he had originally designed as an illustration for Crowley's *Confutation of Nicolas Shaxton* (Figure 8).[22] He must have concealed this valuable piece of printing equipment when he went underground during Mary's reign. The woodcut augments Foxe's transcript through its vivid, visual record of her actual death.

[22] *A & M* (1563), p. 666. See above, p. 80. Both woodcuts contain an identical hairline crack.

The illustration contrasts the Askew execution as a testimonial of true faith with the apostasy of Shaxton, who preaches his recantation sermon from a pulpit at Smithfield. In the second edition, Foxe amplifies this contrast by introducing dialogue between Askew and Shaxton into his moralized conclusion in order to heighten the effect of the circumstances shown in the illustration. His practice follows that of Tacitus and Eusebius, who introduced long speeches that stated what individuals should have said under particular circumstances according to rules of rhetorical decorum. In going beyond Askew's personal narrative, Foxe draws on Crowley's 1548 pamphlet for specific details.

Foxe dramatizes the "Tragical History" of Edward Seymour and the death of Edward VI, portraying them as elect Protestant saints, according to the conventions of *de casibus* tragedy. His account preserves the carefully cultivated public image of Seymour rather than the inside portraits preserved in MSS Stowe 1066 and Harley 2194. Foxe had already introduced Edward's reign in terms of the *theatrum mundi* conceit: "a new face of things began now to appear, as it were in a stage, new players coming in, the old being thrust out" (V, 703). Comparison between Seymour and Humphrey, "the good duke of Gloucester," incorporates the dramatic pattern of the *Mirror for Magistrates*, which Shakespeare would incorporate into his history plays. The moral purpose of the "lamentable and tragical narration" of Seymour's destruction is to admonish

. . . no man to plant any trust or assurance upon the brickle pillars of worldly prosperity, how high soever it seemeth, considering that there is no state so high, but it hath his ruin. . . . no man can always stand in this so ruinous a world, the surest way is, for every man to

choose his standing so, that his fall may be the easier.
(VI, 282)

Although he acknowledges Seymour's flaws, Foxe idealizes
the execution account at the core of the narrative. In the
commentary that he adds to his eyewitness testimony, he
draws Christlike parallels to the attainder trial at Westminster Hall:

> . . . he patiently and quietly did suffer, neither storming
> inwardly in stomach, nor reviling them with words again;
> but like a lamb, following the true Lamb and example
> of all meekness, was contented to take all things at their
> hands. . . . the patience of this good duke was marvel-
> lous in forbearing his enemies, so also was his discretion
> and temperance. . . .

It is through Foxe's closing character sketch that Seymour
would be remembered in later centuries as "a man of nature singularly given to peace" and "void of all pride and
ambition" (VI, 292, 295, 297).

Foxe follows Reformation apologetics in his interpretation of the tragic loss of Edward VI as a "plague" sent by
God in retribution for England's sins. He draws his account of the last words of the "godly child" directly from
the broadside prayer printed immediately after the king's
death (A & M, VI, 352). The ensuing persecutions "fulfill" contemporary prophecies of doom and retribution, first
in the death of the "true Christian woman" Lady Jane Grey
and then in the seemingly unending sufferings of Latimer,
Ridley, Cranmer, Hooper, and all the other Protestant
martyrs whose accounts take up more than one third of the
history of the church "from the yeare of our Lorde a thou-
sande, unto the tyme nowe present." With minor variations, these Marian martyrologies follow the conventional

[441]

paradigm established by Bale's edition of the Anne Askew *Examinations*.

Aside from Dudley, whose last words are pointedly omitted, Gardiner and Bonner function as the chief villains in the Reformation drama. Described by Foxe as agents of Antichrist, they continue to perform the same role under Mary. Foxe claims to omit false rumors from his account of the fall of Gardiner as "the enemy of God's word":

> I will not here speak of that which hath been constantly reported to me touching the monstrous making and mis-[s]haped fashion of his feet and toes, the nails whereof were said not to be like to other men's, but to crook downward, and to be sharp like the claws of ravening beasts. (VII, 586)

Nevertheless, in the manner of More's history of Richard III, the text includes unsupported details about deformities that are said to reflect spiritual monstrosity. Foxe attributes his account of the providential punishment of this Tudor Achitophel to "a certain hearsay." This testimony could not possibly be accurate, however, because of the death of the third Duke of Norfolk on 25 August 1554. According to the lurid report that Foxe derives from a "certain worthy and credible gentlewoman," Gardiner joined the old duke on 19 October 1554, the day on which Latimer and Ridley were burned north of the Oxford city wall. Upon receipt of the news of the deaths of their antagonists, the two are reported to have sat down to dinner in a celebratory mood:

> . . . and the bishop began merrily to eat. But what followed? The bloody tyrant had not eaten a few bits, but the sudden stroke of God's terrible hand fell upon him in such sort, as immediately he was taken from the table, and so brought to his bed; where he continued the

space of fifteen days . . . [and] was brought to a wretched
end. . . . A spectacle worthy to be noted and beholden
of all such bloody burning persecutors. (VII, 593)

Despite its obvious historical inaccuracy, this report
complements Foxe's overall dramatic structure. As one of
the rare *de casibus* tragedies in the collection, this account
of Gardiner's death furnishes a contrast to the repetitive
"comedic" pattern of the innocent suffering and martyrdom of the Protestant witnesses. The artistic shaping of
this prideful fall invites comparison with the "saintly"
composure of the Protestant heroes. According to Foxe's
providential interpretation, Gardiner had served throughout the Reformation conflict as the unwilling agent of a
wrathful God against his iniquitous people. Despite the
naive inaccuracies of this partisan portrait, current historical research supports Tudor animus toward the adroit politician whom the gospellers called "wily Winchester."[23]

THE LEGACY OF ENGLISH REFORMATION LITERATURE

Memory of the Edwardian revival lived on into the Elizabethan age and seventeenth century, as increasingly dim
recollections of historical events were transmuted into art.
What endured was a nostalgic vision of a legendary period
of freedom and truth, which, had it not been cut short,
might have fulfilled millenarian dreams of a perfect Protestant kingdom. For the rest of the sixteenth century, the
king's reputation as a messianic deliverer was fed by Gal-
fridian prophecies of his Arthurian return.[24] A broadside
ballad entitled *The Most Rare and Excellent History of the*

[23] Stephen Gardiner, *A Machiavellian Treatise*, ed. and trans. P. S.
Donaldson (Cambridge, 1975); see Elton, pp. 393-94.

[24] Thomas, *Religion and Decline*, pp. 419-22.

Dutchesse of Suffolkes Calamity (1624) idealizes Edward's reign as a golden age of tranquillity and peace. It sensationalizes the deaths of Cranmer, Ridley, and Hooper, the threats to Princess Elizabeth during Mary's reign, and the exciting escape of the Duchess of Suffolk via Billingsgate prior to the happy homecoming of the exiles under Elizabeth as queen. Thomas Drue's *Life of the Dutches of Suffolke* (1631), "as it hath bene divers and sundry times acted," similarly dramatizes the hairbreadth escape of the duchess from persecution by Gardiner and Bonner.

Anne Askew joined the Duchess of Suffolk as a Protestant heroine in the Elizabethan edition of her *Examinations* (c. 1560), in which the original text is supplemented with "The Ballade whiche Anne Askewe made and sange, whan she was in Newgate" (D2^r-3^r). The popular ballad "I am a Woman Poor and Blind" (c. 1624) represents the final transformation of Anne Askew's ordeal. All that remains of the Henrician dissenter is the generalized figure of a pathetic victim "poor and blind," whereas her antagonist survives only in the vestigial form of a pernicious gardener who attempts to blast "the seed of Christs true verity" in the garden of her body. Characterized only by her dying testimonial, this scarcely humanized embodiment of faith popularizes the radical Reformation as it was dimly remembered by the Puritan opponents of Archbishop Laud and Charles I.

The enduring literary legacy of the Reformation came neither in the form of topical ballads and plays nor in specific influences other than the prayer book and English Bible. By the end of the sixteenth century most readers ignored mid-Tudor texts, which they considered to be stylistically crude. Although particular works of Reformation literature were forgotten, literary traditions that they had popularized lived on into the Restoration. Distinctively

Protestant themes, genres, and conventions shaped the main tradition of English literature from the time of Sidney until Milton. The epistemological problem of the Reformation is, for example, a central concern of Marlowe, Donne, Milton, Bunyan, and many others. Later works return again and again to the Protestant dilemma; justification by faith and imputed grace are incessant concerns in this literature. Predestinarian theology contributed to skepticism concerning a humanity mysteriously divided into the elect and reprobate. Despite the perplexities of many individual tragedies of despair and damnation, the paradoxical balance between freedom of the will and divine providence ensured the "comedic" pattern of the universal drama.

The first printed poetry of the youthful Edmund Spenser articulated Reformation themes. During the year prior to the final publication of Bale's *Image of Both Churches*, Henry Bynneman published Spenser's translations of epigrams and sonnets in *A Theatre [for] Voluptuous Worldlings* (1569). The Dutch Huguenot Jan van der Noot dedicated the collection to Queen Elizabeth as the "Virgin *Astraea* . . . descended from heaven to builde hir a seate in this your moste happie countrey of *England*" (A6ʳ). The text includes Spenser's versions of sonnets by Petrarch and fifteen allegorical visions of Rome by Joachim du Bellay, with an apocalyptic commentary that van der Noot drew largely from Bale's *Image* and Bullinger's *In Apocalypsim conciones centum* (Basel, 1557). The compiler applies to Elizabeth the millennial prophecies of her brother's reign. Four woodcuts in the *Theatre* descend from Dürer's original Revelation series: the Seven-Headed Beast, the Whore of Babylon, the Faithful Man on the White Horse, and Two Angels beholding the New Jerusalem. When William Ponsonby published Spenser's minor poetry in 1591 in order to capitalize on the success of the first volume of *The*

[445]

Faerie Queene, the *Complaints* included revisions of the early translations from Petrarch and du Bellay.

Spenser ignored Sidney's distaste for native literary tradition. For example, the "twelve Aeglogues proportionable to the twelve monethes" in *The Shepheardes Calender* harmonize the imported tradition of neoclassical verse with native diction, forms, and conventions. Spenser dedicated the work to Sidney, who heralded it as the first example of the Elizabethan literary revival. Sidney nevertheless rejects Spenser's style because of its violation of neoclassical canons: "That same framing of his stile to an old rustick language I dare not alowe, sith neyther *Theocritus* in Greeke, *Virgill* in Latine, nor *Sanazar* in Italian did affect it." According to E. K., Spenser's imitation of "our olde Englishe Poetes" has its source in editions of texts popular during the Reformation, such as *The Canterbury Tales* and *Piers Plowman*.[25] The May, July, and September eclogues reshape the antipapal conventions of Reformation satire. In giving the name Piers to the Protestant interlocutor of May, Spenser constructs his character as a variation of the Protestant Plowman whom he would have known through *The Vision of Pierce Plowman* and *The Plowman's Tale*. Piers's fable of the deceitful Fox comes from the tradition of Reformation attacks on the Catholic Fox by Turner, Bale, and Baldwin.

Spenser self-consciously adopted the mantle of the Protestant visionary poet. In *The Shepheardes Calender* he identified himself as the successor to Tityrus (Chaucer, according to E. K.) and "the Pilgrim that the Ploughman playde a whyle." A. C. Hamilton notes that the reference alludes to the climactic vision in *Piers Plowman*, which Crowley

[25] *Essays*, ed. Smith, I, 196; *Shepheardes Calender*, April, l. 19, gloss; see June, l. 81, gloss, and passim.

interpreted as a prophecy of the English Reformation.[26] Judith Anderson asserts, in her revisionist argument, that *Piers Plowman* exerted a direct influence on *The Faerie Queene*, which is discernible in the common "expansion of the personal voice of the poet and the development of characters more fully personal in themselves." She argues that such personalization of characters, ideas, and the role of the poet or narrator transforms English allegory into increasingly subjective and autobiographical forms of poetic expression that anticipate the personal symbolism of Romantic poetry.[27] Yet in the absence of a concrete pattern of unique connections between the texts, Anderson's learned argument rests on thematic and imagistic analogies between the two poems. One need not rely on source-influence argument in order to relate the poems fruitfully. Could it be that Langland and Spenser are linked primarily by a shared pattern of archetypal biblical images and commonplaces? Their common use of Revelation, with its Joachimist commentary tradition, can explain the close parallels between *Piers Plowman* and Spenser's "Legende of Holinesse." The ubiquity of Revelation imagery in explorations of inner consciousness may account for the affinities between Dante's *Commedia* and *Piers Plowman*, which the reformers read anachronistically as crypto-Protestant works, and *The Faerie Queene* and *Pilgrim's Progress*. A shared pattern of biblical imagery enabled readers to interpret *Piers Plowman*, *The Faerie Queene*, and *Paradise Lost* as Protestant apocalypses.

[26] "The Visions of *Piers Plowman* and *The Faerie Queene*," in *Form and Convention in the Poetry of Edmund Spenser*, ed. William Nelson (New York, 1961), p. 3. See *Shepheardes Calender*, February, l. 92, gloss; epilogue; and passim.

[27] *The Growth of a Personal Voice: "Piers Plowman" and "The Faerie Queene"* (New Haven, 1976), pp. 2-4 et seq.

The translations in the *Theatre for Worldlings* fore-shadow Spenser's fully developed apocalyptic vision in Book One of *The Faerie Queene*. His choice of the legend of St. George as the vehicle for the unfolding of Christian virtue announces the nationalistic associations of the tale of the Red Cross Knight. The English Bible is the most impor-tant source for the allegory, as Spenser's Elizabethan ico-nography reduplicates praise of Edward VI as the ideal ruler. The imagery of the quest that leads the knight to his vision of the New Jerusalem and the climactic battle with the dragon, as well as the figures of Una, Duessa, and Archimago, come directly out of Revelation and the tradition of Bale's *Image of Both Churches*.[28] Foxe's *Actes and Monuments* is thus the closest Elizabethan analogue to Spenser's apocalyptic vision.[29]

The recognition of Reformation ideas and imagery in Spenser's works need not reduce the complexity of his art to the intricate historical allegory that the Padelford-Greenlaw school uncritically read into *The Faerie Queene*. Nevertheless, it does help to explain how contemporary readers interpreted Spenser and why the Puritans were so fond of his orthodox poem. John Dixon's 1597 marginalia to the first volume of *The Faerie Queene* show that Tudor readers would recognize Book One's derivation from Rev-elation and interpret the allegory, at least on one level, in terms of the return to Eden after the persecutions of Mary's reign. This unique contemporary commentary wholly ignores Spenser's neoclassicism and imitation of the Ital-ianate epics of Tasso and Ariosto. Equating Gloriana with

---

[28] J. W. Bennett, *The Evolution of "The Faerie Queene"* (Chicago, 1942), chap. 9; J. E. Hankins, *Source and Meaning in Spenser's Allegory: A Study of "The Faerie Queene"* (Oxford, 1971), pp. 205-27.

[29] Frank Kermode, *"The Faerie Queene*, I and V," *Bulletin of the John Rylands Library*, 47 (1964), 123-40.

Queen Elizabeth and Cleopolis with London, Dixon contrasts Una and Duessa as the true church and the false
(*FQ*, I.i.3 and 9; ii.40; x.59; and passim). If the dragon's
defeat by the knight in Canto Eleven represents "Antichristian religion over throwne, and the maintainer their
of Q[ueen] Ma[ry] by death victored" (*FQ*, I.xi.motto),
then Elizabeth's reign marks a return to the apostolic purity of the radical Reformation. Dixon equates the service
of the Red Cross Knight to Gloriana during "six yeares in
warlike wize" with "the time of the raingne of phil[ip]
and marye" (*FQ*, I.xii.18). The gloss on the marriage of
Una and the knight leaves no doubt about Dixon's interpretation of the book as Reformation allegory: "The Church
and the Lambe Christe united by god himselfe. a happy
knotte wherby peace hath beine Continewed 39 yea[res]:
the holy citie ore temple of god are Light with the glory
of god: which is the Lambe" (*FQ*, I.xii.36).[30]

Critics have recognized the survival of Reformation tragic
modes in Elizabethan and Jacobean drama, and recent studies
chart the dramatic influence of Protestant ideas. The *de
casibus* pattern of fortunate rise and tragic fall, with its
central image of Fortune and her wheel, pervades the plays
of Shakespeare and his contemporaries;[31] one may perceive
the providential structuring of such works as *The Mirror
for Magistrates* behind this scheme.[32] Such enigmatic figures as Richard III, Macbeth, Claudius in *Hamlet*, and
Bosola seem to operate as reprobate instruments of divine
judgment, whereas a play like *Doctor Faustus* explores the

[30] *The First Commentary on "The Faerie Queene,"* ed. Graham Hough
(Stansted, 1964).

[31] Willard Farnham, *The Medieval Heritage of Elizabethan Tragedy*
(Berkeley, 1936).

[32] L. B. Campbell, *Shakespeare's "Histories": Mirrors of Elizabethan Policy* (San Marino, Calif., 1947).

enormity of the gulf between God and man and the countervailing possibility of redemption through an act of faith.[33] Yet one need not trace back to Luther and Calvin the dramatic exploration of predestinarian ideas and of the problem of divine justice in a universe that may deny salvation to human beings lacking free will. Such ideas had been domesticated in works of literature and translation that appeared during the mid-Tudor period.

The ideals of gospelling poetry survived into the seventeenth century. Although the low, popular style of Sternhold and Crowley was very old-fashioned by 1600, such poets as John Donne, George Herbert, and Henry Vaughan employed paraphrases and exegetical conceits that reflected the Reformation ideal of the Bible as a layman's book. Herbert's Erasmian advice that the rural parson urge his parishioners to sing psalms at work recommends the use of *The Whole Book of Psalms*. Despite the stylistic and thematic virtuosity with which Herbert elaborates varied states of spiritual turmoil, his poems typically achieve a point of resolution that offers scarcely more than biblical paraphrase. The conclusion of "The Collar," for example, tranquilly dramatizes the consolation in Psalm 102:

> But as I rav'd and grew more fierce and wilde
> At every word,
> Me thoughts I heard one calling, *Child!*
> And I reply'd, *My Lord*.[34]

Similarly Vaughan's poems imitate the scriptural plainness of Herbert's endings.

<hr />

[33] See Sanders, *Dramatist and the Received Idea*; Hunter, *Shakespeare and the Mystery of God's Judgments*; and Roy Battenhouse, *Marlowe's "Tamburlaine": A Study in Renaissance Moral Philosophy* (Nashville, 1941).

[34] Coburn Freer, *Music for a King: George Herbert's Style and the Metrical Psalms* (Baltimore, 1972), pp. 10, 200-201.

The Protestant plain style lived on not only in the prayer book, *Book of Homilies*, and English Bible, but in the prose of Elizabethan and seventeenth-century Puritans. Both the authorized translations (the Bishops' Bible and the King James version), which derive from Tyndale's early Tudor idiom, and the independent Puritan translation in the Geneva Bible employ the *sermo humilis*. The ribald pamphlets of the Martin Marprelate controversy adapted both the stylistic plainness and theological invective of Reformation satire to the 1580s dispute between the Puritans and the bishops. Such pasquinades as Thomas Nashe's *Pierce Penilesse His Supplication to the Divell* (1592) identify lowborn Piers with the anonymous Puritan opposition. By the seventeenth century, however, the Protestant plain style had become consciously artistic in its imitation of archaic biblical diction that had long since passed out of colloquial usage.

Even though the Elizabethan Puritans broke the united Protestant front that existed during Edward VI's reign, they still viewed the monarch as the source of religious reform. Over the passage of time, radical appeals for reform came to be read as attacks on a conservative prelacy rather than as defenses of royal supremacy. Such works as *Philargyrie of Greate Britayne* contained the seeds of this shift. Through the martyrology that Foxe derived from Bale's *Brefe Chronycle*, Sir John Oldcastle emerged as a Puritan hero. Anthony Munday's *Sir John Oldcastle* (1599) comes out of this tradition of Reformation apologetics. During the religious crisis at the end of Elizabeth's reign, Shakespeare drew the figure of Sir John Falstaff out of the alternative tradition that identified Oldcastle as an outlaw and robber, which appeared in Holinshed's *Chronicles*. It is possible that the affront that Shakespeare directed toward the Puritans through Falstaff—the "Reverend Vice"—

stemmed from Foxe's version of Oldcastle's confession to the youthful sins of pride, gluttony, lechery, and avarice.[35] When in 1613 Andrew Bostock attacked Crowley's interpretation of *Piers Plowman*, he linked Oldcastle and Wyclif as members of "a sect of Rebe[ls] . . . against the Soviraign" (above, Chapter 7, n. 20).

When James VI of Scotland wrote Βασιλικόν Δῶρον (Edinburgh, 1599), few Englishmen questioned royalist assumptions dating back to the Reformation. Longstanding tradition contends that at the Hampton Court Conference he, as James I of England, denounced the moderate Puritans and warned them that if they did not conform he would "harry them out of the land." According to this view, the Puritans distrusted the monarch as an agent of reform after 1604. In actual fact, the king endorsed many Puritan reforms that originated in the Reformation platform of the Edwardian gospellers. Despite their continued faith in the monarchy, by 1614 the Puritans had broken with the bishops, whom they now identified with Antichrist, because of their embitterment over episcopal failure to enact reforms promised by the king.[36] The image of the godly prince, as established under Edward VI, nonetheless appears in Puritan panegyrics throughout James's reign. Michael Drayton praised the king's religious zeal in *To the Majestie of King James. A Gratulatorie Poem* (1603). Joshua Sylvester dedicated his translation of du Bartas's *Devine Weekes & Workes* (1605) to James as the ideal Christian king and poet. On the model of du Bartas, the king had already assumed the role of Davidic singer in his own ver-

---

[35] L. M. Oliver, "Sir John Oldcastle: Legend or Literature?" *Library*, 5th ser., 1 (1947), 179-83; see Bevington, *Drama and Politics*, pp. 256-57.

[36] William M. Lamont, *Godly Rule: Politics and Religion 1603-60* (1969), pp. 28-31, 46, 48; see Christopher Hill, *Antichrist in Seventeenth-Century England* (Oxford, 1971), chap. 2.

sification of the Psalms. Pietistic royal iconography survived into the reign of Charles I in George Wither's dedication of *A Collection of Emblemes* (1635), as well as via particular emblems (see Book I, Illustration 32).

Puritan agitators could read their own minds in Reformation texts. For example, the copy of *Rhithmi vetustissimi* at the Bodleian Library contains an English translation of Bale's preface and *Apocalypsis Goliae*. Attracted by the potential of the work as satire against the bishops, the Puritan translator prepared his manuscript for publication and inscribed the title page: "Anno domini 1546 nunc autem de nuvo [novo] impressi in usum ecclesiae Dei. 1623."[37] The copy lacks casting-off marks, however, and the absence of any extant text or record of publication suggests that it was never reissued.

Protestant radicals had reversed their traditional support of the monarchy by the middle of the seventeenth century. Because of the High-Church policies of Charles I and Archbishop Laud, as well as the imposition of external authority upon ministers and congregations, Puritan opposition to the king became widespread by the late 1630s. John Ponet's *Shorte Treatise of Politike Power* (Strasbourg, 1556) was first reprinted in 1639 (Paris?) on the eve of the English Civil War as a Puritan argument against the monarchy. When John Milton wrote *Of Reformation* (1641), his first antiprelatical tract, he severed the earthly kingdom from the reign of Christ the King. Still the holder of millennial expectations, he argues that reform is impossible until the eradication of monarchal government

> . . . at that day when thou the Eternall and shortly-expected King shalt open the Clouds to judge the severall Kingdomes of the World, and . . . put an end to

[37] "1546, now printed again in service to the church of God. 1623" (MS Bodl. 538).

all Earthly *Tyrannies*, proclaiming thy universal and milde *Monarchy* through Heaven and Earth.[38]

Milton and other Puritans supported regicide in 1649. When Ponet advocated tyrannicide, few reformers followed his carefully qualified advocacy of disobedience to the evil prince. Opinion had shifted by the time John Gauden, Bishop of Exeter, issued Ε'ικὼν Βασιλικὴ. *The Pourtraicture of His Sacred Majestie* (1648) in the name of Charles I. When Milton answered these forged words of the "royal martyr," his Ε'ικονοκλάστης *in Answer to* Ε'ικὼν Βασιλικὴ (1649) articulated as formal Parliamentary policy a position much more radical than that of Ponet. Particular doctrinal demands of the revolutionary Puritans differed little, in principle, from the program of religious reform that Cranmer and Seymour had instituted under Edward VI. But during the century following Edward's reign, the godly king had become the royal Antichrist in the eyes of Protestant radicals.

After a process of growing disillusionment during the Commonwealth, Milton's millennial expectations were dashed forever by the restoration of the monarchy in 1660. As he completed *Paradise Lost*, he repeatedly contrasted the kingdom of heaven with the monarchy of this world. The Reformation opposition between king and pope had evolved into conflict between God and king. The reader initially meets Satan as a rebel against "the throne and monarchy of God" (I.42), who attempts to substitute demonic government for divine majesty. During the Restoration defeated Puritans could apply Belial's depravity to the court of Charles II:

[38] *Complete Prose Works*, ed. D. M. Wolfe et al. (New Haven, 1953- ; 8 vols.), I, 616.

> In courts and palaces he also reigns
> And in luxurious cities, where the noise
> Of riot ascends above their loftiest towers,
> And injury and outrage: and when night
> Darkens the streets, then wander forth the sons
> Of Belial, flown with insolence and wine.
>
> (I.497-502)

In *Paradise Regained*, the same allusion offers a similar possibility for satirical application:

> Have we not seen, or by relation heard,
> In courts and regal chambers how thou lurk'st . . . ?
>
> (II.182-83)

Milton's position is not simply post-Restoration—as early as the 1630s he linked the licentiousness of the revelers in *Comus* with the libertinism of Cavalier courtiers.

Paradise Lost offers a clear example of the survival of Reformation themes and conventions in later literary tradition. Although Milton inverts early English Protestant iconography, with its emphasis on royalist panegyric, he integrates the ideas and program of the Tudor gospellers into the epic. Reference to "good Josiah" contradicts the royal epithets that Milton consistently attaches to Satan and the devils; however, he divorces the godly king from temporal kingship.[39] The tragic pattern of the epic comes from the Bible and the Reformation tradition of *de casibus* tragedy. So also the "comedic" possibilities of original sin and life in the fallen world incorporate the Edwardian tension between permission and control, freedom of the will and predestination. The individual problems and dilemmas of Reformation epistemology underlie Milton's thought. The

[39] I.418; see I.261, 315, 342, 348, 359-60, 392, 694, 720-21, 735, 792; II.4, 43, 296, 467, 510, 673.

apocalyptic vision of *Paradise Lost* corresponds to that of John Bale. Milton's reader differs little from his Edwardian forebears as he contemplates the fall of man and expulsion from Eden. Protestant faith never offers certainty, yet it extends almost infinite possibilities as Adam and Eve leave Paradise:

> The world was all before them, where to choose
> Their place of rest, and providence their guide:
> They hand in hand with wandering steps and slow,
> Through Eden took their solitary way.
>
> (XII.646-49)

Appendix I: Reformation Manuscript Dedications

B.L. MSS Royal

20 A. XIV.   Belmaine, Jean,[1] trans., "Le Livre des
Prières Ecclésiastiques, et adminis-
tration des sacramens, et autres Ceri-
monies et façon de faire dont on use
en l'Église d'Angleterre," 1553. The
prayer book in French.

2 D. III.   Brionaeus, Martin,[2] trans., "Ecclesiastes, et Cantica Canticorum Salo-
monis Elegiaco Carmine," n.d.

8 B. VII.   Bucer, Martin,[3] "De Regno Christi,"
1550. New Year gift.

12 D. V.   Colas, Hiérome,[4] "De Republica Nec-
non de prima humanae societatis,"
1548. Dedicated to Cranmer, with
Latin verses addressed to Edward VI.

7 D. XX.   Deleen, Wouter,[5] Lectures on Genesis 1-
3, in Latin, c. 1550. New Year gift.

12 A. VII.   Denisot, Nicholas,[6] "Carmina ad Edwardi Regis," 1547. Latin verses on
the death of Henry VIII and accession of Edward VI.

[1] The king's French tutor.

[2] The author of *Totius terrae sanctae descriptio* (Paris, 1540).

[3] Regius Professor of Divinity, Cambridge University (1549-51).

[4] French tutor to the children of Thomas Wriothesley, first Earl of
Southampton.

[5] A native of Brabant attached to the royal household, who was appointed
a minister of the Dutch Church in London in 1550.

[6] French tutor to the daughters of Edward Seymour.

17 D. III.	Forrest, William,[7] "The Pleasaunt Poesye of Princelie Practise," 1548. Addressed to Edward VI; dedicated to Edward Seymour. With a portrait of Forrest giving his volume to the king.
17 B. XL.	Gerrard, Philip,[8] "An exhortation unto kyng edward the sixt for the reformation of rentes with yn all hys realmes & dominions," c. 1553.
17 C. VII.	Hart, John,[9] "The unreasonable writing of our inglish toung," 1551.
17 A. XXXIII.	Holinshed, Ottuell,[10] "On the ringdiall," 1553. New Year gift.
16 E. IV.	Julien, Jerosme,[11] "Les Estrenes du conforte despoir présentées," 1552. French verses as New Year gift.
16 E. XXXII.	Le Roy, Louis,[12] trans., "Deux Livres d'Isocrathes,"[13] 1550. With illuminated royal arms.
12 A. LIV.	Olivarus, Petrus,[14] "Ratio Legendae Historiae," n.d.
15 C. I.	———, Topographical indices to *Trogus Pompeius* and the *Epistles* of Cicero, 1546.[15] New Year gift to the Prince of Wales.

[7] An Erastian Catholic priest and court poet, later chaplain to Queen Mary.

[8] Yeoman of the Privy Chamber. Gerrard dedicated *A Godly Invective in the Defence of the Gospell* (1547) to Edward VI.

[9] Orthographic reformer and member of the College of Arms.

[10] Fellow of Trinity College, Cambridge.

[11] A native of Argenten in Normandy.

[12] Later Professor of Greek at the Collège Royal.

[13] Printed in Paris, with different dedications, in 1551 and 1568.

[14] A native of Valencia and editor of Pomponius Mela, *De situ orbis, libri tres* (Paris, 1536).

[15] Dated "ex museo nostro Londonensi."

16 E. XXIII.	Ploych, Pierre du,[16] "Petit recueil des homaiges, honneurs, et recognoissances deubs par les hommes à Dieu le créateur," c. 1550-53.
16 E. XXXVII.	————, "Petit recueil très utile et très nécessaire, De l'éstat des princes," c. 1550. New Year gift.
17 C. X.	Thomas, William,[17] trans., "Voiages to Tana and Persia" by Giosafat Barbaro, c. 1550.
17 B. XXXV.	Anon., Treatise on Evils of the Realm, c. 1547-50.[18]

PRINCESS ELIZABETH

16 E. I.	Belmaine, Jean, trans., "L'Epistle de Basile le grand à S. Gregoire théologien de la vie solitaire," 1547.

PRINCESS MARY

13 B. X.	Morren, John,[19] trans., "Martyrologii et Menologii ex graece,"[20] c. 1547-53.
18 A. LX.	Parker, Henry,[21] trans., "The dreme of Sypyon [Scipio] taken owt of the syxte boke of Cicero Intytled de Republyca,"[22] c. 1547-53.

[16] A teacher of French, resident at St. Bernard's College, Oxford, later refounded as St. John's College.

[17] Clerk of the Privy Council.

[18] Possibly addressed to Henry VIII.

[19] Member of Corpus Christi College, Oxford.

[20] A translation of Corpus Christi College Library MS CXL.

[21] Tenth Baron Morley.

[22] One of a series of New Year gifts addressed to the princess under Henry VIII (see MSS Royal 17 A. XLVI, 17 A. XXX, 17 C. XII, 17 C. XVI, 18 A. XV, and 18 A. LX).

Appendix I

Edward Seymour

B.L. MS Add. 9000.	Edward VI, "Recueil des principales places de la sainte Escriture, qui traitent de foy en Dieu nostre père, et créateur. Traduites d'Angloys en Françoys." 12 December 1548. Entirely in the king's hand. The first two leaves of "A lencontre les abus du monde" (B.L. MS Add. 5464) contain an unfinished portion of the dedication and preface to MS Add. 9000. 13 December 1548-14 March 1549. This attack against the papacy and idolatry is entirely in the king's hand.
MS Royal 17 A. XXI.	Forrest, William, "Certaigne Psalmes of Davyd in meeatre added to maister Sterneholdis and oothers," 1551.
MS Royal 17 D. III.	———, "The Pleasaunt Poesye of Princelie Practise," 1548. Dedicated to Seymour; addressed to Edward VI.
MS Royal 18 B. XXVII.	Gibson, William,[23] trans., "A boke of the authoritie and an absolute perfection of the holy scripture by henry Bullinger,"[24] c. 1548-50.
B.L. MS Sloane 1207	Gray, William, New Year gift in verse (fols. 7^r-8^v), c. 1547-52.
C.U.L. MS Dd. 9. 31.	———, New Year gift in verse, c. 1547-52.
MS Royal 17 C.V.	Martyr, Peter,[25] "Of the sacramente of Thankesgeving," 1548. Compiled from various works and translated.

[23] Master of Sherborne School in Dorset.

[24] A translation of book one of *De Scripturae sanctae aucthoritate* (Zurich, 1538).

[25] Regius Professor of Divinity, Oxford University, 1548-53.

Appendix I

MS Royal 17 D. XIII.	Parker, Henry, Commentary on Ecclesiastes, c. 1547-50.
MS Royal 17 C. IX.	Philpot, John,[26] trans., "An oration of Coelius the second Curio [the Basel reformer] for the trew and auncyent authoritie of Christ his churche," c. 1550-51.
Goldsmiths' Library (University of London) MS No. 10	Anon., "Policies to Reduce this Realme of Englande unto a Prosperus Wealthe and Estate," 1549.

Anne Stanhope, Duchess of Somerset

MS Royal 17 B. XVIII.	Cecil, Mildred, trans., "An Homilie or Sermon of Basile the great," c. 1548.
C.U.L. MS Nn. 4.43	Courtney, Edward,[27] trans., "A Treatice most profitable of the benefitt that true christianes receyve by the deathe of JESUS CHRISTE"[28] by Aonio Paleario, 1548.
MS Royal 17 A. VI.	Hamonde, Christopher,[29] Scriptural Sentences and Devotions, c. 1547-52.

[26] Archdeacon of Winchester and member of the royal household.

[27] Earl of Devonshire (c. 1526-56). Imprisoned in the Tower of London (November 1538-3 August 1553) along with his father Henry, who was executed in 1538 for plotting the death of Henry VIII. As grandson and great-grandson of Edward IV, the Courtneys had a claim to the throne. This dedication manuscript represents a gesture of conciliation to Edward VI and his regime. The king's marginalia show that he read the document.

[28] A translation of *Trattato utillissimo del benefacio di Giesu Christo crocofisso* (Venice, 1543), a Protestant tract banned in Italy.

[29] Student at the Inner Temple.

Appendix II: Reformation Woodcuts

Despite the general decadence of book illustration in Tudor England, woodcuts played a major role in works issued by Protestant scholar-publishers such as John Bale, Robert Crowley, John Day, and Walter Lynne. Many of their illustrations were tailor-made to fit particular publications. Thus they broke with the practice of using conventional woodcuts which had prevailed since Caxton's time. Prior to Edward's reign wood blocks were rarely cut to order, and they were used repeatedly in order to print gratuitous illustrations that bore little relationship to text. They tended to be small (usually no more than three or four inches square) and to lack fine detail, crosshatching, and shading. Many of Caxton's blocks were carved in the Low Countries. De Worde inherited those blocks and used them throughout his career. Although Pynson introduced a few Holbein woodcuts, for the most part he relied on the originals and copies of Caxton cuts. Moving freely between London printing shops, wood blocks were worn down over the passage of time. Hodnett limits his census to texts printed before 1535 because de Worde and Pynson had ceased operations by that date. Few new blocks were made after their deaths, and the 1535 ban on old religious pictures made most blocks useless (Hodnett, p. vi). After 1535, Berthelet as King's Printer included no woodcuts in his books.

The Reformation revival of woodcut art owes its impetus to Continental craftsmen. Dutch artisans cut the blocks for *Summarium* that Bale brought back to England (Figures 5-7). When Stephen Mierdman emigrated from Antwerp to London c. 1548-49, he brought with him wood blocks designed for the 1535 Coverdale Bible and his own edition of *Het Nieuwe Testament* (1545). The latter illustrations derive from the Bible cuts used by the Antwerp printers Vosterman, Liesveldt, and Mierdman's master Crom. Mierdman's Revelation illustrations descend from the series Cranach designed for Luther's New Testament. German and Dutch woodcut tradition reflects the Protestant movement away from the sensational devotional images of the late Middle Ages. Protestant Bible illustrations stress the preaching of Christ the man and the transmission of the Word by the evangelists and apostles. Mierdman used his woodcuts in editions of Bale's *Image* printed in Antwerp and London. Day's 1548 New Testament and 1549 folio Bible that Mierdman printed for Day and Seres contain cuts from the Coverdale Bible and Dutch New Testament (see Figures 9-10). The fine, large woodcuts for Psalms and Isaiah come from the 1537 Matthew Bible that Crom printed in Antwerp for Grafton and Whitchurch. Mierdman's illustrations for the Jugge New Testaments are from the same sources.

Holbein's influence survives in the reuse of the title-page border from the 1535 Coverdale Bible (Figure 2) in the 1549 Matthew version printed by T. Raynalde and W. Hill. Lynne uses at least three Holbein blocks in his publications. Cranmer's *Catechism* contains two woodcuts bearing Holbein's name or initials (T6^r, 2D1^r). Lynne's translation of Urbanus Regius' *Lytle Treatise* (Mierdman, 1548) carries another. In *Holbein and Henry VIII*, Roy Strong suggests that Holbein designed a series of woodcuts during the 1530s for an antipapal text that never appeared (pp. 16-17; plates 12-14). Mierdman could have imported them with the printing stock that he brought from Antwerp.

Reformation publishers commissioned excellent examples of Tudor woodcut art. They include very large illustrations that employ fine detail, shading, and crosshatching. Crowley must have ordered the title-page woodcut for *Philargyrie of Greate Britayne* (Figure 14) and the musical score for his *Psalter*. A large illustration of the Holy Spirit overthrowing the pope and monastic orders (Figure 11) appears in Lynne's *Beginning and Endynge of All Popery* and his amended edition of Ochino's *Tragoedie*. As publisher of those texts, Lynne must have commissioned and retained the block. John Day possessed the fine initial capital E from the 1551 Becke Bible (Figure 15) and the illustration of Anne Askew's execution from Crowley's *Confutation of Nicolas Shaxton* (Figure 8). He must have retained them during Mary's reign, for he reused the same blocks in Foxe's *Actes and Monuments* (1563).

Appendix III: The Scottish Propaganda Campaign

Seymour and his two secretaries, Cecil and Smith, directed a propaganda campaign in favor of Edward VI's claim to the Scottish throne that was more coherently organized than any similar effort prior to the 1570s. Grafton printed all of their English texts. Geoffrey of Monmouth's legendary history of the origin of England and Scotland as a united kingdom provided their major source of arguments. James Harrison enunciated Edward's alleged rights in *An Exhortacion to the Scotts* immediately before Seymour invaded Scotland on 4 September 1547; he served Seymour as a spy in Scotland and wrote the work for payment at the order of the Privy Council.[1] Harrison deliberately lies in addressing his Scots audience as disinterested fellow countrymen (F5ʳ). His major argumentative device is the massing of such "indifferent" authorities as Caesar's *Commentaries*, Tacitus's *Agricola*, Bede's *Historia ecclesiastica gentis Anglorum*, and Gildas's *De excidio et conquestu Britanniae* (B6ᵛ). He fabricates these sources, however, in order to conceal his exclusive reliance on Geoffrey. Harrison counters the mythical history of the Stuart dynasty found in the first book of Hector Boethius's *Scotorum historiae* (Paris, 1526). Boethius follows the fourteenth-century *Chronica Gentis Scotorum* of John of Fordun in tracing the Scottish dynasty back to Gathelus, an Athenian prince, and Scota, daughter

---

[1] *Acts*, ed. Dasent, II, 22-23; *Calendar of State Papers, Scotland*, ed. M. J. Thorpe (1858; 2 vols.), I, 64.

of the Pharaoh of the Exodus and eponymous founder of Scotland (2A3^v-4^r). No small irony underlies Harrison's use of one fabrication to counter another (E4^{r-v}).

Written in haste by William Patten, the first English tract to follow the Battle of Pinkie (10 September 1547) was *The Expedicion into Scotlande of Edward, Duke of Soomerset* (30 June 1548; with a dedication to Paget). Appointed to the Marshalsea Tribunal along with Cecil during the invasion, Patten credits his companion with a role in shaping his account:

> Mary, since my cumming home indede, his gentilnes being such as too communicate his notes with me (I have I confes) bene thearby, bothe much a certeyned in many thinges I douted, and sumwhat remembred of that, which els I mought hap to have forgotten. (P5^r)

In contrast to Harrison's *Exhortacion*, Patten's choice of journal format limits description to strict chronological sequence. His separation of factual description of the expedition from the chauvinistic analysis of his preface represents a new departure in Renaissance historiography.[2] Patten interprets the invasion as a skirmish in the general Reformation battle against the papacy. Allusion to Virgil's famous epithet "parcere subiectis et debellare superbos" (*Aeneid* VI. 853) lends Seymour the millennial trappings of the just imperial ruler who is stern in victory and magnanimous in peace. In the context of tag lines from biblical prophecies, Seymour becomes an agent of divine punishment against the Roman Antichrist represented by the Guise faction controlling Scotland (B7^{r-v}).

Richard Grafton published *Epistle or Exhortacion to Un-*

---

[2] W. R. Trimble, "Early Tudor Historiography, 1485-1548," *JHI*, 11 (1950), 39-40.

itie and Peace (5 February 1548) under Seymour's name within one week of Patten's *Expedicion*. An attribution in a manuscript by Thomas Martin plausibly ascribes composition to Thomas Smith.[3] As his major argumentative device, Seymour adopts a fraternal stance in urging the Scots to "have us rather as brothers, than enemies, rather countreymenne, than conquerors" (A6ᵛ-7ʳ). Perhaps he arranged for publication so soon after Patten's threatening discourse in order to pose as a man of peace after the recent warfare. Certainly Foxe offers such an interpretation when he calls Seymour "a man of nature singularly given to peace" (*A & M*, V, 297). Smith's Latin translation, *Epistola exhortatoria ad pacem* (5 March 1548), justified English territorial claims to a Continental audience.

After the departure for France of Mary, Queen of Scots, Seymour abandoned his plans for a royal marriage alliance by returning to the medieval dynastic argument. A genealogy tracing Edward's descent back to Brutus (MS Royal 18 A. LXXV) appears to have been the initial fruit of a 1548 commission to research the Scottish claim.[4] A collection of precedents by John Mason followed in 1549 (B.L. MS Add. 6128). *An Epitome of the Title that the Kynges Majestie of Englande hath to the Sovereigntie of Scotlande* (1548) was the published result of the 1548 commission. Although internal evidence ascribes the text to "Nicholas Bodrugan otherwise Adams" (A2ʳ), Thomas Smith undoubtedly wrote it. The French Ambassador states that Smith headed Seymour's genealogical commission.[5] The ascrip-

[3] As cited in *Athen. Cantab.*, I, 373.

[4] *Acts*, ed. Dasent, II, 225.

[5] *Correspondence politique de Odet de Selve 1546-1549*, ed. Lefevre-Pontalis (Paris, 1888), p. 461, as quoted in Mary Dewar, *Sir Thomas Smith: A Tudor Intellectual in Office* (1964), p. 48. Dewar establishes Smith's authorship without question.

tion may represent an attempt like that of Harrison to disguise Seymour sponsorship.

The *Epitome*'s dedication to Edward VI includes the protector in its general praise of the Seymours who, in the manner of the Tudor dynasty, receive a spurious British genealogy going back to an Eldulph de Samour who slew Hengest and defeated Saxon tyranny at the time of Aurelie Ambrose. Renouncing partisan English sources, the author acknowledges reliance on "indifferent" sources including the Scottish authorities Veremund, Camphil, Cornelius de Hibernia, and Hector Boethius (A3^r-4^r). Although Boethius cites the first three writers in *Scotorum historiae*, he filled a gap of over 700 years in John of Fordun's chronicle with invented speeches and fictional detail. None of his sources survives. Although they could all conceivably have been lost, he probably invented them on the analogy of Geoffrey of Monmouth's "vetustissimus liber." One may conjecture that the author of *Epitome* accepted Boethius's authorities in the spirit in which they were offered. Despite his citation, the author of *Epitome* draws the bulk of his material without acknowledgment from Geoffrey. Distorting Boethius at will, he rejects any discrepancies between the *Scotorum historiae* and Geoffrey's *Historia* in the latter's favor. For example, he substitutes eponymous foundation of Scotland by the Scythians for Boethius's derivation from Scota (compare *Epitome*, b3^r, b6^r, with *Scotorum historiae*, 2A3^v-4^r). Similarly, *The Complaynt of Scotland* (Paris, c. 1550), an anonymous Scottish reply, counters the Tudor claims by inventing an alternative line of descent from the Saxon usurpers, Hengest and Sergest.

Appendix IV: The First English Metrical Psalter

Robert Crowley compiled the first complete metrical psalter in English, in part to recover the lyricism of biblical song. By the end of the Middle Ages, the Psalms were chanted in prose because their original status as Hebrew song had been forgotten. Many Protestants opposed all use of poetry or song in church services because they were thought to lack scriptural authority. To an educated scholar like Crowley, however, no prose rendering could approximate the original. In addition to its accuracy, Crowley chose the *Biblia Sacrosancta* as his source because Leo Jud returned the hymns attributed to King David to verse form. Although Jud's Psalms are nonmetrical, his extremely elegant, line-by-line translation imitates the long lines of Hebrew verse. Bullinger insisted on the lyrical nature of the Psalms in his preface to the Jud Bible. Like his Lutheran predecessors, he contrasts the Psalms to secular poetry in an attempt to substitute divine song for profane lyrics: "The wisdom of God that drew together all disciplines wished both to touch on music and to treat it purely if perchance it could draw men away from music that was more impure and clearly lascivious."[1] Jud's commentary converts the Erasmian principles of *Paraclesis* into a Reformation defense of the Bible as literature. Although they deal primarily with the literal sense, his glosses point out

---

[1] "Voluit autem sapientia dei quae omnes disciplinas perstrinxit & musicam attingere, pureque tractare, si forte a musica impuriore ac plane lascivia homines abstrahere posset" (β4ᵛ).

such rhetorical word-schemes as *zeugma, apostrophe, paronomasia, synechdoche, antonomasia,* and *sarcasmos* (Psalms 4:2, 9:6, 9:18, 12:8, 21:7, 56:8, and 66:1).

Crowley made his translation with the *Biblia Sacrosancta* open before him. He omitted nothing from his original and never knowingly changed its meaning. In imitation of Cranmer's purpose of making "open and playne" that which other translations have left "obscure and harde," he substitutes the flattened style of the *sermo humilis* for the heightened eloquence of his source. He sometimes clarifies his meaning by incorporating one of Jud's marginal glosses into the translation. For example, Crowley draws the note "Et semen eius ad benedictionem" into his translation of "posteri eius opime habent": ". . . his seede and posteritie, have of al thynges theyr fyll" (Psalm 37:28). He usually translates each of Jud's long lines into one fourteener couplet, which is a compressed stanza containing in each line the alternating four-beat and three-beat lines of ballad measure. Crowley's four-beat phrases are always direct and sometimes eloquent, but he tends to pad the three-beat phrases in order to fill his lines and obtain rhymes. Thus he translates "Voce mea ad DOMINUM clamabo, & respondebit mihi de monte sancto suo" (Psalm 3:4) with the following couplet:

And with my voyce upon the Lorde, I wil both call and
   crye:
And he oute of hys holy hyll, wyll heare me by and by.

Elsewhere he translates "Corrosa est facies mea prae indignatione, atquae vetusta facta est propter omnes hostes meos" (Psalm 6:7) as

My face is wrynckled throughe anger, & indignacyon:
And it is made exceadinge olde, throughe myne enemyes
   eche one.

Psalm 23:2 exemplifies the superiority of the *Psalter* to other English translations. Although the Great Bible reads "in a grene pasture," Crowley's "in pasture full of grasse" follows the more accurate rendering of the *Biblia Sacrosancta*: "in pascuis herbidis."

Crowley designed the *Psalter* as a companion to the *Book of Common Prayer*. His perpetual calendar for determining the dates of movable feasts (✠1ᵛ) imitates the prayer book calendar. Even though *The Whole Book of Psalms* (1562) by Sternhold and Hopkins eventually followed the prose psalter in editions of the prayer book, it is less skillfully adapted to the Anglican liturgy. Crowley includes translations of the six *Cantica Prophetarium* from the Sarum psalter that Cranmer retained in the prayer book: *Te Deum, Benedictus, Magnificat, Nunc Dimittis, Quicunque Vult,* and *Benedicite.* Because of their ancient place in the liturgy, these biblical lyrics found their way into many later Protestant songbooks. The last canticle in particular documents the cautious conservatism of Cranmer's liturgy. Because it comes from the Vulgate text for Daniel 3:57-88 and lacks support from Hebrew sources, Protestant Bible translations excluded the text.

Crowley supplements the *Biblia Sacrosancta* with the Great Bible and the prayer book when he versifies *Benedictus, Magnificat, and Nunc Dimittis.* His eclectic gathering is governed as much by metrical as by scholarly considerations. In the canticles he more casually alters wording, omits phraseology, and introduces line fillers and doublets in order to find rhymes. His greater freedom may be inherent in the inaccuracy of his sources, which ignore the metrical nature of the songs from the Greek New Testament. *Benedicite* illustrates some of the drawbacks of ballad translation. Crowley's greater license in versifying the prayer book translation from the Sarum psalter may spring from the text's lack of canonical authority. His struggle to find

sixteen different rhymes (saye, aye; nede, dede; styll, wyll;
hye, eternally; ever, maner; name, same; more, lore; store,
evermore; Lorde, accorde; ye, be; aye, alwaye; evermore,
lore; alwaye, staye; Misael, Israell) forces him to sacrifice
the cumulative rhetorical power of the Latin refrain: "lau-
date et superexaltate eum in saecula." Although he conflates
the Sarum psalter with the prayer book in translating the
Te Deum and *Quicunque Vult*, he often passes over Cranmer's liturgy in order to follow the Latin original. Exclusive reliance on the Sarum text may account for the relative
success of Crowley's *Te Deum*. But *Quicunque Vult* is a
signal failure. Crowley's fourteener couplets collapse under
the weight of the Trinitarian dogma of the Athanasian Creed:

> Whoso wyl be saved muste kepe before all other thynge:
> The Catholyke & commune fayth that of the trueth doeth
> sprynge.
> Which fayth unlesse a man do kepe whole and undefiled:
> No doubt he shall for ever more perishe and be dampned.
> And the fayth catholycke is this, that we worshippe truly:
> One God in three persons & the same three in unitie.
> And that neither confoundynge the persons makynge them
> one:
> Nor yet dividyng the substaunce that is but one alone.
> For the father and sonne are two distynct persons in
> dede:
> And from them boeth the holy goste is also divided.
> Yet of these three persons ther is but one divinitie:
> Equale glorie & in lyke sorte eternal majestie. . . .

Appendix V: Robert Crowley: A Bibliography

A. GENUINE WORKS

1548   *The Confutation of the Mishapen Aunswer to the Bal-*
lade, called the Abuse of the blessed sacrament, Day
and Seres (*STC* 6082). Quotes Miles Hogarde's
"The Abuse of the Sacrament of the Aultare."

The Confutation of the .XIII. Articles, whereunto Ni-
colas Shaxton subscribed, Day and Seres (*STC*
6083). Illustrated.

An Informacion and Peticion agaynst the Oppressours of
the Pore Commons, Day (*STC* 6086 and 6086.5).

c. 1548   *Explicatio petitoria, aduersus expilatores.* Trans. J.
Heron. Mierdman (*STC* 6085). A Latin trans-
lation of the above work.

1549   *The Psalter of David newely translated into Englysh metre,*
Grafton and Mierdman for Crowley (*STC* 2725).
In verse. Dedicated to Owen Oglethorpe. Con-
tains music.

A New Yeres Gyfte, wherein is taught the knowledge of
our selfe and the feare of God, Grafton for Crowley (*STC* 6087). In verse.

The Voyce of the Laste Trumpet blowen bi the seventh
angel wherin are contayned xii. lessons to twelve
several estates of menne, Grafton for Crowley (*STC*
6094). In verse.

1550   *One and Thyrtye Epigrammes, wherein are bryefly touched*
so many abuses, Grafton for Crowley (*STC* 6088
and 6088.3). In verse.

The Voyce of the Laste Trumpet . . . , Grafton for
Crowley (*STC* 6095). In verse.

[473]

The Way to Wealth, wherein is taught a remedy for sedicion, Mierdman for Crowley (*STC* 6096).

c. 1550 *Pyers Plowmans Exhortation, unto the lordes, knightes and burgoysses of the Parlyamenthouse*, Scoloker (*STC* 19905). Attributed to Crowley by Barbara Johnson.

1551 *Philargyrie of Greate Britayne*, Grafton for Crowley (*STC* 6089.5). In verse. Illustrated. Although it was printed anonymously, John Bale attributes this work to Crowley in *Catalogus*, I, 728.

Pleasure and Payne, Heaven and Hell, Grafton for Crowley (*STC* 6090). In verse.

1566 *An Apologie, or Defence, of those Englishe writers which Cerberus chargeth wyth false doctrine*, Denham for Bynneman (*STC* 6076 and 6077). A Puritan tract.

A Briefe Discourse against the outwarde apparell of the popishe church, Denham? (*STC* 6078). Issuing it anonymously, Denham was fined for printing the edition (Arber, I, 316). A second edition (*STC* 6079) was printed in Emden.

1567 *The Opening of the Wordes of the Prophet Joell, in his second and third chapters*, Bynneman for Charlewood (*STC* 6089). Crowley wrote this in 1546.

1569 *A Setting Open of the Subtyle Sophistrie of T. Watson*, Denham (*STC* 6093). A reply to the 1553 Lenten sermons that Watson preached before Queen Mary.

1573 *33 Epigrams, verye notably describing the abuses of our tyme*, J. Awdeley (*STC* 6088.7). In verse.

1575 *A Sermon Made in the Chappel at the Gylde Halle in London*, J. Awdeley (*STC* 6092). The election day sermon before the Lord Mayor and aldermen of the City of London.

1578 *A Briefe Discourse against . . . Apparell* (*STC* 6080).

1581 *An Aunswer to Six Reasons, that T. Pownde required*

to be *aunswered*, Charlewood (*STC* 6075 and 6075.5). One of Crowley's anti-Roman Catholic prison disputations.

A Breefe Discourse, concerning those foure usuall notes, whereby Christes catholique church is knowne, Charlewood (*STC* 6081).

1586 *Fryer John Frauncis of Nigeon in Fraunce*, Charlewood (*STC* 6091). An anti-Roman Catholic polemic.

1588 *A Deliberat Answere Made to a Rash Offer, which a popish catholique, made to a learned protestant*, Charlewood for Woodcock (*STC* 6084).

B. DUBIOUS WORKS

1546 *A Supplication of the Poor Commons* (*STC* 23435.5; reprinted in 10884). Attributed to Crowley and Brinkelow by W. Carew Hazlitt, *Collections and Notes* (1876), V, 155.

c. 1547 *Dialogue between Lent and liberty*, Day? (*STC* 6084.5). Although attributed to Crowley less than ten years after his death in Maunsell's *Catalogue* (p. 41), the fragment is unlike his other works in both style and content. If Crowley did not write this, he may have translated, edited, or imprinted it.

C. EDITIONS

c. 1547 William Tyndale, *The Supper of the Lorde after the true meanyng of the sixte of Johnn*, Day? (*STC* 24469-24471). Although dated 1533, these editions are evidently from the mid-century and contain an epistle signed by Crowley.

1550 *The Vision of Pierce Plowman*, Grafton for Crowley (*STC* 19906-19907a). Attributed to William Langland.

John Wyclif, *The True Copye of a Prolog wrytten about two C. yeres paste by J. Wycklife*, Grafton for Crowley (*STC* 25588).

1559   Thomas Lanquet, *An Epitome of Cronicles . . . continued to the reigne of Quene Elizabeth, by Robert Crowley*, Seres and Marshe (*STC* 15217.5).

1582   Francis Seager, *The Schoole of Vertue, and booke of good nourture for chyldren, and youth to learne theyr dutie by*, Denham (*STC* 22136). Crowley added a preface in acrostic verse and "certaine praiers and graces" in meter.

D. IMPRINTS

1550   Peter Pickering, *A Myroure or Glasse for all Spiritual Ministers* (*STC* 19897.3).

William Salisbury (or Salesbury), *Ban Wedy I Dynny Air. . . . A certaine case extracte out of the auncient law of Hoel da, kyng of Wales whereby it maye gathered* [sic] *that priestes had lawfully maried wyves at that tyme*, Grafton for Crowley (*STC* 21612). The Protestant printer Edward Whitchurch also printed early Welsh texts.

————, *The Baterie of the Popes Botereulx, commonlye called the high altare*, Grafton for Crowley (*STC* 21613). An attack on the Roman Catholic high altar.

————, *A Briefe and a Playne Introduction, teachyng how to pronounce the letters in the British tong*, Grafton for Crowley (*STC* 21614).

1551   *Kynniver Llith a Ban* (*STC* 2983). Salisbury's translation of the gospels into Welsh.

William Samuel, *The Abridgemente of Goddes Statutes in Myter*, Grafton for Crowley (*STC* 21690.2). In verse.

Pore Shakerlaye, *The Knoledge of Good and Ivyle, other wyse calyd Ecclesiastes* (*STC* 2761.5). In verse.

APPENDIX V

E. LOST IMPRINTS

1550   Lady Elizabeth Fane's metrical paraphrases of twenty-one Psalms and 102 proverbs. Listed by Joseph Ames in *Typographical Antiquities* (1749), p. 271.

c. 1550   Peter Pateshull, *Vita fratrum mendicantium*, trans. R. Kylington. A commentary on Hildegard's prophecy against the friars by an Augustinian doctor who flourished at Oxford University c. 1387. Wyclif apparently swayed Pateshull to preach against his order. Listed among Crowley's imprints in Bale's *Index* (pp. 322, 353).

F. ENDORSEMENTS, PREFACES, AND DEDICATIONS

c. 1575   Richard Rice, *An Invective againste Vices taken for vertue*, Kyngston for Kirkham (*STC* 20973). Crowley's preface recommends Rice's Puritan morality.

1578   John Wharton, *Whartons Dreame*, Charlewood for Conyngton (*STC* 25295). Along with John Foxe and others, Crowley endorsed this apocalyptic poem.

1581   Anthony Gilby, *A Pleasaunt Dialogue, betweene a souldior of Barwicke and an English Chaplaine* (*STC* 11888). Gilby dedicated this Puritan protest to Crowley.

Thomas Lovell, *A Dialogue between Custom and Veritie*, Allde (*STC* 16860). Crowley wrote the preface and received Lovell's dedication of this anonymous versified tract against dancing and minstrelsy.

[477]

List of Reformation Literary Texts, c. 1525-1575

This is a selective list of literary works, editions, and translations by early Tudor reformers. It also includes important works that influenced early English Protestant literary tradition. Catholic authors are marked with an asterisk. The word "Anonymous" at the end of an entry indicates that the now known author, translator, or editor was not named in the publication. The list includes most of the early printed books cited in the text. First editions are cited unless otherwise noted. Place of publication is London unless otherwise listed. Brackets enclose manuscripts that were not published during the Renaissance. See *STC* and *NCBEL*, I, for further bibliographical information.

*Allen, William. *A Defense and Declaration Touching Purgatorie.* Antwerp, 1565.

————. *A Treatise Made in Defense of the Lauful Power of Priestho[o]d to Remitte Sinnes.* Louvain, 1567.

Anonymous. *Complaynt of Scotland, The.* Paris, c. 1550.

————. *Court of Venus, The.* c. 1538. With *The Pilgrim's Tale.*

————. *Godly Queene Hester, A New Enterlude of.* 1561. Written c. 1527.

————. *Impacyente Poverte, A Newe Interlude of.* 1560. Written c. 1550.

————. *[Love Feigned and Unfeigned.]* Written c. 1547-49.

————. *New Custome, A New Enterlude Entituled.* 1573. Written c. 1570.

————. *Nice Wanton, A Preaty Interlude Called.* 1560. Written c. 1547-53.

————. *Somebody and Others, or The Spoiling of Lady Verity.* c. 1550. Fragment. Trans. from *La Vérité Cachée.* See Peter Houle in Select Bibliography, Part I.

————. *Wyll of the Devyll, The.* c. 1548.

Ascham, Roger. *Apologia pro caena dominica.* 1577.

————. *Disertissimi viri Rogeri Aschami familiarum epistolarum libri tres.* 1576.

————. *A Report and Discourse of the Affaires of Germany.* c. 1570.

————. *The Scholemaster.* 1570.

————. *Toxophilus.* 1545.

Askew, Anne. *Examinations.* Ed. John Bale. 2 vols. Marburg (i.e., Wesel), November 1546; 16 January 1547. Includes Bale's commentary.

Asser, Joannes. *Alfredi regis res gestae ab Asserio conscriptae.* Ed. Matthew Parker. 1574.

Avale, Lemeke. *A Commemoration or Dirge of Bastarde Edmonde Bon[n]er.* 1569.

Baldwin, William. *The Funeralles of King Edward the Sixt.* 1560. Written 1553.

————. *A Marvelous Hystory Intitulede, Beware the Cat.* 1570. Written 1553.

————, ed. *A Memorial of Suche Princes, as Since the Tyme of King Richard the Seconde, Have Been Unfortunate in the Realme of England.* c. 1554. Suppressed. 6 eds. (c. 1554-1578).

————. 2nd ed., rev. and completed. 1559. With the title *A Myrroure for Magistrates.* Includes tragedies by Baldwin, George Ferrers, Thomas Chaloner, and Thomas Phaer.

————. 3rd ed., rev. 1563. Adds "Induction" by Thomas Sackville and tragedies by Baldwin, Master Cavyl, Thomas Churchyard, John Dolman, Ferrers, Sackville, and Francis Seager.

————. *A Treatise of Morall Phylosophie.* 20 January 1547/8. 24 eds. (c. 1548-1640).

Bale, John. *Acta Romanorum Pontificum.* Basel, July 1558.

————. *The Actes of Englysh Votaryes.* 2 pts. Wesel (i.e., Antwerp), 1546; London, 1551.

————. *An Answere to a Papystycall Exhortacyon.* Antwerp, c. 1548. Anonymous.

[479]

Bale, John. *The Apology of Johan Bale agaynste a Ranke Papyst.* c. 1550.

———. *A Brefe Chronycle concernynge the Examinacyon of Syr Johan Oldecastell.* Antwerp, 1544.

———. *A Brefe Comedy concernynge the Temptacyon of our Lorde.* Wesel, c. 1547. Compiled 1538.

———. [*A Briefe Comedy or Enterlude of Johan Baptystes.*] Compiled 1538.

———. *A Christen Exhortacion unto Customable Swearers.* Antwerp, c. 1543.

———. *A Comedy concernynge Thre Lawes.* Wesel, c. 1548. Compiled 1538.

———. *A Declaration of Edmonde Bonners Articles concerning the Cleargye of London.* 1561.

———. *A Dialoge to be had at a Table betwene Two Chyldren.* 1549.

———. *The Epistle Exhortatorye of an Englyshe Christiane.* Antwerp, c. 1544. Ascribed to Henry Stalbridge (pseud.).

———. *An Excellent and a Right Learned Meditacion.* Rouen (i.e., London?), 1554. Attributed to Bale. From the "Michael Wood" press.

———. *An Expostulation agaynste a Franticke Papyst of Hamshyre.* c. 1552.

———. *Illustrium maioris Britanniae scriptorum summarium.* Ipswich (i.e., Wesel), 31 July 1548. A variant gives Wesel as the place of publication.

———. *The Image of Both Churches.* Antwerp, c. 1545.

———. [*Index Britanniae scriptorum.*] c. 1549-57.

———. [*King Johan.*] Compiled 1538; revised 1558-62.

———. *A Mysterye of Inyquyte contayned within the Heretycall Genealogye of P. Pantolabus.* Geneva (i.e., Antwerp), 1545. From the "Michael Wood" press.

———. *The Pageant of Popes.* Trans. John Studley. 1574. A translation of *Acta Romanorum Pontificum.*

———. *Scriptorum Illustrium maioris Brytanniae . . . Catalogus.* 2 vols. Basel, September 1557; February 1559.

————. *A Soveraigne Cordial for a Christian Conscience.* 1554.

————. *A Tragedye Manyfestyng the Chefe Promyses of God unto Man.* Wesel, c. 1547. Compiled 1538.

————. *The Vocacyon of Johan Bale to the Bishoprick of Ossorie.* Rome (i.e., Wesel?), December 1553. Imprinted "before the castell of S. Angell."

————. *Yet a Course at the Romyshe Foxe.* Zurich (i.e., Antwerp), 1543. Ascribed to James Harrison (pseud.). See William Turner, *The Huntyng of the Romishe Fox* and *The Rescuynge of the Romishe Foxe.*

Barlow, William. *A Propre Dyaloge betwene a Gentillman and an Husband Man.* Marburg (i.e., Antwerp), c. 1529. Also attributed to William Roy. From the "Hans Luft" press.

————. *Rede Me and Be Nott Wrothe.* Strasbourg, 1528. Anonymous. Also attributed to Roy.

Barnes, Robert. *The Whole Workes of W. Tyndall, John Frith, and Doct. Barnes.* Ed. John Foxe. 1573.

————. *A Supplicatyon unto Henrye the Eyght.* c. 1534. Answered by Thomas More's *Confutacyon*, pt. 2.

Becon, Thomas. *Worckes.* 3 vols. 1560-64.

————. *The Castell of Comforte.* c. 1549.

————. *A Christmas Banquet.* 1542. Ascribed to Theodore Basille (pseud.).

————. *A Confortable Epistle to Goddes Faythfull People in Englande.* Strasbourg (i.e., Wesel?), 1554. Printed "at the signe of the golde Bibel."

————. *The Flower of Godlye Praiers.* c. 1550.

————. *The Fortresse of the Faythfull agaynst the Cruel Assau[l]tes of Povertie.* 1550.

————. *A Fruitful Treatise of Fasting.* c. 1551.

————. *The Governans of Vertue.* 1538.

————. *The Jewell of Joye.* c. 1550.

————. *A Newe Dialog betwene thangell of God, & the Shepherdes in the Felde.* c. 1547.

————. *A New Postil conteinyng Most Godly Sermons upon the Sonday Gospelles.* 1566.

Becon, Thomas. *The Physyke of the Soule.* 1549.

———. *The Pomander of Prayer.* 1558. Anonymous.

———. *The Principles of Christen Religion.* c. 1550.

———. *The Relikes of Rome, concernynge Church Ware and Matters of Religion.* c. 1560.

———. *The Sycke Mannes Salve.* c. 1560. 26 eds. (c. 1560-1632).

———. *The Solace of the Soule.* 1548.

———. *The True Defence of Peace.* 1542. Ascribed to T. Basille (pseud.).

Bible. Latin. *Biblia Sacrosancta.* Trans. Leo Jud et al. Zurich, 1543.

———. English. Coverdale Bible. Cologne?, 4 October 1535.

———. "Matthew" Bible. [Coverdale and Tyndale versions.] Antwerp, 1537. Ed. John Rogers under the probable pseudonym Thomas Matthew.

———. "Matthew" version. Rev. Richard Taverner. 1539.

———. Great Bible. Paris and London, April 1539. Rev. Coverdale from the "Matthew" version.

———. First Day Bible ["Matthew" version, rev. Edmund Becke]. 17 August 1549.

———. Second Day Bible [Taverner and Tyndale versions, rev. Becke]. 6 octavo pts. 1549-51.

———. Third Day Bible [Taverner and Tyndale versions, rev. Becke]. 23 May 1551.

———. Geneva Bible. Geneva, 1560. Trans. William Whittingham, with William Cole, Miles Coverdale, Anthony Gilby, Christopher Goodman, Thomas Sampson et al.

———. Bishops' Bible. 1568. Rev. Matthew Parker et al. from the Great Bible.

———. Authorized Version. 1611.

———. O.T., English. *The Fyrst Boke of Moses Called Genesis.* Trans. Tyndale. Marburg (i.e., Antwerp), 1530. From the "Hans Luft" press.

———. *The Prophete Jonas.* Trans. Tyndale. Antwerp, c. 1531.

———. Metrical Versions, Psalms. *Goostly Psalmes.* By Miles Coverdale. c. 1536. From German metrical versions.

————. *Davids Harpe*. By Thomas Becon. 1542. Ascribed to Theodore Basille.

————. *Psalter*. Trans. Robert Crowley. 20 September 1549.

————. *Certayne Psalms*. Paraphrased by Thomas Sternhold. c. 1549. Contains nineteen Psalms.

————. *Certayne Psalmes called thee* [sic] *Penytentiall Psalmes*. Trans. Thomas Wyatt. 31 December 1549.

————. *Certayne Psalmes*. By William Hunnis. 1550.

————. *Certayne Psalmes*. By Francis Seager. 1553.

————. *One and Fiftie Psalmes of David*. Geneva, 1556. The Geneva Psalter.

————. *The Whole Booke of Psalmes*. Ed. John Hopkins. 1562. "The Old Version." Approx. 525 eds. (1562-1640). Includes versions by Thomas Becon, John Craig, John Hopkins, William Kethe, John Marckant, Thomas Norton, John Pullain, Thomas Sternhold, William Whittingham, and Robert Wisdom.

————. *The Whole Psalter*. Trans. Matthew Parker. c. 1567.

————. Proverbs. *Certayne Chapters of the Proverbes of Salomon by T. Sternholde* [or rather by John Hall]. Ed. John Case. 1549-50.

————. *Certayne Chapters of the Proverbes of Salomon*. By John Hall. 1550.

————. Ecclesiastes. *The Knoledge of Good and Ivyle*. By Pore Shakerlaye. 1551.

————. Canticles. *The Canticles or Balades of Salomon*. By William Baldwin. 1 June 1549.

————. N. T., Greek. *Novum Testamentum*. Ed. and trans. into Latin by Erasmus. Basel, 1516. Includes *Paraclesis*.

————. German. *Das Newe Testament Deutzsch*. Trans. Martin Luther. Wittenberg, 1522. Includes woodcuts attributed to Lucas Cranach.

————. Dutch. *Het Nieuwe Testament*. Antwerp, 1545.

————. English. Trans. William Tyndale, helped by William Roy. Cologne, 1525. Fragment.

————. 2nd ed. Worms, c. 1526.

————. Day New Testament [Tyndale version]. 1548.

Bible. *The Paraphrases of Erasmus*. 2 vols. 31 January 1548; 16 August 1549.

————. Metrical Versions, Acts. *Actes of the Apostles*. By Christopher Tye. 1553.

Bodrugan, Nicholas. *An Epitome of the Title that the Kynges Majestie of Englande hath to the Sovereigntie of Scotlande*. 1548. Attributed to Sir Thomas Smith.

Book of Common Prayer. *The Booke of the Common Prayer and Administracion of the Sacramentes, and Other Rites and Ceremonies of the Churche*. 7 March 1549.

————. 2nd version. After 27 October 1552.

————. 3rd version. 1559.

Book of Homilies. *Certayne Sermons, or Homilies*. 31 July 1547. Includes sermons attributed to Thomas Becon, Edmund Bonner, Thomas Cranmer, John Harpesfeld, and Hugh Latimer.

————. *The Seconde Tome of Homelyes*. 1563. Includes sermons by Matthew Parker, James Pilkington, and others.

————. *Certayne Sermons or Homilies*. 1623. Includes the Edwardian and Elizabethan collections.

Bradford, John. *All the Examinations of John Bradforde*. 1561.

————. *Bradfords Beades, Contayning Godly Meditations*. 1597.

————. *The Complaint of Veritie*. 1559.

————. *A Frutefull Treatise against the Feare of Death*. 1560s.

————. *A Godlye Medytacyon*. 1559.

————. *Godlie Meditations upon the Lordes Prayer*. 1562.

————. *Godly Meditations uppon the Ten Commaundementes*. 1567.

————. *The Hurte of He[a]ring Masse*. c. 1561.

————. *A Sermon of Repentance*. 1553.

————. *Two Notable Sermons, the one of repentance, and the other of the Lordes supper*. 1574.

————. *A Worthy Sermon upon the Lords Supper*. 1621.

Brinkelow, Henry. *The Complaynt of Roderyck Mors for the Redresse of Certeyn Wycked Lawes*. Strasbourg?, c. 1542.

————. *The Lamentacion of a Christian against the Citie of London*. 1542. Ascribed to Roderick Mors (pseud.). "Printed at Jericho in the land of Promes by Thome Trauth."

Bucer, Martin. *The Gratulation of M. Martin Bucer unto the Churche of Englande.* 1549.

——. *The Mynd and Exposition of M. Bucer uppon these Wordes of S. Mathew.* Emden, 1566.

——. *A Treatise How by the Worde of God, christian mens almose* [i.e., alms] *ought to be distributed.* Printed abroad, c. 1557.

Bullinger, Heinrich. *Briefe Concordance.* Trans. Walter Lynne. 1550. With Leo Jud and others.

——. *The Christen State of Matrimonye.* Trans. Miles Coverdale. 1541. Anonymous.

——. *Commonplaces of Christian Religion.* Trans. John Stockwood. 1572.

——. *An Holsume Antidotus agaynst the Anabaptistes.* Trans. Jean Veron. 1548.

——. *In Apocalypsim conciones centum.* 1561.

——. *A Hundred Sermons upon the Apocalips.* 1561.

——. *The Judgement of H. Bullinger Declaring it Lawfull to Weare the Apparell Prescribed.* 1566.

——. *A Most Necessary and Frutefull Dialogue between the Seditious Libertin and the True Christian.* Trans. Jean Veron. Worcester, 1551.

——. *A Most Sure and Strong Defence of the Baptisme of Children.* Trans. Jean Veron. Worcester, 1551.

——. *The Olde Fayth.* Trans. Miles Coverdale. 1547.

——. *A Treatise or Sermon Concernynge Magistrates.* Trans. Walter Lynne. 1549.

——. *Two Epystles, one of H. Bullinger, another of Johan Calvyne.* 1548.

Calvin, Jean. *Catechismus ecclesiae Geneuensis.* 1562.

——. *Certain Homilies Conteining Profitable Admonition for this Time.* [London], 1553. "Imprinted at Rome before the castle of S. Angel at the signe of s. Peter."

——. *Commentaries upon the Prophet Daniell.* Trans. Arthur Golding. 1570.

——. *An Epistle of Godly Consolacion.* Trans. Edward Seymour. 5 April 1550.

Calvin, Jean. *A Faythfull and Moste Godly Treatyse concernynye* [sic] *the Sacrament.* Trans. Miles Coverdale. c. 1549.

―――. *The Institution of Christian Religion.* Trans. Thomas North. 1561.

―――. *A Little Booke Concernynge Offences.* Trans. Arthur Golding. 1567.

―――. *Of the Life or Conversation of a Christen Man.* Trans. Thomas Broke. 1549.

―――. *The Psalmes of David and Others.* Trans. Arthur Golding. 1571. With Calvin's commentaries.

―――. *A Short Instruction agaynst the Pestiferous Errours of Anabaptistes.* 1549.

―――. *Whether Christian Faith Maye be Kepte Secret in the Heart, without confession thereof openly.* Rouen (i.e., London?), 1553. From the "Michael Wood" press.

Carion, Johann. *The Thre Bokes of Cronicles.* Trans. Walter Lynne. 1550. "Carion's Chronicle."

Cartwright, Thomas. *A Replye to an Answere Made of M. Doctor Whitegift.* c. 1574. Init. T. C.

―――. *A Second Admonition to the Parliament.* 1572. Anonymous.

―――. *The Second Replie agaynst Maister Whitgiftes Second Answer.* Zurich, 1575.

Catechism. *Catechismus brevis.* 1553. Attributed to John Ponet. Set forth by royal authority.

―――. *A Short Catechisme.* 1553. Printed with the Forty-two Articles.

*Cavendish, George. *Life of Cardinal Wolsey.* 1641. Written c. 1554-58.

―――. *[Metrical Visions.]* Written c. 1552-54.

Cecil, William. *The Execution of Justice in England.* 1583.

Champneys, John. *The Harvest is at Hand.* 1548.

Chaucer, Geoffrey. *The Workes of Geffray Chaucer Newly Printed, with Dyvers Workes Never in Printe Before.* Ed. William Thynne. 1532.

―――. 2nd ed., rev. 1542. Includes *The Plowman's Tale.*

————. Ed. John Stow. 1561. With revisions and expansions.

————. Supposititious Works. *Jack Upland.* c. 1536.

————. *The Plowman's Tale.* c. 1535.

Cheke, John. [New Testament. Matthew and Mark 1.] Trans. c. 1550.

————. *D. Ioannis Chrysostomi homiliae duae.* 1543. Second homily trans. Thomas Chaloner, 1544.

————. *D. Ioannia Chrysostomi de providentia Dei ac de fato orationes sex.* 1545.

————. *De obitu doctissimi doctoris M. Buceri: Epistolae duae.* 1551.

————. *De pronuntiatione graecae potissimum linguae disputationes cum Stephano Wintoniensi.* Basel, 1555.

————. *The Hurt of Sedicion.* 1549. Anonymous.

————. *Leonis imperatoris De bellico apparatu liber e graeco in latinum conversus I. Checo interp.* Basel, 1554.

Churchyard, Thomas. *The Contention bettwyxte Churchyeard and Camell, upon David Dycers Dreame. Newlye Imprinted.* 1560. Reprints the c. 1552 flyting (*STC* 5225.5, 4527.6, 5252, 4527.4, 5258, 25668.5, 18969.5, 4999.5, 4527.8, 23251.5, 4527.2, 5246, 1654).

————. *Davy Dycars Dreame.* c. 1552.

————. *A Myrrour for Man.* c. 1552.

Cicero, Marcus Tullius. *The Booke of Freendeship.* Trans. John Harington. 1550.

Coverdale, Miles. *Certain Most Godly Letters of Such True Saintes as Gave Their Lyves.* 1564.

————. *The Christen Rule; or state of all the worlde.* c. 1547. Anonymous.

————. *A Confutacion of that Treatise, which one J. Standish made agaynst the protestacion of D. Barnes.* [Zurich], c. 1541.

————. *An Exhortacion to the Careinge of Chrystes Crosse.* c. 1550.

————. *Fruitfull Lessons.* 1593.

————. *The Order that the Churche in Denmarke Doth Use.* c. 1550.

Coverdale, Miles, trans. *The Defence of a Certayne Poore Christen Man*. Nuremberg (i.e., Antwerp?), 1545. From German.

————, trans. *A Faythfull and True Pronostication*. c. 1547.

Cranmer, Thomas. *All the Submyssyons and Recantations of T. Cranmer*. 1556. In English and Latin.

————. *An Answere against the False Calumniacion of Richarde Smyth*. c. 1551.

————. *An Answer unto a Crafty Cavillation by S. Gardiner*. 1551. Reprints Gardiner's *Explication and Assertion*.

————. *A Confutation of Unwritten Verities*. 1558. Trans. E. P. A reply to Richard Smith.

————. *The Copy of Certain Lettres Sent to the Quene*. Emden, c. 1556.

————. *A Defence of the True and Catholike Doctrine of the Sacrament*. 1550.

————. *Defensio verae et catholicae doctrinae de sacramento*. Trans. John Cheke. 1553.

————. *The Institution of a Christen Man*. 1537. "The Bishops' Book." Sometimes attributed to Cranmer.

————. *Reformatio legum ecclesiasticarum*. 1571. Ed. John Foxe et al.; trans. John Cheke and Walter Haddon. Anonymous.

————. *The Recantation of Cranmer translated out of Latin*. 1556. From *All the Submyssyons and Recantations*.

————, trans. *Cathechismus. That is to say; a shorte instruction into christian religion*. 1548. From Justus Jonas.

Crowley, Robert. See Appendix V.

Dudley, John. *The Saying of John Late Duke of Northumberlande Uppon the Scaffolde*. 1553.

Edward VI. *The Prayer of Kynge Edwarde the Syxte*. 10 July 1553.

————. *A Prayer Sayd in the Kinges Chappel*. 19 June 1553.

England, Church of. *Articles Agreed on by the Bishoppes, in the Synod*. 1553. The Forty-two Articles. Promulgated by Cranmer.

————. *Articuli de quibus in synodo Londinensi 1562 convenit*. 1563. The Thirty-nine Articles. Derived directly from the Forty-two Articles.

————. *Injunctions Gyven by the Auctoritie of the Kynges Highnes to the Clergie.* 1536.

————. *Injunctions for the Clergy.* 1538.

————. *Injunccions Geven by Edward the VI.* 31 July 1547.

Erasmus, Desiderius. [*Adagia.*] *Proverbes or Adagies with Newe Addicions, Gathered out of the Chiliades of Erasmus.* Ed. Richard Taverner. 1539.

————. *Apophthegmes.* Trans. Nicholas Udall. 1542.

————. [*Apophthegmata.*] *Flores aliquot sententiarum ex variis collecti scriptoribus.* Trans. Richard Taverner. 1540. Selections in Latin and English.

————. *The Censure and Judgement of Erasmus: whyther dyvorsemente stondeth with the lawe of God.* Trans. Nicholas Lesse. c. 1550.

————. *Commonplaces of Scripture Ordrely Set Forth.* Trans. Richard Taverner. 1538.

————. [*Enchiridion.*] *A Booke Called in Latyn Enchiridion and in Englysshe the Manuell of the Christen Knyght.* 1533.

————. *A Shorte Recapitulacion or Abridgement of Erasmus Enchiridion.* Abridged by Miles Coverdale. Antwerp?, 1545. From the press of "Adam Anonimus."

————. [*Paraclesis.*] *An Exhortation to the Diligent Studye of Scripture.* Trans. William Roy. Marburg (i.e., Antwerp), 1529. Anonymous. From the "Hans Luft" press.

————. *The Praise of Folie. Moriae encomium.* Trans. Thomas Chaloner. 1549.

————. *Two Dyaloges.* Trans. Edmund Becke. Canterbury, 1550.

Fish, Simon. *The Summe of the Holye Scripture and Ordynance of Christen Teachyng.* Antwerp, 1529.

————. *A Supplicacyon for the Beggars.* c. 1529. Anonymous. Answered by More's *Supplycacyon.*

————. *A Supplication of the Poore Commons.* 1546. Reprints *A Supplicacyon for the Beggars.*

Flacius Illyricus, Matthias. *Epistola de Morte Pauli Tertii Pontifex Maximus.* Piacenza (i.e., Basel), c. 1549-50. Attributed to Publius Aesquillus.

Flacius Illyricus, Matthias. *Wonderfull Newes of the Death of Paule the .III.* Trans. William Baldwin. c. 1552.

*Forrest, William. *A New Ballade of the Marigolde.* c. 1553.

Foxe, John. *Actes and Monuments of these Latter and Perillous Dayes.* 20 March 1563. "The Book of Martyrs." 7 eds. (1563-1632).

———. 2nd ed., rev. and enlarged. 2 vols. 1570.

———. *Christus Triumphans.* Basel, 1556.

———. *Commentarii Rerum in Ecclesia Gestarum.* Strasbourg, 1554.

———. *De non plectendis morte adulteris consultatio.* 1548.

———. *Rerum in Ecclesia Gestarum Commentarii, Pars Prima.* Basel, 1 September 1559. Henricus Pantaleon completed the text with *Martyrum historia. Pars secunda* (Basel, 1563).

Frith, John. *The Whole Workes of W. Tyndall, John Frith, and Doct. Barnes.* Ed. John Foxe. 1573.

———. *A Boke Made by J. Frith Answering unto M. Mores Lettur.* 1533. A reply to More's attack against Simon Fish.

———. *An other Boke against Rastel.* c. 1533.

———. *The contentes of thys booke: a letter unto the faythfull followers of Christes gospel.* c. 1540.

———. *A Disputacion of Purgatorye.* c. 1533.

———. *A Mirrour or Glasse to Know Thyselfe.* c. 1533.

———. *A Myrroure or Lokynge Glasse wherein you may beholde the Sacramente of baptisme described.* 1533 (i.e., 1548?).

———. *A Pistle to the Christen Reader; the revelation of antichrist.* Marburg (i.e., Antwerp), 1529.

———. *The Preparacyon to the Crosse, wyth the preparacion to deeth.* c. 1530. Anonymous.

*Gardiner, Stephen. *Ad Bucerum de impudenti eiusdem pseudologia conquestio.* Louvain, 1544.

———. *Ad Martinum Bucerum epistola.* Louvain, 1546.

———. *An Admonishion to the Bishoppes of Winchester, London, and Others.* Rouen (i.e., London?), 1553. From the "Michael Wood" press.

———. *The Communication betweene my Lord Chauncelor and Judge Hales.* Rouen (i.e., London?), 1553. From the "Michael Wood" press.

———. *Confutatio cavillationum quibus sacrosanctum eucharistiae sacramentum*. Paris, 1552. Anonymous. Reply to Cranmer.

———. *De pronunciatione linguae graecae et latinae*. Basel, 1555. Printed with Cheke's treatise by C. S. Curio.

———. *De vera obedientia*. 1535.

———. *De vera obedientia: An Oration*. Trans. John Bale. Rouen (i.e., London?), 1553. From the "Michael Wood" press.

———. *A Declaration of such True Articles as George Joye hath gone about to confute*. 1546.

———. *A Detection of the Devils Sophistrie, wherwith he robbeth the unlearned people, of the true byleef, in the sacrament of the aulter*. 1546. Answered by Antony Gilby.

———. [*Examination of the Hunter*.] Printed in William Turner's reply, *The Rescuynge of the Romishe Fox*. Apparently circulated only in manuscript.

———. *An Explication and Assertion of the True Catholique Fayth, touchyng the moost blessed sacrament of the aulter*. Rouen, 1551. Reprinted in Cranmer's reply.

———. *Responsio venerabilium sacerdotum Henrici Ioliffi & Roberti Ionson ad articulos Ioannis Hoperi una cum confutationibus Hoperi et replicationibus Stephani Gardineri*. Antwerp, 1564. Mostly by Gardiner.

Gascoigne, George. *A Hundreth Sundrie Flowres*. 1573. Includes *The Adventures of Master F. J.*

———. *A Delicate Diet for Daintiemouthde Droonkardes*. 1576.

———. *The Droomme of Doomes Day*. 1576.

———. *The Glasse of Governement*. 1575.

———. *The Posies*. 1575.

———. [*The Princelye Pleasures at the Courte at Kenelwoorth*.] 1576.

———. *The Spoyle of Antwerpe*. c. 1576.

———. *The Steele Glas*. 1576.

———. *The Tale of Hemetes the Hermite*. 1579. Printed in Abraham Fleming's trans. of Synesius' *A Paradoxe*.

Gerrard, Philip. *A Godly Invective in the Defence of the Gospell*. 1547.

Gilby, Anthony. *An Answer to the Devellish Detection of S. Gardiner*. 1547. Init. A. G.

Gilby, Anthony. *A Briefe Treatice of Election and Reprobation*. c. 1575.

———. *A Commentary upon the Prophet Mycha*. 1551.

———. *A Pleasaunt Dialogue, betweene a souldior of Barwicke and an English Chaplaine*. 1581. Init. A. G.

———. *A Treatise Wherein the Doctrine of God is Handled*. 1581.

Googe, Barnaby. *Eglogs, Epytaphes, and Sonettes*. 1563.

———. *A Newe Booke Called the Shippe of Safegarde*. 1569.

———, trans. *The Zodiake of Life* by Marcellus Palingenius. 1565.

Grafton, Richard. *An Abridgement of the Chronicles of England*. 1562.

———. *A Chronicle at Large*. 2 vols. 1569. Title page to Vol. 2 dated 1568.

———. *A Manuell of the Chronicles of England*. 1565.

Grey [really Dudley], Lady Jane. *An Epistle of the Ladye Jane to a Learned Man*. London?, 1554. Contains a transcript of her interrogation by John Feckenham, an epistle to her sister, and her last words on the scaffold.

Grimald, Nicholas. *Archipropheta: tragoedia*. Cologne, 1548.

———. *Christus redivivus: comoedia tragica*. Cologne, 1543.

Guevara, Antonio de. *The Diall of Princes*. Trans. Thomas North. 1557. From the French of René Bertaut.

———. *A Dispraise of the Life of a Courtier*. Trans. Francis Brian. 1548.

———. *The Golden Boke of Marcus Aurelius*. Trans. John Bourchier, Lord Berners. 1534. From the French of Bertaut.

Hall, Edward. *The Union of the Two Noble and Illustrious Families of Lancaster and York*. 1542. Fragment.

———. 2nd ed. 1548.

Harrison, James. *An Exhortacion to the Scottes*. 1547.

Hart, Henry. *A Godly Newe Short Treatyse Instructyng Every Parson, howe they shulde trade theyr lyves*. 1548.

Henry VIII. *Assertio septem sacramentorum adversus M. Lutherum*. 1521. Sometimes attributed to More.

———. *A Necessary Doctrine and Erudition for any Christen Man*. 1543. "The King's Book." Attributed to Henry VIII.

*Heywood, John. *The Spider and the Flie, a Parable.* 1556.

Hilarie, Hugh. *The Resurreccion of the Masse with the Wonderful Vertues of the Same.* Strasbourg (i.e., London or Wesel), 1554. Also attributed to John Bale and Thomas Becon.

*Hogarde, Miles. *The Abuse of the Blessed Sacrament of the Aultare.* Printed in Crowley's *Confutation of the Mishapen Aunser.*

——. *The Assault of the Sacrament of the Alter.* 1554. Written in 1549.

——. *A Mirror of Love.* 1555.

——. [*A Myrroure of Myserie.*] Dated 1557.

——. *A Newe ABC Paraphrasticallye Applied.* 1557.

——. *A New Treatyse in Maner of a Dialoge whiche sheweth the excellency of mannes nature.* c. 1550.

——. *A Treatise Declaring Howe Christ by perverse preachyng was banished out of this realme.* 1554.

——. *A Treatise Entitled the Pathwaye to the Towre of Perfection.* 1554.

Hooper, John. *An Answer unto my Lord of Wynchesters Booke.* Zurich, 1547. In reply to Stephen Gardiner.

——. *A Briefe and Cleare Confession of the Christian Faith.* 1581. Issued as part of J. Baker, *Lectures.*

——. *Certeine Comfortable Expositions upon the xxiii, lxii, lxxiii and lxxvii psalmes.* 1580.

——. *A Declaracion of Christe.* Zurich, 1547.

——. *A Declaration of the Ten Holy Commaundementes.* Zurich, 1548.

——. *An Exposition upon the 23. psalmes.* 1562.

——. *A Funerall Oratyon made the xiiii. day januarii.* 1549.

——. *Godly and Most Necessary Annotations in the xiii Chapyter to the Romaynes.* Worcester, 1551.

——. *A Godly Confession and Protestacion of the Christian Fayth.* c. 1551.

——. *An Homelye to be Read in the Tyme of Pestylence.* Worcester, 1553.

——. *A Lesson of the Incarnation of Christe.* 1549.

Hooper, John. *An Oversight and Deliberacion upon the Prophete Jonas.* 1550.

———. *The Wordes of Maister Hooper at His Death.* 1559.

Howard, Henry, Earl of Surrey. *Songes and Sonettes, Written by Henry Haward late Earle of Surrey, and Other.* 1557. 8 eds. (1557-87). Known as Tottel's *Miscellany.* Includes verse by Francis Brian, Geoffrey Chaucer, John Cheke, Thomas Churchyard, Nicholas Grimald, John Hall, John Harington, John Heywood, Thomas Norton, Anthony St. Leger, Thomas Vaux, and Thomas Wyatt.

Hurlestone, Randall. *Newes from Rome.* c. 1550.

Ingelend, Thomas. *A Pretie and Mery New Enterlude: Called the Disobedient Child.* c. 1570. Written c. 1560?

Jewel, John. *Apologia ecclesiae anglicanae.* 1562. Anonymous.

———. *An Apologie, or Aunswer in Defence of the Church of England.* Anonymous. Trans. 1562. Later trans. Ann, Lady Bacon (1564).

Joye, George. *An Apologye made to Satisfye W. Tindale, of hys new Testament.* 1535.

———. *A Compendyouse Somme of the Very Christen Relygyon.* 1535.

———. *George Joye Confuteth Winchesters False Articles.* Wesel (i.e., Antwerp), 1543.

———. *A Present Consolacion for the Sufferers of Persecucion.* 1544. Init. G. J.

———. *The Refutation of the Byshop of Winchesters Derke Declaration of His False Articles.* 1546. Answers Gardiner's *Declaration.*

———. *The Subversion of Moris False Foundacion.* Emden (i.e., Antwerp), 1534.

———. *The Unit[i]e and Scisme of the Olde Chirche.* Antwerp, 1543.

———, ed. *The Exposicion of Daniel the Prophete.* Geneva (i.e., Antwerp), 1545. From Melanchthon et al.

Kethe, William. *Of Misrules Contending, With Gods Worde by Name.* c. 1553.

———. *A Ballet Declaringe the Fal of the Whore of Babylone Intytuled Tye Thy Mare Tom Boye.* c. 1548.

———. *William Keth His Seeing Glasse.* Printed abroad, c. 1555.

Kirchmeyer, Thomas [Thomas Naogeorgus]. *Pammachius.* Wittenberg, 1538.

———. [Trans. John Bale.] c. 1538-39. A lost work.

———. *The Popish Kingdome, or Reigne of Antichrist.* Trans. Barnaby Googe. 1570.

Knell, Thomas. *An A B C to the Christen Congregacion.* c. 1550.

———. *An Answer to a Papisticall Byll, Cast in the Streetes of Northampton.* 1570. Anonymous.

———. *An Epitaph upon the Life & Death of D. Bon[n]er, Bisshop of London.* 1569.

———. *An Historicall Discource of the Life and Death of Doctor Story.* 1571.

———. *Pithy Note to Papists.* 1570.

Knox, John. *An Admonition that the Faithful Christians in London, Newcastel Barwycke & Others, May Avoide Gods Vengeaunce.* Wittenberg (i.e., London?), 1554.

———. 2nd ed. Rome (i.e., Wesel?), 1554. With *A Confession & Declaration of Praiers* (on the death of Edward VI). Imprinted "before the castel of s. Aungel at the signe of sainct Peter."

———. *The Apellation from the Cruell Sentence of the False Bishoppes.* Geneva, 1558.

———. *A Percel of the .VI. Psalme Expounded.* London?, 1554.

———. *A Faythfull Admonition unto the Professours of Gods Truthe in England.* Kalykow (i.e., Emden), 1554.

———. *The First Blast of the Trumpet against the Monstruous Regiment of Women.* Geneva, 1558. Anonymous.

———. *The History of the Reformation of Religion Within the Realm of Scotland.* 1587. Anonymous.

Lanquet, Thomas. *An Epitome of Cronicles.* 1549. "Cooper's Chronicle." Continued to the reign of Edward VI by Thomas Cooper.

———. 2nd ed., rev. 5 April 1559. Continued to the reign of Queen Elizabeth by Robert Crowley.

Lanquet, Thomas. 3rd ed., rev. 1560. Continued to the death of Queen Mary. Crowley's continuation replaced with one by Cooper.

Latimer, Hugh. *The Fyrste Sermon of Mayster Latimer, Preached before the Kynges Grace.* Ed. Thomas Some. 1549.

————. *The Second [third, fourth, fifth, sixth, seventh] Sermon Preached before the Kynges Majestie.* 1549.

————. *Twenty-Seven Sermons Preached by Latimer.* 1562. 2 pts. Ed. Augustine Bernher; preface by Thomas Some.

————. *Seven Sermons made upon the Lordes Prayer.* 1572. Preached before the Duchess of Suffolk.

————. *The Sermon that Latimer made to the Clergie, in the Convocation.* 1537. Trans. from Latin.

————. *A Moste Faithfull Sermon Preached before the Kynges Majestye.* 1550.

————. *A Notable Sermon* [on the Plough] *of Maister Latemer, preached in the shroudes at Paules Churche.* 1548. Printed with the arms of the Duchess of Suffolk.

————. *A Sermon Preached at Stamford.* 1550.

Leland, John. *Assertio inclytissimi Arturii regis Britanniae.* 1544.

————. *[Commentarii de Scriptoribus Britannicis.]*

————. *[The Itinerary of John Leland.]* c. 1540.

————. *The Laboryouse Journey & Serche for Englandes Antiquitees.* Ed. John Bale. 1549. Includes Bale's commentary.

Lever, Thomas. *A Fruitfull Sermon Made in Poules Churche at London in the shroudes the seconde daye of February.* 1550.

————. *A Meditacion upon the Lordes Prayer.* 1551.

————. *A Sermon Preached at Pauls Crosse, the .xiiii. day of December.* 1551.

————. *A Sermon preached the Thyrd Sonday in Lent before the Kynges Majestie.* 1550.

————. *A Treatise of the Right Way from Danger of Synne.* 1571.

Luther, Martin. *The Chiefe Articles of the Christen Faythe.* Trans. Walter Lynne? 1548.

————. *An Exposicion upon the Songe of the Blessed Virgine Mary, Called Magnificat.* Trans. J. Hollybush (pseud., i.e., Miles Coverdale). 1538.

———. *A Frutefull Exposition of the Kyngdom of Christ.* Trans. Walter Lynne. 1548. With a sermon on Matthew 9 by Urbanus Regius.

———. *A Frutfull Sermon of the Angelles.* Trans. John Foxe. c. 1548.

———. *A Propre Treatyse of Good Workes.* c. 1535.

———. *A Ryght Notable Sermon, made uppon the Twent[i]eth Chapter of Johan of absolution and the true use of the keyes.* Trans. Richard Argentine. Ipswich, 20 January 1548.

———. [*A Treatise on Christian Liberty.*] c. 1537. A lost edition.

———. *A Very Comfortable Sermon Concerning the Comming of Christ.* Trans. Thomas Becon. 1570.

———. *A Very Excellent Exposition upon the [Twenty-third] Psalme.* Trans. Miles Coverdale. 1537.

Lynne, Walter, trans. *The Beginning and Endynge of All Popery.* c. 1548. Derived from Andreas Osiander's German translation of the Joachimist *Vaticinia.*

———. *A Briefe Collection of Textes of the Scripture as Do Declare the Happie Estate of Them that be Vyseted wyth Sycknes.* 1549. With two sermons by Luther.

———, trans. *The Vertuous Scholehous of Ungracious Women.* c. 1548. From German. With a sermon on matrimony by Luther.

L[ynyng], U[rban]. *The Pleasaunt Playne and Pythye Patheway Leadynge to a Vertues and Honest Lyfe.* c. 1552. (*STC* 15113.5.)

Map, Walter (?). *Rhithmi vetustissimi de corrupto ecclesiae statu.* Ed. John Bale. Antwerp, 1546. An edition of *Apocalypsis Goliae.*

Mardeley, John. *A Breife Recantacion of Maystres Missa.* 1 June 1548. Init. J. M. (*STC* 17137.)

———. *A Declaration of the Power of Gods Worde.* 1548.

———. *Here is a Shorte Resytal of Certayne Holy Doctours whych proveth that the naturall body of christ is not in the sacrament . . . collected in myter.* c. 1548.

[497]

Mardeley, John. *Here Beginneth a Necessarie Instruction for all Covetous Ryche Men*. c. 1548.

Margaret of Navarre. *A Godly Medytacyon of the Christen Sowle*. Trans. Princess Elizabeth. Ed. John Bale. Wesel, April 1548.

Moone, Peter. *A Short Treatyse of Certayne Thinges Abused in the Popysh Church*. Ipswich, 1548.

————. Verse sermon against papists. Ipswich, 1548. Anonymous. Fragment.

*More, Thomas. *The Workes Wrytten in the Englysh Tonge*. Ed. William Rastell. 1557.

————. *The Answere to the Fyrst Parte of the Poysened Booke Named the Souper of the Lorde*. 1534. A reply to Tyndale. Answered by George Joye's *Subversion of Moris False Foundacion*.

————. *The Apologye of Syr T. More Knyght*. 1533. Answers Saint German's *Treatise Concernynge the Division betwene the Spirytualitie and Temporalitie*. Answered by Saint German's *Salem and Bizance*.

————. *The Confutacyon of Tyndales Answere*. 2 pts. 1532-33. A reply to Tyndale's *Answere* and Barnes's *Supplicatyon*.

————. *The Debellacyon of Salem and Bizance*. 1533. Answers Saint German's *Salem and Bizance*.

————. *A Dialoge of Comfort against Tribulacion*. 18 November 1553.

————. *A Dyalogue Wherin be Treatyd Dyvers Maters, as of the veneration & worshyp of ymagys*. 1529. Replied to by Tyndale's *Answere*.

————. *A Letter Impugnynge the Erronyouse Wrytyng of J. Frith*. 1533. Answered by Frith's *Boke* and Tyndale's *Souper of the Lorde*.

————. *The Supplycacyon of Soulys*. Before 25 October 1529. A reply to Fish's *Supplicacyon for the Beggars*. c. 1529.

————. [*Utopia*.] *Libellus vere aureus de optimo reip. statu, deque nova insula Utopiae cura P. Aegidii nunc primum editus*. Louvain, 1516.

―――. *A Fruteful and Pleasaunt Worke of the Beste State of a Publyque Weale, and of the Newe Yle Called Utopia.* Trans. Ralph Robinson. 1551.

Noot, Jan van der. *A Theatre [for] Voluptuous Worldlings.* Trans. Theodore Roest and Edmund Spenser. 1569.

Norton, Thomas. *A Disclosing of the Great Bull.* 1570. Anonymous.

―――. *The Tragedie of Gorboduc.* 1561. Written with Thomas Sackville.

―――. *A Warning agaynst the Dangerous Practises of Papistes.* c. 1569. Anonymous.

Ochino, Bernardino. *Sermons of Barnardine Ochine of Siena.* Trans. Ann, Lady Bacon. 1548. Contains five sermons.

―――. *Sermons of the Ryght Famous and Excellent Clerke Master B. Ochine.* Trans. Richard Argentine. Ipswich, 1548. Contains six sermons different from the Bacon translation.

―――. *Fouretene Sermons.* Trans. Ann, Lady Bacon. Ed. G. B. [William Baldwin?]. c. 1551.

―――. *Sermons of Barnardine Ochyne, Concerning the Predestination and Election of God.* Trans. Ann, Lady Bacon, and Richard Argentine. c. 1570. Contains twenty-five sermons. Includes all sermons in the collections above.

―――. *A Tragoedie or Dialoge of the Unjuste Usurped Primacie of the Bishop of Rome.* Trans. John Ponet. Before 10 October 1549.

―――. 2nd issue, rev. After 10 October 1549. Deletes references to "the lorde Protector."

Oporinus, Joannes. *Librorum Index.* 2nd ed. Basel, 1567.

Ovidius Naso, Publius. *The Fyrst Fower Bookes of Metamorphosis.* Trans. Arthur Golding. 1565.

―――. *The .XV. Bookes of Metamorphosis.* Trans. Golding. 1567.

Parker, Matthew. *De antiquitate Britannicae ecclesiae.* 1572.

―――. *Howe We Ought to Take the Death of the Godly. A sermon made in Cambrydge at the buriall of the noble clerck. D. M. Bucer.* c. 1551.

Parr, Catherine. *Prayers Stirryng the Mynd unto Heavenlye Medytacions.* 1545.

————. *Prayers or Medytacions.* 1545.

————. *The Lamentacion of a Sinner.* 1547. Ed. William Cecil, with a preface.

Patten, William. *The Calender of Scripture.* 1575.

————. *The Expedicion into Scotlande of Edward, Duke of Soomerset.* 30 June 1548.

Phillips, John. *A Balad Intituled, a Cold Pye for the Papists.* c. 1570.

Piers Plowman. *A Godly Dyalogue & Dysputacion betwene Pyers Plowman, and a Popysh Preest.* c. 1550.

————. *I Playne Piers Which Can Not Flatter.* c. 1550.

————. *Pierce the Ploughmans Crede.* 1553.

————. *Pyers Plowmans Exhortation, unto the lordes, knightes and burgoysses of the Parlyamenthouse.* c. 1550. Attributed to Robert Crowley.

————. *The Praier and Complaynte of the Ploweman unto Christe.* Ed. William Tyndale? or George Joye? Antwerp, c. 1531.

————. *The Vision of Pierce Plowman.* Ed. Robert Crowley. 3 eds. 1550. Attributed to William Langland.

————. 4th ed. Ed. Owen Rogers. 1561. With *Pierce the Ploughmans Crede.*

Ponet, John. *An Apologie Fully Aunsweringe D. Steph. Gardiner and Other Papists.* Strasbourg, 1555.

————. *A Defence for Mariage of Priestes.* 1549.

————. *A Notable Sermon Concerninge the Ryght Use of the Lordes Supper.* 1550.

————. *A Shorte Treatise of Politike Power.* Strasbourg, 1556.

Proctor, John. *The Fal of the Late Arrian.* 1549.

Punt, William. *A New Dialoge Called the Endightment agaynste Mother Messe.* 1548. Init. W. P. 3 eds. (17 December 1548–2 January 1549).

Ramsey, John. *A Corosyfe to be Layed Hard unto the Hartes of all Faythfull Professours of Christes Gospel.* c. 1548.

————. *A Plaister for a Galled Horse.* 1548.

Regius, Urbanus. *A Comparison betwene the Olde Learnynge &*
the Newe. Trans. William Turner. Southwark, 1537.

―――. *A Declaration of the Twelve Articles of the Christen Faythe.*
Trans. Walter Lynne. 1548.

―――. *An Instruccyon of Christen Fayth.* Trans. John Foxe. c.
1548.

―――. *A Lytle Treatise wherin he declareth the dyversyte be-*
twene ryght worshyppyng and ceremonis invented by mannis
institucion. Trans. Walter Lynne. 1548.

―――. *The Sh[i]elde of Salvacion.* Trans. Thomas Becon. c.
1548.

Ridley, Nicholas. *A Brief Declaracion of the Lordes Supper.* Emden, 1555.

―――. *Certein Godly, Learned, and Comfortable Conferences,*
betwene N. Rydley and H. Latimer. Emden, 1556.

―――. *A Frendly Farewel, which master doctor Ridley, did write*
unto all his true lovers and frendes in God, a litle before that
he suffred. Ed. John Foxe. 1559.

―――. *A Pituous Lamentation of the Miserable Estate of the Church*
of Christ in Englande, in the time of the late revolt from the
gospel. 1566.

Roy, William. See Erasmus, *Paraclesis*, and William Barlow.

Sachs, Hans. *A Goodly Dysputatyon betwene a Christen Shomaker*
and a Popysshe Parson. Trans. Anthony Scoloker. Ipswich,
1548.

Saint German, Christopher. *Salem and Bizance.* 1533. Anonymous. A reply to More's *Apologye.* Answered by More's
Debellacyon of Salem and Bizance.

―――. *A Treatise Concernynge the Division betwene the Spiryt-*
ual[i]tie and Temporal[i]tie. c. 1532. Anonymous. Answered by More's *Apologye.*

―――. *A Treatyse Concerninge the Power of the Clergye, and the*
Lawes of the Realme. c. 1535. Anonymous.

Samuel, William. *An Abridgement of All the Canonical Books of*
the Olde Testament, written in Sternholds meter. 1569.

―――. *The Abridgemente of Goddes Statutes in Myter.* 1551. A
précis of the Pentateuch.

Samuel, William. *The Love of God.* c. 1559.

———. *The Practise Practiced by the Pope and His Prelates.* c. 1550.

———. *A Warnyng for the Cittie of London.* c. 1550.

Seager, Francis. *The Schoole of Vertue.* c. 1550.

———. 3rd ed. Ed. Robert Crowley. 1582. With Crowley's "Praiers and Graces" in meter.

Seymour, Edward. *An Epistle or Exhortacion to Unitie & Peace, sent to the inhabitauntes of Scotlande.* 1548.

———. *Epistola exhortatoria ad pacem.* 1548. A translation.

Shepherd, Luke. *Antipus.* c. 1548.

———. *The Comparison betwene the Antipus and the Antigraphe.* c. 1548.

———. *Doctour Doubble Ale.* c. 1548.

———. *A Godlye and Holesome Preservatyve against Desperation.* c. 1548.

———. *John Bon and Mast Person.* 1547.

———. *Pathose.* c. 1548.

———. *Phylogamus.* c. 1548.

———. *A Pore Helpe, the Buklar and Defence of Mother Holy Kyrke.* c. 1548.

———. *The Upcheringe of the Messe.* c. 1548.

Sherry, Richard. *A Treatise of Schemes & Tropes.* 13 December 1550.

Skelton, John. *Pithy Pleasaunt and Profitable Workes.* Ed. John Stow. 1568.

*Smith, Richard. *A Brief Treatyse Settynge forth Divers Truthes.* 1547.

———. *Of Unwryten Verytyes.* 1548. Anonymous.

Smith, Thomas. *De republica Anglorum. The Maner of Governement of England.* 1583.

———. *A Discourse of the Commonweal of the Realm of England.* 1581. Anonymous. Attributed to Smith. Written 1549. (*STC* 23133.)

Starkey, Thomas. [*A Dialogue between Reginald Pole and Thomas Lupset.*] Written 1530s.

Stevenson, William. *A Ryght Pithy, Pleasaunt and Merie Come-*

die: Intytuled Gammer Gurtons Nedle. 1575. Init. Mr. S., M[aste]r of Art. Attributed to Stevenson.

Stow, John. *Annales, or a Generall Chronicle of England.* 5th ed. 1631. Continued by Edmund Howes.

———. *A Survay of London,* 1598.

Thomas, William. *The Historie of Italie.* 1549.

———. *The Vanitee of this World.* 1549.

Tilney, Emery. *Here Beginneth a Song of the Lordes Supper.* c. 1550. Init. E. T.

Turberville, George. *Epitaphes, Epigrams, Songs and Sonets.* 1567.

Turner, William. *The Huntyng & Fyndyng Out of the Romishe Fox.* Basel (i.e., Bonn), 1543. Ascribed to William Wraghton (pseud.). See John Bale's *Yet a Course at the Romyshe Foxe.*

———. *The Rescuynge of the Romishe Foxe Other Wyse Called the Examination of the Hunter Devised by Steven Gardiner.* Winchester (i.e., Bonn), 1545. A sequel to the above. From the "Hanse hit prik" press. A reply to Gardiner's *Examination.*

———. *The Names of Herbes.* 1548. In Greek, Latin, English, German, and French.

———. *A New Booke of Spirituall Physik.* Emden, 1555. "Imprented at Rome by the vaticane churche, by Marcus Antonius Constantius. Otherwyse called, thraso miles gloriosus."

———. *A New Dialogue Wherein is Conteyned the Examination of the Masse.* 1548. 4 eds. (c. 1548-49).

———. *A New Herball.* 1551.

———. *A Preservative agaynst the Poyson of Pelagius, lately renued by the Annabaptistes.* 1551. With poems by Thomas Becon, Randall Hurlestone, and Thomas Norton.

Tyndale, William. *The Whole Workes of W. Tyndall, John Frith, and Doct. Barnes.* Ed. John Foxe. 1573.

———. *An Answere unto Sir Thomas Mores Dialoge.* Antwerp, 1531. A reply to More's *Dyaloge of the Veneration of Ymagys.* Answered by More's *Confutacyon.*

Tyndale, William. *A Briefe Declaration of the Sacraments.* c. 1548. Written c. 1533.

———. *A Compendious Introduccion unto the Pistle to the Romayns.* Worms, 1526. Anonymous.

———. *An Exposicion uppon the V. VI. VII. Chapters of Mathew.* Antwerp, c. 1533. Init. W. T.

———. *The Exposition of the Fyrste Epistle of Seynt Jhon.* Antwerp, 1531. Init. W. T.

———. *The Obedience of a Christen Man.* Marburg (i.e., Antwerp), 1528. From the "Hans Luft" press.

———. *The Parable of the Wicked Mammon.* Marburg (i.e., Antwerp), 1528. From the "Hans Luft" press.

———. *A Path Way into the Holy Scripture.* c. 1536. Anonymous.

———. *The Practyse of Prelates.* Marburg (i.e., Antwerp), 1530. Init. W. T.

———. *The Souper of the Lorde.* Nuremberg (i.e., Antwerp?), 1533 [or London, 1546?]. Anonymous. With a reply to More's attack on John Frith. Answered by More's response to *The Souper of the Lord.*

———. 2nd ed. Ed. Robert Crowley. n.p., 1533 (i.e., London, 1547?). With a preface by Crowley. The third and fourth editions (n.p., 1533 [London, 1547?]) contain Crowley's preface.

Udall, Nicholas. *An Interlude upon the History of Jacob and Esau.* 1557. Attributed to Udall. Written c. 1547-53. (*STC* 14326.5.)

———. [*A Merye Enterlude Entitled Respublica.*] Attributed to Udall. Written 1553.

———. *A New Enterlude called Thersytes.* c. 1562. Attributed to Udall.

———. *Ralph Roister Doister.* c. 1566. Written c. 1552.

Vermigli, Peter Martyr. *A Discourse Concernynge the Sacrament of the Lordes Supper.* Trans. Nicholas Udall. 1550.

———. *An Epistle unto the Duke of Somerset Written in Latin.* Trans. Thomas North. 1550.

———. *Petri Martyris Vermilii, . . . loci communes.* 1576.

———. *The Common Places.* Trans. A. Marten. 1583.

———. *Tractatio de sacramento eucharistiae.* 1549.

———. *A Treatise of the Cohabitacyon of the Faithfull with the Unfaithfull.* Trans. Thomas Becon? Strasbourg, 1555. Anonymous.

Virgilius Maro, Publius. [*Aeneid.*] *The Seven First Bookes of the Eneidos.* Trans. Thomas Phaer. 1558.

———. *The Nyne Fyrst Bookes of the Eneidos.* Trans. Phaer. 1562.

———. *The Whole XII Bookes of the Aeneidos.* Trans. Phaer and Thomas Twyne. 1573.

Voragine, Jacobus de. *The Golden Legend.* Trans. William Caxton. 1483.

Wager, Lewis. *A New Enterlude of the Life and Repentaunce of Marie Magdalene.* 1566. Written c. 1550.

Werdmueller, Otto. *A Spyrytuall and Moost Precyouse Pearle.* Trans. Miles Coverdale. 1550. Ed. Edward Seymour, with a preface. With appended prayers by Thomas Becon. 10 eds. (1550-1605).

Wever, R. *An Enterlude Called Lusty Juventus.* c. 1550.

Whitgift, John. *An Answere to a Libel Intituled an Admonition.* 1572. A reply to Thomas Cartwright.

———. *The Defense of the Aunswere to the Admonition.* 1574. A reply to Thomas Cartwright.

Wilson, Thomas. *The Arte of Rhetorique.* January 1553. 8 eds. (1553-85).

———. *The Rule of Reason.* 1551. 7 eds. (1551-93).

———. *Vita et obitus duorum fratrum Suffolciensium, Henrici et Caroli Brandoni duobus epistolis explicata.* 1551. With a letter by Walter Haddon.

Wyatt, Sir Thomas. *A Boke of Balettes.* c. 1549. See *STC* 24650-24650.5.

Wyclif, John. *The Dore of Holy Scripture.* 1540. The general prologue of the Wyclifite Bible. Anonymous. Attributed to John Purvey.

Wyclif, John. *The True Copye of a Prolog*. Ed. Robert Crowley. 28 May 1550. Another edition, from a different manuscript.

————. *Wycklyffes Wycket*. Nuremberg (i.e., London), 1546. 4 eds. (c. 1546-48).

Zwingli, Ulrich. *Certeyne Preceptes*. Trans. Richard Argentine. Ipswich, 1548.

————. *A Short Pathwaye to the Understanding of the Scriptures*. Trans. Jean Veron. Worcester, 1550.

————. *The Ymage of Bothe Pastoures*. Trans. Jean Veron. 1550.

Select Bibliography

Place of publication is London unless otherwise stated. "Cambridge" refers to Cambridge, England.

I. Primary Sources

Baldwin, William, et al. *The Mirror for Magistrates*, ed. L. B. Campbell. Cambridge, 1938.

———. *"Beware the Cat,"* and *"The Funerals of King Edward the Sixth,"* ed. W. P. Holden. New London, Conn., 1963.

Bale, John. *Select Works*, ed. H. Christmas. Parker Society, Vol. 36. Cambridge, 1849.

———. *King Johan*, ed. H. B. Adams. San Marino, Calif., 1969.

Becon, Thomas. *Works*, ed. J. Ayre. Parker Society, Vols. 2-4. Cambridge, 1843-44.

Bevington, David, ed. *The Macro Plays*. New York and Washington, 1972.

Book of Common Prayer. *The Book of Common Prayer 1559*, ed. John E. Booty. Charlottesville, Va., 1976.

———. *The First and Second Prayer Books of Edward VI*, intro. D. Harrison. 1968.

Cavendish, George. *The Life and Death of Cardinal Wolsey*, ed. R. S. Sylvester. EETS, o.s. 243. Oxford, 1959.

———. *Life of Cardinal Wolsey and Metrical Visions*, ed. S. W. Singer. 2 vols. 1825.

———. *Metrical Visions*, ed. A.S.G. Edwards. Publications of the Renaissance Text Society, Vol. 9. Columbia, S.C., 1980.

The Court of Venus, ed. R. A. Fraser. Durham, N.C., 1955.

Cranmer, Thomas. *Works*, ed. J. E. Cox. Parker Society, Vols. 12, 24. Cambridge, 1844-46.

[507]

Creeth, E., ed. *Tudor Plays*. New York, 1966.

Crowley, Robert. *Philargyrie of Greate Britayne*, ed. John N. King. *ELR*, 10 (1980), 46-75.

———. *Select Works*, ed. J. M. Cowper. EETS, e.s. 15. 1872.

Donne, John. *Poems*, ed. H.J.C. Grierson. 2 vols. Oxford, 1912.

Edward VI. *The Chronicle and Political Papers*, ed. W. K. Jordan. Ithaca, N.Y., 1966.

———. *Literary Remains*, ed. J. G. Nichols. 2 vols. Roxburghe Club. 1857.

Elizabeth I. *Poems*, ed. L. Bradner. Providence, R.I., 1964.

Erasmus, Desiderius. *Christian Humanism and the Reformation: Selected Writings*, ed. J. C. Olin. New York, 1965. Includes *Paraclesis*.

———. *The Praise of Folie*, trans. T. Chaloner, ed. C. H. Miller. EETS, o.s. 257. 1965.

Feuillerat, A., ed. *Documents Relating to the Revels at Court in the Time of King Edward VI and Queen Mary. Materialien zur Kunde des älteren Englischen Dramas*, Vol. 44. Louvain, 1914.

Foxe, John. *Acts and Monuments*, ed. S. R. Cattley. 4th ed., rev. and corrected by J. Pratt. 8 vols. 1877.

———. *Two Latin Comedies: "Titus et Gesippus" and "Christus Triumphans,"* ed. John Hazel Smith. Ithaca, N.Y., 1973.

Gardiner, Stephen. *Letters*, ed. J. A. Muller. Cambridge, 1933.

———. *A Machiavellian Treatise*, ed. and trans. P. S. Donaldson. Cambridge, 1975.

Gransden, K. W., ed. *Tudor Verse Satire*. 1970.

Grimald, Nicholas. *Life and Poems*, ed. L. R. Merrill. New Haven, 1925.

Hall, John. *The Court of Virtue (1565)*, ed. R. A. Fraser. 1961.

Heywood, John. *"Works" and Miscellaneous Short Poems*, ed. B. A. Milligan. Urbana, Ill., 1956.

Hooper, John. *Early Writings*, ed. S. Carr. Parker Society, Vol. 20. Cambridge, 1843.

———. *Later Writings*, ed. C. Nevinson. Parker Society, Vol. 21. Cambridge, 1852.

SELECT BIBLIOGRAPHY

Houle, Peter J., ed. "A Reconstruction of the English Morality Fragment *Somebody and Others*," *PBSA*, 71 (1977), 259-77.

Howard, Henry, Earl of Surrey. *Poems*, ed. E. Jones. Oxford, 1964.

———— et al. *Tottel's Miscellany (1557-1587)*, ed. H. E. Rollins. 2nd ed., rev. 2 vols. Cambridge, Mass., 1965. A critical edition of *Songes and Sonettes*.

Hughey, Ruth, ed. *Arundel-Harington Manuscript of Tudor Poetry*. 2 vols. Columbus, Ohio, 1960.

————. *John Harington of Stepney: Tudor Gentleman: His Life and Works*. Columbus, Ohio, 1971.

Impatient Poverty, ed. R. B. McKerrow. *Materialien zur Kunde des älteren Englischen Dramas*, Vol. 33. Louvain, 1911.

Jacob and Esau, ed. J. Crow and F. P. Wilson. *Malone Society Reprints*, Vol. 96. Oxford, 1956. Attributed to Nicholas Udall.

Langland, William. *The Vision of William Concerning Piers the Plowman*, ed. W. W. Skeat. 2 vols. Oxford, 1886.

Latimer, Hugh. *Works*, ed. G. E. Corrie. Parker Society, Vols. 16, 20. Cambridge, 1844-45.

————. *Selected Sermons*, ed. A. G. Chester. Charlottesville, Va., 1968.

Love Feigned and Unfeigned, ed. A. Esdaile. *Malone Society Collections*, Vol. 1. Oxford, 1907.

Migne, J. P., ed. *Patrologiae cursus completus. Series latina*. 221 vols. Paris, 1844-64.

Milton, John. *Complete Prose Works*, ed. D. M. Wolfe et al. 8 vols. New Haven, 1953-

————. *Poems*, ed. J. Carey and A. Fowler. 2 vols. 1969.

More, Sir Thomas. *The Complete Works*, ed. R. S. Sylvester et al. 14 vols. New Haven, 1963-

————. *Thomas More's Prayer Book*, ed. Louis L. Martz and R. S. Sylvester. New Haven, 1969. Includes facsimiles of More's marginalia.

Parker, Henry, Baron Morley, trans. *Tryumphes of Fraunces Petrarcke*, ed. D. D. Carnicelli. Cambridge, Mass., 1971.

Sidney, Sir Philip. *The Countess of Pembroke's Arcadia ("The Old Arcadia")*, ed. J. Robertson. Oxford, 1973.

———. *Miscellaneous Prose*, ed. Katherine Duncan-Jones and Jan van Dorsten. Oxford, 1973.

———. *Poems*, ed. William A. Ringler, Jr. Oxford, 1962.

Smith, G. G., ed. *Elizabethan Critical Essays*. 2 vols. Oxford, 1904.

Somerset, J.A.B., ed. *Four Tudor Interludes*. 1974.

Spenser, Edmund. *The Faerie Queene*, ed. A. C. Hamilton. 1977.

———. *Minor Poems*, ed. E. de Selincourt. Oxford, 1910.

Tyndale, William. *Doctrinal Treatises*, ed. H. Walter. Parker Society, Vol. 43. Cambridge, 1848.

Wager, Lewis. *Marie Magdalene*, ed. F. I. Carpenter. Chicago, 1902.

Wickham, Glynne, ed. *English Moral Interludes*. 1976.

Wyatt, Sir Thomas. *Collected Poems*, ed. Joost Dalder. 1975.

II. REFERENCE WORKS AND BIBLIOGRAPHIES

à Wood, Anthony. *Athenae Oxonienses*. 2 vols. 1691-92.

———. 3rd ed., rev. and enlarged by Phillip Bliss. 4 vols. 1813-20.

Adams, H. M. *Catalogue of Books Printed on the Continent of Europe, 1501-1600 in Cambridge Libraries*. 2 vols. Cambridge, 1967.

Arber, Edward, ed. *A Transcript of the Registers of the Company of Stationers of London; 1554-1640 A.D.* 5 vols. 1875-94.

Bale, John. *Index Britanniae Scriptorum*, ed. R. Poole and M. Bateson. Oxford, 1902.

Dictionary of National Biography, ed. Leslie Stephen and Sidney Lee. 63 vols. 1885-1900.

Duff, E. Gordon. *A Century of the English Book Trade*. 1905.

Fuller, Thomas. *The History of the Worthies of England*. 4 pts. 1662.

Gaskell, Philip. *A New Introduction to Bibliography*. Oxford, 1972.

SELECT BIBLIOGRAPHY

Harbage, Alfred. *Annals of the English Drama*, rev. Samuel Schoenbaum. Philadelphia, 1964.

Hodnett, Edward. *English Woodcuts: 1480-1535*. 1935.

Leland, John. *Commentarii de Scriptoribus Britannicis*, ed. A. Hall. Oxford, 1709.

The New Cambridge Bibliography of English Literature, ed. George Watson. Vol. 1. Cambridge, 1974.

A New English Dictionary on Historical Principles, ed. J.A.H. Murray et al. 11 vols. Oxford, 1884-1933.

Percy, Thomas. *Reliques of Ancient English Poetry*. 3 vols. 1765.

Rider, Philip R. *A Chronological Index to the Revised Edition of the Pollard and Redgrave Short-Title Catalogue, 1475-1640*. Vol. 2. De Kalb, Ill., 1978.

A Short-Title Catalogue of Books Printed in England, Scotland, & Ireland, and of English Books Printed Abroad, 1475-1640, comp. A. W. Pollard and G. R. Redgrave. 1926.

Short-Title Catalogue. 2nd ed., rev. and enlarged by W. A. Jackson and F. S. Ferguson, completed by K. F. Pantzer. 3 vols. 1976-

Strype, John. *Ecclesiastical Memorials*. 3 vols. Oxford, 1721.

Warton, Thomas. *The History of English Poetry*. 3 vols. and vol. 4, unfinished. 1774-81.

Williams, Franklin B., Jr. *Index of Dedications and Commendatory Verses in English Books before 1641*. 1962. Addenda in Supplement to *The Library* (March 1975).

III. BOOKS AND ARTICLES

Anglo, Sidney. *Spectacle, Pageantry, and Early Tudor Policy*. Oxford, 1969.

Auerbach, Erich. *Literary Language and Its Public in Late Latin Antiquity and in the Middle Ages*, trans. R. Manheim. New York, 1965.

———. *Scenes from the Drama of European Literature: Six Essays*, trans. R. Manheim. New York, 1959. Includes "Figura."

Bauckham, Richard. *Tudor Apocalypse*. Abingdon, 1978.

Bevington, David. *From "Mankind" to Marlowe: Growth and Structure in the Popular Drama of Tudor England.* Cambridge, Mass., 1962.

————. "Popular and Courtly Traditions on the Early Tudor Stage." *Medieval Drama*, ed. N. Denny. Stratford-upon-Avon Studies, Vol. 16. 1973.

————. *Tudor Drama and Politics: A Critical Approach to Topical Meaning.* Cambridge, Mass., 1968.

Brightman, F. E. *The English Rite.* 2 vols. 1915.

Brook, Stella. *The Language of the Book of Common Prayer.* 1965.

Bush, M. L. *The Government Policy of Protector Somerset.* 1975.

Butterworth, Charles. *The Literary Lineage of the King James Bible: 1340-1611.* Philadelphia, 1941.

Campbell, L. B. *Divine Poetry and Drama in Sixteenth-Century England.* Berkeley, Calif., 1959.

————. "Humphrey Duke of Gloucester and Elianor Cobham His Wife in the *Mirror for Magistrates.*" *Huntington Library Bulletin*, no. 5 (1934), 119-55.

————. "The Suppressed Edition of *A Mirror for Magistrates.*" *HLB*, no. 6 (1934), 1-16.

Chambers, E. K. *The Elizabethan Stage.* 4 vols. Oxford, 1923.

————. *The Mediaeval Stage.* 2 vols. Oxford, 1903.

Chester, A. G. *Hugh Latimer: Apostle to the English.* Philadelphia, 1954.

Christianson, Paul. *Reformers and Babylon: English Apocalyptic Visions from the Reformation to the Eve of the Civil War.* Toronto, 1978.

Curtius, Ernst R. *European Literature and the Latin Middle Ages*, trans. W. Trask, 1953.

Davies, W. T. "A Bibliography of John Bale." *Oxford Bibliographical Society, Proceedings and Papers*, 5 (1936), 201-81.

Devereux, E. J. "The Publication of the English *Paraphrases* of Erasmus." *Bulletin of the John Rylands Library*, 51 (1969), 348-67.

Dickens, A. G. *The English Reformation.* 2nd ed., rev. 1967.

Elton, G. R. *Reform and Reformation England, 1509-1558.* 1977.

Fairfield, L. P. *John Bale: Mythmaker for the English Reformation*. W. Lafayette, Ind., 1976.

———. *"The vocacyon of Johan Bale* and Early English Autobiography," *RQ*, 24 (1971), 327-40.

Feasey, E. I. "The Licensing of the *Mirror for Magistrates.*" *Library*, 4th ser., 3 (1923), 177-93.

———. "William Baldwin." *MLR*, 20 (1925), 407-18.

Ferguson, Arthur B. *The Articulate Citizen and the English Renaissance*. Durham, N.C., 1965.

Firth, Katharine R. *The Apocalyptic Tradition in Reformation Britain: 1530-1645*. Oxford, 1979.

Gardiner, Harold C. *Mysteries' End: An Investigation of the Last Days of the Medieval Religious Stage*. New Haven, 1946.

Germann, Friedrich. *Luke Shepherd, ein Satirendichter der englischen Reformationszeit*. Augsburg, 1911.

Haile, G. H. "Luther and Literacy." *PMLA*, 91 (1976), 816-28.

Haller, William. *Foxe's Book of Martyrs and the Elect Nation*. 1963.

———. " 'Hail Wedded Love.' " *ELH*, 13 (1946), 79-97.

——— and Malleville Haller. "The Puritan Art of Love." *HLQ*, 5 (1942), 235-72.

Hardison, O. B. *Christian Rite and Christian Drama in the Middle Ages*. Baltimore, 1965.

Harris, J. W. *John Bale: A Study in the Minor Literature of the Reformation*. Urbana, Ill., 1940.

Heiserman, Arthur. *Skelton and Satire*. Chicago, 1961.

Hill, Christopher. *Antichrist in Seventeenth-Century England*. Oxford, 1971.

———. *The World Turned Upside Down: Radical Ideas during the English Revolution*. 1972.

Hoak, D. E. *The King's Council in the Reign of Edward VI*. Cambridge, 1976.

Jordan, W. K. *Edward VI*. 2 vols. 1968-70.

Josipovici, Gabriel. *The World and the Book: A Study of Modern Fiction*. 1971.

Kelly, R. L. "Hugh Latimer as Piers Plowman." *SEL*, 17 (1977), 13-26.

Kermode, Frank. *"The Faerie Queene,* I and V." *Bulletin of the John Rylands Library,* 47 (1964), 123-50.

Kernan, Alvin. *The Cankered Muse: Satire of the English Renaissance.* New Haven, 1959.

King, John N. "Freedom of the Press, Protestant Propaganda, and Protector Somerset." *HLQ,* 40 (1976), 1-9.

————. "Protector Somerset, Patron of the English Renaissance." *PBSA,* 70 (1976), 307-31.

————. "Robert Crowley: A Tudor Gospelling Poet." *YES,* 8 (1978), 220-37.

————. "Robert Crowley's Editions of *Piers Plowman*: A Tudor Apocalypse." *MP,* 73 (1976), 342-52.

Knappen, M. M. *Tudor Puritanism.* Chicago, 1939.

Langston, B. "Essex and the Art of Dying." *HLQ,* 13 (1950), 109-29.

Lewalski, B. K. *Protestant Poetics and the Seventeenth-Century Religious Lyric.* Princeton, 1979.

Lewis, C. S. *The Allegory of Love.* Oxford, 1936.

————. *English Literature in the Sixteenth Century Excluding Drama.* Oxford, 1954.

Loach, Jennifer. "Pamphlets and Politics, 1553-8." *Bulletin of the Institute of Historical Research,* 48 (1975), 31-44.

———— and Robert Tittler, eds. *The Mid-Tudor Polity c. 1540-1560.* 1980.

McConica, J. K. *English Humanists and Reformation Politics under Henry VIII and Edward VI.* Oxford, 1965.

McCusker, Honor. *John Bale: Dramatist and Antiquary.* Bryn Mawr, Pa., 1942.

Maclure, Millar. *The Paul's Cross Sermons: 1534-1642.* Toronto, 1958.

Nelson, William. *Fact or Fiction: The Dilemma of the Renaissance Storyteller.* Cambridge, Mass., 1973.

Owst, G. R. *Literature and Pulpit in Medieval England.* Oxford, 1933.

SELECT BIBLIOGRAPHY

Peter, John. *Complaint and Satire in Early English Literature.* Oxford, 1956.

Phillips, John. *The Reformation of Images: Destruction of Art in England, 1535-1660.* Berkeley and Los Angeles, 1973.

Raby, F.J.E. *A History of Christian-Latin Poetry from the Beginnings to the Close of the Middle Ages.* Oxford, 1927.

Rasmussen, Carl. " 'Quietnesse of Minde': A Theatre for Worldlings as a Protestant Poetics." *Spenser Studies*, 1 (1980), 3-27.

Reeves, Marjorie. *The Influence of Prophecy in the Later Middle Ages: A Study in Joachimism.* Oxford, 1969.

Ringler, William A., Jr. *"Beware the Cat* and the Beginnings of English Fiction." *Novel*, 12 (1979), 113-26.

————. "The First Phase of the Elizabethan Attack on the Stage, 1558-1579." *HLQ*, 5 (1942), 391-418.

Roston, Murray. *Biblical Drama in England.* 1968.

Scheper, George L. "Reformation Attitudes toward Allegory and the Song of Songs." *PMLA*, 89 (1974), 551-62.

Smith, Hallett. "English Metrical Psalms in the Sixteenth Century and their Literary Significance." *HLQ*, 9 (1946), 249-71.

Stevens, John E. *Music and Poetry in the Early Tudor Court, 1480-1530.* 1961.

Strong, Roy. *The Cult of Elizabeth.* 1977.

————. "Edward VI and the Pope: A Tudor Anti-Papal Allegory and Its Setting." *Journal of the Warburg and Courtauld Institutes*, 23 (1960), 311-13.

————. *The Elizabethan Image.* 1969.

————. *Holbein and Henry VIII.* 1967.

Sylvester, R. S. "Cavendish's *Life of Wolsey*: The Artistry of a Tudor Biographer." *SP*, 57 (1960), 44-71.

Trench, Wilbrahim F. "William Baldwin." *Modern Quarterly of Language and Literature*, 1 (1899), 259-67.

Turville-Petre, Thorlac. "Nicholas Grimald and *Alexander A.*" *ELR*, 6 (1976). 180-86.

Tuve, Rosamund. "Sacred 'Parody' of Love Poetry, and Herbert." *Studies in the Renaissance*, 8 (1961), 249-90.

[515]

Wall, John N., Jr. "The 'Book of Homilies' of 1547 and the Continuity of English Humanism in the Sixteenth Century." *Anglican Theological Review*, 58 (1976), 75-87.

Wawn, Andrew. "The Genesis of *The Plowman's Tale*." *YES*, 2 (1972), 21-40.

Weiner, Andrew. *Sir Philip Sidney and the Poetics of Protestantism: A Study of Contexts*. Minneapolis, 1978.

White, Helen C. *Social Criticism in Popular Religious Literature of the Sixteenth Century*. New York, 1944.

Wickham, Glynne. *Early English Stages, 1300 to 1660*. 3 vols. 1959-80.

Williams, Franklin B., Jr. "Lost Books of Tudor England." *Library*, 5th ser., 33 (1978), 1-14.

Williams, Penry. *The Tudor Regime*. Oxford, 1979. Chap. 8 concerns the establishment of Protestantism.

Wilson, F. P. *The English Drama: 1485-1585*, ed. G. K. Hunter. Oxford, 1969.

Yates, Frances A. *Astraea: The Imperial Theme in the Sixteenth Century*. 1975.

Yost, John K. "Protestant Reformers and the Humanist *Via Media* in the Early English Reformation." *JMRS*, 5 (1975), 187-202.

Biblical Texts Cited

Page numbers are given in italics.

BIBLICAL TEXTS CITED

Index

Most works are indexed under their authors or probable authors. Short titles are used for many works. Biblical texts cited appear in a special index.

INDEX

in, 21, 72, 102; use of satirical imprints and colophons in, 50, 66, 287, 372, 379n.25, 418-19; use of pseudonyms in, 56, 65-66, 287, 372-74, 381. *See also* List of Reformation Literary Texts

propaganda: relative absence of Catholic, 89, 413; against Scotland, 465-68. *See also* Protestant propaganda

prophecy: literary conventions of, 260, 335-38, 380, 383; poetry and, 220-21, 340, 345; *Piers Plowman* as, 247-48, 325, 331, 335-40; and Joachimist tradition, 198-206; and prognostication, 335-37, 353; in Canticles, 370-71; influence of, 407

prophet: Old Testament, 341, 345; David as, 221

Protestant propaganda, 82, 194, 337; authorization of, 88-89; government sponsorship of, 27, 94-95, 102, 107; and Thomas Cromwell, 48-53, 377. *See also* Edward VI, as ideal ruler; attack on the mass; satire, antipapal

proverb, 360, 365-66, 381, 387, 389, 396

Psalms, 209-25 passim, 368, 452. *See also* Index of Biblical Texts Cited; Penitential Psalms; Crowley, *Psalter*; Thomas Sternhold; Sternhold and Hopkins

pseudonyms, *see* printing, use of pseudonyms in

publishing, *see* printing

Punt, William, 288-90

Puritan Revolution, 6, 32, 90-91, 453-54

Puritanism, 451-54; origins of, 6-8, 15, 30-32, 319, 355n, 431-34; and literature, 8, 277-78, 319, 433-34

Puttenham, George, 232, 344; and native literary tradition, 12-13, 108, 256, 340

Pythagoras, 364, 393

Rabelais, François, 171, 185, 257, 264, 388

Raleigh, Sir Walter, 18, 114, 237

Ramsey, John, 102

Rastell, William, 413

readership of printed books, *see* printing

rebellions of 1549, 28, 77, 92, 135, 188, 312

Regius, Urbanus, 463

relics, Protestant, 70, 72, 421, 438. *See also* images, and relics; martyrology

Revelation, 61, 131, 190, 198, 325, 356. *See also* Index of Biblical Texts Cited; *Image of Both Churches*

Richard I (Richard Lionheart), 198-99

Richard II, 162, 324, 415

Richard III, 247, 416, 442

Richmond, Duchess of, *see* Mary Fitzroy

Ridley, Nicholas, 134n.8, 135, 137n.12, 172, 242, 357; execution of, 438, 441-42

LIBRARY OF CONGRESS CATALOGING IN
PUBLICATION DATA

King, John N., 1945-
English Reformation literature.

Bibliography: p.
Includes index.
1. English literature—Early modern, 1500-
1700—History and criticism.   2. Reformation—
England.   I. Title.
PR411.K48   820′.9′002   81-47929
ISBN 0-691-06502-0   AACR2